GREAT
AMERICAN
STORIES,
POEMS
& ESSAYS

Compiled by Hugh Graham

GREAT
AMERICAN STORIES, POEMS & ESSAYS

Compiled by Hugh Graham

CASTLE

Copyright© 1956 & 1949 by The Spencer Press, Inc.
Previously published under the title An American Treasury and 1000 American
Things

This edition is published in the United States of America in 1985 by Castle,
a division of Book Sales, Inc., 110 Enterprise Ave., Secaucus, N.J. 07094, by
arrangement with Lexicon Publications, Inc. and Galahad Books, Inc.

Library of Congress Catalog Card Number: 85-070378

ISBN: 0-89009-886-7

The CASTLE Trademark is registered in the U.S. Patent and
Trademark Office.

Printed and bound in the U.S.A.

G. P. PUTNAM'S SONS for permission to reprint *From New York to Paris*, from "We," by Charles A. Lindbergh. Copyright, 1927, by Charles A. Lindbergh.

THE REILLY & LEE CO. for permission to reprint *America* from the book "Collected Verse of Edgar A. Guest," copyright, 1934, by The Reilly & Lee Co., Chicago.

RINEHART & COMPANY, INC., for permission to reprint *Nathan Hale*, from "There Were Giants in the Land," by Nancy Hale. Copyright, 1942; *One Hour of Glory*, from "Familiar Faces," by Mary Roberts Rinehart. Copyright, 1940, 1941, by Mary Roberts Rinehart.

PAUL R. REYNOLDS & SON for permission to reprint *Ann Story* by Dorothy Canfield Fisher, copyright, 1946, by Stores Publishing Company, Inc.; *A New Englander* by Dorothy Canfield Fisher, copyright, 1940, by The Reader's Digest Association, Inc.

THE RONALD PRESS COMPANY for permission to reprint *The Lincoln Memorial*, from "The Course of American Democratic Thought," by Ralph Henry Gabriel. Copyright, 1940, by The Ronald Press Company.

THIS WEEK MAGAZINE and the author for permission to reprint *Beyond Price* by Hugh B. Cave. Copyrighted 1941 by the United Newspapers Magazine Corporation.

We wish to thank the following copyright owners for permission to reprint certain selections in this book: Thomas Alva Edison Foundation, Inc., Emporia Gazette, Ford Motor Company, Elbert Hubbard II, Virgil Markham, Dr. Charles William Mayo, Frederick T. McKeon, Clifford Meigs, Helen Channing Pollock, Will Rogers, Jr., and Mrs. Newton Booth Tarkington.

We also wish to thank the following authors for permission to reprint their selections in this book: George Matthew Adams, Maxwell Anderson, Marjorie Barrows, Bernard M. Baruch, Gail Brook Burket, Rabbi Barnett R. Brickner, Thomas Curtis Clark, Ruth Crary, August Derleth, John Dewey, R. L. Duffus, George Eaton, Albert Einstein, Raymond Blaine Fosdick, Robert I. Gannon, S.J., Charles Buxton Going (for *Columbus* from "Star-Glow and Song," published by Harper & Brothers), Mrs. J. Borden Harriman, Bishop Edwin Holt Hughes, Helen Keller, Charles F. Kettering, Adelaide Love, Edgar Lee Masters, Angelo Patri, Homer Saint-Gaudens, Walter Dill Scott, James Stevens and Nancy Byrd Turner.

Contents

Publisher's foreword

OUR AMERICA is a glorious land!

Our America is sugar maples in Vermont, buckeye trees in Ohio, palm trees in Florida and giant sequoias in California. Fleets sailing out of Gloucester and airliners bound southwest for Phoenix are America. America also is Mark Twain and Ol' Man River, the rolling Mississippi, and Thoreau beside quiet Walden Pond. The very soul of our country can be found in the milking shed, the hardware store, the village meeting hall, the highway gas station, the local movie theatre, the church choir loft, and on the steps of the front porch.

What makes a nation great? Not its land, not its mines, not its rivers, not its machinery, not its money—important as these things are. Only people make a nation great—people like you and your family and your forbears.

In short, you and the neighbors on your street are the strength of the nation and the hope of the world—and to you we dedicate this book.

The reader who cares for our heritage of freedom, our immortal past and our unlimited future, will find in this volume—in this blending of legends, essays, speeches, ballads, short stories and other cross-sections of Americana, a personal message and a testament of faith in our country.

Everyone has felt the charm of stories that begin, "In the olden times—." It is these olden times in America, so comparatively recent and yet so completely vanished, that we recapture in the poetry of Whitman, Lowell, Whittier and Longfellow; and in the prose of Emerson, Harte, Irving and Hawthorne. Here is the America that we now see on Christmas cards, the America of husking bees and quilting parties, of sleigh rides on narrow country roads, the America, too, of Indians lurking in the woods near lonely farms.

The present day is also here in the fine writing of Carl Sandburg, Thomas Wolfe, Stephen Vincent Benét, Vachel Lindsay, Robert Frost, Thornton Wilder, Edgar Lee Masters and many others. Their work reveals their love of America, of democracy and of freedom. Through their creative efforts thousands of Americans have gained a greater understanding of what their country means to them, for their writing is in touch with common human needs.

We have a mighty story to tell about our country, to a world which knows only fragments of that story. The purpose of these selections is to present in prose and poetry the ideals of American democracy. In these pages we hope to express in some small measure what millions of our fellow Americans feel: that we have in this country a way of life that is unique and precious, a way of life of which we can be infinitely proud.

GREAT
AMERICAN
STORIES,
POEMS
& ESSAYS

Compiled by Hugh Graham

AMERICA THE BEAUTIFUL
KATHARINE LEE BATES

O beautiful for spacious skies,
  For amber waves of grain,
For purple mountain majesties
  Above the fruited plain!
    America! America!
  God shed His grace on thee,
And crown thy good with brotherhood
  From sea to shining sea!

O beautiful for pilgrim feet,
  Whose stern, impassioned stress
A thoroughfare for freedom beat
  Across the wilderness!
    America! America!
  God mend thine every flaw,
Confirm thy soul in self-control
  Thy liberty in law!

O beautiful for heroes proved
  In liberating strife,
Who more than self their country loved,
  And mercy more than life!
    America! America!
  May God thy gold refine,
Till all success be nobleness,
  And every gain divine!

O beautiful for patriot dream
  That sees beyond the years
Thine alabaster cities gleam
  Undimmed by human tears!
    America! America!
  God shed His grace on thee,
And crown thy good with brotherhood
  From sea to shining sea!

1

MEET A GREAT AMERICAN—THE BELL

By Donald Culross Peattie

This story of the symbol of our country's liberty was written in 1942.

I HAD CROSSED the continent to see it—the most holy relic of American history. I stood in line, hat in hand, the day Bataan fell, to look for the first time at the Liberty Bell.

I waited among other Americans —Pennsylvania Dutch, Iowans, Negroes, Armenians, Hungarians— to see the symbol of what makes worth while all our sacrifices. I saw the look on their faces, like a flag hung out in front of every house. I suppose I'd hung my own flag out, too, for we smiled at one another. This is the place where we can be our proudest —this Independence Hall in Philadelphia, where both the Declaration and the Constitution were proclaimed.

So there it was! It hung from its beam of solid, hand-hewn black walnut, its shattered frame clinging by a fragile isthmus of ancient metal, its great tongue still.

Three armed guards never take their eyes off the bell, day or night. Mounted on a mahogany truck fitted with smooth-rolling steel casters, it could be rushed away quickly in case of an air raid. To the enemy, its shrine would be an inviting target, for in letters indelibly blazoned around its crown it says: "PROCLAIM LIBERTY THROUGHOUT ALL THE LAND UNTO ALL THE INHABITANTS THEREOF."

That verse from the twenty-fifth chapter of Leviticus, chosen in 1751, was a bold prediction as well as a command. The man who selected it has remained too long unnoticed. He was Isaac Norris, Speaker of the Assembly of the Colony of Pennsylvania. Step by step he fought for American liberties, yet did not live to hear his bell cry aloud the verse he chose for it.

Old Isaac Norris was chairman of a committee to get a bell from London Town that could be heard far and wide. He placed his order with Lister, the most famous bell founder of England, for a bell of about 2000 pounds.

But perhaps the times were not yet ripe for liberty, for when the bell was hung in 1752 it cracked at the first stroke of the clapper. The Philadelphians asked Charles Stow and John Pass to melt the bell and remold it. They added American copper to make the metal less brittle. The tone of their first bell was wretched, and they had to cast a third one. The result was a fine bell, to all sounds and appearances. It is twelve feet in circumference around the lip and seven feet six inches around the crown. The metal is three inches thick at the lip, the clapper three feet two inches long. The overall weight is 2080 pounds.

When their bell was hung at last, Philadelphians rejoiced. The bell was rung on every possible occasion. Neighbors complained of the brazen tumult and architects feared the vibrations would unsettle the graceful bell tower. But the ringing went on, announcing occasions of joy and sorrow, or summoning the citizens to the public square to hear the

2

news. It was the town crier and the newspaper.

It spoke to the people and for the people, for there is no musical instrument so democratic as a bell. Its single tone expresses unison. And the Liberty Bell is the great voice of this people, which no other on earth can shout down or command to be still.

These noisy days of the bell's youth were stirring times. The Colonies were increasingly aroused by the encroachment of the British government on their hard-bought New World liberties. The bell was forever tolling alarum and excursion.

It rang in 1757 when Franklin went to England to seek redress for American grievances. It was muffled in 1765 as the *Royal Charlotte*, with a protecting man-of-war, came bearing those hated stamps up the Delaware. When Parliament forbade the Colonies to manufacture iron and steel, hats and woolen goods, the bell roared forth the national rage. It was muffled again, in sympathy, when the port of Boston was closed.

Nine months later, on April 25, 1775, it brought people flocking to the public square to hear how the Redcoats had been routed at Lexington six days before. Now indeed the great bronze throat might truly "proclaim Liberty."

Yet, in strict historical accuracy, the Liberty Bell did not ring on July 4, 1776. The Declaration of Independence was accepted by final vote on that day, but it was not read aloud by Colonel John Nixon in front of Independence Hall until July 8, to the tune of cheers, musket shots, fireworks and a ringing of bells —the voice of the Liberty Bell shouting above them all.

The big bronze crier was not allowed to rest in its tower. In September of 1777 it became apparent that the British were going to take Philadelphia, and Congress ordered the bell removed. In a rickety army wagon it began its wild flight over wretched roads and hills. The wagon broke down and the sacred bell had a bad fall. At last it was smuggled to safety in Allentown and secretly buried under the floor of the Zion Reformed Church. Independence Hall was made a prison for patriots, and had the bell remained there it might have been melted into a gun to be turned against American soldiers.

It was back in place to clang joy over the surrender of Cornwallis and from then on it was not long still. It rang, muffled, for the death of Washington. It bellowed forth the election of Jefferson. It mourned the death of Hamilton and of Lafayette. On July 4, 1826, it pealed forth the fiftieth anniversary of the Declaration of Independence.

Then in 1835, on July 8, the anniversary of the day when it had first proclaimed liberty, as the bell tolled the death of Chief Justice John Marshall, suddenly it cracked —never to be heard again.

And never again to be silent. For it is the incarnation of our democracy. It has traveled more than 20,000 miles on exhibition. Little towns through which it passed in the night lit bonfires along the railroad track so that people might get a glimpse as it rolled slowly by.

For the Liberty Bell is almost a person, an immortal hero that was born in our greatest hour, lived through our glorious youth, retreated, advanced, sang, shouted, fought and fell, in the line of duty, silent after eighty-three years of glory.

The Liberty Bell is an American. A great American like Washington, Jefferson, Lincoln. A plain American like any of us or all of us. It is the one bell in the world in whose presence every man takes off his hat. It is the bell for which all the world is listening now.

BATTLE-HYMN OF THE REPUBLIC
JULIA WARD HOWE

Mine eyes have seen the glory of the coming of the Lord:
He is trampling out the vintage where the grapes of wrath are stored;
He hath loosed the fateful lightning of His terrible swift sword;
   His truth is marching on!

I have seen Him in the watch-fires of a hundred circling camps;
They have builded Him an altar in the evening dews and damps;
I can read His righteous sentence by the dim and flaring lamps;
   His day is marching on!

I have read a fiery gospel, writ in burnished rows of steel:
"As ye deal with my contemners, so with you my grace shall deal;
Let the Hero, born of woman, crush the serpent with His heel,
   Since God is marching on!"

He has sounded forth the trumpet that shall never call retreat;
He is sifting out the hearts of men before His judgment-seat:
O, be swift, my soul, to answer Him! Be jubilant my feet!
   Our God is marching on!

In the beauty of the lilies Christ was born across the sea,
With a glory in His bosom that transfigures you and me;
As He died to make men holy, let us die to make men free,
   While God is marching on!

One Hour of Glory

By MARY ROBERTS RINEHART

*T*ONY WAS RATHER AMUSED when he received the letter from Grandfather Rogers. It was sent to him at the State Department, where Tony was something or other in a division called Protocol; that is, he helped the governors of states to lay wreaths hither and yon, and even now and then had appeals from frantic hostesses who had made a mistake in an important dinner party.

"But you can't ask an ambassador and the Chief Justice together," Tony would say. "They rank the same."

"How are they ever to meet, if they can't go to the same dinner?"

"They don't meet," Tony would reply cheerfully. "That's what keeps the Supreme Court free from foreign influences. Better get sick, Mrs. Jones. It can't be done."

All in all, Tony had his place in a great democracy. Aside from that, he was a cheerful young man, who wore a morning coat and top hat quite well, could hold a teacup in one hand and a piece of chocolate layer cake in the other without disaster, had been married for some years to a pretty and highly social young woman named Muriel, and had the usual if vague hope for a foreign post. An ambition which, to tell the truth, was largely Muriel's.

It is hardly surprising, then, that Muriel was not amused at the news.

"Look," Tony said. "We're going to have a visitor, darling."

"Not Aunt Emma," wailed Muriel. "I couldn't bear it, Tony. I really couldn't."

"Not Aunt Emma," said Tony. "It's my Grandfather Rogers."

"Grandfather Rogers?" she said

vaguely. "I thought he was dead or something." Then the thing burst on her in full force, so to speak. "Good heavens, Tony, that one! He must be a hundred."

"He's in his nineties; but I gather from his letter that he's still pretty spry."

Muriel looked at him helplessly. "In his nineties!" she said. "What on earth am I to do with him? I can't nurse him. In the very middle of the season, too. You've got to put him off, Tony. You've got to. We're out almost every night. And I don't like old men. At the best they talk too much, and at the worst they're deaf as a post."

"Not Grandfather Rogers, even if he is ninety-six," said Tony calmly. "Now listen to me, my girl. He's the last relative I've got, and he's making a sort of pilgrimage. He wants to see Father's grave and Harry's, over in Arlington. And he wants to see Washington, where he camped in 'sixty-three, and hasn't been since. And I think, incidentally, that he wants to see me. I'm the only one he has left."

Muriel brightened slightly. She was not mercenary; but Tony's job did cost money—clothes and cars and dinner parties, and so on. "Has he anything to leave you?" she inquired with interest.

"My rapacious darling!" said

5

Tony fondly. "No, he hasn't. He has his pension and a small farm. I used to go there when I was a kid. He's rather a grand old boy; but all you'll get out of him will be some eggs and butter. He'll probably bring them with him."

Which was precisely what Grandfather Rogers did bring when Tony met him at the station. At first Tony did not know him. He had remembered a tall, elderly figure, erect and soldierly, with a full set of quite dreadful white-porcelain teeth. As a matter of fact, had it not been for the teeth, Tony might have passed him by. But he caught a glimpse of them as they got out of the day coach, and found a cheerful but very old man more or less behind them. He still stood erect, but he had shrunk. There was, however, nothing senile about the faded blue eyes of Grandfather Rogers.

"I expect you're Tony," he said, in a cracked but not feeble voice. "Wait till I say good-bye to the conductor. He's a nice fellow. Had a father in my old regiment."

He left Tony for a moment and shook hands with the conductor. "Look me up while I'm here, Ed," he said. "This is my grandson. He'll be glad to see you."

"Thanks. Maybe I will. Have a good time."

Tony gave a quick thought to Muriel and then, so to speak, tossed her overboard. For it was evident that Grandfather Rogers had, in the course of the last eight hours, made a good many friends. They crowded around him, and when he was finally extricated, Tony was clutching an ancient suitcase, and Grandfather Rogers had a large basket covered with a napkin.

"If it's not too far, we can walk," he said. "I'd like to stretch my legs."

Tony chuckled. "It's quite a way," he said. "Anyhow, I've got my car here."

But getting Grandfather Rogers out of the station was still not simple. He stopped at the locomotive and looked up at the engineer in the cab.

"Made a good run, son," he said. "Right on the minute, too."

The engineer put a finger to his peaked cap in salute.

"Glad you liked it," he said, and smiled.

Tony gave the old suitcase to a porter; but they were still not ready to go. At the entrance to the station Grandfather Rogers stopped and gazed toward the Capitol. It was dusk by that time, and the great dome rose, white and luminous, straight across the plaza. It was always impressive, even to Tony. He turned to the old man, to find him standing at salute. But when he spoke, his voice was matter-of-fact enough.

"Looks like the place is changed some since I saw it in 'sixty-three," he said casually. "Brought some eggs and butter. Thought your wife might like them. Every woman likes fresh eggs to cook with. Some of them were warm when I packed them."

He eyed Sam, the chauffeur, rather suspiciously when he took the basket. "Who are you?"

"I'm the chauffeur," said the colored gentleman. "Name's Sam."

"All right, Sam," said Grandfather Rogers. "You watch those eggs. There's a heap of nourishment in them."

Sam grinned, and Tony got the old man into the car. Seated, he seemed almost small. He gazed out the car window, and once he passed his hand over his eyes, as though the

6

noise and lights confused him. Almost all he said was to ask if Arlington Cemetery was near.

"Thought I'd go and see the graves," he said. "Won't see them again, you know. I'm getting on."

"You look pretty husky for your age."

"Well, I've seen a lot of living," he said, and lapsed into silence.

Tony was a trifle anxious when they reached the house, and Grandfather Rogers was obliged to relinquish the basket to Henry, the butler. But Muriel was a good girl. She came into the hall and kissed the old man on his withered cheek, and she did not so much as blush when, his overcoat removed, he was revealed as wearing a red-flannel chest protector, tied with strings around the neck.

"Katie makes me wear it since I had pneumonia," he explained. "Katie's my housekeeper. You'd think to hear her I was getting childish in my old age."

Muriel dutifully smiled; but she cast a rather desperate look at Tony, who ignored it.

She had ordered the butler to serve tea by the fire in the library, and she kept a determined smile on her face even when Grandfather Rogers brought up the subject of the war. The State Department did not talk about the war except behind closed doors. But Grandfather Rogers, after eating everything in sight—the teeth were at least useful—sat back, replete at last, and brought the subject up.

"What's this mess in Europe, Tony? Are we going to get into it?"

"Not if we can help it," answered Tony carefully.

"Help it? How can we help it? If it keeps up, we'll go in to stop it, be-cause we can't stand any more murder. That's America, son."

"Well, perhaps it is," said Tony pacifically. It was quite a long time since he had considered what America really was, his mind mostly having been turned to the happenings abroad.

Grandfather Rogers put down his third cup of tea and got up. It was a slow process, but he made it.

"I guess maybe, if you don't mind, I'll go to bed," he said. "It's been a long day."

"Bed?" said Muriel blankly. "Won't you want some dinner? We're in tonight."

"Dinner? Great Scott, what have I just had?"

"Tea," said Muriel, not looking at Tony, who was grinning delightedly. "We always have tea at five o'clock. Dinner's at eight."

"That's bedtime on the farm," said Grandfather Rogers, "but I guess I'll make it."

He did make it, but the evening was not a success. He seemed slightly oppressed by Henry, the butler, and by the ritual of the table. He looked away when Muriel lighted a cigarette, and some time after the meal he made the startling discovery that she was wearing pajamas. After that he was careful not to look at her legs. At nine-thirty he yawned, and Tony suggested bed to him. He got up gratefully.

"See you at breakfast," he said, and made a formal good night, still avoiding Muriel's legs.

Muriel and Tony had quite a talk after he had gone. That is, Muriel talked, and Tony listened. She said quite firmly that she was willing to make the old man comfortable, but that he was impossible otherwise.

"I'm thinking of your career,

Tony," she said. "He would ruin it. If you are proposing to exhibit him around Washington, I'll go to Aiken. That's flat."

"What's the matter with him? He's a gentleman, even if he doesn't like your pants," said Tony cheerfully. "As a matter of fact, I hadn't thought of exhibiting him. He'd hate it."

On which truce of sorts they went to bed.

Grandfather Rogers was also in bed. His teeth were in a glass of water beside him, and he lay in Muriel's guest bed under Muriel's pink silk eiderdown comfort and felt extremely lonely. When Henry, the butler, looked in later to see if he was all right, Grandfather Rogers hailed him as a friend.

"Come in and sit down," he said. "I'd like to talk to you. Sit down, man, I won't bite you. If you'll look at that glass on the table, you'll see why."

Henry gave a rather sickly smile. He sat down, although he looked like a kangaroo ready to leap at the least alarm.

"I've been watching you tonight," said Grandfather Rogers. "Englishman, eh? Been a soldier, haven't you?"

"Most of my life, sir."

"Must seem queer to be passing plates, eh?"

Henry smiled. "It's better than starving," he said.

Grandfather Rogers learned quite a lot about Henry that night, including his possession of the Victoria Cross. The old man was highly interested.

"I got a medal myself once," he said, in his cracked old voice. "Katie's got it tucked away somewhere. Never did me any good that I can see."

But he fell asleep quite suddenly in the middle of Henry's retreat from Mons, and Henry put out the lights and raised the window before he tiptoed out.

When Grandfather Rogers opened his eyes again, Henry was standing by the bed, and the old man blinked at him.

"Sorry," he said. "Must have dozed off for a minute."

Henry smiled. "It's morning, sir. I've brought your breakfast."

Grandfather Rogers sat up in bed and looked. It was certainly morning, and there was a tray on a table. Moreover, Henry showed every indication of placing it on the bed. Grandfather Rogers eyed it indignantly.

"Great Scott," he said. "I'm not paralyzed, am I? You take that down and tell the hired girl I've been up for my breakfast ever since my mother weaned me. What time is it?"

He ate his breakfast downstairs that morning, to the annoyance of the household. Also he went up later and made his own bed, thus greatly embarrassing the chambermaid. When he came down again, he found Muriel in the hall, dressed to go out. She greeted him without enthusiasm.

"Tony wants you to have Sam and the car today," she said. "I do hope you can amuse yourself."

"I thought I'd go to Arlington."

As this definitely was not amusement, Muriel felt uncomfortable. She was still more uncomfortable when Grandfather Rogers, having donned his chest protector and old overcoat, shook Henry's hand before leaving the house.

"Maybe you don't know it," he said to Muriel, "but this fellow here's got quite a war record. Get him to

8

show you his medal."

Henry looked unhappy, but Muriel rallied and took it in her stride. "You must do that sometime, Henry," she said brightly. "I had no idea you were a soldier."

The old man went out, leaving what amounted to domestic chaos behind him. Henry apologized gravely.

"I'm sorry, madam," he said. "The old gentleman seemed lonely last night, and he wanted to talk. It won't happen again."

And then something, which under the State Department veneer was really Muriel, emerged and surprised her. "I understand, Henry. I—I really would like to see your medal someday. And I'm sure Mr. Rogers would, too."

Henry, however, was back, so to speak, in the Division of Protocol. He merely bowed. "Thank you, madam," he said, and called a taxi for her.

So Grandfather Rogers had the car that day. He sat in front beside Sam and, by and large, Sam learned a good bit about the Civil War. Also Grandfather Rogers learned a lot about Washington. They cruised first among the great stone buildings; but Grandfather Rogers seemed unimpressed. Only at the Lincoln Memorial, when Sam had helped him up the steps, he stood for a long time gazing up with his old eyes into the tragic, kindly face. Then he saluted, and, turning smartly, marched out again. Sam was waiting, and the old man looked out over the city.

"Wonder how *he'd* have liked it, Sam?" he said. "He wasn't much for show."

He was a little tired and more than a little cold when they reached the cemetery.

"I've got a son and a grandson here," he told Sam. "Tom died of typhoid in the Spanish War, and they brought his boy back from France and put him here, too. That was Tony's brother. My wife died when that happened. She'd banked a lot on Harry."

"Sure tough," said Sam.

The old man was silent after that. He was seeing Millie when the news came about Tom. She was sick, and he couldn't leave her. But she had wanted Tom in Arlington, and so they had buried him there. Millie had gone about like a ghost for months. Then she had pulled out of it, although she never forgot. It was Harry's death that had finished her. She'd fallen over with a heart attack when the telegram came. . . . Three graves, he thought. That was what a man had left if he lived long enough. Millie lay over the hill from the farm, and he had missed her every day for more than twenty years.

He had some difficulty in locating his graves. He found Tom's first and stood bareheaded beside it.

"Here he is, Millie," he said. "If you can hear me, he's here, and he's all right. Either he's busy somewhere else, or he's just asleep. You know how he liked to sleep."

But he stood longer beside Harry's, among that marching army of small white headstones. All these boys, he thought. Young once and full of life, and now lying there lost, and men and women still missing them. To what end? That he and others like him should stand there on a winter hillside, at the end of their lives and alone.

He was shivering when he went back to the car, and his ancient legs

9

were not too steady.

"Better go home, sir," said Sam, tucking the rug about him. "Kind of a strain, all this. And it's cold, too."

But Grandfather Rogers wanted to see the Tomb of the Unknown Soldier, and it was there that he first saw the Moselys. Not that they were the Moselys to him then. They were merely a boy and a girl, standing hand in hand, watching the sentry on his endless patrol. It was the expression on their faces that caught his attention. They looked, he thought, like lost children. They did not even speak until an elderly woman got out of an old car, laid some carnations at the foot of the tomb, and after standing a moment in silence, went away again. Then the boy stirred.

"So that's war and glory," he said. "A bunch of flowers freezing against a piece of marble."

"It's more than that," said the girl quietly. "To fight to save the country—"

"If it's worth saving," said the boy bitterly, and moved abruptly away.

It upset Grandfather Rogers. They were too young for that sort of thing. In their early twenties, probably—just the age Harry had been when he went to France. When he got into the car, he was shivering with cold, and Sam tucked him up carefully. The old man did not notice. He was gazing out over the city across the river. Then, halfway down the hill, he saw the young couple again. They were still hand in hand, and on an impulse he stopped the car.

"How about a lift into town?" he inquired. "Kind of cold for walking."

They hesitated, as though somehow kindness was unexpected. Then the girl smiled and agreed. They got in, and he saw that they were both thinly clad and pinched with cold.

"Thanks a lot," she said. "What a nice car! I never expected to ride in one like it."

"It's not mine," said Grandfather Rogers hastily. "Belongs to my grandson. I have an old one myself. Kind of willful, but goes now and then."

"We had one like that," said the girl. "We sold it for twenty-five dollars."

They were easier after that. They introduced themselves—John and Margery Mosely—and said they were in town for only a little while. Then for some reason they became silent, and Grandfather Rogers saw the boy take the girl's hand under the robe and hold it. But they accepted his offer of a hot drink at a drugstore, and when they separated, Margery thanked him nicely.

"You've been very kind," she said. "When I saw you at the Tomb, I thought you looked kind."

He did not see them again for several days. He stayed on at Tony's insistence, although he was often homesick for the old familiar things of the farm. He was rather lonely, to tell the truth. Both Tony and Muriel were busy, and even Henry remained aloof. Grandfather Rogers, dining alone in state when Tony and Muriel had gone out, would try to get him to talk.

"What's wrong with this country, Henry? Just as rich as it ever was, isn't it? Got everything. What's the trouble with it?"

"I couldn't say, sir," Henry would reply. "Will you have some more of the chicken?"

He filled his time as best he could. One day Sam took him to Mount Vernon, and he was cheered to learn that George Washington had also

10

worn false teeth, and had hated them as he did.

He made friends, of course. He made them everywhere. He would talk in his friendly fashion to tourists, to streetcar and bus conductors, to taxi drivers slapping themselves to keep warm. Some of them called him "colonel," and he would straighten under his old overcoat and smile, showing his teeth in all their perfection.

"Not a colonel, son, although I saw some fighting in my time."

They liked him. Sometimes he even took his lunch with them, sitting on a high stool at a counter. Behind his back they called him "Grandpap."

"Took Grandpap to the Capitol today."

"How'd he like it?"

"He liked the statuary."

That was a laugh. They had no illusions, especially the taxi drivers. They had consorted too long with the great and near-great. But behind the laugh was a sort of amused tenderness.

Then one day on the street he met John and Margery Mosely again. They looked better, less pinched, and Margery had a new outfit and looked very nice in it. Grandfather Rogers noticed it at once.

"Well, bless my soul," he said. "Here you are again. I see you've been doing some shopping."

There was a note of defiance in John's voice when he replied. "She's had something coming to her for a long time," he said. "Anyhow, we're going away soon. I wanted her to have one last fling."

"Going home, eh?"

"Yes," said Margery softly. "Going home."

He took them to the movies that afternoon, getting his money out of an old-fashioned purse to do so. It was a comedy, and they all enjoyed it. It did not occur to the old man that it was their mutual loneliness that had brought them together; or that they were three derelicts, washed up on the same shore until some tide would separate them forever. So he was rather astonished to see tears in Margery's eyes when they said goodbye at the hotel where they were staying.

"Thanks," she said. "Thanks a lot. And maybe we will see you again—sometime."

"Of course you will," said Grandfather Rogers. And because for some reason he felt uneasy, he patted her on the shoulder. "Have a nice time," he told her. "You're both young, and you've got each other. That's a lot to be thankful for."

Then he left them and went on, his kind old face beaming on all and sundry.

"Taxi, colonel?"

"No, thanks, son. I'm stretching my legs a bit."

"Looks like they're long enough already, colonel. I'm going home anyhow. Maybe I can drop you. No charge."

He was more cheerful that night. After all, in spite of its troubles, America was a pretty friendly place. Tony had brought him a new book, *Heroes of Four Wars*, and after he and Muriel had gone out as usual, the old man tried to read it by the library fire. But he was drowsy. The book fell to the floor, and he slept.

The next day the weather changed. It had been cold and sunny, as only Washington can be in winter. In the small circle near the house children in long leggings and small, thick coats had played, and Grandfather

Rogers had regularly stopped to watch them. At such times he wished that Tony and Muriel had a child to carry on the name; but after a day or two of observing Muriel's life, he saw that a child did not belong in it. He would sigh and go on.

Then the snow came—a soft, wet snow, which took the latent heat out of the air and left it raw and penetrating. For the first time since his arrival the old man was housebound. He was lonely and unhappy.

One day he wrote to Katie: "I am having a fine time. Tony and his wife are taking good care of me, and I wear the chest protector as per instructions, although I gather from Muriel's face that she doesn't care much for it. Don't laugh, but they have a butler here, and he helps me into my pants. Makes me feel like a fool. They tried to feed me in bed, too, but I put an end to that.

"This is a fine city, but I guess it cost the taxpayers of the country plenty to build it. Well, easy come, easy go.

"Yours,

"Alexander Cameron Rogers.

"P.S. Don't worry about my being lonely. I have made quite a few friends, although I doubt if Tony's wife would care for some of them."

As events proved, Muriel did not. One day she gave a tea for the wife of what Tony called his boss. She had been a long time in getting that eminent lady, and all morning the house was in a turmoil. Then at four o'clock she called Tony frantically on the telephone.

"What am I to do?" she wailed. "He's all over the place, and I simply can't have him around, Tony."

"Give him Sam," said Tony. "He might like a drive."

"I need Sam."

Tony grunted. "Well, it's your party," he said. "I don't suppose any of your women would drop dead if they did see him. They're a sturdy lot."

Muriel banged down the receiver.

But she was relieved when at five o'clock Henry gravely reported that Mr. Rogers had put on his overshoes and chest protector and gone out. She hurried into the library, hid Grandfather Roger's ancient pipe, emptied the ash tray, and raised the window for a moment.

"You can bring those roses in now," she told Henry. "We may not use this room, but I want the whole house to look nice."

The party was a great success. Everybody who was anybody came. A long line of automobiles extended up and down the street; Sam was on the pavement opening car doors; and best of all, there was no sign of Grandfather Rogers. Then, practically one hour later, over the chatter of women and the click of teacups, Muriel proudly showed her honor guest the lower floor of the house.

"Such a nice house," said that great lady, with her tired official smile. "How well you have done it."

"It was a mess when we took it," said Muriel, and threw open the library door. The library, so to speak, was her *tour de force*. It had, she considered, atmosphere. And certainly at the moment it had plenty of atmosphere. Muriel stood transfixed in the doorway.

Standing in front of the fire was Grandfather Rogers who had removed his overcoat but not his chest protector; and sitting in a large handsome chair was what was unmistakably a taxi driver. He was holding a glass of hot toddy, and as

12

they looked, he raised it.

"Well, here's to you, colonel," the taxi driver said happily.

Muriel closed the door, and the great lady smiled, not so officially.

"Such a nice room," she murmured. "And thank you for the party, my dear. I've really enjoyed it."

Which she probably had, since she smiled—not officially—most of the way home.

Muriel spent the evening sulking in bed, and Grandfather and Tony had dinner together. The old man was happy. Tony talked quite a little about Europe—not giving away any official secrets, of course—but he had little to say about America.

"Now, look, son," said Grandfather Rogers. "We used to think this was a great country. Nothing we couldn't do. Now the courage has gone out of us. What's the matter with us?"

But Tony's mind was on Europe, and on Muriel, in tears upstairs.

"Europe's in a pretty mess," he said absently.

Grandfather Rogers said irritably: "Better forget it and get busy about America. It's cost a lot to build and save. Go over to Arlington someday, son. It might make you think."

Tony went so often to Arlington with quite a number of important visitors that this left him unimpressed. He drew out of his pocket an invitation to a White House reception, with Grandfather Rogers's name written in to match the engraving, and handed it to him. But the old man eyed it coldly.

"What for?" he said suspiciously. "I don't hold with that fellow there, and I don't care if he knows it."

Tony grinned. "You don't have to kiss him," he said. "Just shake hands and move on. They'll have the Marine Band. You'll like that."

It was actually the band that decided Grandfather Rogers.

The next few days passed slowly for him. He went out one day and was forcibly fitted with an evening suit for the great occasion. And another day he saw the Moselys again. John had a new overcoat; but for all their new clothes, they looked more like lost children than ever. Before he could reach them, they got on a streetcar, leaving him more puzzled than before. He had a queer, apprehensive feeling that day, as though they had gone for good; as though indeed, having picked them out of nowhere, he had lost them there.

But he had not lost them.

It was the afternoon of the reception at the White House when he realized that. Everything had been perfectly normal up to that time. He had been out, spending some time standing by the Grant monument near the Capitol. He thought it very handsome, especially the horses, although he had never seen General Grant, and his memory of that war had been mostly of dirt and hunger and slogging along on foot. When he got back, he found Henry hanging up the dress suit and putting the studs in the stiff shirt. He sat down and eyed the outfit unfavorably.

"I'll look like a black rooster in that," he grumbled. "All tail and no front."

Henry ventured to smile. "That's the way I felt, sir, the first time I wore one."

"When was that?" Grandfather Rogers inquired, interested. "Thought you English were born in them."

Henry hesitated. Then he said: "It was after the war, sir. I'd saved a little, but it was almost gone. There were no jobs, and medals were selling for ten shillings or less. So I decided to have one last fling, as you might say. That's when I got the evening clothes. I'd never had any before."

Grandfather Rogers eyed him with interest. "And then what?" he asked.

Henry looked apologetic. "You know how it is, sir. I was young and pretty desperate. I had a good time for a week or so. After that I meant—well, there was always the river, sir."

But Grandfather Rogers was getting up out of his chair. He had a quite dreadful look on his face.

"I'm a darned old fool, Henry," he said, and marched out of the room and out of the house.

When Tony, carrying a new dress tie, came home at six, he looked into the library and found it empty. Muriel, of course, was not in.

"Where is Mr. Rogers?" he asked Henry. "In his room?"

"No, sir. He left the house some time ago."

"Good Lord," said Tony, annoyed. "He knows he's going out tonight, doesn't he?"

"Yes, sir, he knows, all right. The clothes are in his room. He saw them."

Tony ordered a whisky-and-soda and lighted a cigarette. He was vaguely uneasy, but the old boy had seemed pretty capable of looking after himself. When Henry brought his drink, however, he questioned him.

"Did he say where he was going?"

"No, sir. I was fixing his shirt, and—" Henry gulped—"I don't know what happened, sir. He acted as if he'd just remembered something. He said he was a darned old fool, if you'll excuse the expression."

"Well, it's a darned nuisance, any-how," said Tony.

He was not really anxious. He smoked a cigarette and looked at the paper, which was saying unpleasant things about the Administration, as usual. But when he looked into the hall closet to see the condition of his top hat, he saw Grandfather Rogers's chest protector on the floor. He picked it up, and he was still holding it when Muriel arrived.

"He's gone. And without this," he said.

"Gone where? Home?" said Muriel hopefully.

"No. Just out, no one knows where. I've a notion to call the police."

"And get in the papers? Don't be silly. What could happen to him?"

"That's what I intend to find out," said Tony grimly.

He did not call the police, however. He went up to the old man's room first; but there was no clue there. The room itself seemed mutely to protect him. It looked bare, as though the old man's living in it had left little or no impression on it; as though, indeed, great age asked little and required little. Except for the hired evening clothes, which looked oddly out of place, there were only a pair of worn hairbrushes, a small photograph of his dead wife, a second suit of clothing in the closet, a few undergarments, a toothbrush, and a tin of something to keep false teeth from slipping. Tony surveyed the room with a sense of guilt.

And he's had so little from us, he thought. A bed and food. Good Lord, if anything has happened to him—

It was eight o'clock, and in spite of Muriel and the press, Tony was calling the police, when Grandfather

Rogers finally returned. There was no excitement about his return. He simply rang the doorbell, and Henry found him standing there. Henry kept his relief out of his voice.

"We've been worried about you, sir," he said. "Steady, sir. Not sick, are you?"

He reached out and caught the old man by the arm; but Grandfather Rogers shook him off.

"I'm all right," he said testily. "I want to sit down, that's all. I'm tired."

It was there that Tony found him, looking weary and incredibly old, while Henry hovered over him.

"Sorry, Tony," he said slowly. "Just let me rest here for a minute. I've been kind of busy."

Tony eyed him. He was pale, and the scar of an old bullet wound stood out, livid, on his wrinkled face.

"Don't want to bother you, but do you care to talk about it?" Tony asked.

"Not yet. Maybe later."

Tony put an arm around the thin shoulders. "Better tell me, old soldier," he said. "Better get to bed, too. Henry and I will take you up. No party tonight."

But Grandfather Rogers shook his head, and this time he smiled. "Can't waste that dress suit, can we? It would break Henry's heart."

An hour later they were on the way to the White House. The drive was uneventful, except that outside the White House Grandfather Rogers lowered a window and hailed a policeman standing there.

"Hi, Bill," he called in his cracked voice. "Got it all fixed. Everything's hunky-dory."

The policeman stared. He did not know the old man in his finery. Then he grinned. "Good for you, colonel," he said.

Tony, puzzled, mutely thanked his gods that Muriel was not there, and the car drove on.

If the White House and its pageantry impressed Grandfather Rogers that night, he did not show it—the uniforms and foreign decorations everywhere, the brilliance of the Marine Band, the clothes and jewels of the women as the line moved slowly forward. And people looked at him, Tony noticed; at his erect figure, his fine old head. Suddenly he was proud of him. He was a fighter. They had all been fighters, his people. He and his kind had fought for this country, and it still belonged to them. Maybe he'd been forgetting that. Maybe a lot of people had been forgetting it.

It was not until after Grandfather Rogers had shaken the presidential hand that anything happened. Jammed into the East Room, they came face to face with one of the Cabinet officers, and the Secretary looked interested when he heard Grandfather Roger's name.

"Rogers?" he said. "I don't suppose you could be related to Alexander Cameron Rogers?"

"That's my name, sir," said the old man stiffly.

"Great Scott!" he said. "I was reading about you only today. New book, *Heroes of Four Wars*. Had no idea you were still—" He coughed and turned to Tony. "Where's his decoration, Tony? He's got the Medal of Honor. Ought to have worn it tonight."

Grandfather Rogers looked at him. "It was a long time ago, Mr. Secretary," he said. "Price of medals has gone down since."

The Secretary looked bewildered.

So did Tony. However, the news passed through the room. People began to gather around the old man. The circle grew. It became a crowd, and the crowd almost a riot. But if it was Grandfather Rogers's one hour of glory, he did not show it. Now and then he smiled, showing his porcelain teeth, and when word came that the President—who was upstairs by that time and probably in bed—would like to see him the following day, he merely nodded acquiescence.

"Got something to say to him," he said rather grimly.

But suddenly he looked very tired, as though the will power that had carried him so far had all at once failed him. In the midst of the ovation he turned to Tony.

"Get me out of here, son," he said.

That took time, however. They did not want to let him go. More and more people came. The wife of Tony's boss was among them, looking thrilled but also amused.

"I think we've met before, Mr. Rogers," she said. "That is, I've seen you."

The old man looked blank; but the great lady glanced at Tony and gave him what amounted to a grin.

"Imagine your hiding such a celebrity, Tony," she said. "I happened on him only by accident. At your house. You may have heard about it."

"And how!" said Tony, looking proud and excited.

He got the old man outside by main force. But by that time nothing astonished Tony, even when a taxi driver drove up to receive a lady in a tiara, and Grandfather Rogers leaned out of the crowd to call to the driver.

"How's the boil?" he inquired with interest.

"Fine," said the driver. "It busted today."

So it did not surprise Tony to find that they were not going directly home that night.

"I'd like to go to the railroad station, son," said Grandfather Rogers. "Won't take long."

"Somebody you know going away?"

In the darkness the old man smiled. "Yes. But not so far as they expected. Two young people I happened to meet," he added. "Couldn't get work and wouldn't go on relief. They sold what little they had and then came here for one last fling. It would have been, too, if it hadn't been for Henry."

"Henry?" said Tony, astonished. "What has Henry got to do with it?"

"He said there was always the river," said Grandfather Rogers mildly. "You might learn a little about the folks around you sometime, son. They're likely to be interesting."

"What about these young people?"

"They're all right. We found them on the bridge, that policeman and I. Nice fellow, Bill. He's got five kids." He leaned back and yawned. "Anyhow, it's all fixed. They're going to the farm tonight. They'll like it there. Plenty to eat and plenty to do. There's a lot of room in this country still," he added, and yawned again.

Tony sat very still. He felt guilty. He and Muriel on their everlasting frivolous round, and the old man going about alone and getting close to the great common level of humanity. Even his job—how important was it? What did it matter in a world full of human anxiety and suffering?

He reached over and touched Grandfather Rogers's withered old hand. "You're a grand guy," he said. "And a great person, sir. I guess I've learned a few things tonight."

He did not go into the station. He had a feeling that this thing concerned only three people—two of them very young and one incredibly old. But there was a new gentleness when, on Grandfather Rogers's return, he carefully tucked the rug about the old man's legs.

"Everything all right, sir?"

"Everything fine," said Grandfather Rogers.

He was very weary. His legs ached, and his hand where it had been squeezed. Also his teeth bothered him. In the darkness he took them out, wrapped them in a handkerchief, and tucked them in the pocket of his tailcoat.

"If I yelp, you'll know they've bit me," he told Tony, and in a moment he was fast asleep.

A week later he went home to the farm. It had been a big week, with people calling to see him, including a foreign ambassador or two, an elderly member of the Supreme Court, and practically the entire membership of the Army and Navy Club. Muriel, on one occasion, heard him tell an ambassador about his hired dress suit; but as the ambassador laughed heartily, it was apparently all right.

Henry packed for him, and at the last moment Grandfather Rogers, instead of shaking hands, gave him a military salute, and Henry returned it stiffly.

"Good-bye, major," said Grandfather Rogers. "And good luck to you."

"Good-bye, colonel," said Henry, smiling. "I shall miss you, sir." They shook hands then, and Henry's back was straight as he marched into the house.

Both Muriel and Tony took the old man to the train. Perhaps Muriel had not expected that half the taxidrivers at the station would gather around him to say good-bye, or that he would shake Sam warmly by the hand before he left him. But Tony was not surprised. Nor was he surprised when, on the way to his car, the old man went forward to the engine and looked up at the engineer in the cab.

"How've you been?" he said affably.

"Pretty good. How'd you like the big town?"

"All right," said Grandfather Rogers and went back to his car.

It took some time to get him settled on the train, however. This time he was traveling by Pullman; but he had to look up Ed first. Ed greeted him warmly.

"Well, I suppose you saw the President," he said, grinning.

"Saw him! Suffering snakes, I had a visit with him," said Grandfather Rogers proudly. "Told him some things, too."

"You don't say," said Ed, with interest. "What did you tell him?"

But it was time for the train to go. Grandfather Rogers was rather astonished when Muriel put her arms around him and kissed him. He would have been even more astonished had he heard her in the car on the way home. She slid a hand into Tony's, and he saw there were tears in her eyes.

"I wish I'd been kinder to him, Tony. That's what he is—kind. Isn't he?"

Tony considered that gravely. "I'll tell you what he is, my girl," he said. "He's an American. At least he's America before it went high-hat.

I suppose, in a way, the old boy's Democracy as it ought to be."

Feeling embarrassed by this, he kissed Muriel and grinned. "There's good stuff in you, darling. Every now and then it comes out. As now," he added, and dried her eyes for her.

On the train Grandfather Rogers made himself comfortable. For a little while he thought of John and Margery Mosely. He saw them again in the dark on the bridge, still holding hands and gazing down at the Potomac River. He had been just in time, he and the policeman Bill. But it had been Bill who had got to them first.

"Here, what are you doing?" he had demanded roughly.

"Whose business is that?" John had said, looking desperate and defiant.

And then Bill's voice had softened. "There's an old party here got kind of worried about you kids. Come on, colonel, here they are."

Well, it was all right now. Margery had cried a lot, but it had probably done her good. A minute or two more, and they'd have been gone, poor children; fussed up with life and not knowing what it was all about. Like the whole country now. Just growing pains. The country was all right. All it needed was time.

He settled down in his seat, and after a while, finding himself unobserved, he took out his teeth and put them away. Then he put on his spectacles and looked at the book on his knee, *Heroes of Four Wars*. What made· a hero, anyway? Tom and Harry in Arlington, and Henry holding a man's pants and asking him how he liked chicken. Even John Mosely, facing eternity for Margery and himself rather than go on relief. All brave, but all waste somehow. He sighed.

Nevertheless, he opened the book and started to read: "In the last hundred years the United States has engaged in four wars. In all of these it has seen many acts of valor. This book . . ."

But the car was warm and the motion of the train soothing. The book slid from his hands to his knees and from his knees to the floor.

When Ed came back to hear what he had said to the President, Grandfather Rogers was fast asleep. Ed carefully drew the window shade and left him there.

THE SPIRIT OF AMERICA
By ANGELO PATRI

AHEAD are the children of the next generation. We are to carry to them the Spirit of America. We must show them what went before, what lies ahead. We must lead them to seek through the dimness of centuries, a gleaming line of silver white. It is the line of the Crusaders, steady, straight and strong, the quest for the Holy Grail, the search for Freedom.

Back there, glimmering faintly in the dawn of history, stand the gods, their very names lost in the long ago.

There are the prophets, and the teachers, and the law-givers, a mighty host.

There is Moses, and those who followed him out of bondage.

There are the martyrs.

Now the line brightens and broadens. We are nearer. We can see some of the faces. There are Columbus, Washington, Lafayette, Garibaldi.

There is Lincoln.

There is Roosevelt.

There are the countless hosts who fought on the world's battlefields. We know them well.

The light streams from their faces. Their helmets gleam. Their swords flash fire. A fearless, dauntless, invincible army, they march on, and on and on to the fullness of Freedom. They live.

They are with us, children of America. They urge us on. They command us to go forward.

Man has slaved through the ages that we might be free. He has battled that we might have peace. He has studied that we might know. He has left us the heritage of the ages that we in our turn might carry it on.

Ahead of us are the children of the next generation. It is for them that we must live. It is for them that we must go on.

We are the torchbearers of Liberty. We, too, must take our place in the search for Freedom, the quest for the Holy Grail.

It is for this, we, the children of America, were born.

AND THOU, AMERICA
WALT WHITMAN

And thou, America,
Thy offspring towering e'er so high, yet higher Thee above all towering,
With Victory on thy left, and at thy right hand Law;
Thou Union holding all, fusing, absorbing, tolerating all,
Thee, ever Thee, I sing!

Thou, also Thou, a World,
With all thy wide geographies, manifold, different, distant,
Rounded by Thee in one—one common orbic language,
One common indivisible destiny for All . . . .

Behold, America!
Behold! thy fields and farms, thy far-off woods and mountains.
As in procession coming . . . .

Behold, in Oregon, far in the North and West,
Or in Maine, far in the North and East, thy cheerful axemen,
Wielding all day their axes.
Behold, on the lakes, thy pilots at their wheels, thy oarsmen,
How the ash writhes under their muscular arms! . . .

And thou, the Emblem, waving over all! . . .
Now here and hence in peace, all thine, O Flag!
And here and hence for thee, O universal Muse! and thou for them!
And here and hence, O Union, all the work and workmen thine!
None separate from Thee—henceforth One only, we and Thou!

19

REMEMBER the Alamo!—*Colonel Sidney Sherman*

AN AMERICAN kneels only to his God.—*Colonel William Crittenden*

THE GREATEST GLORY of a freeborn people is to transmit that freedom to their children.—*William Harvard*

PERFECT FREEDOM is as necessary to the health and vigor of commerce, as it is to the health and vigor of citizenship.—*Patrick Henry*

I PLEDGE ALLEGIANCE to the Flag of the United States of America and to the Republic for which it stands, one Nation, indivisible, with liberty and justice for all.
—*Bellamy* and *Upham*

AMONG THE NATURAL RIGHTS of the colonists are these: first a right to life, secondly to liberty, thirdly to property; together with the right to defend them in the best manner they can.—*Samuel Adams*

BUT WHILE I DO LIVE, let me have a country, or at least the hope of a country, and that, a free country.—*Webster*

THE PEOPLE'S GOVERNMENT, made for the people, made by the people, and answerable to the people.—*Webster*

THE PRINCIPLE of spending money to be paid by posterity, under the name of funding, is but swindling futurity on a large scale.—*Jefferson*

WE ARE APT to believe what is pleasant rather than what is true.—*Penn*

INDEPENDENCE now and independence forever.—*Webster*

THEN JOIN HAND in hand, brave Americans all;
By uniting we stand, by dividing we fall.
—*John Dickinson*

LIBERTY

I HAVE not begun to fight!—*John Paul Jones*

HOLD the fort, for I am coming!—*General William T. Sherman*

WE SELL OUR BIRTHRIGHT whenever we sell our liberty for any price of gold or honor.—*Whipple*

TELL THE MEN to fire faster and not to give up the ship; fight her till she sinks. (His last words)—*Captain James Lawrence*

DRIVEN FROM EVERY OTHER CORNER of the earth, freedom of thought and the right of private judgment in matters of conscience direct their course to this happy country as their last asylum.—*Samuel Adams*

ANY GOVERNMENT IS FREE to the people where the laws rule and the people are a party to the laws. For liberty without obedience is confusion, and obedience without liberty is slavery.—*Penn*

GENERAL TAYLOR never surrenders. (Reply to Mexican General Santa Anna before battle of Buena Vista, 1847)—*Thomas Leonidas Crittenden*

DON'T FIRE unless fired upon; but if they mean to have war, let it begin here! —*Captain John Parker*

THE CONSTITUTION in all its provision looks to an indestructible Union composed of indestructible States.—*Chase*

WE HAVE MET the enemy, and they are ours.—*Commander Oliver H. Perry*

AND NE'ER shall the sons of Columbia be slaves,
While the earth bears a plant, or the sea rolls its waves.
—*Robert Treat Paine*

THEY HAVE A RIGHT to censure, that have a heart to help.—*Penn*

21

Between Americans

By NORMAN CORWIN

AMERICAN. This program is between Americans. That's where the title comes in. We hope you like it, but you don't have to. At any rate, nobody's goin' to make you stick around and listen to it. That's one of the advantages of being an American.

We invite you to think that one over for a moment; and while you're exercisin' your inalienable right to tune us out or let us ride, we'll help ourselves to a music cue. *Music: A little prelude which starts out as American as Kansas City but suddenly and inexplicably goes Oriental on us.*

AMERICAN. What that Chinese music was doin' there I don't know. Never know what to expect these days. But then, a little mixin' of strain never bothered any real American. Not when we've got States named after French kings and English queens, or lifted right out of the Latin language like Montana or out o' the Spanish like Nevada. Now you take Vermont. Vermont is the French for Green Mountain—*vert* for green, *mont* for mountain—simple as all that. They call it the Green Mountain State, don't they?

It's a good thing there were some Indians around once to give us some original names, or we'd be in bad shape. You know, if we was to hold a convention of all the people who live in foreign-soundin' American towns, we could fill quite a sizable stadium. Among the delegates registerin' on the first day would be—

LONDONER. Me, I'm the delegate from London—Minnesota.

DUBLINITE. I'm in from Dublin—New Hampshire.

BERLINER. Flew in this morning from Berlin—Oregon.

ROMAN (*after some confusion*). Whose turn, me? I'm from Rome—Mississippi.

TOKIOITE. I'm from Tokio—Texas.

SHANGHAIAN. I came alla way from Shanghai—West Virginia.

WARSAVIAN. Warsaw—Georgia.

MOSCOVITE. Ah'm the delegate representin' Moscow—Kentucky.

TORONTONIAN. My town is Toronto—Kansas.

LISBONIAN. As for me, Lisbon—Maine.

MADRILENO. Delegate from Madrid—Alabama—reportin'.

STOCKHOLMER. I'm from Stockholm—South Dakota.

BOMBAYITE. Drove down this afternoon from Bombay—New York.

BAGDADDY. Hitch-hiked here from Bagdad—Florida.

AMERICAN. All right, gentlemen, now that you've registered, you may all be seated.

Sound of people being seated.

AMERICAN. Now that's all the preliminaries there's goin' to be tonight. We're through with the introductions, the overture, and the official registration, so now we can get down to the text . . . which is, roughly speakin', this:

People are thinkin' about their

22

country pretty hard these days . . . some of them for the first time in their lives. People are wonderin' where we're headed. Men are bein' called on to defend America, and a lot of them are thinkin' in terms of what there is to defend.

Well now, America means a lot of things to a lot of people. Most Americans are solid patriots, only they don't know it. They don't have to wear a red-white-and-blue button in their lapels to prove it. They don't have to fall on their faces every time they hear a popular patriotic tune. They don't need nobody to prod 'em in the back with a bayonet so's they'll take their hats off when the flag goes by. They don't have to agree with, or even listen to, people like this—

ORATOR. (*Bombastic and fulsome double-talk, unintelligible except for accent and inflection, which are caricatured.*)

AMERICAN. We got a good hunch most people prefer the quiet kind of speaker like the fellow who got up on a platform in a Pennsylvania town one day and said—

LINCOLN. The world will little note, nor long remember what we say here.

AMERICAN. That was the Gettysburg address he was referrin' to; and as a matter of fact, he didn't get such good reviews the next mornin'. Take, for example, the write-up in the Harrisburg *Patriot:*

PATRIOT. We pass over the silly remarks of the President: for the credit of the nation, we are willing that they shall no more be repeated and thought of.

AMERICAN. If you think that's bad, listen to what the Chicago *Times* had to say:

TIMES. The cheek of every American must tingle with shame as he reads the silly, flat, and dishwatery utterances of the man who has to be pointed out to intelligent foreigners as the President of the United States.

AMERICAN. O' course, the rival paper in Chicago—the *Tribune*—took the opposite point of view. Rival papers often do:

TRIBUNE. The remarks of President Lincoln will live among the annals of men.

AMERICAN. The *Trib* gave it four stars, and they was right. The Gettysburg address did survive.

Now, that business of callin' a president a ham is really somethin' to be proud of. I mean, the right to print a piece saying a president makes a sound like dishwater. That's important. Nobody dragged the editors off to jail even if they was wrong. Today there's a terrific lot of opinion on the loose, and the poll-makers are pursuin' it—at a Gallup, you might say. Comes under the headin' of free press. As soon as anybody starts gaggin' the press—any press—watch out! Americans don't like that.

And by the way, we got a nerve to be callin' ourselves Americans all the time, when we're really only United Staters. We're a little selfish about that. Do you know that a citizen of Punta Arenas on the Strait of Magellan has as much right to sing *America the Beautiful* as you have? Under his technical rights any Latin American could sing like this—

Music: "America the Beautiful" sung in heavy Spanish accent, accompanied by orchestra. Hold for ten seconds; then drop and sustain briefly under:

AMERICAN. It's America down there

23

in Chile, too. All the way down the spine of the Andes. And if any of you folks are hearin' this down in Mexico or Honduras or Salvador or Argentina, or even if you're an Eskimo in the Arctic, we hope you'll overlook our callin' ourselves Americans as though we was the only ones in the hemisphere. We do that just because it's so much easier to say than anything else, and also because it sounds so good.

And by the way—before we leave the subject—what about the original Americans: the Indians? They're the only race which the scientists honor by the name of *homo americanus*. Not even George Washington and Tom Jefferson were *homo americanuses*. The only real Americans left today, if you want to get good and tough and anthropological about it, is a minority group.

There's a forgotten race for you. Even the forgotten man has forgotten the forgotten race.

Music: Indian motif in.

AMERICAN. How about the Indian on the nickel? And the buffalo who roamed the back of the great American jit? Seems a shame. No two ways about it—we *have* forgotten them hundred-per-cent Americans who went down to quarantine to meet the *Mayflower*. We don't see them around in person very much these days, but their ghosts are still with us.

Music: Up briefly, the instrumentation going slightly shrill for the following paragraph and returning to normalcy after it.

AMERICAN. Maybe the red men are forgotten, maybe not. (*Low and confidential.*) But between you an' us an' this program, it's said that near Boonesboro, Kentucky, on certain nights in November by the light of the waning moon, some very peculiar ghost-meetin's go on in the woods south of the river; also in certain parts of the Alleghenies, between the hours of sundown and the comin' of the mornin' mists. Yes, and if you happen to be listenin' to this in a car drivin' along Highway 99 in Wyomin'—that man you passed walkin' down the road a few miles back wasn't a man at all!

(*Reflectively.*) They were a brave people, the Indians. Fought a losin' fight against great odds. Wanted nothin' more'n to keep their land and their way of life— fightin' the fight so many people of all races have had to fight since, the fight to keep free and independent, the fight to stop men from the outside who want to "civilize" somebody else *their* way.

Perhaps today the Indian looks down from a reasonably happy huntin' ground—and wonders— wonders whether right here at home among the people who took their place there are any tribes still strugglin' to be free—whether in any part of this inherited country a man is any less a man because of his color or of his race.

Music: Up and to a quiet conclusion.

AMERICAN (*on a new tack*). Have you ever asked yourself what America means to you? Does it mean 1776? *Columbia the Gem of the Ocean*? Big business? The Bill of Rights? Uncle Sam? Chances are it means none

24

of these things. Chances are it means somethin' very personal to each of you . . . somethin' close to your heart which you'd miss like the very blazes if you was stranded abroad. It might have nothin' at all to do with quotes from Madison or Acts of Congress. It might be just the feelin' about crisp autumns in New England and the smell of burnin' leaves . . . it might be the memory of the way they smooth off the infield between the games of a double-header . . . it might be a thing as small as your little finger.

Have you ever been abroad an' run out of American cigarettes? . . .

Fade in a background of Spanish conversation simultaneously with:

CLERK. *No, Señor, solo hablo español.*

TOURIST. Well, anyway, do you carry cigarettes?

CLERK. *Ah, cigarillos—sí, tenemos bastante aquí.*

TOURIST. Naw, I just want cigarettes. I'll take these. How much?

CLERK. *Veinte centavos.*

TOURIST. Keep the change.
Sounds of opening package.

TOURIST. Got a light there, Seenior?

CLERK. *Sí, como no, Señor—un momento.*

Sound of scratching a match.

TOURIST. Hey—what is this—soft coal? (*Spits tobacco grains from lips.*) Pfoo! Tastes like an old shoe. Here, you can smoke the rest of them.

AMERICAN. There y'are—America might mean a tight-packed cigarette which tastes good; it might mean the way a hotdog man slaps mustard on a frank; it might mean goin' with your wife to the Orpheum on bank nite, or takin' your girl to the annual barn dance and social at Tuckerman's barn. Plenty you listeners know what I'm talkin' about.

Music: Fade in square-dance music, under:

PROMPTER. All join hands.
Circle eight till you get straight.
Knock down Sal and pick up Kate.
First couple lead the couple on the right.

Wave the ocean, wave the sea,
Wave that pretty girl back to me.
Swing your opposite, now your own,
Couple up four in a little bitty ring,
Do see, lady, you pretty little thing.

On to the next, don't be slow,
Make that wooden leg jar the flo'.
On the corner with your left hand,
Meet your partner, right and left grand.

Music: Dance effect fades under:

AMERICAN. Do you hear people speak of home defense? This is home, buddy, the home to be defended— this square dance down the glen a piece, in old man Tuckerman's barn—this is the America of all the couples dancin' there tonight— this is what "the nation" means to Butch and Fred and Jenny and Elvira; this is America to all the boys and girls from Malvern County and their folks at home sittin' up, out on the porch, waitin' for them.

What do you suppose America means to that auto repair man in the grease-caked dungarees who works in the garage on the corner of Willow and Elm Streets? It means, quite likely, crawlin' (*fading*) under that 1936 Buick and draggin' an electric light bulb on a long extension after him. . . .

Slight echo throughout the following:

PETE. Joe, hand me that wrench.
JOE (*off*). What wrench?
PETE. The wrench at your feet—right there.
JOE. Where? I don't see no wrench.
PETE. Y' blind? Where you lookin'? No! Behind ya!
JOE. Well, whyncha say so? Here y'are.

Sound of wrench being thrown and landing on stone floor.

PETE. 'At's more like it.

Desultory clanking as Pete swings into action under the car. Effect continues under:

AMERICAN. Sure—that's America to Pete and Joe . . . piston job, transmission job, valve job, jack it up and change the tire, new fan belt, check the pump—and on Saturday night, take the girl down to Joyland Dance Park. It means repairs to those boys, and cans of oil, and carburetor mixtures. And to Jack Prentiss, who owns the Buick that Pete is fixing and who lives down on the beach near the Coast Guard station, America means the sound and the sight and the smell of high tide under the full moon, with occasionally the melancholy note of the buoy driftin' up when the wind's blowin' in from the ship channel.

Sneak in sound of waves and faint buoy whistle under the last sentence. After these are established:

Music: Moon motif, behind speech.

AMERICAN. It means the age-old sound of the sea—the same sound folks are hearin' this very moment up around Penobscot Bay, an' Marblehead, an' Chincoteague Inlet, down by Calibogue Sound, and on Boca Chica, and then clean over to the other coast, by Guadalupe and Carmel.

Pause for sound alone.

AMERICAN. Yes—wind and wave and sand and rock and riptide and undertow—that's America to Jack Prentiss and all the thousands o' folks settled on the coastlines between Eastport, Key West, Point Isabel, and Birch Bay.

Fade entire effect as speaker continues.

AMERICAN. America is all things to all her people—prairie to Nebraskans, coal to Scranton miners, cameras and raw celluloid to the picture boys in Hollywood, the stink of crude oil to the men who work the wells, relief checks to the unemployed, a mike and stopwatch to a radio production man, a B.M.T. express to Brooklyn office clerks.

Sure, sure. That's the way it goes. Or isn't it? What does this country mean to you? It might mean anything—anything at all. It might mean a course in highfalutin' poetry at Harvard. . . .
LECTURER. Today, gentlemen, we will consider the influence of Whitman on the development of poetry

26

in America. By 1870, after twelve years of incessant attack against squeamish overrefinements, (*fading*) Whitman really began to create an active distaste for literary affectation. . . .

AMERICAN. Or else it might be an argument between two baseball fans as to which is better, the Yankees or the Red Sox:

FIRST FAN. Yeah, but look—the Yanks are a bunch of old men and cripples.

SECOND FAN. (*Laughs scornfully.*)

FIRST FAN. They won't last, I tell ya, they won't last. Wait'll it gets good and hot, aroun' the middle o' July. Wait'll 'em double-headers begin pilin' up.

SECOND FAN. Don't make me laff, Eddie. Lissen, Di Mag is havin' the best season he ever had. He's an old man, huh? Keller hittin' a dozen homers! I'd like to be a cripple like that. New home run record for the club. Won't last, huh? Who's the Red Sox got as good as Di Mag? Name one guy.

FIRST FAN. I'll name two: Ted Williams.

SECOND FAN. A good hitter—no gettin' away from that. But you say he's better than Di Mag?

FIRST FAN. How about the pitchin'? (*Fading.*)

SECOND FAN. Wait a minute—do you say he's—

FIRST FAN. Cronin's a smart guy. He knows how to . . .

AMERICAN. Or it could be a poker game in Charlie Ferriter's law office upstairs over the five-and-ten-cent store on a rainy afternoon; or a meetin' of the Kiwanis Club in the Mansion House on Thursday . . . or the news store on the corner . . . or a great symphony concert sent out over everybody's air, playin' the music of all the world's great composers regardless of their race or nationality. F'rinstance, somethin' by a German Jew named Mendelssohn . . . somethin' you couldn't play in certain countries on the other side. . . .

Music: Opening of "Reformation" Symphony. Hold for about fifteen seconds; then bring down behind:

AMERICAN. Now let's stop a minute an' figure this out. Is it an accident that makes just bein' a citizen in this comparatively young country so attractive to so many people? To the world's greatest skater, from Norway? To the world's greatest mathematician, from Germany? To the world's greatest orchestra conductor, from Italy? Is it an accident that a thousand million people all around the world would give everything they own to be in your shoes—a free citizen of this country—right this very minute? . . . Well, why is that? Is it the weather here? Let's ask some of the natives. You, from New York. How's the weather out your way?

NEW YORKER. I like it all right, only the summers give me a pain. Sticky and hot. And then we usually get a stretch of terrible overcast weather around April and November. Sometimes ten days go by without the sun coming out once.

AMERICAN. And you, from Miami, Florida?

FLORIDIAN. Climate's fine, except

27

you have to watch out for hurricanes.

AMERICAN. The gentleman from Kansas?

KANSAN. Summers get pretty hot and winters pretty cold. Tornadoes raise a ruckus every once in a while.

AMERICAN. Los Angeles? You?

ANGELINO. Wonderful climate! Magnificent!

AMERICAN. Don't you ever get tired of all that sunshine?

ANGELINO. No, sir, not a bit.

AMERICAN. Never rains?

ANGELINO. A little precipitation, maybe, but no rain.

AMERICAN. No earthquakes?

ANGELINO. Just little ones. Are you interested in some real estate?

AMERICAN. No, thanks. . . . And you from San Francisco, how about it there?

FRISCAN. Best climate in the world. Tops.

AMERICAN. Lots of sunshine?

FRISCAN. Lots.

AMERICAN. Lots of fog?

FRISCAN. Lots.

AMERICAN. All right, then it's not the weather that makes us so attractive. Is it maybe our wine, women, and song? Let's ask the experts. You, there, you expert on women!

EXPERT ON WOMEN. American women are beautiful, certainly. But we've never produced any classic or historic beauty. We have no legendary figure to compare with Helen of Troy, or with any of the Greek or Roman Venuses, or with Egypt's Cleopatra. As far as fiction is concerned, we can offer nobody to stand up against Italy's Juliet, or Germany's Isolde, or France's Roxanne. Certainly not Scarlet O'Hara.

AMERICAN. All right, that's fine, Doc; thanks very much. Now, what about our wines—is that what makes America so attractive from the outside looking in? How about it, expert?

EXPERT ON WINES. American wines are excellent. But then, of course—meaning no offense—have you ever heard of French Champagne, of Burgundy, or Liebfraumilch . . .

AMERICAN. Okay, okay. Can it be our *song*? Maestro?

MAESTRO. America can well be proud of its composers and of its wealth of folk music. But the fact of the matter is that we have yet to produce a single world-great symphony, whereas Finland has produced seven, Germany and Austria half a hundred, the Russians about twelve, the French two or three, England two or three, Bohemia . . .

AMERICAN. Not song, then. Neither wine, women, nor song.

So what is it, then?

Well, it's this, when you come right down to it. It's the fact of nearly a hundred fifty million people tryin' to live up to the expectations of a handful of great men who lived and died a hundred fifty years ago—men who were so fed up with the kind of government they'd been gettin' they sat down and wrote a new constitution for themselves and their children—a democratic constitution. Unfortunately, we don't always live up to that document. There's some people who'd like to stiff-arm the Constitution right out of the books, others who deliberately twist it and turn it until it

28

means somethin' quite different from what Franklin an' Jefferson meant it to mean—like the devil quotin' the Scriptures to his own purpose. There's intolerance and bigotry in certain places—and a lot o' things there shouldn't be; but we people, by and large, are still tryin' to live by the rules—some of the best rules we've seen around in a long time.

Of course, there are other things that make our Union a good one to belong to. It's a beautiful country, even though it has a lot of incorrigible bad lands and corrigible slums. Aren't many countries have as much in them to look at and wonder about as this one. Lakes and mountains and deserts and rivers and beaches and capes and forests . . . Cape Cod and the Sierra Nevada . . . Gloucester and Death Valley . . . the Great Lakes and the Rockies . . . Old Orchard and the Great Plains . . . Williamsburg and Yosemite . . . steel mills at Pittsburgh and geysers at Yellowstone . . .

Music: Sneak in a strain of a half-defiant character, dark to begin with, but brightening as it proceeds, under:

AMERICAN. This can be a kind of a *fierce* country, too. Ever see the way its mountains frown down sometimes? Know what they're frownin' at? Rumors they heard about petty intrigue—about political bosses and shysters and fakers and grafters and men who make a business of gyppin' the people. Ever see the way the skies suddenly get black and thunder roars and the lightnin' throws itself around? That's the spirit of the country saying what there is to say about a lynching. Ever see a storm whuppin' it up acrost the Great Lakes? That's how the American winds feel about anybody who denies anybody else a fair trial, or free speech, or the right to assemble, or the right to worship as one sees fit.

Music: Up to a powerful conclusion.

AMERICAN. In the final analysis, there can be no analysis. Many a great thinker and poet has attempted it, but the country's too big for any one man. There's Walt Whitman, and Carl Sandburg and Tom Wolfe, and they all felt the magnitude and magnificence of the nation that got put together piece by piece. Like a jig-saw puzzle . . . they felt it, and wrote about it in unforgettable ways; but still it's bigger'n any of them or any of us. Whitman hit it on the nose when he said it was bigger'n the President and his Cabinet and the District of Columbia . . . it's not Park Avenue or Broadway or Forty-second Street or the Loop or the Golden Triangle—it's other things, many, many, many other things.

VOICES. Mill towns . . . steel towns . . . tobacco towns . . . mining towns . . . oil towns . . . cotton towns . . . farmhouses . . . railroad sidings . . . statues on the common . . . tourist houses on the edge of town, along the state highway . . . swimming holes . . . gas stations . . . strollers on Main Street . . . kettles of sorghum molasses . . . Sunday papers . . . season tickets to concerts . . . auctioneers . . . night courts . . . radios, parades, tooth paste, shaving cream, dogs, cats, skyscrapers, subways, cornfields,

29

offices, hotel rooms, airports, hospitals, factories, cemeteries . . .

AMERICAN. Oh, we could go on for weeks with this and never come any closer to a workin' definition of America, or to any real understandin' of its total meanin'. Look —how can you add up all the red and yellow neon signs, the smell of all the eggs and bacon fryin' in the morning, the bargain specials, the lessons learned, the cows let in from pasture, the mileage clocked up on automobile speedometers, the rainfall and the snowfall and the winddrift?

It's much too big for you or me or any of us who happen to stand alone or in small cliques. It's much too great for any person or any party—too much loved by its people—loved in spite of an' because of its faults an' virtues an' its past mistakes an' future promises.

America is not a map, a poem, a post of Legionnaires, an almanac, a mural, a buildin' in the heart of Washington . . . it's a territory possessed by people possessed by an ideal.

Well, that's all, listeners. Just wanted to talk between Americans for a half hour of an evenin'. No big finish here; no brass section bringin' down the curtain. Just a little music to separate me from the announcer who follows with the closin' announcement.

Good night, Americans.

Music: A quiet conclusion.

THE STAR-SPANGLED BANNER
FRANCIS SCOTT KEY

O! say can you see by the dawn's early light,
What so proudly we hailed at the twilight's last gleaming,
Whose broad stripes and bright stars, through the perilous fight,
O'er the ramparts we watched were so gallantly streaming?
And the rocket's red glare, the bombs bursting in air,
Gave proof through the night that our flag was still there;
O! say does that star-spangled banner yet wave,
O'er the land of the free, and the home of the brave?

On the shore dimly seen through the mists of the deep,
Where the foe's haughty host in dread silence reposes,
What is that which the breeze, o'er the towering steep,
As it fitfully blows, half conceals, half discloses?
Now it catches the gleam of the morning's first beam,
In full glory reflected now shines in the stream.
'Tis the star-spangled banner, O! long may it wave
O'er the land of the free, and the home of the brave.

And where is that band who so vauntingly swore
That the havoc of war and the battle's confusion,

A home and a country, shall leave us no more?
Their blood has washed out their foul footsteps pollution;
No refuge could save the hireling and slave,
From the terror of flight, or the gloom of the grave;
And the star-spangled banner in triumph doth wave,
O'er the land of the free, and the home of the brave.

O, thus be it ever when freemen shall stand,
Between their loved home and the war's desolation,
Blest with victory and peace, may the heaven-rescued land,
Praise the Power that hath made and preserved us a nation.
Then conquer we must, when our cause it is just,
And this be our motto,—"In God is our trust,"
And the star-spangled banner in triumph shall wave,
O'er the land of the free, and the home of the brave.

SAIL ON, O SHIP OF STATE!
HENRY WADSWORTH LONGFELLOW

Thou, too, sail on, O Ship of State!
Sail on, O Union, strong and great!
Humanity with all its fears,
With all its hopes of future years,
Is hanging breathless on thy fate!
We know what Master laid thy keel,
What Workmen wrought thy ribs of steel,
Who made each mast, and sail, and rope,
What anvils rang, what hammers beat,
In what a forge and what a heat
Were shaped the anchors of thy hope!
Fear not each sudden sound and shock,
'Tis of the wave and not the rock;
'Tis but the flapping of the sail,
And not a rent made by the gale!
In spite of rock and tempest's roar,
In spite of false lights on the shore,
Sail on, nor fear to breast the sea!
Our hearts, our hopes, are all with thee,
Our hearts, our hopes, our prayers, our tears,
Our faith, triumphant o'er our fears,
Are all with thee,—are all with thee!

31

FIFTY-FOUR, forty, or fight!—*William Allen*

PROTECTION and patriotism are reciprocal.—*Calhoun*

LIBERTY exists in proportion to wholesome restraint.—*Webster*

WHAT IS WANTED is not more law, but a better public opinion.—*James Blaine*

WE MUTUALLY PLEDGE to each other our lives, our fortunes, and our sacred honour.—*Jefferson*

LET US NEVER FORGET that cultivation of the earth is the most important labour of man. Unstable is the future of the country that has lost its taste for agriculture. If there is one lesson of history which is unmistakable, it is that national strength lies very near the soil.—*Webster*

THE UNITED STATES is the only country with a known birthday. All the rest began, they know not when, and grew into power, they know not how. If there had been no Independence Day, England and America combined would not be so great as each actually is. There is no Republican, no Democrat, on the Fourth of July,—all are Americans. All feel that their country is greater than party.—*James Blaine*

YOU SHALL BE GOVERNED by laws of your own making, and live a free, and if you will, a sober and industrious people. I shall not usurp the right of any, or oppress his person.—*Penn*

LET US AT LEAST do our duty, and like honest men (who value freedom) use our utmost care to support liberty, the only bulwark against lawless power.—*General Andrew Hamilton*

WHEN THE PRESS is free and every man able to read, all is safe.—*Jefferson*

EQUAL RIGHTS for all, special privileges for none.—*Jefferson*

OF LIBERTY

DAMN the torpedoes! . . . Go ahead!—*Admiral Farragut*

FACE the other way, boys; we're going back!—*General Sheridan*

WE ASK no quarter and shall give none.—*Colonel Christopher Greene*

WE SHALL TAKE the fort or die there! Forward, Fifty-fourth!—*Colonel Shaw*

MEN, YOU ARE ALL MARKSMEN—don't fire until you see the whites of their eyes!
—*General Putnam*

THE GOVERNMENT OF THE UNION, then, is emphatically and truly a government
of the people. In form and in substance it emanates from them. Its powers are
granted by them, and are to be exercised directly on them and for their benefit.
—*John Marshall*

THAT PATRIOTISM WHICH, catching its inspiration from the immortal
God, and, leaving at an immeasurable distance below all lesser,
grovelling, personal interests and feelings, animates and prompts
to deeds of self-sacrifice, of valour, of devotion, and of death itself:
that is public virtue; that is the noblest, the sublimest of all public
virtues!—*Henry Clay*

NO. THIS IS A SERVICE for my country, and it doesn't matter whether
I do it as an officer or as a plainsman. The big thing is to do it.
—*Kit Carson*

THE WILL OF THE PEOPLE is the only legitimate foundation of any
government, and to protect its free expression should be our first
object.—*Jefferson*

WAR BE IT, then; millions for defense, sir, but not one cent
for tribute.—*Pinckney*

I strike my flag. (Last words)—*Commander Isaac Hull*

33

Keep 'Em Marching, Giuseppe

By JACK SHER

*I*F YOU have nothing better to do right now, you might be amused by this tale of Giuseppe Gusselli, a little gnome of a shoemaker, who is the dearly beloved of that historic village called Barsten, in Middlesex County, Massachusetts.

The people of Barsten, like all inhabitants of old New England towns, are tolerant of tourists visiting their Revolutionary landmarks, and they are proud of the statues and time-worn signs which tell of the heroism of their ancestors. But, today, scarcely a tourist leaves this hamlet without also being shown the shoe shop of Giuseppe Gusselli, although it is the smallest and very last establishment on the main street.

Here, until a few months ago, Giuseppe Gusselli could be seen every day by the simple expedient of walking past his tiny shop. When the wind blew through the streets of the town, wintry raw and cold, Giuseppe's face, seen through the window, was usually bright pink from the heat of the glowing, pot-bellied stove, which stood near his nicked, iron shoejacks. In the summer, Giuseppe could be viewed only through the open door, because his wife, Maria Helena, would be perching her huge bulk perilously on a small chair directly in front of the window.

Until the words "National Defense" began to appear with regularity in the local paper and on the tongues of Barsten's citizens, Giuseppe Gusselli, by nature of his excellent work, did a fair business, considering the fact that there were two rival shoemakers on the same street. With the appearance of these words, however, the bells above the door of Giuseppe's tiny shop jingle-jangled less regularly. Customers stayed away.

At first, Giuseppe took the boycott with silent resignation, a resignation mingled with the hope that the people of Barsten eventually would take cognizance of the fact that his Italian ancestry was several generations removed from the followers of Mussolini.

For Giuseppe had been born some fifty miles from Barsten, in the rear of a shoe shop not unlike his own. On his wife's side, there was the fact that her grandfather had fought with the Union under Hooker. Looking at the record more closely, Giuseppe had voted Republican for the past twenty-nine years and, long before the events at Ethiopia, had publicly, if not loudly, disowned and denounced the present Italian government as "un-American."

As the boycott tightened, a worried look took the place of the smile which usually spread even into the wrinkles around Giuseppe's bright, living-blue eyes. The smells from Maria's kitchen behind the shop became weaker and weaker, sometimes barely strong enough to penetrate as far as his workbench. At last, when there were only five pairs of shoes on his shelves and three of those already resoled, Giuseppe closed the door upon his shop and ventured out into the main street of Barsten.

Almost as if it were intent on adding to his misery, the wind, unusually frisky that morning, captured his cap several times and wound the tail of his coat—a garment much too long for his small body—around his legs in such a way as nearly to upset him. Giuseppe passed the shops of his competitors, James Warren and Wickliff Carter, sighed as he noted the long rows of shoes on their shelves, and went up the street to the garage of Ben Smith, one of his few loyal and remaining customers.

Ben was busily engaged in separating a precious tube of rubber from a rim. Giuseppe, standing first on one foot and then the other, waited until Ben had disengaged the tire with a last, resounding ring and, straightening up, noticed him.

"H'ya, Joseph?" Ben said cheerfully.

Giuseppe extended his hand solemnly. Ben grasped it with a smile, wrung it heartily, and returned it to the shoemaker a little the worse for wear. Giuseppe swallowed several times and then spoke in his high, small, but strangely musical voice. "You are a good customer, Ben," he said. "I have always given you good service?"

"The best!" Ben said emphatically, tapping the sole of one heavy shoe. "The very best. The soles wear like iron." Then, noticing the countenance of the shoemaker, he said, "Something wrong, Joseph?"

Giuseppe nodded, and searched miserably for words. The more he talked, the more shame and embarrassment crept into his voice. Ben listened, shook his head, frowned, spat, and, finally, stared angrily at the people passing by on the walk in front of his garage.

"I'll be cussed!" Ben said. "C'mon inside, Joseph. We got to figure this out."

Giuseppe followed Ben through the garage and back into the little glass-enclosed cubicle Ben called an office. Ben sat down and put both his feet up on a scratched metal desk. Giuseppe sat gingerly on the edge of the other chair, looking as if he expected someone to enter, suddenly, and claim it.

"Anybody ought to know you're a loyal American," Ben growled. Giuseppe nodded. "Anybody could see that," Ben went on. "But some folks 'n this region are plain dumb, besides being backward." Ben pondered. "Won't do no good to tell 'em, though," he muttered. "Does more harm 'n good, when you start shoutin' about where you stand."

The two men sat in silence, Ben's frown getting deeper by the minute.

"Seems like your name's against you, Joseph," Ben said hesitantly. "Don't suppose you could change it to somethin' like—like—" Ben groped for a name, gave up in disgust, and added, "Wouldn't do a bit of good, anyway, seein' as everybody'd know you're still Gusselli." Ben's face brightened. "You're a citizen, aren't you?" Giuseppe nodded vigorously. "Well, then," Ben said with relief, "you just paste your papers right up there in your store window, where everybody can see 'em."

"I was born here," Giuseppe said simply.

Ben banged on the desk. "That does it!" he said angrily. "You're prob'ly more American than I am and nobody's gonna push you around!"

He stood up and paced back and forth in the little office. As he did so,

35

a slight breeze fluttered the corner of a large piece of white paper pasted on the glass partition. The paper caught Ben's eye. "I've got it, Joseph!" he shouted.

Almost swooping him off his feet, Ben whirled Giuseppe out of the office and around the partition and planted him in front of the piece of paper. It was a letter, a very imposing-looking document, bearing the letterhead of a governmental agency in Washington, D.C.

"See that!" Ben boomed. "There's somethin' proves how American I am!" Giuseppe just looked more confused. "Just as soon as this National Defense came up," Ben explained, "I wrote a letter to them people in Washington and offered to pitch in and help—told 'em just what I did, and could I do something? Well, sir"—Ben patted the letter importantly—"like they say in that letter, they ain't got nothin' for me to do right now, but thanks just the same for my patriotic offer." Ben pointed proudly to the signature on the letter. "Guess everybody knows who that is."

Giuseppe read the letter slowly and carefully. "Yes," he said, "that's a good letter."

"Don't hurt business none, either," Ben said. "Everybody that comes in here gets around to readin' it. Jim Baxter over at the grocery store has one almost exactly like this. He's got it plastered in the window, out front."

"Yes?" Giuseppe asked.

"Don't you get it?" Ben asked excitedly. "You got to write to this fellow and get a letter back—like this one. Then you paste it in your window and everybody knows where you stand." Ben slapped Giuseppe on the back.

All the way back to his shop Giuseppe ransacked his brain for the right words for his letter. He thought of Maria and hoped this news would bring a smile, no matter how short-lived, to her round face.

That night, in honor of the letter which was to be written, the delicious smells of Maria's highly spiced dishes once more wafted and stirred through the shop, pungently drowning out even the tangled odors of Giuseppe's glue and dye and leather. Waiting for his supper, Giuseppe leaned against his battered stitching machine and began composing his letter.

After the table had been cleared and the cloth removed, Maria brought forth a pen, a bottle of ink, and some paper. Then Maria sat down on the other side of the table and watched, not without anxiety and a certain amount of amazement at his daring, as her husband began to write very slowly.

Giuseppe had been writing for an hour, writing and crossing out and making small noises and writing again, before he looked up. "Maria," he said, "do you think I should put down how much I charge for the soles and the heels?"

Maria looked startled and then pleased that he should ask her advice. Finally, after concentrating on it for a full fifteen minutes, she said, "Yes, Joseph, you should put it in."

"I have already," Giuseppe smiled. "Ben said to tell them everything about myself."

The following morning, Giuseppe took his letter to Miss Burns, a public stenographer in the Barsten House, whose heels he had straightened on more than one occasion. In a few minutes she typed the letter which it had taken him so long to write. He signed the letter, Miss Burns placed it in an addressed envelope, and Giuseppe hurried to the post office and dropped it into the slot.

When the first week had gone by and Giuseppe had not received an answer, he became so fraught with worry and despair that Maria had trouble getting him to eat. Twice the following week he went to see Ben Smith.

"These things take time," Ben reassured him. "Might be a whole month before you hear from them."

"A whole month?" Giuseppe asked forlornly.

"Yes, sir," Ben said. "They're mighty busy."

The night after Giuseppe's last visit Ben got into his car and collected six pairs of shoes from his relatives. Two pairs of the shoes hardly needed repairing, but, all the same, he took them to Giuseppe and insisted he wanted them done as quickly as possible.

Giuseppe was working on the last pair of those shoes when the letter arrived. The postman rapped on the glass, waved the letter, and slipped it under the door. Giuseppe sat as if he had frozen to his chair. "Maria," he said weakly. Then, in a louder voice, "Maria!"

Maria approached the letter gingerly. She picked it off the floor and handed it to Giuseppe solemnly. There was no stamp on it. In the upper left-hand corner, in plain black letters, was the same wording as that on the letterhead in Ben's office. It was addressed to:

Giuseppe Gusselli

Gusselli Shoe Works

Barsten, Mass.

Giuseppe carried it back into their living quarters and sat down at the table. He closed his eyes, opened them again, and, holding his breath, shak-ily slit open one end of the envelope. Maria sat down opposite him, her mouth slightly open.

Giuseppe read the letter aloud, beginning with the letterhead, and ending with the signature.

"Dear Mr. Gusselli," it began. "We are happy to inform you that your bid has been accepted. We are shipping you two thousand (2,000) pairs of regulation Army shoes, which are to be repaired and returned to Fort —— within two weeks of the date on which you receive the aforementioned shoes."

Giuseppe read it again, this time to himself. When he came to the word "bid" he stared at it stupidly. When he came to the words "two thousand" he gasped, and his hands shook so that the letter rattled. He dropped the letter and got to his feet unsteadily. He moved around the room in a daze, muttering, "Two thousand pairs, two thousand pairs."

For the first time in years Giuseppe was nowhere in sight when the bells over the door jangled. Ben Smith found him seated at the table again, staring at the letter.

"What's the trouble, Joseph?" Ben asked.

"I don't understand," Giuseppe said in a small voice, pointing at the letter.

Ben picked it up and began reading, half aloud. His voice trailed off. "I'll be cussed!" he said at last. "This here is a government order— sort of." Giuseppe stared at him with unbelieving eyes. Ben scratched his head. "What the devil kind of a letter did you write them people?"

Giuseppe fumbled in his hip pocket and produced the carbon copy of the letter Miss Burns had typed. Ben studied it. Then he began to chuckle.

"Holy smokes, Joseph!" he said.

37

"You got here how much you charge to fix shoes and looks like they figured you were making them a proposition."

Giuseppe shuddered. He stood up, standing as a condemned man would stand, and said, as if in prayer, "Two thousand pairs—"

"Why not?" Ben said gleefully. "You can do it, Joseph. Fact is, you're set for life!"

Giuseppe shook his head. "In a year," he said. "In a year, I could do it." His eyes widened with horror. "But two thousand pairs—in two weeks—!"

"Hire a helper," Ben said. "Get the other shoemakers in town to help you. They'll be glad to take some off your hands."

And so, a few hours later, Giuseppe poked his small, worried face into the shop of his nearest competitor, Wickliff Carter, and, seeing he was alone, stepped inside timidly. The big New Englander, who looked more like a sea captain than a shoemaker, stared dubiously at the letter Giuseppe held out to him.

"Two thousand pairs, huh?" he said scowling. "You can't do it."

Giuseppe nodded and explained the purpose of his call.

Carter frowned and pointed at his shelves which were packed with shoes of all sorts. Carter thought for a moment. "Tell you what," he said finally. "I'll take twenty-five pairs off your hands."

"Twenty-five—" Giuseppe said hopelessly.

Carter shrugged. "That's the best I can do," he scowled again. "I got my own business to think about. Can't be neglectin' that."

Giuseppe thanked his rival and went on up the street to James Warren's shop. That bustling, round-faced man, whose shop bore evidence of even brisker business than Carter's, rubbed his mustache, swore, laughed at Giuseppe's plight, and finally agreed to take 30 pairs of shoes. His desperation mounting by the minute, Giuseppe hurried to Ben Smith's garage, where the two men sat for hours in frantic consultation.

"Tell you what," Ben said, by that time his own desperation almost as great as his friend's. "You go back and get rested and ready for work. I'll get you help on them shoes, if it's the last thing I do."

But that night Ben stormed into Giuseppe's shop, his temper at the boiling point. "I've seen everybody in town," he said bitterly. "Nobody's got no time to help you, Joseph. Even saw Williams, head of the bank." Ben shook his head. "He says puttin' up money for a factory is impractical. 'less you have more time and a larger order."

"A larger order!" Giuseppe breathed. "A factory!"

"Yeah," Ben said disgustedly. "I thought that was the answer. But it's no soap." He sighed. "Joseph, the only thing we can do is send them government fellows a wire and tell 'em you can't handle the job."

Tears came to Giuseppe's eyes. "I wanted to do that job for those government people," he said softly.

"It's impossible!" Ben exclaimed.

And so Giuseppe accompanied Ben to the telegraph office. After the wire was sent they shook hands and parted ways, two forlorn figures moving in opposite directions. . . .

For the first time in twenty-nine years Giuseppe didn't get up the next morning. Curious townspeople, having heard about the 2,000 pairs of shoes, gathered in front of the shop about noon, chattering and worrying. Several of them decided, after

38

much discussion, that Giuseppe might have been miserable enough to have committed some harm to his person and that the sheriff should be called.

Sheriff Lowery had almost reached the shop, when the huge Army truck rolled up the main street and came to a stop before the crowd on the pavement. Several soldiers jumped off the back of the truck and one of them began pounding on the door. To the crowd's great relief, Giuseppe's frightened face appeared in the window. Then he opened the door.

"Gusselli?" the soldier asked authoritatively. Giuseppe nodded. "Got an order here for you—two thousand pairs of shoes. Where do you want 'em?"

"But—I—" Giuseppe began feebly.

"Well," the soldier boomed, "where do we put 'em?"

Giuseppe waved his arms and fled back to his bed. The soldier scratched his head.

"Guess he wants you to put 'em in his shop," a citizen suggested.

The soldier peered inside. "In there?" he asked. "Well," he said doubtfully, "we can try."

When Maria finally persuaded Giuseppe to get out of bed and take a look at his shop, all his equipment, his buffer, his stitching machine, his shoe-jacks, and his skiver were completely out of sight. There was only a narrow path from the living-room door to the street door. Like a sleep-walker, Giuseppe stepped unseeingly into that path, and, the next moment, was almost smothered in an avalanche of shoes, which slithered and bumped and leaped at him from hastily stacked piles that reached to the ceiling. Maria, wisely, stayed within the confines of their living quarters.

Frantically, his every movement bringing more shoes down upon him until he felt as though he had been caught in quicksand, Giuseppe fought his way to the street door. In all the crowd gathered there he saw only one face, Ben Smith's, and staggered toward his friend.

Ben caught him and held him up by the shoulder of his coat and stuck a telegram into his hand. "It just came," Ben said. "Don't worry, Joseph. Guess they'll take these off your hands, now."

Giuseppe fumbled at the telegram, but his hands were shaking so badly that Ben had to open it. He read it aloud, his voice booming at the start and trailing off with incredulity:

"Cannot cancel order. Shoes arrive noon. Four thousand more pairs on way."

At first there was a hush over the crowd. Then everyone began talking at once. Giuseppe just stood there, looking first at one face, then another, but not really seeing any of them. Finally a youngster in the crowd giggled and shouted, "Hey, Ge-Ge! You'd better get busy, if you're gonna get those shoes done!"

"Attaboy, Giuseppe!" a skinny youth in a pork-pie hat yelled. "Keep 'em marching!"

A few people tittered.

Giuseppe looked at them. He swallowed several times. "Yes," he said in a small, birdlike voice, "I'd better get busy."

Some of the crowd broke into loud laughter. Then people began drifting away, most of them smiling and shaking their heads. Ben Smith followed Giuseppe inside and watched the little shoemaker as he began clearing shoes away from his machines.

"What are you doing, Joseph?" Ben asked.

"I have to get them out of the way," Giuseppe said, "so I can go to work."

"Listen!" Ben cried. "You can't finish all them shoes in two weeks. Not a chance!"

Giuseppe nodded. "I know," he said softly. "But I must try."

"But there's four thousand more coming!" Ben said.

"I know." Giuseppe shuddered slightly, but he didn't stop working.

"You just can't do it, Joseph," Ben said a little wildly.

"I must try," Giuseppe said, and there was a hint of stubbornness in his voice. "It is for our defense."

By the time Ben left the shop, after hours of hopeless argument, Giuseppe had cleared a little space around his equipment and, holding his small, bent shoulders as firm and square as he could get them, had set to work on the first pair of army shoes. He had only 1,999 pairs to go.

At first, the citizens of Barsten thought Giuseppe Gusselli's labor a huge joke. They gathered in front of his shop and watched him in amazement, chuckling and laughing and ridiculing him with such encouragement as, "Hey, Giuseppe! Think you'll get 'em done before the war's over?" But Giuseppe worked on doggedly and, when the last person in Barsten had retired for the night, the light in Giuseppe's tiny shop was still burning.

When three days had gone by and Giuseppe was still at his work, the temper of the onlookers changed. They stood in almost reverent silence, now and then whispering in wonder at the little shoemaker's unrelenting toil. Some of them were uneasy, muttering, "He'll kill himself, that little fool." But the tone of their comments had changed from scorn to respect.

Late on the fourth night, at the instigation of several prominent citizens, Sheriff Lowery tried to persuade Giuseppe to give up his back-breaking and impossible struggle against the shoes. The sheriff argued and pleaded. But the little shoemaker's thin, gnarled hands never faltered at their work.

After the sheriff's failure, Carter and Warren were drafted, almost forcibly, into visiting their diminutive rival. But these two, in spite of pleas, bribes, and threats, interrupted Giuseppe's work only long enough for him, silently, to hand them the shoes they had respectively promised to repair.

On the seventh day of Giuseppe's labor, with the people of Barsten almost literally holding their collective breath in awe, a Town Meeting was called to decide what should be done to save the little shoemaker from working himself to death. For, on the morning of that day, two more Army trucks had appeared with the promised 4,000 pairs of shoes, which, had they been deposited in Giuseppe's shop, would have buried him or burst the walls. They had been stored in Ben Smith's garage, until, as Giuseppe had said weakly, but bravely, "until I am ready for them."

The Barsten Meeting was packed, the overflow gathering in the streets outside. Ben Smith was there and Mayor Burke and the banker, Williams, and Grocer Baxter and Homer T. Thrupp, who owned the town canning factory. From the platform they looked down into the anxious faces of good people who were thinking, even while Mayor Burke talked so eloquently, that Giuseppe might be keeling over in his shop at that very moment.

Ben Smith was the last to speak.

He began with Giuseppe's first visit to his garage. When he got to the part about the boycott, he indulged in some deliberate and pointed cussing. And, for the first time since its erection in 1771, cussing was not only allowed but meekly accepted within the walls of this historic meeting place. Then, Ben's voice became a little softer.

"We're supposed to be Americans," he said. "We got names that sound American, and some of us have ancestors that roamed around these parts in 1776. These ancestors weren't natural-born Americans like us. Before they were Americans, they were just men and women who wanted to be free." Ben paused. "And they got to fighting for that freedom, and when they won it they were Americans.

"Sure—we put up statues to some of them Americans," Ben said. "We roped off places where they fought and died and put up signs saying what they did, but"—Ben's eyes grew hard and bright—"maybe we've got so much history and tradition around us that we take being Americans for granted. Maybe we don't remember often enough that them first Americans were real people, fighting for real things, and that they never knew what it was to quit until they got 'em!"

There was a hush in the hall.

"Then," Ben said, "along comes a little guy like Joseph and reminds us. You know," he said slowly, "I been figurin' and figurin' how a little guy like him could keep goin' like he has —seven days, now, with hardly any sleep. And then it come to me, how he's been doin' it. He's been doin' it because he ain't alone!"

Ben stood perfectly motionless, his eyes searching the crowd. "No," he said, "Joseph ain't workin' alone. He's workin' with the strength of all the guys in our past—with Washington and them soldiers at Valley Forge, with Tom Paine and Ben Franklin. And he ain't gonna lose," he said fiercely, "because we ain't gonna let him!"

Williams stood up, his eyes glistening, "I'll put up the money for a repair factory, Ben," he said.

Ben shook his head. "Won't do no good," he said. "You can't build a factory and get it running overnight, and that first batch of shoes has to be in by the end of this week."

"Well," Mayor Burke cried, "what are we going to do?"

"That," said Ben, "depends. Are there any Americans left in this town with a little of their time and money to invest?"

The noise indicated that such people were present . . . .

After midnight, Barsten is usually quiet and deserted. But, on this particular night, a few minutes after the Town Meeting was adjourned, the streets were alive with citizens streaming toward their homes. In a little while lights began to go on in the houses all over town.

On the main street, four men walked silently toward the small shoe shop. There Giuseppe was still working relentlessly, his face white and strained, his blue eyes fixed and bloodshot. When the bells above his door jangled, he looked up with a start into the determined faces of Ben Smith, Banker Williams, Jim Baxter, and Sheriff Lowery.

"We've come for you, Joseph," Ben said, kindly but firmly.

Then the four men bore down on him. Three of them reached the little shoemaker, picked him up, heedless of his struggles, and carried him to

41

the street. They had to step over the prostrate form of Banker Williams, who in his eagerness had tripped over a pile of shoes and fallen flat on his face.

Giuseppe was carried to Jim Baxter's home, where he was divested of his clothes and, still struggling, forced into bed. And, just in case he might defy the social graces and flee, Lady-Godiva-like, back to his shop, Mrs. Baxter and three other similarly big-bosomed, strong-armed ladies were posted around the bed.

By the time the three men returned to Giuseppe's shop, the main street of Barsten was choked with automobiles, over 200 of them, jockeying for position. Not a horn was honked, and, miraculously, scarcely a fender was scraped as the long line formed. Every driver sat quietly in his seat, waiting for action.

The first car in line pulled up before Giuseppe's shop. Its occupant scrambled out of it, entered the shop, returned with an armload of shoes, which he deposited in his car. Banker Williams, standing at the curb holding a map of New England, saluted the driver.

"Lexington," he said. "Godspeed!"

The car leaped away and another took its place. When it was ready to go, Banker Williams looked at his map again.

"Concord," he said, and repeated, "Godspeed!"

All through the night the cars streamed out of Barsten, loaded with shoes, headed north, east, south, and west over paved highways and dirt roads. In Shrewsbury, a recalcitrant cobbler was reminded that he might not be there at all if General Artemas Ward had not once arisen from a sickbed there and ridden 100 miles through the night to win a battle in Cambridge. In Medford, a shoe-maker complaining about being awakened at such an ungodly hour, was told about a man named Revere, who, at just such an ungodly hour, had once aroused the whole town. At Great Barrington, a man toiled un-willingly all night over shoes, while his guardian kept comparing him, threateningly, to General Burgoyne, who had once been similarly held captive in a house across the street.

As far away as Boston, near Bunker Hill, and on the street of the Old North Church and close by the Liberty Tree on the Commons, under the watchful eyes of Barsten men, busy shoemakers cut and hammered and stitched and shaped and polished on regulation, Government Issue, United States Army shoes.

As it has been shown, some worked not entirely of their own free will, even at Concord and Lexington, somewhat resenting being routed out of their beds in the middle of the night. Some worked good-naturedly, when those presenting the shoes took time to tell them the tale of Giuseppe Gusselli. A few worked because business was slack and they were glad to have even such impatient and demanding customers.

The first Barsten car returned thirty-six hours after the departure of Banker Williams, and its owner checked in the first batch of repaired shoes with Ben Smith. Banker Williams, having been the last to leave on the longest trip, was the last to return. He arrived just four hours before an Army truck rattled to a stop before Giuseppe's shop.

The sergeant in charge swung off the truck and pounded on Giuseppe's door. Finally, swaying a little and frightened, Giuseppe opened the door and stared at the soldier.

42

"I got orders to pick up two thousand pairs of kicks," the sergeant barked.

"Kicks?" Giuseppe asked blankly.

"Shoes," the sergeant said. "Where are they?"

"I have only these," Giuseppe whispered, stepping aside and pointing to a pile of 200 pairs or so.

"Quit kiddin'," the sergeant roared. "Where's the rest of them?"

"I don't know," Giuseppe said.

The sergeant opened his mouth, shut it again, pulled off his fatigue cap, and scratched his head, glaring at Giuseppe. Giuseppe waited, resigned to his fate.

Ben Smith appeared suddenly. "Right this way, Sergeant," he said. "They're all up in my garage—six thousand pairs, less these two hundred—as good as new."

The sergeant's mouth came open again. He squinted suspiciously at Giuseppe, whose mouth was also open. "You mean to tell me that little squirt fixed up all them shoes in two weeks?" he demanded.

Ben grinned. "Ain't it surprisin' what one little guy can do, when he puts his mind to it?"

The sergeant shook his head. "I don't get it," he scowled. "Anyway, I only got orders to pick up two thousand pair. The others'll have to wait."

Ben's scowl matched the sergeant's. "You'd better get a couple more trucks up here, fast," he snapped, "or them guys in Washington are gonna hear from the people in this town about holdin' up National Defense orders."

Giuseppe now has a new shop, employing eight men steadily on the flow of shoes which the Government keeps sending him.

And that is all there is to the story of Giuseppe Gusselli, except to add that when the check from the Government arrived, he implored Ben Smith to give him the names of all those who robbed his place that night. Ben hasn't been able to remember a single name. But Giuseppe hasn't given up. He still stops people on the street and says in his high, small voice, "I am Giuseppe Gusselli and I'm sure I owe you some money." Then, not being able to get anyone to accept so much as a penny, he continues along the street, walking with dignity, as befits an honored citizen of a historic American town.

From *THANATOPSIS*
William Cullen Bryant

So live, that when thy summons comes to join
The innumerable caravan that moves
To the pale realms of shade, where each shall take
His chamber in the silent halls of death,
Thou go not, like the quarry-slave at night,
Scourged to his dungeon, but, sustained and soothed
By an unfaltering trust, approach thy grave
Like one who wraps the drapery of his couch
About him, and lies down to pleasant dreams.

WORDS OF GREAT AMERICANS:

MAKE haste slowly.

HUNGER is the best pickle.

DISPLAY is as false as it is costly.

ENERGY and persistence conquer all things.

WHAT is serving God? 'Tis doing good to man.

WITHOUT FREEDOM OF THOUGHT there can be no such thing as wisdom, and no such thing as public liberty without freedom of speech; which is the right of every man, as far as by it he does not hurt or control the right of another; and this is the only check it ought to suffer and the only bounds it ought to know.

THERE was never a good knife made of bad steel.

THE STING of reproach is the truth of it.

THERE'S a time to wink as well as to see.

WHO pleasure gives shall joy receive.

HONESTY is the best policy.

REMEMBER that time is money.

LOST TIME is never found again.

SEARCH others for virtues,
thyself for vices.

44

BENJAMIN FRANKLIN

LIGHT purse, heavy heart.

HOPE of gain lessens pain.

GOD helps them that help themselves.

WE MAY GIVE advice, but we cannot give conduct.

LOOK before, or you'll find yourself behind.

I NEVER WAS WITHOUT some religious principles. I never doubted, for instance, the existence of the Deity; that He made the world, and governed it by His Providence; that the most acceptable service of God was the doing good to man; that our souls are immortal; and that all crime will be punished, and virtue rewarded, either here or hereafter.

THE GREAT SECRET OF SUCCEEDING in conversation is to admire little, to hear much; always to distrust our own reason, and sometimes that of our friends; never to pretend to wit, but to make that of others appear as much as possibly we can; to hearken to what is said, and to answer to the purpose.

HALF a truth is often a great lie.

NECESSITY never made a good bargain.

NEVER dig more than plough-deep.

LITTLE strokes fell great oaks.

GOD governs, and he is good.

EAT to live;
don't live to eat.

Ann Story

By DOROTHY CANFIELD FISHER

*I*F YOU WANTED to give Chinese readers some idea of who George Washington was, you wouldn't start with Washington, himself. You'd start with some account of the colonial America in which he grew up. You would be pretty sure nobody could make head or tail of Washington's character and life story, without knowing something about why Americans of his day—some of them — fought the Revolutionary War. I don't think anybody could make head or tail of Ann Story's character and deeds, without some idea of why the people, who settled Vermont, recklessly risked their lives to fight against remaining subjects of the British crown and—as hotly— against becoming "York State folks," to use our own phrase.

I don't mean that Ann Story is in the same class with George Washington. Or anywhere near that. The very fact that she is not, that she was only one among many stout-hearted frontier women of our early history, is the point of her story.

So let me stand back far enough to get a run at it, before I take the jump into the tale of Ann Story, who she was, what she means. Means to Vermonters? Yes, but to you, too, no matter where you live in the U.S.A. She is spiritually one of your great-grandmothers. Perhaps she is in actual fact, for she had five children, whom she brought up, every one of them, to strong, useful maturity. They all married, had children and moved with their families here and there in our country, as is the American way.

The French-and-Indian War (the last one in which our colonial ancestors fought for the British) ended in 1763. The ferment of opinion, political, economic and social, which boiled into our Revolution, was bubbling hotly (among younger people) in the settlements to which the colonial soldiers returned after they were mustered out at Quebec. That was only ten years before the Boston Tea Party, twelve years before the shooting at Lexington and Concord and the rhetorical demand by Ethan Allen for the surrender of Ticonderoga. Men who had been young soldiers in 1763 were still radical younger generationers when, a decade later, they set out to make homes in the Vermont forests.

Vermont was then new country— an unbroken wilderness of forests. Its only roads were lakes and streams and a few Indian trails made by wandering hunters. The hunting and fishing were fabulously rich. And wherever the huge trees were cut down, Vermont land was strong, deep and black. Up from the towns of Massachusetts and Connecticut they came, these adventurous young men with their cheerful, hardy wives and children, following old Indian trails to a new freedom.

For there was more in the migration to Vermont of men like Ethan Allen and his brother, and Seth

Warner and Matthew Lyons, and Ann Story's husband, than just the random itching feet of returned soldiers, and the stories of rich land and plentiful game. They were looking for new land and good hunting, yes, but they were also on fire with the love of liberty, a word which they spelled and pronounced with a capital L, and for which they were, literally, ready to give their lives.

When before long, they wrote a constitution for their new state, these buckskin-clad farmers laid down their rifles and their axes to write into it (the first time in the Western Hemisphere) a clause forbidding human slavery in any form. The rising wind of the passion for human freedom, for the recognition of the dignity of each human being, sang loudly in the ears of these family men, then British colonials, soon to become Americans, who pushed into Vermont along Indian trails.

Those early Vermonters were all very much the same kind of folk—younger sons and daughters of literate Connecticut and Massachusetts farmers, and they all followed much the same pattern during their first years in Vermont. It is a pattern we, their descendants, know all about, for they were literate like their parents and left behind letters, diaries, account-books, many varieties of written records. In addition, the oral tradition is vivid and unbroken. How the Vermont forests were turned into the mellow home farms now all around us we know from the talk, as well as from yellowed letters, account-books and deeds.

Ann Story was a notable figure of her times (notable to her fellow Vermonters), she lived to be seventy-five years old, and was visited and interviewed and "written up" many times. So we have an unusually complete written record of her.

Usually the first to come into Vermont was the father of the family. He brought a helper, a son, if he had one old enough to be a help to him, or a brother, or a friend who also planned to settle in Vermont. If the waterways were right, they came by canoe. But mostly they traveled with a pack-horse, carrying the minimum of tools and supplies—axes, wedges, levers, seed for the first crop of grain, and Indian corn, a kettle or two (very precious), a frying-pan (or spider), blankets, and a very small iron-ration of food to fall back on, on the infrequent days when neither game nor fish could be had.

Thus, in September, 1774, did Ann Story's husband, Amos, arrive at the spot in the dense forest which was to become the town of Salisbury, Vermont. With him was his son, Solomon, then thirteen years old. Together through that long, cold, dark Vermont winter, they felled trees, built a strong log-house out of the great oak and maple trunks, and constructed a chimney. As spring came on, the man and boy called the new home done, and turned to clearing a field in the forest, to plant wheat for the family bread the next winter.

And as they toiled together, forward-looking, creative-minded, peaceable young father and sturdy son, disaster struck. A huge sugar maple (we know exactly what kind of tree it was, for this is one of the details of the story, told and written down over and over) did not fall as

47

Amos Story had thought it would. As it plunged downward, its great branches roaring in its fall, it turned and, crashing to the earth, pinned Amos' body beneath it. He died instantly.

The nearest human being lived in a clearing where the town of Middlebury now stands—miles away. The young woodsman knew where the trail ran, followed it, and brought back one Benjamin Smauley (we know the names of the people in this story) and his two sons. They carried Amos Story's body to lie beside the grave of one of Smauley's daughters who, at twenty years of age, had lost her way in the forest and starved to death before she could be found—this as a reminder to the boy of what the wilderness meant. After the funeral, the fourteen-year-old boy set off on foot to go back to tell his mother.

The many accounts of this homespun epic which have come down to us, are entirely factual. The details of what was done we know fully. But not what was felt. Nobody ever told us about the day when young Ann Story (for she was thirty-three when her husband died) back in the Connecticut town, weary with waiting for news, watching the road anxiously, saw her eldest son, footsore, dusty, ragged, his head hanging, trudging in on the highway from the north. But that is the last pathos in this tale. From that point on the story rings with vitality.

Ann Story had planned with her husband the creation of the new home in the north woods, where their boys and girls could grow up children of free and independent landowners. Her sorrow over his death seemed to her a mighty motive for carrying out that plan. With-out him, she did what they had thought to do together. Buying a pack-horse with the money from the sale of most of her household gear, she gathered her brood around her and set out—a young widow with three sons and two daughters, Hannah and Susanna, Samuel, Ephraim and Solomon—such stout old Yankee-Bible names—their ages running from fourteen down.

Ann carried a rifle over her shoulder as her husband would have done, and so did her first-born, because, after plunging into the Vermont forests, they depended largely on what game they could shoot for food. They slept out at night, around a camp-fire, over which, turn by turn, one of them kept watch. Steadily, slowly, held back by the short steps of the younger children, drawn forward by Ann's vision of earned independence, day after day, week after week, they pushed forward through the great dark trees.

It was about a year after her husband had reached the spot in the forest which was to be their home farm—in the latter part of 1775—that Ann Story led her children into the ragged, bramble-overgrown clearing, saw the log-cabin built by her husband and knelt beside its hearth to strike out the spark which would light the first home fire. Little and bigger, boy and girl, every one of the five stood around her, safe.

She set to work at once to provide for her children, inside the home and out of it. They all grew to be as at home in the woods as the squirrel and partridge. The boys helped as they could to clear the land of the monstrous great trees, to plant the crops for the food there was no other way to get, to cut up the mountains of firewood against the long hard Vermont winter. The little girls helped too, with might and main, cooking, mending, picking and drying wild fruits, making soap out of grease and the lye from the wood-ashes, using this soap to keep the family clothes and home spotlessly clean, smoking the haunches of the deer their mother and the boys shot, trying out the great slabs of fat from the occasional bear brought down by their mother who, like any other pioneer, kept her musket as close to her hand as her ax.

On a diet of venison, fish, bear-fat, wild fruit, Indian corn mush and maple-syrup Ann Story's children grew strong, hardy, muscular, alert, and as boldly courageous as their mother who was said, by those who knew her, just not to know the meaning of fear. As her grief for her husband's death was buried deeper under the incredible activity and responsibility of every day, she herself grew, too, not taller like the children, but stronger, in mind and body and spirit. An old settler, reminiscing about her in his last years said, "She was a busting great woman who could cut off a two-foot log as quick as any man in the settlement." She had always been good-looking and as she grew in power, she took on a stately handsomeness which became legendary. With her tanned, bright-eyed, skilled and disciplined boys and girls about her (she taught them to read in the Bible she had brought in the pack-saddle, from the old home) she was a model mother, the admiration of all who passed that way.

But she was more. She was a citizen. And a patriot. All her bold, generous heart was set on that independence for her country, which she coveted for her children and worked so hard to get for them. She had political opinions in times that showed the stuff men and women were made of. In the Revolutionary struggle, she was passionately on the side of self-government by the people.

A Justice of the Supreme Court of the District of Columbia, speaking forty years ago at the dedication in Salisbury of the monument in Ann Story's honor, said of her: "She gave herself, heart and soul, to the great cause of the people against their tyrants . . . She was brave and strong, and what her mind approved, her arm did not tremble to execute."

What was at stake? For Vermont settlers it was the right to own their land as free men and not be forced into the semi-feudal dependence of those who lived as tenant farmers in New York, dependent on patroons. For Americans in general what was at stake was their right to self-government, not to obedience to an overseas political authority over which they had no control. Ann Story was ready to stand by those causes with as forthright a civic conscience and courage as, in her personal life, she had shown in taking care of her children.

As soon as the sickening news was heard that the British had enlisted the Indians to fight for them against the Colonial rebels, and were sending them out on war-parties to raid, burn and kill, those few Vermont families who were building up their homes in the region north of Rutland, knew that they would not be safe, scattered in the wilderness as they were, and close to the Canadian border. Giving up their dearly earned log-homes, abandoning their painfully cleared fields, they moved to the southern part of the state, where the settlements were more numerous. But not Ann Story.

It was her home-place, begun by the father of her children, developed by her own efforts. It was all she had for her sons and daughters. It was more. It was an outpost of the fighting front. Because of its position on the very frontier line, she could be of use in the battle for freedom. She was already a valued aid and adviser to the loosely organized guerrilla fighters called The Green Mountain Boys. To them, as she boldly announced her determination to stay on, she said, in a phrase well-known to us, "Give me a place among you, and see if I am the first to desert my post." She stayed on. And in the spring of 1776, the Indians came, torch and tomahawk in hand.

The Story children had been trained to act as sentinels, and there were enough of them so that, in every direction around the house, some watchful young Story ear was cocked for suspicious sounds. One of them came running—but silently—to tell his mother in a whisper that an Indian war-party, about half a mile away, was pillaging and setting fire to the cabin of a neighbor (one of those who had gone south for safety, leaving his home empty). The river was high with melted snow, had overflowed its banks and flooded low-lying parts of the forest. Working at top speed, Ann and her children loaded their big canoe with the most vital household belongings—blankets, the precious iron "kittle" and spider, the bags of seed soon to be planted, the wooden tub of maple-sugar,

and bear-grease. Stepping in themselves, they paddled swiftly off on the floodwaters in amongst the dense trees, which hid them, but through which they could see everything done by the Indians, who soon came whooping into the clearing. The Story family watched them ravage the carefully kept home, and with relishing shouts, set it on fire in a dozen places. When the cabin was quite burned down, they shouldered their booty and were off.

Ann and her children waited cautiously till it was safe to return to the desolation which had been their home. We do not need to try to imagine what they felt as they stood by the smouldering logs, for Ann's own words have come down to us through people who heard her tell the story with terse Vermont understatement. She evidently did not even consider the possibility of giving up and beating a retreat to safety. Nor did she waste an instant's time in laments. "If the smoking ruins of our home disheartened us, the hope arose that the Indians had made so little in this excursion, they might not visit the region any more. So we began cutting and laying up small trees, such as the children and I could handle, and it was not long before we had quite a comfortable cabin, made of poles instead of logs, on the spot where the former one had stood."

In the daytime the Story children and their mother could go on, growing food, preparing it, keeping house (and incidentally gathering valuable information for the guerrilla forces on their side) because they could stand guard and at the first sound of danger could take to their canoe and paddle noiselessly out of sight. But at night?

People thought that now, of course, Mistress Story would not stay on, that she could not but abandon the half-created home and move south for safety. But stay on she did, as patriot. Her house of poles—but a home nonetheless, clean and snug and smelling pleasantly of good food cooking, became like the switchboard of a modern telephone system. To it came singly, or in small groups, men who looked like trappers or hunters, dropping in casually for a chat with the Widow Story over a dish of her excellent venison stew. But they left an important message to be passed on orally to other buckskin-clad, musket-carrying men who were to drop in, some days or weeks later. Or, while the children scattered into the woods in a wide circle, all around the clearing, to keep watch, a canoe would come up the creek, loaded with kegs of gunpowder, which would be hastily rolled out and hidden, till a party of the Green Rangers later arrived with the right password. Often the men dropped in just to get what information Ann and her active children had picked up about British or Indian movements, for the children were everywhere and Ann acquired an F.B.I. ability to piece together isolated odd items to make a clear whole. Or, perhaps the visitors came just to get Ann Story's slant on some new move, political or military. For of course, as always happens, her judgment grew in value with experience and observation.

As to what the family did at night, nobody knew for a long time. Ann kept her own counsel and the children were as mum as young partridges hiding in the dry leaves at their mother's command. But we now know the device.

The banks of the Otter Creek, where their home stood, were high above the water. Selecting a place where tall old trees stood thickly, their roots intertwining into a strong, wiry network, the Storys began to dig an underground passageway into the bank. Prisoners digging escape tunnels have trouble hiding the fresh dirt. The Story diggers just slid it into the swift-flowing stream. The mouth of the passage, at the water level, they made just large enough to let the canoe float in, the passengers all lying flat. And they kept that entrance thickly planted with overhanging bushes, so it would not be seen by any of the men in canoes, pro-British, Indian or pro-American, who used the Otter as a road into and out of the northern wilderness. A place to sleep was dug out at one side, well above the level of the water. Here the roots of the trees acted as a natural arch to hold up the roof, over what was a sizable underground room.

Mistress Story placed the cave on the far side of the stream from their cabin, so that, entered as it was from the water, no sign of trodden leaf or broken stick could betray it to the sharpest Indian trackers. A well-worn path led down, naturally enough, to where the canoe lay moored.

Every night, after dark, they filed silently down, stepped into the canoe, pushed it out without a sound, and glided between the high wooded banks, around a bend in the Otter. With one deft paddle stroke, the light craft was swung around and slid in under the overhanging bushes. The Storys were gone, all six of them, as if they had evaporated.

And then one day one of her children returned from a far-ranging woods expedition, reporting that he had heard somebody crying. Going cautiously to see, noiseless on his moccasined feet, he had peeped through the leaves from a distance and had seen a woman, a white woman, sunk in a heap on the forest floor, sobbing.

Ann Story reflected. It might be an Indian trick. But it might not be. Musket on shoulder, guided by the child, both of them as silent as cloud-shadows, she made her way to a place where she could see and not be seen. The child's story was true. The mother waited a long time, with Indian patience, standing invisible in the forest, till she was sure it was no trick. Then she stepped forward.

What a moment for that girl, abandoned by her Indian captors, when the "busting," stately Ann stood before her, in her brown homespun!

The girl had come from a settlement, far inside the American lines, which had been raided by Indians in the service of the British. The prisoners were hurried along the trail to Canada. And this girl (here is one name that has not come down to us, so I can only call her the girl) was far advanced in pregnancy. She tried desperately to keep up with the swift dog-trot of the Indians, quite as much afraid of being left to starve in the wilderness as of their tomahawks. But she had finally fallen so far behind, as to be out of their sight. And they had gone on. It was less trouble to leave her there to perish than to turn back and split her skull.

Ann Story knew that the young woman's time was near. There was nothing for it but to add another to the incredible sum of responsibilities on her strong shoulders. The young mother was taken in, the baby was born—Ann Story midwife—and like all babies, he was anything but self-controlled and disciplined. One of the stock sayings of her contemporaries about Ann Story was that "she feared neither Tory, Indian nor wild beast," because she felt herself to be stronger than they. But she could not keep a baby from crying when he felt like crying. The soundless caution of the canoe-approach to the underground shelter, the whispers of their talk in the cave, were often broken by the baby's lusty yells when something displeased him. You can imagine what the Storys' situation now became.

But Ann never thought of the possibility of evading this responsibility. Babies and their mothers must be cared for, come what may. For the present, till the mother could walk, there was no way of moving them on to another place of safety. So there the baby stayed, crying when the spirit moved him.

And he was the hinge on which a small, but not unimportant piece of American history swung into place— the right place.

The American Revolution was not at bottom a struggle between the colonists and Great Britain. It was between those, everywhere, who steadfastly believed that people should be free to govern themselves, and those who did not. In the colonies— in Vermont, too, so new that the bark was still on it—there were plenty of people who took no stock in the republican ideas which, with

Cromwell, had shaken the English state to its foundations, and who hated and feared the principles of the American Revolution, so dear to Ann Story—and to us, her descendants.

A band of these royalists were, unknown even to the wide-spread intelligence system of the Green Mountain Rangers, leaving the various Vermont settlements in which they lived, starting north, to go to Canada, to join the British Army, to take to them and their allies, the Indians, exact, detailed information about the location and defenses of the American settlements in Vermont and about the movements, organizations and resources of the guerrilla fighters. Their success might very well have meant the wiping out of those settlements altogether. Traveling separately, to avoid detection, they were on the last lap of the journey, crossing the no-man's strip of the extreme frontier where Ann Story lived, and kept her eyes open.

But they went by night. All the keen Story eyes were underground, asleep. The northbound anti-Americans would have slipped through, unobserved, if just before dawn one morning, that baby had not taken it into his head to cry. At the sound, coming from the ground under his feet, one Ezekiel Jenny, following the trail north along the riverbank, stopped and stood still in his tracks. He was of that region, known to Ann Story, and well acquainted with her way of life. So this, he thought in exultation, was the key to the secret of the Storys' vanishing at night.

He tiptoed to the edge of the water, hid himself in the bushes, looking keenly up and down the river, as the dawn slowly broke. Before long, sure enough, just under where he stood, the tip of a canoe was silently pushed through the bushes. It hung there a moment, probably to make sure no one was passing. Then with a swift thrust, it was in midstream, and shot towards the bend of the river and the landing place.

Now, thought Ezekiel Jenny, putting his musket on the cock, and darting across the neck of land to lie in wait for the unsuspecting party, now is the time to make that pestiferous woman rebel talk. Crouched in the bushes, beside the landing place, he waited till Ann had stepped out of the canoe and then springing up, he presented the muzzle of his gun at her very breast, and attempted to terrorize her into betraying her allies.

Let Ann speak for herself here. Her own inimitably dry words have come down to us: "I gave evasive and dissatisfactory replies to his questions. This exasperated Jenny and he threatened to shoot me on the spot; but to all his threats I bid defiance, and told him I had no fears of being shot by so consummate a coward as he; and finally he passed along down the creek." And so it was that Ann Story contemptuously dismissed a bully.

Ezekiel did not shoot her. He had other things to do that day, and had interrupted his hurried secret journey only on a chance. He sped on his way, not dreaming that the woman would take note of which way he went, that she had inside information enough to guess what his purpose was, and means of giving notice of his presence in the region.

What she did was to snatch a flyleaf from her Bible, the only paper she had, write a hasty note on it, and send one of her boys flying swift-footed along a short-cut trail, to the nearest Green Mountain Ranger. In no time, Daniel Foot, Samuel Bentley and other Americans, had snatched their muskets from the pegs over the home-hearth, and set off in pursuit. From my little girlhood I have always hoped that the men let that Story boy who took them the message go along with them. I'm sure he would not have felt he needed to get his mother's permission.

Silent as any wild inhabitant of the forests so familiar to them, those American settlers, turned in an instant from family men to guerrilla fighters, followed the trail of the unsuspecting would-be English soldiers. When night fell, the royalists were far enough north beyond the last cabins to venture to make camp and lie down to sleep around their fire. Without a sound, the Green Mountain Rangers closed in around them, and then, on a signal, broke upon them with yells and musket-firing.

But not to kill. Their prisoners had intended the betrayal of American families to fire and tomahawks. But their capture had prevented that. There was no need to kill them. Prosaically, and we think, gloriously, the Rangers marched their prisoners across country to Fort Ticonderoga, then in American hands, and "gave them up to the proper constituted authorities."

Ann Story's monument stands on the spot where her husband built their first log-cabin home. On it are these plain unrhetorical words:

Ann Story
In grateful memory of her
Service in the struggle of the
Green Mountain Boys
for Independence.

You might think that those who designed the monument would have put on it that well-known saying of hers to the defenders of Vermont, when she was being urged to turn her back on danger, to be wholly mother and not citizen and patriot —"Give me a place among you and see if I am the first to desert my post."

But to endure, that doesn't need to be carved in stone. It is well-remembered in our hearts.

PIONEER MOTHER
Gail Brook Burket

The greatest words could not record
The epic of her years,
Nor tell of hope and hardihood
She shared with pioneers.
She lived a life of stalwart faith,
Expressed in phrase and deed.
Christ walked beside her as she went
To help a friend in need.
Enshrined beyond all tribute words
Of transitory pen,
Her life has been inscribed by love
Within the hearts of men.

NATHAN HALE
By Nancy Hale

"THE BOY was only a couple of years out of New Haven when he joined up. He'd hardly got started. He'd been teaching school, you know, up at East Haddam and then down in New London, and it looked as if he was shaping up into a fine teacher. He'd made a lot of friends everywhere he went, and the girls always liked him. They say he was a good-looking boy.

"Then the war came. Things had looked bad to us Americans for a long time, but when the first gun was fired on that April day it seemed to light a sudden strong fire in everyone's heart. It seemed to call out—'Americans!' The boy's brothers, John and Joseph, volunteered first off. It was a patriotic family—the father'd been a Deputy in the old Connecticut Assembly. The boy himself had signed up with the school for a year. He wasn't the kind to let people down, but he did write and ask to be released from his contract two weeks early. He joined up in July, as a Lieutenant in Webb's Seventh Connecticut.

"Well you know how things went after that. The boy was in camp up near Boston all winter. It wasn't an exciting siege. But there was a lot to do getting the men to re-enlist. Most of their terms of enlistment ran out in December. The General was worried about it. Our boy offered the men in his company his own pay for a month if they'd stay that much longer. Anyway, the siege was maintained.

"He got a leave in the winter and went home. Maybe that was when he got engaged. Alicia Adams. A lovely girl; they would have made a handsome couple. When spring came the enemy evacuated Boston and our army went down to New York, where real trouble was threatening. The boy'd been made a captain by that time. He was twenty-one years old.

"Our Long Island campaign was just this side of disastrous. Morale was none too good, afterwards. I don't suppose the General was in a worse spot in the whole war than he was for those three weeks right after the Battle of Long Island. There we lay, facing the enemy across the East River, and no way of knowing what they had up their sleeve. Surprise was what we feared. The answer to that was companies of rangers, to scout around and find out what was up. Knowlton's Rangers were organized, and our boy switched over to it. He wanted action, you see.

"But the rangers weren't enough. The General wanted to know two things: when the enemy was planning to attack, and where. Nobody could tell him. The General let it be known that he'd welcome volunteers to spy.

"Now, people didn't take kindly to the word 'spy' around these parts. It didn't mean excitement or glamour or any of those things. It meant something degrading. It was a job they gave to bums, who didn't care. But the General said he wanted a spy. Well, our boy volunteered. His friends tried to talk him out of it. They spoke of the indignity; they also told him he'd make a terrible spy—a frank, open boy like him.

"But his idea was, the job was necessary. That was the great thing. It's being necessary seemed to him to make it honorable. He was sent through the enemy lines dressed up like a Dutch schoolmaster.

"He didn't make such a bad spy, after all. He got what he went after, and hid the drawings in his shoes. He was on his way back, crossing their lines, when they caught him. They found the information on him. He admitted he was over there to spy. You know what a spy gets. They hanged him in the morning. He wrote some letters to the family at home, but they were destroyed before his eyes, they say. But in his last moment, they let him say what he wanted to. And later one of their officers told one of our officers what he'd said.

"There he was, with the noose around his neck. He hadn't got much done. He'd got caught on the first big job of his life. He wasn't going to marry Alicia Adams, nor to have any children, nor to do any more teaching, nor to finish fighting this war. He stood there in the morning air, and he spoke and said who he was, his commission and all. And then he added, 'I only regret that I have but one life to lose for my country.' "

You could tell the story like that, simply, because it is a simple story, and when you'd finished you'd have told about all there is to tell about Nathan Hale. There isn't even a contemporary picture of him. Most of the friends to whom he wrote didn't keep his letters. He was just a young American who'd gone to war, who'd lived for twenty-one ordinary enough years before—in the day's work—he died for his country.

One of his brothers, Enoch, was my great-great-grandfather.

When I was a child there was a small bronze statue, about four feet high, that stood in the corner of the living room at home. It was just about my height, but it wasn't another child. It was a young man, with his wrists tied behind him and his ankles bound. I passed it several times a day, every day of my childhood. Sometimes I used to touch the bronze face. It was a small-scale replica of the Nathan Hale statue at Yale.

I must have been told his story, because I always knew it. But my father never went on about it, if you know what I mean. There his story was; for what it might mean to you. Some of my other ancestors were the kind of characters that have a whole legend of anecdotes surrounding them, pointed, stirring, or uproarious. But the young man with his hands bound had died at twenty-one, a patriot, as stark and all alone and anecdoteless as young men of twenty-one must be.

Once I was set upon the knees of an old gentleman whose grandmother had been Alicia Adams. She had married and had children, and lived to be eighty-eight, a pretty, sparkling old lady. And when she died she said, "Where is Nathan?" But about the young man himself there were no family reminiscences, no odd little jokes, no tales beyond the short, plain story of his life and death. He had had no time to do anything memorable but die.

Nevertheless . . . it was my job as a child to fill the kitchen scuttle with coal from the cellar. I was not a brave child, and to me the long corners of the cellar seemed menacing and full of queer, moving shadows— Wolves? Robbers? I cannot remember when I first started taking the thought of Nathan Hale down cellar with me, for a shield and buckler. I thought, "If he could be hanged, I can go down cellar." The thing was, he was no impossible hero; he was a member of the family, and he was young too. He was a hero you could take along with you into the cellar of a New England farmhouse. You felt he'd be likely to say, "Aren't any wolves or robbers back there that I can see."

Well, I am grown up now and I know very little more about Nathan Hale than I did then. There are, of course, a mass of details about his short life. A devoted scholar named George Dudley Seymour has spent years in collecting all that can be collected about him. There's a wartime diary. They know his friends. He played football and checkers at camp. He drank wine at Brown's Tavern and cider at Stone's. But when you add all these little things you only affirm the peculiar simplicity of the story.

Hale is a symbol of all the young American men who fight and who die for us. Partly, he is a symbol because he was the first of our heroes in the first of our own wars. He was the first to show the world what Americans are made of. The reason they destroyed his letters home at the time of his death was, they said, so that "the rebels should not know they have a man who can die so firmly." He showed them.

He is no Washington or Jefferson, although he ranks with the heroes. Washington was a great general and Jefferson was a genius. All of our nation's heroes are great men who are great by their minds and by their deeds and by their careers. All except Hale. His special gift to his country, and to us who love that country, was the manner of his death.

He is the young American. He is the patron of all the young Americans who have grown up, as he did, in the quiet self-respecting families; who have gone to college and done well, and had fun, too; who have started out along their life's careers, well spoken of, promising; and then broken off to join their country's forces in time of war, without an instant's hesitation; knowing what must be done and who must do it. He was no different than they. He was an American boy. Everything that can be said of them can be said of him. In the letters of his friends written about him after his death, certain words keep cropping up. They sound oddly familiar. "Promising . . . patriotic . . . generous . . . modest . . . high-spirited . . . devoted . . ." His friends fitted the words to Hale. They fit Americans.

Nothing was more American in Hale than his taking on the duties that led to his death. It was a dirty job, spying. Nobody wanted it. He took it. There's something about that, taking on a dirty job that's got to be done, that rings a bell. It's an American custom of American heroes. He wasn't a remarkably articulate boy. His letters are nothing special. He just jotted things in his diary. But he became the spokesman for young American fighting men who have to die for their country. He chanced to say the thing they think; the thing they mean, when there's not even a split second to think. He stood there at Turtle Bay on Manhattan Island. Don't think he declaimed. He wasn't that kind. He had those few moments, and he was thinking about all the different things that were ending for him. He said and I think it was more like a remark:

"I only regret . . ."

57

ATLAS HAD a great reputation, but I'd like to have seen him try to carry a mattress upstairs.—*Kin Hubbard*

HUMOR is gravity concealed behind the jest.—*Johan Weiss*

COMMON SENSE is instinct, and enough of it is genius.—*Josh Billings*

A WITTY WRITER is like a porcupine: his quill makes no distinction between friend and foe.—*Josh Billings*

THERE IZ TWO things in this life for which we are never fully prepared; and this iz twins.—*Josh Billings*

KISSING AN UNWILLING pair of lips is as mean a victory as robbing a bird's nest, and kissing too willing ones is about as unfragrant a recreation as making bouquets out of dandelions.—*Josh Billings*

DON'T TAKE the bull by the horns, take him by the tail; then you can let go when you want to.—*Josh Billings*

FOR A MALE PERSON bric-a-brac hunting is about as robust a business as making doll clothes.—*Samuel Clemens*

THE VERY THING than men think they have got the most of, they have got the least of; and that is judgment.—*Josh Billings*

WHO RECALLS when folks used to git along without somethin' if it cost too much?—*Kin Hubbard*

IT OFTEN REQUIRES more bravery to tell the simple truth than it does to win a battle.—*Josh Billings*

ECONOMY IS a savings bank, into which men drop pennies, and get dollars in return.—*Josh Billings*

LAUGHTER

I DON'T KARE how mutch a man talks, if he only says it
in few words.—*Josh Billings*

THERE'S many a knock gits across in a jest.—*Kin Hubbard*

IT IS BETTER to know nothing than to know what ain't so.—*Josh Billings*

HAIN'T WE GOT all the fools in town on our side? And ain't that a
big enough majority in any town?—*Samuel Clemens*

LOTS O' FOLKS don't know when ther well off, but ther's ten times as many who
don't know when they hain't well off.—*Kin Hubbard*

THERE IS NO radical cure for the busybody, no more than there is for the fleas
on a long-haired dog—if you get rid of the fleas you have got the dog left, and
if you get rid of the dog you have got the fleas left, and so, where are you?
—*Josh Billings*

A REASONABLE AMOUNT o' fleas is good fer a dog—keeps him from broodin'
over bein' a dog.—*Edward Noyes Westcott**

NATURE never makes enny blunders. When she makes a phool
she means it.—*Josh Billings*

ABOUT THE ONLY THING we have left that actually discriminates in favor of the
plain people is the stork.—*Kin Hubbard*

INCREDULITY is the wisdom of a fool.—*Josh Billings*

THE WORST waste of breath, next to playin' a saxophone,
is advisin' a son.—*Kin Hubbard*

NOBUDDY HAS ever been able to describe a play
without makin' me tired.—*Kin Hubbard*

*From "David Harum" by Edward Noyes Westcott, reprinted by permission of Appleton-Century-Crofts, Inc.

I AM SENDING A PERSON OF DISTINCTION
NANCY BYRD TURNER

The Governor of Virginia took his pen
In hand, his long-quilled, solemn pen, and wrote
To Pennsylvania's Governor a note.

Trouble was brewing at the border again;
The settlers asked for aid. Someone must go,
Someone of spirit and strength, to make an ending
Once and for all of this aggression; so
Dinwiddie wrote to Hamilton he was sending
A person of distinction, who would deal
Capably with the matter; and set his seal
And signed his name.

               Upon an early day
The Person of Distinction started forth
On his long errand. Far the journey lay,
Four hundred mounting miles to west and north,
With peril on every hand and death at heel.
His company would be mustered on the way;
He made the start afoot, Dinwiddie's man,
With gun and knapsack. Eyes alert to scan
Thicket and copse, he went—age, twenty-one;
Height, six feet in his socks; name, Washington.

The road he took was an old trail that started
High in the Blue Ridge, crossed a valley, and climbed
Into the Alleghenies. He had timed
His going with dawn . . . . Toiling, he gained a steep,
Halted, and looked behind. The sun was lifting,
The little valley towns were still asleep,
Lost in their darkness; but the fog had parted.

He turned and looked ahead: the great mist, shifting,
Moved like a curtain drawn. Long, long he stood,
Staring. Below him meadow and field and wood,
River and plain stretched on unendingly
To the sky's edge. How many miles unrolled
In rivers unnamed, and ranges yet untold,
And forests dark with midnight, to the sea?
How long before the far coast caught the dawn?

Silent, the Governor's messenger stared on,
The slow fog cleared, the picture sharpened and shone....
His native land, waiting her destiny,
He with her .... As the last gloom broke and thinned,
Dispersed before a long, far-gathering wind,
Down in the valley a traveler, looking high,
Said: "Yonder a tall man stands against the sky."

SOME INTIMATE LETTERS OF GEORGE WASHINGTON

To Mrs. Martha Custis, later his wife:
July 20, 1758

WE HAVE begun our march for the Ohio. A courier is starting for Williamsburg, and I embrace the opportunity to send a few words to one whose life is now inseparable from mine. Since that happy hour when we made our pledges to each other, my thoughts have been continually going to you as another self. That an all-powerful Providence may keep us both in safety is the prayer of your faithful and affectionate friend.

To Mrs. George William Fairfax, his early love:
12th *September,* 1758

DEAR MADAM: Yesterday I was honored with your short but very agreeable favor of the first instant. How joyfully I catch at the happy occasion of renewing a correspondence which I feared was disrelished on your part, I leave to time, that never failing expositor of all things, and to a monitor equally faithful in my own breast, to testify.

If you allow that any honor can be derived from my opposition to our present system of management, you destroy the merit of it entirely in me by attributing my anxiety to the animating prospect of possessing Mrs. Custis when—I need not tell you, guess yourself. Should not my own honor and the country's welfare be the excitement? 'Tis true, I profess myself a votary of love. I acknowledge that a lady is in the case, and further I confess that this lady is known to you ....

To Robert Cary & Co.:
6 *June,* 1768

GENTLEMEN: My old chariot having run its race, and gone through as many stages as I could conveniently make it travel, is now rendered incapable of any further service. The intent of this letter, therefore, is to desire you will bespeak me a new one.

As these are kind of articles that last with care against a number of years, I would willingly have the chariot you may now send me made in the newest taste, handsome, genteel and light; yet not slight, and consequently unserviceable; to be made of the best seasoned wood, and by a celebrated workman. The last importation which I have seen, besides the customary steel springs, have others that play in a brass barrel and contribute at one and the same time to the ease and ornament of the carriage. One of this kind, therefore, would be my choice; and green being a color little apt, as I apprehend, to fade, and grateful to the eye, I would give it the preference, unless any other color more in vogue and equally lasting is entitled to precedence. In that case I would be governed by fashion . . . .

If such a chariot as I have here described could be got at second hand, little or nothing the worse for wear, but at the same time a good deal under the first cost of a new one, it would be very desirable.

(*The cost of the chariot was £103, but the harness, covers, blinds, and other extras brought the cost to £133.*)

To Mrs. Martha Washington:
Philadelphia,
18 June, 1775.
MY DEAREST: I am now set down to write to you on a subject which fills me with inexpressible concern, and this concern is greatly aggravated and increased, when I reflect upon the uneasiness I know it will give you. It has been determined in Congress, that the whole army raised for the defence of the American cause shall be put under my care, and that it is necessary for me to proceed immediately to Boston to take upon me the command of it.

You may believe me, my dear Patsy, when I assure you, in the most solemn manner, that, so far from seeking this appointment, I have used every endeavor in my power to avoid it, not only from my unwillingness to part with you and the family, but from a consciousness of its being a trust too great for my capacity, and that I should enjoy more real happiness in one month with you at home, than I have the most distant prospect of finding abroad, if my stay were to be seven times seven years . . . . I, therefore, beg that you will summon your whole fortitude, as it must add greatly to my uneasy feelings to hear that you are dissatisfied or complaining at what I could not avoid . . . .

To Lund Washington:
20th September, 1783.
DEAR LUND: For my own part, I never did, nor do I believe I ever shall, give advice to a woman, who is setting out on a matrimonial voyage; first, because I never could advise one to marry without her own consent; and, secondly, because I know it is to no purpose to advise her to refrain, when she has obtained it. A woman very rarely asks an opinion or requires advice on such an occasion, till her resolution is formed; and then it is with the hope and expectation of obtaining a sanction, not that she means to be governed by your disapprobation, that she applies . . . .

To Mrs. Mary Washington, his mother:
15th February, 1787.
HONORED MADAM: My house is at your service, and I would press you most sincerely and most devoutly to accept it, but I am sure, and candor requires me to say, it will never answer your purposes in any shape whatsoever. For in truth it may be compared to a well resorted tavern, as scarcely any strangers who are going from north to south, or from south to north, do not spend a day or two at it. This would, were you to be an inhabitant of it, oblige you to do one of three things; first, to be always dressing to appear in company, second, to come into the room in a dishabille, or third, to be, as it were, a prisoner in your own chamber. The first you'd not like; indeed, for a person at your time of life it would be too fatiguing. The second, I should not like. And the third more than probably, would not be pleasing

in any room; for what with the sitting up of company, the noise and bustle of servants, and many other things, you would not be able to enjoy that calmness and serenity of mind, which in my opinion you ought now to prefer to every other consideration in life.

To *John Jay*:

Mount Vernon,
10th *March*, 1787.

DEAR SIR: Among men of reflection, few will be found, I believe, who are not beginning to think that our system is more perfect in theory than in practice; and that notwithstanding the boasted virtue of America it is more than probable we shall exhibit the last melancholy proof, that mankind are not competent to their own government without the means of coercion in the sovereign.

To *Alexander Spotswood*:

Mount Vernon,
13th *February*, 1788.

DEAR SIR: I think with you, that the life of a husbandman of all others is the most delectable. It is honorable, it is amusing, and, with judicious management, it is profitable. To see plants rise from the earth and flourish by the superior skill and bounty of the laborer fills a contemplative mind with ideas which are more easy to be conceived than expressed.

To *the Marquis de Chastellux*:

Mount Vernon,
25th *April*, 1788.

MY DEAR MARQUIS: In reading your very friendly and acceptable letter, of 21st December, 1787, which came to hand by the last mail, I was, as you may well suppose, not less delighted than surprised to meet the plain American words, "my wife." A wife! Well, my dear Marquis, I can hardly refrain from smiling to find you are caught at last . . . . Now you are well served for coming to fight in favor of the American rebels, all the way across the Atlantic Ocean, by catching that terrible contagion—domestic felicity—which time, like the small pox or the plague, a man can have only once in his life; because it commonly lasts him (at least with us in America—I don't know how you manage these matters in France) for his whole life time. And yet after all the maledictions you so richly merit on the subject, the worst wish which I can find in my heart to make against Madame de Chastellux and yourself is, that you may neither of you ever get the better of this same—domestic felicity —during the entire course of your mortal existence.

To *Arthur Young*:

Mount Vernon,
4th *December*, 1788.

SIR: As to what you suggest at the close of your letter, respecting the publication of extracts from my correspondence in your annals, I hardly know what to say. I can only say for myself, that I have endeavored, in a state of tranquil retirement, to keep myself as much from the eye of the world as I possibly could. I have studiously avoided, as much as was in my power, to give any cause for ill-natured or impertinent comments on my conduct: and I should be very unhappy to have anything done on my behalf (however distant in itself from impropriety), which should give occasion for one officious tongue to use my name with indelicacy. For I wish most devoutly to glide silently and unnoticed through the remainder of life. This is my heart-felt wish; and these are my undisguised feelings. After having submitted them confidentially to you, I have such a reliance upon your prudence, as to leave it with you to do what you think, upon a full consideration of the matter, shall be wisest and best. I am, etc.

GEORGE WASHINGTON IN HIS OWN WRITINGS

Written When Seventeen Years Old

MY PLACE of residence is at present at his Lordships where I might, was my heart disengaged, pass my time very pleasantly as there's a very agreeable young lady lives in the same house (Colonel George Fairfax's wife's sister) but as that's only adding fuel to fire, it makes me the more uneasy, for by often and unavoidably being in company with her, revives my former passion for your low land Beauty, whereas was I to live more retired from young women I might in some measure eliviate my sorrows by burying that chaste and troublesome passion in the grave of oblivion or eternal forgetfulness, for, as I am very well assured, that's the only antidote or remedy that I shall be relieved by or only recess that can administer any cure or help to me as I am well convinced was I ever to attempt any thing I should only get a denial which would be only adding grief to uneasiness.

Letter from George Washington to "Dear Robin," 1748.

ENTERTAINMENT
West Point, 16 August, 1779

DEAR DOCTOR:

I have asked Mrs. Cochran and Mrs. Livingston to dine with me tomorrow; but am I not in honour bound to apprise them of their fare? As I hate deception, even where the imagination only is concerned, I will. It is needless to premise that my table is large enough to hold the ladies. Of this they had occular proof yesterday. To say how it is usually covered, is rather more essential; and this shall be the purport of my letter.

Since our arrival at this happy spot, we have had a ham, (sometimes a shoulder) of bacon, to grace the head of the table; a piece of roast beef adorns the foot; and a dish of beans, or greens, (almost imperceptible,) decorates the center. When the cook has a mind to cut a figure, (which I presume will be the case tomorrow,) we have two beefsteak pies, or dishes of crabs, in addition, one on each side of the center dish, dividing the space and reducing the distance between dish and dish to about six feet, which without them would be about twelve feet apart. Of late he has had the surprising sagacity to discover that apples will make pies; and it's a question, if, in the violence of his efforts, we do not get one of the apples, instead of having both of beefsteak. If the ladies can put up with such entertainment, and will submit to partake of it on plates, once tin but now iron—(not become so by the labor of scouring), I shall be happy to see them; and am, dear Doctor, yours, etc.

FRANKNESS

... I never say any thing of a man that I have the smallest scruple of

64

saying—*to him.* *To Robert Morris.*

HE SAYS AT FIFTY-FOUR

... I do not recollect that in the course of my life I ever forfeited my word, or broke a promise made to any one. ... *To William Triplett.*

CRITICISM

... While the eyes of America, perhaps of the world, are turned to this government and many are watching the movement of all those, who are concerned in its administration, I should like to be informed, through so good a medium, of the public opinion of both men and measures, and of none more than myself; not so much of what may be thought commendable parts, if any, of my conduct, as of those which are conceived to be of a different complexion. The man, who means to commit no wrong, will never be guilty of enormities; consequently he can never be unwilling to learn what is ascribed to him as foibles. If they are really such, the knowledge of them in a well-disposed mind will go half way towards a reform. If they are not errors, he can explain and justify the motives of his actions.

To David Stuart.

I STRIKE

... But after all, is not Lawrence Lewis on the point of matrimony? Report says so, and if truly, it would be an effectual bar to a *permanent* establishment in my business, as I never again will have two women in my house when I am there myself ....

To Bruges Ball, 1793.

LOVE AT SIXTY-ONE

... Love is said to be an involuntary passion, and it is therefore contended that it cannot be resisted.

This is true in part only, for like all things else, when nourished and supplied plentifully with aliment, it is rapid in its progress; but let these be withdrawn and it may be stifled in its birth or much stinted in its growth. For example, a woman (the same may be said of either sex) all beautiful and accomplished, will, while her hand and heart are undisposed of, turn the heads and set the circle in which she moves on fire. Let her marry, and what is the consequence? The madness *ceases* and all is quiet again. Why? Not because there is any diminution in the charms of the lady, but because there is an end of hope. Hence it follows, that love may and therefore ought to be under the guidance of reason, for although we cannot avoid first impressions, we may assuredly place them under guard; and my motives for treating on this subject are to show you, while you remain Eleanor Parke Custis, spinster, and retain the resolution to love with moderation, the propriety of adhering to the latter resolution, at least until you have secured your game, and the way by which it may be accomplished.

To Eleanor Parke Custis.

From FAREWELL ADDRESS

... THE UNITY of government, which constitutes you one people, is also now dear to you. It is justly so; for it is a main pillar in the edifice of your real independence, the support of your tranquility at home, your peace abroad; of your safety; of your prosperity; of that very liberty which you so highly prize. ... You should properly estimate the immense value of your national Union to your collective and individual happiness ...

WASHINGTON
Nancy Byrd Turner

He played by the river when he was young,
He raced with rabbits along the hills,
He fished for minnows, and climbed and swung,
And hooted back at the whippoorwills.
Strong and slender and tall he grew
And then, one morning, the bugles blew.

Over the hills, the summons came,
Over the river's shining rim.
He said that the bugles called his name,
He knew that his country needed him,
And he answered, "Coming!" and marched away
For many a night and many a day.

Perhaps when the marches were hot and long
He'd think of the river flowing by,
Or, camping under the winter sky,
Would hear the whippoorwill's far-off song.
Boy and soldier, in peace or strife,
He loved America all his life!

INSCRIPTION AT MOUNT VERNON

Washington, the brave, the wise, the good,
Supreme in war, in council, and in peace,
Valiant without ambition, discreet without fear,
Confident without presumption.
In disaster, calm; in success, moderate; in all, himself.
The hero, the patriot, the Christian,
The father of nations, the friend of all mankind,
Who, when he had won all, renounced all,
And sought in the bosom of his family and of nature, retirement,
And in the hope of religion, immortality.

A WORD ABOUT WASHINGTON
NANCY BYRD TURNER

He loved his Country, he loved her cause,
   Her honor, her flag, her fame,
He loved the light of her liberty,
   Her new and radiant name;
And it doesn't get into the histories,
But how he loved her trees!

It only got into his journal how
   He cherished them, down to the core
And up with the grain to the topmost bough,
   With all the treasure they bore.
He must have remembered, in battle smoke,
The ripple of new-leaved oak.

He knew the hillside for apple and peach
   And the orchard corner for plums;
He knew to an inch how far apart
   Birches must stand, and gums,
As he knew to a day the budding time
Of maple and larch and lime.

When the wearisome fights were over and done
   He used to hurry home
And get down close to America's sod,
   Touching her clay and loam,
Breathing deep at the root of things,
Forgetting colonels and kings!

History gives us the Gentleman,
   Fine in ruffle and stock,
The General, booted and spurred and bold,
   The Statesman, firm as a rock.
I give you the Countryman, on his knees,
Earth-warmed, setting out trees!

No ONE CAN replace him, sir; I am only his successor.
—Jefferson (on Franklin)

SOME MISGUIDED PEOPLE see nothing wrong in the rule that to the victors belong the spoils of the enemy.—*William Learned Marcy*

LET the bugles sound the *Truce of God* to the whole world forever!
—Charles Sumner

THERE IS MUCH vice and misery in the world, I know; but more virtue and happiness, I believe.—*Jefferson*

MY MEN, yonder are the Hessians. They were bought for seven pounds and ten pence a man. Are you worth more? Prove it. Tonight, the American flag floats from yonder hill or Molly Stark sleeps a widow!—*General John Stark*

ALL RIGHT, just give me some wedges and a mallet, and half a dozen men of my own choosing, and I'll soon take her for you. (Speech before surrender of Fort Oswegatchie)—*General Putnam*

I HAVE THE CONSOLATION to reflect that during the period of my administration not a drop of the blood of a single fellow citizen was shed by the sword of war or of the law.—*Jefferson*

THOMAS JEFFERSON still lives! (The last words of John Adams; Jefferson had died on the morning of that same day.)—*John Adams*

THE DECLARATION THAT OUR PEOPLE are hostile to a government made by ourselves, and for themselves, and conducted by themselves, is an insult.—*John Adams*

WE HAVE LIVED long, gentlemen, but this (the Louisiana Purchase) is the noblest work of our lives.—*Robert R. Livingston*

PRIDE costs us more than hunger, thirst, and cold.—*Jefferson*

WORDS OF GEORGE WASHINGTON

HEAVEN ITSELF has ordained the right.

IT is well. I die hard, but am not afraid to go. (His last words.)

TO PERSEVERE in one's duty and be silent is the best answer to calumny.

MOCK NOT NOR JEST at anything of importance; break no jests that are sharp or biting; and if you deliver anything witty or pleasant, abstain from laughing thereat yourself.

WHAT YOU may speak in secret to your friend, deliver not before others.

SHOW NOT YOURSELF GLAD at the misfortune of another, though he were your enemy. Be not hasty to believe flying reports to the disparagement of any.

UNDERTAKE NOT what you cannot perform; but be careful to keep your promise.

THE COMPANY in which you will improve most will be least expensive to you.

ASSOCIATE WITH MEN of good quality, if you esteem your own reputation; for it is better to be alone than in bad company.

THE FATE of unborn millions will now depend, under God, on the courage and conduct of this Army.

I HOPE I SHALL ALWAYS POSSESS firmness and virtue enough to maintain what I consider the most enviable of all titles, the character of an "Honest Man."

ARBITRARY POWER is most easily established on the ruins of liberty, abused by licentiousness.

LET US RAISE A STANDARD to which the wise and honest can repair; the rest is in the hands of God.

69

The Man Without a Country

By EDWARD EVERETT HALE

I suppose that very few casual readers of the *New York Herald* of August 13, 1863, noticed, in an obscure corner, among the "Deaths," the announcement,

"Nolan. Died on board *U.S.S. Corvette Levant*, Lat. 2° 11′ S., Long. 131° W., on the 11th of May, Philip Nolan."

I happened to observe it, because I was stranded at the old Mission House in Mackinaw, waiting for a Lake Superior steamer which did not choose to come, and I was devouring to the very stubble all the current literature I could get hold of, even down to the deaths and marriages in the *Herald*. My memory for names and people is good, and the reader will see, as he goes on, that I had reason enough to remember Philip Nolan. There are hundreds of readers who would have paused at that announcement, if the officer of the *Levant* who reported it had chosen to make it thus: "Died, May 11, 'The Man without a Country.'" For it was as "The Man without a Country" that poor Philip Nolan had generally been known by the officers who had him in charge during some fifty years, as, indeed, by all the men who sailed under them. I dare say there is many a man who has taken wine with him once a fortnight, in a three years' cruise, who never knew that his name was "Nolan," or whether the poor wretch had any name at all.

There can now be no possible harm in telling this poor creature's story.

Reason enough there has been till now, ever since Madison's administration went out in 1817, for very strict secrecy, the secrecy of honor itself, among the gentlemen of the navy who have had Nolan in successive charge. And certainly it speaks well for the *esprit de corps* of the profession, and the personal honor of its members, that to the press this man's story has been wholly unknown, and, I think, to the country at large also. I have reason to think, from some investigations I made in the Naval Archives when I was attached to the Bureau of Construction, that every official report relating to him was burned when Ross burned the public buildings at Washington. One of the Tuckers, or possibly one of the Watsons, had Nolan in charge at the end of the war; and when, on returning from his cruise, he reported at Washington to one of the Crowninshields,—who was in the Navy Department when he came home,—he found that the Department ignored the whole business. Whether they really knew nothing about it, or whether it was a *Non mi ricordo* determined on as a piece of policy, I do not know. But this I do know, that since 1817, and possibly before, no naval officer has mentioned Nolan in his report of a cruise.

But, as I say, there is no need for secrecy any longer. And now the poor creature is dead, it seems to me worth while to tell a little of his story, by way of showing young Americans of today what it is to be a "Man without a Country."

Philip Nolan was as fine a young officer as there was in the "Legion of the West," as the Western Division of our Army was then called. When Aaron Burr made his first dashing expedition down to New Orleans in 1805, at Fort Massac, or somewhere above on the river, he met, as the Devil would have it, this gay, dashing, bright young fellow, at some dinner party, I think. Burr marked him, talked to him, walked with him, took him on a day or two's voyage in his flatboat, and, in short, fascinated him. For the next year, barracks life was very tame to poor Nolan. He occasionally availed himself of the permission the great man had given him to write to him. Long, high worded, stilted letters the poor boy wrote and rewrote and copied. But never a line did he have in reply from the gay deceiver. The other boys in the garrison sneered at him, because he sacrificed in this unrequited affection for a politician the time which they devoted to Monongahela, hazard, and high-low-Jack. Bourbon, euchre, and poker were still unknown. But one day Nolan had his revenge. This time Burr came down the river, not as an attorney seeking a place for his office, but as a disguised conqueror. He had defeated I know not how many district attorneys; he had dined at I know not how many public dinners; he had been heralded in I know not how many *Weekly Arguses*, and it was rumored that he had an army behind him and an empire before him. It was a great day—his arrival —to poor Nolan. Burr had not been at the Fort an hour before he sent for him. That evening he asked Nolan to take him out in his skiff, to show him a cane-brake or a cottonwood tree, as he said,—really to seduce him; and by the time the sail was over, Nolan was enlisted body and soul. From that time, though he did not yet know it, he lived as a "Man without a Country."

What Burr meant to do I know no more than you, dear reader. It is none of our business just now. Only, when the grand catastrophe came, and Jefferson and the House of Virginia of that day undertook to break on the wheel all the possible Clarences of the then House of York, by the great treason trial at Richmond, some of the lesser fry in that distant Mississippi Valley, which was farther from us than Puget Sound is today, introduced the like novelty on their provincial stage, and to while away the monotony of the summer at Fort Adams, got up, for *spectacles*, a string of courts-martial on the officers there. One and another of the colonels and majors were tried, and to fill out the list, little Nolan, against whom, Heaven knows, there was evidence enough, that he was sick of the service, had been willing to be false to it, and would have obeyed any order to march anywhither with any one who would follow him had the order been signed, "By command of His Exec. A. Burr." The courts dragged on. The big flies escaped,—rightly for all I know. Nolan was proved guilty enough, as I say; yet you and I would never have heard of him, reader, but that, when the president of the court asked him at the close whether he wished to say anything to show that he had always been faithful to the United States, he cried out in a fit of frenzy,

"Damn the United States! I wish

I may never hear of the United States again!"

I suppose he did not know how the words shocked old Colonel Morgan, who was holding the court. Half the officers who sat in it had served through the Revolution; and their lives, not to say their necks, had been risked for the very idea which he so cavalierly cursed in his madness. He, on his part, had grown up in the West of those days in the midst of "Spanish plot," "Orleans plot," and all the rest. He had been educated on a plantation where the finest company was a Spanish officer or a French merchant from Orleans. His education, such as it was, had been perfected in commercial expeditions to Vera Cruz; and I think he told me his father once hired an Englishman to be a private tutor for a winter on the plantation. He had spent half his youth with an older brother, hunting horses in Texas; and, in a word, to him "United States" was scarcely a reality. Yet he had been fed by "United States" for all the years since he had been in the army. He had sworn on his faith as a Christian to be true to "United States." It was "United States" which gave him the uniform he wore and the sword by his side. Nay, my poor Nolan, it was only because "United States" had picked you out first as one of her own confidential men of honor that "A. Burr" cared for you a straw more than for the flatboat men who sailed his ark for him! I do not excuse Nolan; I only explain to the reader why he damned his country, and wished he might never hear her name again.

He never did hear her name but once again. From that moment, Sept. 23, 1807, till the day he died, May 11, 1863, he never heard her name again. For that half-century and more he was a "Man without a Country."

Old Morgan, as I said, was terribly shocked. If Nolan had compared George Washington to Benedict Arnold, or had cried, "God save King George!" Morgan would not have felt worse. He called the court into his private room, and returned in fifteen minutes, with a face like a sheet, to say,

"Prisoner, hear the sentence of the court! The court decides, subject to the approval of the President, that you never hear the name of the United States again."

Nolan laughed. But nobody else laughed. Old Morgan was too solemn, and the whole room was hushed dead as night for a minute. Even Nolan lost his swagger in a moment. Then Morgan added,

"Mr. Marshall, take the prisoner to Orleans in an armed boat, and deliver him to the naval commander there."

The Marshal gave his orders, and the prisoner was taken out of court.

"Mr. Marshal," continued old Morgan, "see that no one mentions the United States to the prisoner. Mr. Marshal, make my respects to Lieutenant Mitchell at Orleans, and request him to order that no one shall mention the United States to the prisoner while he is on board ship. You will receive your written orders from the officer on duty here this evening. The court is adjourned without delay."

I have always supposed that Colonel Morgan himself took the proceedings of the court to Washington City, and explained them to Mr. Jefferson. Certain it is that the President approved them,—certain, that is, if I may believe the men who

72

say they have seen his signature. Before the *Nautilus* got round from New Orleans to the Northern Atlantic coast with the prisoner on board, the sentence had been approved, and he was a man without a country.

The plan then adopted was substantially the same which was necessarily followed ever after. Perhaps it was suggested by the necessity of sending him by water from Fort Adams and Orleans. The Secretary of the Navy—it must have been the first Crowninshield, though he is a man I do not remember—was requested to put Nolan on board a government vessel bound on a long cruise, and to direct that he should be only so far confined there as to make it certain that he never saw or heard of the country. We had few long cruises then, and the navy was very much out of favor; and as almost all of this story is traditional, as I have explained, I do not know certainly what his first cruise was. But the commander to whom he was intrusted, perhaps it was Tingey or Shaw, though I think it was one of the younger men—we are all old enough now—regulated the etiquette and the precautions of the affair, and according to his scheme they were carried out, I suppose, till Nolan died.

When I was second officer of the *Intrepid*, some thirty years after, I saw the original paper of instructions. I have been sorry ever since that I did not copy the whole of it. It ran, however, much in this way:

WASHINGTON [with a date which must have been late in 1807].
Sir: You will receive from Lieutenant Neale the person of Philip Nolan, late a lieutenant in the United States Army.

This person on his trial by court-martial expressed with an oath the wish that he might "never hear of the United States again."

The court sentenced him to have his wish fulfilled.

For the present, the execution of the order is intrusted by the President to this department.

You will take the prisoner on board your ship, and keep him there with such precautions as shall prevent his escape.

You will provide him with such quarters, rations, and clothing as would be proper for an officer of his late rank, if he were a passenger on your vessel on the business of his Government.

The gentlemen on board will make any arrangements agreeable to themselves regarding his society. He is to be exposed to no indignity of any kind, nor is he ever unnecessarily to be reminded that he is a prisoner.

But under no circumstances is he ever to hear of his country, or to see any information regarding it; and you will specially caution all the officers under your command to take care that, in the various indulgences which may be granted, this rule, in which his punishment is involved, shall not be broken.

It is the intention of the Government that he shall never again see the country which he has disowned. Before the end of your cruise you will receive orders which will give effect to this intention.

Respectfully yours,
W. Southard, for the
Secretary of the Navy.

If I had only preserved the whole of this paper, there would be no break in the beginning of my sketch of this story,—for Captain Shaw, if

73

it were he, handed it to his successor in the charge, and he to his; and I suppose the commander of the *Levant* has it today as his authority for keeping this man in this mild custody.

The rule adopted on board the ships on which I have met the "Man without a Country" was, I think, transmitted from the beginning. No mess liked to have him permanently, because his presence cut off all talk of home or of the prospect of return, of politics or letters, of peace or of war, cut off more than half the talk men liked to have at sea. But it was always thought too hard that he should never meet the rest of us, except to touch hats, and we finally sank into one system. He was not permitted to talk with the men unless an officer was by. With officers he had unrestrained intercourse, as far as they and he chose. But he grew shy, though he had favorites; I was one. Then the captain always asked him to dinner on Monday. Every mess in succession took up the invitation in its turn. According to the size of the ship, you had him at your mess more or less often at dinner. His breakfast he ate in his own stateroom—he always had a stateroom—which was where a sentinel or somebody on the watch could see the door. And whatever else he ate or drank, he ate or drank alone. Sometimes, when the marines or sailors had any special jollification, they were permitted to invite "Plain Buttons," as they called him. Then Nolan was sent with some officer, and the men were forbidden to speak of home while he was there. I believe the theory was that the sight of his punishment did them good. They called him "Plain Buttons" because, while he always chose to wear a regulation army-uniform, he was not permitted to wear the army button, for the reason that it bore either the initials or the insignia of the country he had disowned.

I remember soon after I joined the navy I was on shore with some of the older officers from our ship and from the *Brandywine*, which we had met at Alexandria. We had leave to make a party and go up to Cairo and the pyramids. As we jogged along (you went on donkeys then), some of the gentlemen (we boys called them "Dons," but the phrase was long since changed) fell to talking about Nolan, and some one told the system which was adopted from the first about his books and other reading. As he was almost never permitted to go on shore, even though the vessel lay in port for months, his time at the best hung heavy; and everybody was permitted to lend him books, if they were not published in America, and made no allusion to it. These were common enough in the old days, when people in the other hemisphere talked of the United States as little as we do of Paraguay. He had almost all the foreign papers that came into the ship, sooner or later; only somebody must go over them first, and cut out any advertisement or stray paragraph that alluded to America. This was a little cruel sometimes, when the back of what was cut out might be as innocent as Hesiod. Right in the midst of one of Napoleon's battles, or one of Canning's speeches, poor Nolan would find a great hole, because on the back of the page of that paper there had been an advertisement of a packet for New York, or a scrap from the President's message. I say this was the first time I ever heard of this plan, which afterward I had enough and more than enough to do with. I remember it because poor

Phillips, who was of the party, as soon as the allusion to reading was made, told a story of something which happened at the Cape of Good Hope on Nolan's first voyage; and it is the only thing I ever knew of that voyage. They had touched at the Cape, and had done the civil thing with the English Admiral and the fleet; and then, leaving for a long cruise up the Indian Ocean, Phillips had borrowed a lot of English books from an officer, which in those days, as indeed in these, was quite a windfall. Among them, as the Devil would order, was the *Lay of the Last Minstrel*, which they had all of them heard of, but which most of them had never seen. I think it could not have been published long. Well, nobody thought there could be any risk of anything national in that, though Phillips swore old Shaw had cut out the *The Tempest* from Shakespeare before he let Nolan have it, because he said "the Bermudas ought to be ours, and, by Jove, should be one day." So Nolan was permitted to join the circle one afternoon when a lot of them sat on deck smoking and reading aloud. People do not do such things so often now; but when I was young we got rid of a great deal of time so. Well, so it happened that in his turn Nolan took the book and read to the others; and he read very well, as I know. Nobody in the circle knew a line of the poem, only it was all magic and Border chivalry, and was ten thousand years ago. Poor Nolan read steadily through the fifth canto, stopped a minute and drank something, and then began, without a thought of what was coming,

"Breathes there the man, with soul so dead,
Who never to himself hath said—"

It seems impossible to us that any-body ever heard this for the first time; but all these fellows did then, and poor Nolan himself went on, still unconsciously or mechanically,

"This is my own, my native land!"

Then they all saw something was to pay: he expected to get through, I suppose, turned a little pale, but plunged on,

"Whose heart hath ne'er within him burned,
As home his footsteps he hath turned
From wandering on a foreign strand?
If such there breathe, go, mark him well—"

By this time the men were all beside themselves, wishing there was any way to make him turn over two pages; but he had not quite presence of mind for that. He gagged a little, colored crimson, and staggered on,

"For him no minstrel raptures swell;
High though his titles, proud his name,
Boundless his wealth as wish can claim,
Despite these titles, power, and pelf,
The wretch, concentred all in self—"

and here the poor fellow choked, could not go on, but started up, swung the book into the sea, vanished into his stateroom, "And by Jove," said Phillips, "we did not see him for two months again; and I had to make up some beggarly story to that English surgeon why I did not return his Walter Scott to him."

That story shows about the time when Nolan's braggadocio must have broken down. At first, they said, he took a very high tone, considered his imprisonment a mere farce, affected to enjoy the voyage, and all that; but Phillips said that after he came out of his stateroom he never was the same man again. He never read aloud again, unless it was the Bible or Shakespeare, or something else he was sure of. But it was not that merely. He never entered in with the other young men exactly as a companion again. He was always shy afterward, when I knew him,—very seldom spoke, unless he was spoken to, except to a very few friends. He lighted up occasionally—I remember late in his life hearing him fairly eloquent on something which had been suggested to him by one of Fléchier's sermons, but generally he had the nervous, tired look of a heart wounded man.

When Captain Shaw was coming home—if, as I say, it was Shaw— rather to the surprise of everybody they made one of the Windward Islands, and lay off and on for nearly a week. The boys said the officers were sick of salt-junk, and meant to have turtle-soup before they came home. But after several days the *Warren* came to the same rendezvous; they exchanged signals; she sent to Phillips and these homeward bound men letters and papers, and told them she was outward bound, perhaps to the Mediterranean, and took poor Nolan and his traps on the boat back to try his second cruise. He looked very blank when he was told to get ready to join her. He had known enough of the signs of the sky to know that till that moment he was going "home." But this was a distinct evidence of something he had not thought of, perhaps—that there was no going home for him, even to a prison. And this was the first of some twenty such transfers, which brought him sooner or later into half our best vessels, but which kept him all his life at least some hundred miles from the country he had hoped he might never hear of again.

It may have been on the second cruise—it was once when he was up the Mediterranean—that Mrs. Graff, the celebrated Southern beauty of those days, danced with him. They had been lying a long time in the Bay of Naples, and the officers were very intimate in the English fleet, and there had been great festivities, and our men thought they must give a great ball on board the ship. How they ever did it on board the *Warren* I am sure I do not know. Perhaps it was not the *Warren*, or perhaps ladies did not take up so much room as they do now. They wanted to use Nolan's stateroom for something, and they hated to do it without asking him to the ball; so the captain said they might ask him if they would be responsible that he did not talk with the wrong people, "who would give him intelligence." So the dance went on, the finest party that had ever been known, I dare say; for I never heard of a man-of-war ball that was not. For ladies they had the family of the American consul, one or two travellers who had adventured so far, and a nice bevy of English girls and matrons, perhaps Lady Hamilton herself.

Well, different officers relieved each other in standing and talking with Nolan in a friendly way, so as to be sure that nobody else spoke to him. The dancing went on with spirit; and after a while even the

76

fellows who took this honorary guard of Nolan ceased to fear any *contretemps*. Only when some English lady—Lady Hamilton, as I said, perhaps—called for a set of "American dances," an odd thing happened. Everybody then danced contra-dances. The black band, nothing loath, conferred as to what "American dances" were, and started off with "Virginia Reel" which they followed with "Money Musk," which in its turn, in those days should have been followed by "The Old Thirteen." But just as Dick, the leader, tapped for his fiddles to begin, and bent forward, about to say in true negro state, " 'The Old Thirteen,' gentlemen and ladies!" as he had said, " 'Virginny Reel,' if you please!" and " 'Money Musk,' if you please!" the captain's boy tapped him on the shoulder, whispered to him, and he did not announce the name of the dance; he merely bowed, began on the air, and they all fell to, the officers teaching the English girls the figure, but not telling them why it had no name.

But that is not the story I started to tell. As the dancing went on, Nolan and our fellows all got at ease, as I said, so much so that it seemed quite natural for him to bow to that splendid Mrs. Graff, and say,

"I hope you have not forgotten me, Miss Rutledge. Shall I have the honor of dancing?"

He did it so quickly that Fellows, who was by him, could not hinder him. She laughed, and said,

"I am not Miss Rutledge any longer, Mr. Nolan; but I will dance all the same," just nodded to Fellows, as if to say he must leave Mr. Nolan to her, and led him off to the place where the dance was forming.

Nolan thought he had found his chance. He had known her at Philadelphia, and at other places had met her; and this was a godsend. He began with her travels and Europe and Vesuvius and the French; and then, when they had worked down, and had that long talking time at the bottom of the set, he said boldly,—a little pale, she said, as she told me the story, years after,

"And what do you hear from home, Mrs. Graff?"

And that splendid creature looked through him. Jove! how she must have looked through him!

"Home! Mr. Nolan! I thought you were the man who never wanted to hear of home again!" And she walked directly up the deck to her husband, and left poor Nolan alone, as he always was. He did not dance again.

I cannot give any history of him in order; nobody can now, and indeed I am not trying to. These are the traditions, which I sort out, as I believe them, from the myths which have been told about this man for forty years. The lies that have been told about him are legion. The fellows used to say he was the "Iron Mask"; and poor George Pons went to his grave in the belief that this was the author of *Junius*, who was being punished for his celebrated libel on Thomas Jefferson. Pons was not very strong in the historical line. A happier story than either of these I have told is of the war. That came along soon after. I have heard this affair told in three or four ways, and indeed it may have happened more than once. But which ship it was on I cannot tell. However, in one, at least, of the great frigate-duels with the English in which the navy was really baptized, it happened that a round shot from the enemy entered one of our ports square, and took right down the officer of the gun himself, and almost every man of the gun's crew. Now you may say what you choose about courage, but that is not a nice thing to see. But as the men who were not killed picked themselves up, and as they and the surgeon's people were carrying off the bodies, there appeared Nolan, in his shirt sleeves, with the rammer in his hand, and just as if he had been the officer, told them off with authority, who should go to the cockpit with the wounded men, who should stay with him, perfectly cheery, and with that way which makes men feel sure all is right, and is going to be right. And he finished loading the gun with his own hands, aimed it, and bade the men fire. And there he stayed, captain of that gun, keeping those fellows in spirits till the enemy struck, sitting on the carriage while the gun was cooling, though he was exposed all the time, showing them easier ways to handle heavy shot, making the raw hands laugh at their own blunders, and when the gun cooled again, getting it loaded and fired twice as often as any other gun on the ship. The captain walked forward by way of encouraging the men, and Nolan touched his hat, and said,

"I am showing them how we do this in the artillery, sir."

And this is the part of the story where all the legends agree; and the commodore said,

"I see you do, and I thank you, sir; and I shall never forget this day, sir, and you never shall, sir."

And after the whole thing was over, and he had the Englishman's sword, in the midst of the state and ceremony of the quarter-deck, he said,

"Where is Mr. Nolan? Ask Mr. Nolan to come here."

And when Nolan came, the captain said,

"Mr. Nolan, we are all very grateful to you today. You are one of us today; you will be named in the despatches."

And then the old man took off his own sword of ceremony, and gave it to Nolan, and made him put it on. The man told me this who saw it. Nolan cried like a baby, and well he might. He had not worn a sword since that infernal day at Fort Adams. But always afterward on occasions of ceremony, he wore that quaint old French sword of the commodore's.

The captain did mention him in the despatches. It was always said he asked that he might be pardoned. He wrote a special letter to the Secretary of War; but nothing ever came of it. As I said, that was about the time when they began to ignore the whole transaction at Washington, and when Nolan's imprisonment began to carry itself on because there was nobody to stop it without orders from home.

I have heard it said that he was with Porter when he took possession of the Nukahiva Islands. As an artillery officer who had seen service in the West, Nolan knew more about fortifications, embrasures, ravelins, stockades, and all that, than any of them did; and he worked with a right good will in fixing that battery all right. I have always thought it was a pity Porter did not leave him in command there with Gamble. That would have settled all the question about his punishment. We should have kept the islands, and at this moment we should have one station in the Pacific Ocean. Our French friends, too, when they wanted this little watering place, would have found it was preoccupied. But Madison and the Virginians, of course, flung all that away.

All that was near fifty years ago. If Nolan was thirty then, he must have been near eighty when he died. He looked sixty when he was forty; but he never seemed to me to change a hair afterward. As I imagine his life from what I have seen and heard of it, he must have been in every sea, and yet almost never on land. He must have known in a formal way more officers in our service than any man living knows. He told me once with a grave smile that no man in the world lived so methodical a life as he. "You know the boys say I am the 'Iron Mask,' and you know how busy he was." He said it did not do for any one to try to read all the time, more than to do anything else all the time; but that he read just five hours a day. "Then," he said, "I keep up my notebooks, writing in them at such and such hours from what I have been reading; and I include in these my scrapbooks." These were very curious indeed. He had six or eight, of different subjects. There was one of History, one of Natural Science, one which he called "Odds and Ends." But they were not merely books of extracts from newspapers. They had bits of plants and ribbons, shells tied on, and carved scraps of bone and wood, which he had taught the men to cut for him; and they were beautifully illustrated. He drew admirably. He had some of the funniest drawings there, and some of the most pathetic, that I have ever seen in my life. I wonder who will have Nolan's scrapbooks.

Well, he said his reading and his notes were his profession, and that they took five hours and two hours respectively of each day. "Then," said he, "every man should have a diversion as well as a profession. My Natural History is my diversion." That took two hours a day more. The men used to bring him birds and fish, but on a long cruise he had to satisfy himself with centipedes and cockroaches and such small game. He was the only naturalist I ever met who knew anything about the habits of the housefly and the mosquito. All those people can tell you whether they are *Lepidoptera* or *Steptopotera:* but as for telling how you can get rid of them, or how they get away from you when you strike them,—why Linnaeus knew as little of that as John Foy the idiot did. These nine hours made Nolan's regular daily "occupation." The rest of the time he talked or walked. Till he grew very old, he went aloft a great deal. He always kept up his exercise; and I never heard that he was ill. If any other man was ill, he was the kindest nurse in the world; and he knew more than half the surgeons do. Then if anybody was sick or died, or if the captain wanted him to, on any other occasion, he was always ready to read prayers. I have remarked that he read beautifully.

My own acquaintance with Philip Nolan began six or eight years after the war, on my first voyage after I was appointed a midshipman. It was in the first days after our Slave Treaty, while the reigning House, which was still the House of Virginia, had still a sort of sentimentalism about the suppression of the horrors of the Middle Passage, and something was sometimes done that way. We were in the South Atlantic on that business. From the time I joined, I believe I thought Nolan was a sort of lay chaplain,—a chaplain with a blue coat. I never asked about him. Everything in the ship was strange to me. I knew it was green to ask questions, and I suppose I thought there was a "Plain Buttons" on every ship. We had him to dine in our mess once a week, and the caution was given that on that day nothing was to be said about home. But if they had told us not to say anything about the planet Mars or the Book of Deuteronomy, I should not have asked why; there were a great many things which seemed to me to have as little reason. I first came to understand anything about the "Man without a Country" one day when we overhauled a dirty little schooner which had slaves on board. An officer was sent to take charge of her, and after a few minutes he sent back his boat to ask that some one might be sent him who could speak Portuguese. We were all looking over the rail when the message came, and we all wished we could interpret when the captain asked who spoke Portuguese. But none of the officers did; and just as the captain was sending forward to ask if any of the people could, Nolan stepped out and said he should be glad to interpret if the captain wished, as he understood the language. The captain thanked him, fitted out another boat with him, and in this boat it was my luck to go.

When we got there, it was such a scene as you seldom see, and never want to. Nastiness beyond account, and chaos run loose in the midst of the nastiness. There were not a great many of the negroes; but by way of making what there were understand that they were free, Vaughan had had their handcuffs and anklecuffs knocked off, and, for convenience' sake, was putting them upon the rascals of the schooner's crew. The negroes were most of them out of the hold, and swarming all round the dirty deck, with a central throng surrounding Vaughan, and addressing him in every dialect and *patois* of a dialect, from the Zulu click up to the Parisian of Beledeljereed.

As we came on deck, Vaughan looked down from a hogshead, on which he had mounted in desperation, and said,

"For God's love, is there anybody who can make these wretches understand something? The men gave them rum, and that did not quiet them. I knocked that big fellow down twice, and that did not soothe him. And then I talked Choctaw to all of them together; and I'll be hanged if they understood that as well as they understood the English."

Nolan said he could speak Portuguese; and one or two fine looking Kroomen were dragged out, who, as it had been found already, had worked for the Portuguese on the coast at Fernando Po.

"Tell them they are free," said Vaughan; "and tell them that these rascals are to be hanged as soon as we can get rope enough."

Nolan "put that into Spanish"; that is, he explained it in such Portuguese as the Kroomen could understand, and they in turn to such of the negroes as could understand them. Then there was such a yell of delight, clinching of fists, leaping and dancing, kissing of Nolan's feet, and a general rush made to the hogshead by way of spontaneous worship of Vaughan, as the *deus ex machina* of the occasion.

"Tell them," said Vaughan, well pleased, "that I will take them all to Cape Palmas."

This did not answer so well. Cape Palmas was practically as far from the homes of most of them as New Orleans or Rio de Janeiro was; that

80

is, they would be eternally separated from home there. And their interpreters, as we could understand, instantly said, "*Ah non Palmas,*" and began to propose infinite other expedients in most voluble language. Vaughan was rather disappointed at this result of his liberality, and asked Nolan eagerly what they said. The drops stood on poor Nolan's white forehead, as he hushed the men down, and said,

"He says, 'Not Palmas.' He says, 'Take us home; take us to our own country; take us to our own house; take us to our own pickaninnies and our own women.' He says he has an old father and mother who will die if they do not see him. And this one says he left his people all sick, and paddled down to Fernando to beg the white doctor to come and help them, and that these devils caught him in the bay just in sight of home, and that he has never seen anybody from home since then. And this one says," choked out Nolan, "that he has not heard a word from his home in six months, while he has been locked up in an infernal barracoon."

Vaughan always said he grew gray himself while Nolan struggled through this interpretation, I, who did not understand anything of the passion involved in it, saw that the very elements were melting with fervent heat, and that something was to pay somewhere. Even the negroes themselves stopped howling, as they saw Nolan's agony, and Vaughan's almost equal agony of sympathy. As quick as he could get words, he said,

"Tell them yes, yes, yes; tell them they shall go to the Mountains of the Moon, if they will. If I sail the schooner through the Great White Desert, they shall go home!"

And after some fashion Nolan said so. And then they all fell to kissing him again, and wanted to rub his nose with theirs.

But he could not stand it long; and getting Vaughan to say he might go back, he beckoned me down into our boat. As we lay back in the stern-sheets, and the men gave way, he said to me: "Youngster, let that show you what it is to be without a family, without a home, and without a country; and if you are ever tempted to say a word or to do a thing that shall put a bar between you and your family, your home, and your country, pray God in His mercy to take you that instant home to His own Heaven. Stick by your family, boy; forget you have a self, while you do everything for them. Think of your home, boy; write and send, and talk about it. Let it be nearer and nearer to your thought the farther you have to travel from it; and rush back to it when you are free, as that poor black slave is doing now. And for your country, boy," and the words rattled in his throat, "and for that flag," and he pointed to the ship, "never dream a dream but of serving her as she bids you, though the service carry you through a thousand hells. No matter what happens to you, no matter who flatters you or who abuses you, never look at another flag, never let a night pass but you pray God to bless that flag. Remember, boy, that behind all these men you have to do with, behind officers and Government and people even, there is the Country Herself, your Country, and that you belong to Her as you belong to your own mother. Stand by Her, boy, as you would stand by your mother, if those devils there had got hold of her today!"

I was frightened to death by his calm, hard passion; but I blundered out that I would, by all that was holy, and that I had never thought of doing anything else. He hardly seemed to hear me; but he did almost in a whisper say, "Oh, if anybody had said so to me when I was of your age!"

I think it was this half confidence of his, which I never abused—for I never told this story till now—which afterward made us great friends. He was very kind to me. Often he sat up, or even got up, at night, to walk the deck with me, when it was my watch. He explained to me a great deal of my mathematics, and I owe to him my taste for mathematics. He lent me books, and helped me about my reading. He never alluded so directly to his story again; but from one and another officer I have learned, in thirty years, what I am telling. When we parted from him in St. Thomas Harbor, at the end of our cruise, I was more sorry than I can tell. I was very glad to meet him again in 1830; and later in life, when I thought I had some influence in Washington, I moved heaven and earth to have him discharged. But it was like getting a ghost out of prison. They pretended there was no such man, and never was such a man. They will say so at the Department now! Perhaps they do not know. It will not be the first thing in the service of which the Department appears to know nothing!

There is a story that Nolan met Burr once on one of our vessels, when a party of Americans came on board in the Mediterranean. But this I believe to be a lie; or rather it is a myth, *ben trovato*, involving a tremendous blowing up with which he sunk Burr, asking him how he liked to be "without a country." But it is clear from Burr's life that nothing of the sort could have happened; and I mention this only as an illustration of the stories which get agoing where there is the least mystery at bottom.

So poor Philip Nolan had his wish fulfilled. I know but one fate more dreadful; it is the fate reserved for those men who shall have one day to exile themselves from their country because they have attempted her ruin, and shall have at the same time to see the prosperity and honor to which she rises when she has rid herself of them and their iniquities. The wish of poor Nolan, as we all learned to call him, not because his punishment was too great, but because his repentance was so clear, was precisely the wish of every Bragg and Beauregard who broke a soldier's oath two years ago, and of every Maury and Barron who broke a sailor's. I do not know how often they have repented. I do know that they have done all that in them lay, that they might have no country, that all the honors, associations, memories, and hopes which belong to "country" might be broken up into little shreds and distributed to the winds. I know, too, that their punishment, as they vegetate through what is left of life to them in wretched Boulognes and Leicester Squares, where they are destined to upbraid each other till they die, will have all the agony of Nolan's, with the added pang that every one who sees them will see them to despise and to execrate them. They will have their wish, like him.

For him, poor fellow, he repented of his folly, and then, like a man, submitted to the fate he had asked for. He never intentionally added to the difficulty or delicacy of the charge of those who had him in hold. Accidents would happen; but they never

82

happened from his fault. Lieutenant Truxton told me that when Texas was annexed there was a careful discussion among the officers, whether they should get hold of Nolan's handsome set of maps, and cut Texas out of it, from the map of the world and the map of Mexico. The United States had been cut out when the atlas was bought for him. But it was voted, rightly enough, that to do this would be virtually to reveal to him what had happened, or, as Harry Cole said, to make him think Old Burr had succeeded. So it was from no fault of Nolan's that a great botch happened at my own table, when, for a short time, I was in command of the *George Washington* corvette, on the South American station. We were lying in the La Plata, and some of the officers who had been on shore, and had just joined again, were entertaining us with accounts of their misadventures in riding the half wild horses of Buenos Aires. Nolan was at the table, and was in an unusually bright and talkative mood. Some story of a tumble reminded him of an adventure of his own, when he was catching wild horses in Texas with his adventurous cousin, at a time when he must have been quite a boy. He told the story with a good deal of spirit,—so much so, that the silence which often follows a good story hung over the table for an instant, to be broken by Nolan himself. For he asked perfectly unconsciously,

"Pray, what has become of Texas? After the Mexicans got their independence, I thought that province of Texas would come forward very fast. It is really one of the finest regions on earth; it is the Italy of this continent. But I have not seen or heard a word of Texas for near twenty years."

There were two Texan officers at the table. The reason he had never heard of Texas was that Texas and her affairs had been painfully cut out of his newspapers since Austin began his settlements; so that while he read of Honduras and Tamaulipas, and till quite lately of California, this virgin province, in which his cousin had travelled so far, and, I believe, had died, had ceased to be to him. Waters and Williams, the two Texas men, looked grimly at each other, and tried not to laugh. Edward Morris had his attention attracted by the third link in the chain of the captain's chandelier. Watrous was seized with a convulsion of sneezing. Nolan himself saw that something was to pay, he did not know what. And I, as master of the feast, had to say,

"Texas is out of the map, Mr. Nolan. Have you seen Captain Back's curious account of Sir Thomas Roe's *Welcome?*"

After that cruise I never saw Nolan again. I wrote to him at least twice a year, for in that voyage we became even confidentially intimate; but he never wrote to me. The other men tell me that in those fifteen years he "aged" very fast, as well he might indeed, but that he was still the same gentle, uncomplaining, silent sufferer that he ever was, bearing as best he could his self-appointed punishment,—rather less social, perhaps, with new men whom he did not know, but more anxious apparently than ever to serve and befriend and teach the boys, some of whom fairly seemed to worship him. And now it seems the dear old fellow is dead. He has found a home at last, and a country.

Since writing this, and while considering whether or not I would print it as a warning to the young Nolans and Vallandighams and Tatnalls of today of what it is to throw away a country, I have received from Danforth, who is on board the *Levant*, a letter which gives an account of Nolan's last hours. It removes all my doubts about telling this story.

To understand the first words of the letter, the nonprofessional reader should remember that after 1817 the position of every officer who had Nolan in charge was one of the greatest delicacy. The Government had failed to renew the order of 1807 regarding him. What was a man to do? Should he let him go? What, then, if he were called to account by the Department for violating the order of 1807? Should he keep him? What, then, if Nolan should be liberated some day, and should bring an action for false imprisonment or kidnapping against every man who had had him in charge? I urged and pressed this upon Southard, and I have reason to think that other officers did the same thing. But the Secretary always said, as they so often do at Washington, that there were no special orders to give, and that we must act on our own judgment. That means, "If you succeed, you will be sustained; if you fail, you will be disavowed." Well, as Danforth says, all that is over now, though I do not know but I expose myself to a criminal prosecution on the evidence of the very revelation I am making.

Here is the letter:

"*Levant*, 2° 2′ S. @ 131° W.
Dear Fred,—I try to find heart and life to tell you that it is all over with dear old Nolan. I have been with him on this voyage more than I ever was; and I can understand wholly now the way in which you used to speak of the dear old fellow. I could see that he was not strong, but I had no idea the end was so near. The doctor has been watching him very carefully, and yesterday morning came to me and told me that Nolan was not so well, and had not left his stateroom, —a thing I never remember before. He had let the doctor come and see him as he lay there,—the first time the doctor had been in the stateroom,—and he said he should like to see me. Oh, dear! do you remember the mysteries we boys used to invent about his room in the old *Intrepid* days? Well, I went in, and there, to be sure, the poor fellow lay in his berth, smiling pleasantly as he gave me his hand, but looking very frail. I could not help a glance round, which showed me what a little shrine he had made of the box he was lying in. The Stars and Stripes were triced up above and around a picture of Washington, and he had painted a majestic eagle, with lightnings blazing from his beak, and his foot just clasping the whole globe, which his wings overshadowed. The dear old boy saw my glance, and said with a sad smile, 'Here, you see, I have a country!' And then he pointed to the foot of his bed, where I had not seen before a great map of the United States, as he had drawn it from memory, and which he had there to look upon as he lay. Quaint, queer old names were on it in large letters: 'Indiana Territory,' 'Mississippi Territory,' and 'Louisiana Territory,' as I suppose our fathers learned such things; but the old fellow had patched in Texas, too; he had carried his Western boundary all the way to the Pacific, but on that shore he had defined nothing.

" 'Oh, Danforth,' he said, 'I know I am dying. I cannot get home. Surely you will tell me something now? Stop! stop! Do not speak till I say what I am sure you know, that there is not in this ship, that there is not in America—God bless her!—a more loyal man than I. There cannot be a man who loves the old flag as I do, or prays for it as I do, or hopes for it as I do. There are thirty-four stars in it now, Danforth. I thank God for that, though I do not know what their names are. There has never been one taken away; I thank God for that. I know by that, that there has never been any successful Burr. Oh, Danforth, Danforth,' he sighed out, 'how like a wretched night's dream a boy's idea of personal fame or of separate sovereignty seems, when one looks back on it after such a life as mine! But tell me,—tell me something,—tell me everything, Danforth, before I die!'

"Ingham, I swear to you that I felt like a monster that I had not told him everything before. Danger or no danger, delicacy or no delicacy, who was I, that I should have been acting the tyrant all this time over this dear, sainted old man, who had years ago expiated, in his whole manhood's life, the madness of a boy's treason? 'Mr. Nolan,' said I, 'I will tell you everything you ask about. Only, where shall I begin?'

"Oh, the blessed smile that crept over his white face! and he pressed my hand, and said, 'God bless you! Tell me their names,' he said, and he pointed to the stars on the flag. 'The last I know is Ohio. My father lived in Kentucky. But I have guessed Michigan and Indiana and Mississippi,—that was where Fort Adams is; they make twenty. But where are your other fourteen? You have not cut up any of the old ones, I hope.'

"Well, that was not a bad text; and I told him the names in as good order as I could, and he bade me take down his beautiful map, and draw them in as best I could with my pencil. He was wild with delight about Texas, told me how his cousin died there; he had marked a gold cross near where he supposed his grave was, and he had guessed at Texas. Then he was delighted as he saw California and Oregon; that he said he had suspected partly, because he had never been permitted to land on that shore, though the ships were there so much. 'And the men,' said he, laughing, 'brought off a good deal besides furs.' Then he went back—heavens, how far!—to ask about the *Chesapeake*, and what was done to Barron for surrendering her to the *Leopard*, and whether Burr ever tried again,—and he ground his teeth with the only passion he showed. But in a moment that was over, and he said, 'God forgive me, for I am sure I forgive him.' Then he asked about the old war, told me the true story of his serving the gun the day we took the *Java*, asked about dear old David Porter, as he called him. Then he settled down more quietly and very happily, to hear me tell in an hour the history of fifty years.

"How I wished it had been somebody who knew something! But I did as well as I could. I told him of the English war. I told him about Fulton and the steamboat beginning. I told him about old Scott and Jackson; told him all I could think of about the Mississippi and New Orleans and Texas and his own old Kentucky. And do you think, he asked who was in command of the 'Legion of the West.' I told him it was a very gallant officer named Grant, and that by our last news he was about to establish his headquarters at Vicksburg. Then, 'Where was Vicksburg?'

85

I worked that out on the map; it was about a hundred miles, more or less, above his old Fort Adams; and I thought Fort Adams must be a ruin now. 'It must be at Old Vick's plantation, at Walnut Hills,' said he; 'well, that is a change!'

"I tell you, Ingham, it was a hard thing to condense the history of half a century into that talk with a sick man. And I do not now know what I told him,—of emigration, and the means of it; of steamboats and railroads and telegraphs; of inventions and books and literature; of the colleges and West Point and the Naval School,—but with the queerest interruptions that ever you heard. You see it was Robinson Crusoe asking all the accumulated questions of fifty-six years!

"I remember he asked, all of a sudden, who was President now; and when I told him, he asked if Old Abe was General Benjamin Lincoln's son. He said he met old General Lincoln when he was quite a boy himself, at some Indian treaty. I said No, that Old Abe was a Kentuckian like himself, but I could not tell him of what family; he had worked up from the ranks. 'Good for him!' cried Nolan; 'I am glad of that. As I have brooded and wondered, I have thought our danger was in keeping up those regular successions in the first families.' Then I got talking about my visit to Washington. I told him of meeting the Oregon Congressman, Harding; I told him about the Smithsonian and the Exploring Expedition; I told him about the Capitol and the statues for the pediment and Crawford's Liberty and Greenough's Washington. Ingham, I told him everything I could think of that would show the grandeur of his country and its prosperity; but I could not make

up my mouth to tell him a word about this infernal Rebellion!

"And he drank it in, and enjoyed it as I cannot tell you. He grew more and more silent, yet I never thought he was tired or faint. I gave him a glass of water, but he just wet his lips, and told me not to go away. Then he asked me to bring the Presbyterian *Book of Public Prayer*, which lay there, and said with a smile that it would open at the right place,—and so it did. There was his double red mark down the page; and I knelt down and read, and he repeated with me: 'For ourselves and our country, O gracious God, we thank Thee that notwithstanding our manifold transgressions of Thy holy laws, Thou hast continued to us Thy marvelous kindness,'—and so to the end of that Thanksgiving. Then he turned to the end of the same book, and I read the words more familiar to me: 'Most heartily we beseech Thee with Thy favor to behold and bless Thy servant, the President of the United States, and all others in authority,'—and the rest of the Episcopal Collect. 'Danforth,' said he, 'I have repeated those prayers night and morning, it is now fifty-five years.' And then he said he would go to sleep. He bent me down over him, and kissed me; and he said, 'Look in my Bible, Danforth, when I am gone.' And I went away.

"But I had no thought it was the end. I thought he was tired and would sleep. I knew he was happy, and I wanted him to be alone.

"But in an hour, when the doctor went in gently, he found Nolan had breathed his life away with a smile. He had something pressed close to his lips. It was his father's badge of the Order of the Cincinnati.

"We looked in his Bible, and there

was a slip of paper at the place where he had marked the text,

"'They desire a country, even a heavenly: wherefore God is not ashamed to be called their God: for he hath prepared for them a city.'

"On this slip of paper he had written,

"'Bury me in the sea; it has been my home, and I love it. But will not some one set up a stone for my memory at Fort Adams or at Orleans, that my disgrace may not be more than I ought to bear? Say on it,

In Memory of
PHILIP NOLAN,
Lieutenant in the Army of the United States.
He loved his country as no other man has loved her; but no man deserved less at her hands'."

TO BE AN AMERICAN
ARCHIBALD MACLEISH

It is a strange thing—to be an American.
Neither an old house it is, with the air
Tasting of hung herbs and the sun returning
Year after year to the same door and the churn,
Making the same sound in the cool of the kitchen,
Mother to son's wife, and the place to sit
Marked in the dusk by the worn stone at the wellhead—
That—nor the eyes like each other's eyes and the skull
Shaped to the same fault and the hands' sameness.
Neither a place it is nor a blood name.

America is West and the wind blowing.
America is a great word and the snow,
A way, a white bird, the rain falling,
A shining thing in the mind and the gulls' call.
America is neither a land nor a people,
A word's shape it is, a wind's sweep—
America is alone: many together,
Many of one mouth, of one breath,
Dressed as one—and none brothers among them:
Only the taught speech and the aped tongue.
America is alone and the gulls calling.

I AM NOT a Virginian, but an American.—*Patrick Henry*

SIR, I would rather be right than be President.—*Henry Clay*

THE FINAL end of government is not to exert restraint but to do good.—*Choate*

IF ANY ONE desires to know the leading and paramount object of my public life, the preservation of this Union will furnish him the key.—*Henry Clay*

THERE IS THE NATIONAL FLAG. He must be cold, indeed, who can look upon its folds rippling in the breeze without pride of country. If in a foreign land, the flag is companionship, and country itself with all its endearments.—*Charles Sumner*

I NEVER USE the word Nation in speaking of the United States. I always use the word Union or Confederacy. We are not a nation but a *union*, a confederacy of equal and sovereign States.—*Calhoun*

A REPRESENTATIVE DEMOCRACY, where the right of election is well secured and regulated, and the exercise of the legislative, executive, and judiciary authorities is vested in select persons, chosen really and not nominally by the people, will, in my opinion, be most likely to be happy, regular, and durable. —*Alexander Hamilton*

A POWER HAS RISEN up in the government greater than the people themselves, consisting of many and various and powerful interests, combined into one mass, and held together by the cohesive power of the vast surplus in the banks.—*Calhoun*

GOVERNMENT IS a trust, and the officers of the government are trustees; and both the trust and the trustees are created for the benefit of the people.—*Henry Clay*

Now he belongs to the ages. (At the death of Abraham Lincoln, April 15, 1865.)—*Edwin M. Stanton*

AMERICAN STATESMEN

ALL we ask is to be let alone.—*Jefferson Davis*

THE SUREST WAY to prevent war is not to fear it.—*John Randolph*

THE SURRENDER of life is nothing to sinking down into acknowledgment of inferiority.—*Calhoun*

WE JOIN OURSELVES to no party that does not carry the flag and keep step to the music of this Union.—*Choate*

THE ARTS OF POWER and its minions are the same in all countries and in all ages. It marks its victim; denounces it; and excites the public odium and the public hatred, to conceal its own abuses and encroachments.—*Henry Clay*

THE VERY ESSENCE of a free government consists in considering offices as public trusts, bestowed for the good of the country, and not for the benefit of an individual or party.—*Calhoun*

GIVE ME THE MONEY that has been spent in war, and I will clothe every man, woman and child in an attire of which kings and queens would be proud. I will build a schoolhouse in every valley over the whole earth. I will crown every hillside with a place of worship, consecrated to the gospel of peace.
—*Charles Sumner*

BLANDISHMENTS WILL NOT FASCINATE us, nor will threats of a halter intimidate. For, under God, we are determined that, wheresoever, whensoever, or howsoever we shall be called to make our exit, we will die free men.—*Josiah Quincy*

MAN IS a reasoning rather than a reasonable animal.—*Alexander Hamilton*

THE AGE of chivalry has gone; the age of humanity has come.—*Charles Sumner*

NEITHER irony nor sarcasm is argument.—*Choate*

TOM LINCOLN'S SON
NANCY BYRD TURNER

"Tom Lincoln's gawky lad," they said, "won't set the world agog;
He's homely as a stable door and knotty as a log;
Cares not a whit for who says what about his ways and looks—
Full length you'll find him, after work, a-moonin' over books."

"Aye," said another, "so they tell, and grudges half a word.
But knows the ways of woodcraft well as any man I've heard.
He swings a mighty ax, I'm told, that sets the trees a-shake;
And when he splits a rail—that rail is split, and no mistake!"
So . . . nothing much for speed or looks, according to their tale,
But held his tongue, and read his books, and split a splendid rail.
He'd never set the world aflame, they reckoned, every one—
And yet, he'd maybe make his mark, would Thomas Lincoln's son!

NANCY HANKS
ROSEMARY AND STEPHEN VINCENT BENÉT

If Nancy Hanks
Came back as a ghost,
Seeking news
Of what she loved most,
She'd ask first
"Where's my son?
What's happened to Abe?
What's he done?

"Poor little Abe,
Left all alone
Except for Tom,
Who's a rolling stone;
He was only nine
The year I died.
I remember still
How hard he cried.

"Scraping along
In a little shack,
With hardly a shirt
To cover his back,

And a prairie wind
To blow him down,
Or pinching times
If he went to town.

"You wouldn't know
About my son?
Did he grow tall?
Did he have fun?
Did he learn to read?
Did he get to town?
Do you know his name?
Did he get on?"

WE ARE COMING FATHER ABRAAM, THREE HUNDRED THOUSAND MORE

James Sloane Gibbons

We are coming Father Abraam, three hundred thousand more,
From Mississippi's winding stream and from New England's shore;
We leave our plows and workshops, our wives and children dear,
With hearts too full for utterance, with but a silent tear;
We dare not look behind us but steadfastly before,
We are coming, Father Abraam, three hundred thousand more.

Chorus
We are coming, coming our union to restore.
We are coming, Father Abraam, three hundred thousand more.

If you look across the hilltops that meet the northern sky,
Long moving lines of rising dust your vision may descry;
And now the wind an instant tears the cloudy veil aside,
And floats aloft our spangled flag in glory and in pride;
And bayonets in the sunlight gleam, and bands brave music pour,
We are coming Father Abraam, three hundred thousand more.

Chorus
We are coming, coming our union to restore.
We are coming, Father Abraam, three hundred thousand more.

The Battle-Ground

By ELSIE SINGMASTER

*M*ERCIFULLY, Mary Bowman, a widow, whose husband had been missing since the battle of Gettysburg, had been warned, together with the other citizens of Gettysburg, that on Thursday, the nineteenth of November, 1863, she would be awakened from sleep by a bugler's reveillé, and that during that great day she would hear again the dread sound of cannon.

Nevertheless, hearing again the reveillé, she sat up in bed with a scream and put her hands over her ears. Then, gasping, groping about in her confusion and terror, she rose and began to dress. She put on a dress which had been once a bright plaid, but which now, having lost both its color and the stiff, outstanding quality of the skirts of '63, hung about her in straight and dingy folds. It was clean, but it had upon it certain ineradicable brown stains on which soap and water seemed to have no effect. She was thin and pale, and her eyes had a set look, as though they saw other sights than those directly about her.

In the bed from which she had risen lay her little daughter; in a trundle-bed near by, her two sons, one about ten years old, the other about four. They slept heavily, lying deep in their beds, as though they would never move. Their mother looked at them with her strange, absent gaze; then she barred a little more closely the broken shutters, and went down the stairs. The shutters were broken in a curious fashion. Here and there they were pierced by round holes, and one hung from a single hinge. The window-frames were without glass, the floor was without carpet, the beds without pillows.

In her kitchen Mary Bowman looked about her as though still seeing other sights. Here, too, the floor was carpetless. Above the stove a patch of fresh plaster on the wall showed where a great rent had been filled in; in the doors were the same little round holes as in the shutters of the room above. But there was food and fuel, which was more than one might have expected from the aspect of the house and its mistress. She opened the shattered door of the cupboard, and, having made the fire, began to prepare breakfast.

Outside the house there was already, at six o'clock, noise and confusion. Last evening a train from Washington had brought to the village Abraham Lincoln; for several days other trains had been bringing less distinguished guests, until thousands thronged the little town. This morning the tract of land between Mary Bowman's house and the village cemetery was to be dedicated for the burial of the Union dead, who were to be laid there in sweeping semicircles round a centre on which a great monument was to rise.

But of the dedication, of the President of the United States, of his distinguished associates, of the great crowds, of the soldiers, of the crape-banded banners, Mary Bowman and her children would see nothing. Mary Bowman would sit in her little wrecked kitchen with her children. For to her the President of the United States and others in high places who prosecuted war or who tolerated war, who called for young men to fight, were hateful. To Mary Bowman the crowds of curious persons who coveted a sight of the great battle-fields were ghouls; their eyes wished to gloat upon ruin, upon fragments of the weapons of war, upon torn bits of the habiliments of soldiers; their feet longed to sink into the loose ground of hastily made graves; the discovery of a partially covered body was precious to them.

Mary Bowman knew that field! From Culp's Hill to the McPherson farm, from Big Round Top to the poorhouse, she had traveled it, searching, with frantic, insane disregard of positions or of possibility. Her husband could not have fallen here among the Eleventh Corps, he could not lie here among the unburied dead of the Louisiana Tigers! If he was in the battle at all, it was at the Angle that he fell.

She had not been able to begin her search immediately after the battle because there were forty wounded men in her little house; she could not prosecute it with any diligence even later, when the soldiers had been carried to the hospitals, in the Presbyterian Church, the Catholic Church, the two Lutheran churches, the Seminary, the College, the Court-House, and the great tented hospital on the York road. Nurses were here, Sisters of Mercy were here, compassionate women were here by the score; but still she was needed, with all the other women of the village, to nurse, to bandage, to comfort, to pray with those who must die. Little Mary Bowman had assisted at the amputation of limbs, she had helped to control strong men torn by the frenzy of delirium, she had tended poor bodies which had almost lost all semblance to humanity. Neither she nor any of the other women of the village counted themselves especially heroic; the delicate wife of the judge, the petted daughter of the doctor, the gently bred wife of the preacher forgot that fainting at the sight of blood was one of the distinguishing qualities of their sex; they turned back their sleeves and repressed their tears, and, shoulder to shoulder with Mary Bowman and her Irish neighbor, Hannah Casey, they fed the hungry and healed the sick and clothed the naked. If Mary Bowman had been herself, she might have laughed at the sight of her dresses cobbled into trousers, her skirts wrapped round the shoulders of sick men. But neither then nor ever after did Mary laugh at any incident of that summer.

Hannah Casey laughed, and by and by she began to boast. Meade, Hancock, Slocum, were non-combatants beside her. She had fought whole companies of Confederates, she had wielded bayonets, she had assisted at the spiking of a gun, she was Barbara Frietchie and Moll Pitcher combined. But all her lunacy could not make Mary Bowman smile.

Of John Bowman no trace could be found. No one could tell her anything about him, to her frantic letters no one responded. Her old friend, the village judge, wrote letters also, but could get no reply. Her husband was missing; it was probable that he lay somewhere upon this field, the field upon which they had wandered as lovers.

93

In midsummer a few trenches were opened, and Mary, unknown to her friends, saw them opened. At the uncovering of the first great pit, she actually helped with her own hands. For those of this generation who know nothing of war, that fact may be written down, to be passed over lightly. The soldiers, having been on other battle-fields, accepted her presence without comment. She did not cry, she only helped doggedly, and looked at what they found. That, too, may be written down for a generation which has not known war.

Immediately, an order went forth that no graves, large or small, were to be opened before cold weather. The citizens were panic-stricken with fear of an epidemic; already there were many cases of dysentery and typhoid. Now that the necessity for daily work for the wounded was past, the village became nervous, excited, irritable. Several men and boys were killed while trying to open unexploded shells; their deaths added to the general horror. There were constant visitors who sought husbands, brothers, sweethearts; with these the Gettysburg women were still able to weep, for them they were still able to care; but the constant demand for entertainment for the curious annoyed those who wished to be left alone to recover from the shock of battle. Gettysburg was prostrate, bereft of many of its worldly possessions, drained to the bottom of its well of sympathy. Its schools must be opened, its poor must be helped. Cold weather was coming and there were many, like Mary Bowman, who owned no longer any quilts or blankets, who had given away their clothes, their linen, even the precious sheets which their grandmothers had spun. Gettysburg grudged nothing, wished nothing back, it asked only to be left in peace.

When the order was given to postpone the opening of graves till fall, Mary began to go about the battle-field searching alone. Her good, obedient children stayed at home in the house or in the little field. They were beginning to grow thin and wan, they were shivering in the hot August weather, but their mother did not see. She gave them a great deal more to eat than she had herself, and they had far better clothes than her blood-stained motley.

She went about the battle-field with her eyes on the ground, her feet treading gently, anticipating loose soil or some sudden obstacle. Sometimes she stooped suddenly. To fragments of shells, to bits of blue or gray cloth, to cartridge belts or broken muskets, she paid no heed; at sight of pitiful bits of human bodies she shuddered. But there lay also upon that field little pocket Testaments, letters, trinkets, photographs. John had had her photograph and the children's, and surely he must have had some of the letters she had written!

But poor Mary found nothing.

One morning, late in August, she sat beside her kitchen table with her head on her arm. The first of the scarlet gum leaves had begun to drift down from the shattered trees; it would not be long before the ground would be covered, and those depressed spots, those tiny wooden headstones, those fragments of blue and gray be hidden. The thought smothered her. She did not cry, she had not cried at all. Her soul seemed hardened, stiff, like the terrible wounds for which she had helped to care.

Suddenly, hearing a sound, Mary looked up. The judge stood in the doorway; he had known all about her since she was a little girl; something in his face told her that he knew also of her terrible search. She did not ask him to sit down, she said nothing at all. She had been a loquacious person; she had become an abnormally silent one. Speech hurt her.

The judge looked round the little kitchen. The rent in the wall was still unmended, the chairs were broken; there was nothing else to be seen but the table and the rusty stove and the thin, friendless-looking children standing by the door. It was the house not only of poverty and woe, but of neglect.

"Mary," said the judge, "how do you mean to live?"

Mary's thin, sunburned hand stirred a little as it lay on the table.

"I do not know."

"You have these children to feed and clothe and you must furnish your house again. Mary—" the judge hesitated for a moment. John Bowman had been a schoolteacher, a thrifty, ambitious soul, who would have thought it a disgrace for his wife to earn her living. The judge laid his hand on the thin hand beside him. "Your children must have food, Mary. Come down to my house, and my wife will give you work. Come now."

Slowly Mary had risen from her chair, and smoothed down her dress and obeyed him. Down the street they went together, seeing fences still prone, seeing walls torn by shells, past the houses where the shock of battle had hastened the deaths of old persons and little children, and had disappointed the hearts of those who longed for a child, to the judge's house in the square. There wagons stood about, loaded with wheels of cannon, fragments of burst caissons, or with long, narrow, pine boxes, brought from the railroad, to be stored against the day of exhumation. Men were laughing and shouting to one another, the driver of the wagon on which the long boxes were piled cracked his whip as he urged his horses.

Hannah Casey congratulated her neighbor heartily upon her finding work.

"That'll fix you up," she assured her.

She visited Mary constantly, she reported to her the news of the war, she talked at length of the coming of the President.

"I'm going to see him," she announced. "I'm going to shake him by the hand. I'm going to say, 'Hello, Abe, you old rail-splitter, God bless you!' Then the bands'll play, and the people will march, and the Johnny Rebs will hear 'em in their graves."

Mary Bowman put her hands over her ears.

"I believe in my soul you'd let 'em all rise from the dead!"

"I would!" said Mary Bowman hoarsely. "I would!"

"Well, not so Hannah Casey! Look at me garden tore to bits! Look at me beds, stripped to the ropes!"

And Hannah Casey departed to her house.

Details of the coming celebration penetrated to the ears of Mary Bowman whether she wished it or not, and the gathering crowds made themselves known. They stood upon her porch, they examined the broken shutters, they wished to question her. But Mary Bowman would answer no

95

questions, would not let herself be seen. To her the thing was horrible. She saw the battling hosts, she heard once more the roar of artillery, she smelled the smoke of battle, she was torn by its confusion. Besides, she seemed to feel in the ground beneath her a feebly stirring, suffering, ghastly host. They had begun again to open the trenches, and she had looked into them.

Now, on the morning of Thursday, the nineteenth of November, her children dressed themselves and came down the steps. They had begun to have a little plumpness and color, but the dreadful light in their mother's eyes was still reflected in theirs. On the lower step they hesitated, looking at the door. Outside stood the judge, who had found time in the multiplicity of his cares, to come to the little house.

He spoke with kind but firm command.

"Mary," said he, "you must take these children to hear President Lincoln."

"What!" cried Mary.

"You must take these children to the exercises."

"I cannot!" cried Mary. "I cannot! I cannot!"

"You must!" The judge came into the room. "Let me hear no more of this going about. You are a Christian, your husband was a Christian. Do you want your children to think it is a wicked thing to die for their country? Do as I tell you, Mary."

Mary got up from her chair, and put on her children all the clothes they had, and wrapped about her own shoulders a little black coat which the judge's wife had given her. Then, as one who steps into an unfriendly sea, she started out with them into the great crowd. Once more, poor Mary said to herself, she would obey. She had seen the platform; by going round through the citizen's cemetery she could get close to it.

The November day was bright and warm, but Mary and her children shivered. Slowly she made her way close to the platform, patiently she stood and waited. Sometimes she stood with shut eyes, swaying a little. On the moonlit night of the third day of battle she had ventured from her house down toward the square to try to find some brandy for the dying men about her, and as in a dream she had seen a tall general, mounted upon a white horse with muffled hoofs, ride down the street. Bending from his saddle he had spoken, apparently to the empty air.

"Up, boys, up!"

There had risen at his command thousands of men lying asleep on pavement and street, and quietly, in an interminable line, they had stolen out like dead men toward the Seminary, to join their comrades and begin the long, long march to Hagerstown. It seemed to her that all about her dead men might rise now to look with reproach upon these strangers who disturbed their rest.

The procession was late, the orator of the day was delayed, but still Mary waited, swaying a little in her place. Presently the great guns roared forth a welcome, the bands played, the procession approached. On horseback, erect, gauntleted, the President of the United States drew rein beside the platform, and, with the orator and the other famous men, dismounted. There were great cheers, there were deep silences, there were fresh volleys of artillery, there was new music.

Of it all, Mary Bowman heard but little. Remembering the judge, whom she saw now near the President, she tried to obey the spirit as well as the letter of his command; she directed her children to look, she turned their heads toward the platform.

Men spoke and prayed and sang, and Mary stood still in her place. The orator of the day described the battle, he eulogized the dead, he proved the righteousness of this great war; his words fell upon Mary's ears unheard. If she had been asked who he was, she might have said vaguely that he was Mr. Lincoln. When he ended, she was ready to go home. There was singing; now she could slip away, through the gaps in the cemetery fence. She had done as the judge commanded and now she would go back to her house.

With her arms about her children, she started away. Then some one who stood near by took her by the hand.

"Madam!" said he, "the President is going to speak!"

Half turning, Mary looked back. The thunder of applause made her shiver, made her even scream, it was so like that other thunderous sound which she would hear forever. She leaned upon her little children heavily, trying to get her breath, gasping, trying to keep her consciousness. She fixed her eyes upon the rising figure before her, she clung to the sight of him as a drowning swimmer in deep waters, she struggled to fix her thoughts upon him. Exhaustion, grief, misery threatened to engulf her, she hung upon him in desperation.

Slowly, as one who is old or tired or sick at heart, he rose to his feet,

the President of the United States, the Commander-in-Chief of the Army and Navy, the hope of his country. Then he stood waiting. In great waves of sound the applause rose and died and rose again. He waited quietly. The winner of debate, the great champion of a great cause, the veteran in argument, the master of men, he looked down upon the throng. The clear, simple things he had to say were ready in his mind, he had thought them out, written out a first draft of them in Washington, copied it here in Gettysburg. It is probable that now, as he waited to speak, his mind traveled to other things, to the misery, the wretchedness, the slaughter of this field, to the tears of mothers, the grief of widows, the orphaning of little children.

Slowly, in his clear voice, he said what little he had to say. To the weary crowd, settling itself into position once more, the speech seemed short; to the cultivated who had been listening to the elaborate periods of great oratory, it seemed commonplace, it seemed a speech which any one might have made. But it was not so with Mary Bowman, nor with many other unlearned persons. Mary Bowman's soul seemed to smooth itself out like a scroll, her hands lightened their clutch on her children, the beating of her heart slackened, she gasped no more.

She could not have told exactly what he said, though later she read it and learned it and taught it to her children and her children's children. She only saw him, felt him, breathed him in, this great, common, kindly man. His gaze seemed to rest upon her; it was not impossible, it was even probable, that during the hours that had passed he had singled out that little group so near him, that desolate woman in her motley dress, with her children clinging about her. He said that the world would not forget this field, these martyrs; he said it in words which Mary Bowman could understand, he pointed to a future for which there was a new task.

"Daughter!" he seemed to say to her from the depths of trouble, of responsibility, of care greater than her own,—"Daughter, be of good comfort!"

Unhindered now, amid the cheers, across ground which seemed no longer to stir beneath her feet, Mary Bowman went back to her house. There, opening the shutters, she bent and solemnly kissed her little children, saying to herself that henceforth they must have more than food and raiment; they must be given some joy in life.

WHEN LILACS LAST IN THE DOORYARD BLOOMED
WALT WHITMAN

When lilacs last in the dooryard bloomed,
And the great star early drooped in the western sky in the night,
I mourned, and yet shall mourn with ever-returning spring.
Ever-returning spring, trinity sure to me you bring,
Lilac blooming perennial and drooping star in the west,
And thought of him I love.

O powerful western fallen star!
O shades of night—O moody, tearful night!
O great star disappeared—O the black murk that hides the star!
O cruel hands that hold me powerless—O helpless soul of me!
O harsh surrounding cloud that will not free my soul!

In the dooryard fronting an old farm-house near the whitewashed palings,
Stands the lilac-bush tall-growing with heart-shaped leaves of rich green,
With many a pointed blossom rising delicate, with the perfume strong I love,
With every leaf a miracle—and from this bush in the dooryard,
With delicate-colored blossoms and heart-shaped leaves of rich green,
A sprig with its flower I break.

In the swamp in secluded recesses,
A shy and hidden bird is warbling a song.
Solitary the thrush,
The hermit withdrawn to himself, avoiding the settlements,
Sings by himself a song.
Song of the bleeding throat,
Death's outlet song of life, (for well, dear brother, I know,
If thou wast not granted to sing thou would'st surely die.)

98

Over the breast of the spring, the land, amid cities,
Amid lanes and through old woods, where lately the violets peeped from
    the ground, spotting the gray debris,
Amid the grass in the fields each side of the lanes, passing the endless grass,
Passing the yellow-speared wheat, every grain from its shroud in the dark-
    brown fields uprisen,
Passing the apple-tree blows of white and pink in the orchards,
Carrying a corpse to where it shall rest in the grave,
Night and day journeys a coffin.
Coffin that passes through lanes and streets,
Through day and night with the great cloud darkening the land,
With the pomp of the enlooped flags, with the cities draped in black,
With the show of the States themselves as of crape-veiled women standing,
With processions long and winding and the flambeaus of the night,
With the countless torches lit, with the silent sea of faces and the unbared
    heads,
With the waiting depot, the arriving coffin, and the sombre faces,
With dirges through the night, with the thousand voices rising strong and
    solemn,
With all the mournful voices of the dirges poured around the coffin,
The dim-lit churches and the shuddering organs—where amid these you
    journey,
With the tolling tolling bells' perpetual clang,
Here, coffin that slowly passes,
I give you my sprig of lilac.

(Nor for you, for one alone,
Blossoms and branches green to coffins all I bring,
For fresh as the morning, thus would I chant a song for you, O sane and
    sacred death!
All over bouquets of roses,
O death, I cover you over with roses and early lilies,
But mostly and now the lilac that blooms the first,
Copious I break, I break the sprigs from the bushes,
With loaded arms I come, pouring for you,
For you and the coffins all of you, O death!)

O western orb sailing the heaven,
Now I know what you must have meant as a month since I walked,
As I walked in silence the transparent shadowy night,
As I saw you had something to tell as you bent to me night after night,
As you drooped from the sky low down as if to my side, (while the other stars
    all looked on,)
As we wandered together the solemn night, (for something I know not what

kept me from sleep,)
As the night advanced, and I saw on the rim of the west how full you were
    of woe,
As I stood on the rising ground in the breeze in the cool transparent night,
As I watched where you passed and was lost in the netherward black of
    the night,
As my soul in its trouble dissatisfied sank, as where yon sad orb,
Concluded, dropt in the night, and was gone!

Sing on there in the swamp,
O singer bashful and tender, I hear your notes, I hear your call,
I hear, I come presently, I understand you,
But a moment I linger, for the lustrous star has detained me,
The star my departing comrade holds and detains me!
O how shall I warble myself for the dead one there I loved?
And how shall I deck my song for the large sweet soul that has gone?
And what shall my perfume be for the grave of him I love?
Sea-winds blown from east and west,
Blown from the Eastern sea and blown from the Western sea, till there on
    the prairies meeting,
These and with these and the breath of my chant,
I'll perfume the grave of him I love.

O what shall I hang on the chamber walls?
And what shall the pictures be that I hang on the walls,
To adorn the burial-house of him I love?
Pictures of growing spring and farms and homes,
With the Fourth-month eve at sundown, and the gray smoke lucid and
    bright,
With floods of the yellow gold of the gorgeous, indolent, sinking sun, burning,
    expanding the air,
With the fresh sweet herbage under foot, and the pale green leaves of the
    trees prolific,
In the distance the flowing glaze, the breast of the river, with a wind-dapple
    here and there,
With ranging hills on the banks, with many a line against the sky, and
    shadows,
And the city at hand with dwellings so dense, and stacks of chimneys,
And all the scenes of life and the workshops, and the workmen homeward
    returning.

Lo, body and soul—this land,
My own Manhattan with spires, and the sparkling and hurrying tides, and
    the ships,

The varied and ample land, the South and the North in the light, Ohio's
     shores and flashing Missouri,
And ever the far-spreading prairies covered with grass and corn.
Lo, the most excellent sun so calm and haughty,
The violet and purple morn with just-felt breezes,
The gentle soft-born measureless light,
The miracle, spreading, bathing all, the fulfilled noon,
The coming eve delicious, the welcome night and the stars,
Over my cities shining all, enveloping man and land.
Sing on, sing on you gray-brown bird,
Sing from the swamps, the recesses, pour your chant from the bushes,
Limitless out of the dusk, out of the cedars and pines.
Sing on, dearest brother, warble your reedy song,
Loud human song, with voice of uttermost woe.
O liquid and free and tender!
O wild and loose to my soul—O wondrous singer!
You only I hear—yet the star holds me, (but will soon depart,)
Yet the lilac with mastering odor holds me.

Now while I sat in the day and looked forth,
In the close of the day with its light and the fields of spring, and the farmers
     preparing their crops,
In the large unconscious scenery of my land with its lakes and forests,
In the heavenly aerial beauty, (after the perturbed winds and the storms,)
Under the arching heavens of the afternoon swift passing, and the voices of
     children and women,
The many-moving sea-tides, and I saw the ships how they sailed,
And the summer approaching with richness, and the fields all busy with
     labor,
And the infinite separate houses, how they all went on, each with its meals
     and minutia of daily usages,
And the streets how their throbbings throbbed, and the cities pent—lo,
     then and there,
Falling upon them all and among them all, enveloping me with the rest,
Appeared the cloud, appeared the long black trail,
And I knew death, its thought, and the sacred knowledge of death.

Then with the knowledge of death as walking one side of me,
And the thought of death close-walking the other side of me,
And I in the middle as with companions, and as holding the hands of
     companions,
I fled forth to the hiding receiving night that talks not,
Down to the shores of the water, the path by the swamp in the dimness,
To the solemn shadowy cedars and ghostly pines so still.

And the singer so shy to the rest received me,
The gray-brown bird I know received us comrades three,
And he sang the carol of death, and a verse for him I love.
From deep secluded recesses,
From the fragrant cedars and the ghostly pines so still,
Came the carol of the bird.
And the charm of the carol rapt me,
As I held as if by their hands my comrades in the night,
And the voice of my spirit tallied the song of the bird.

Come, lovely and soothing death,
Undulate round the world, serenely arriving, arriving,
In the day, in the night, to all, to each,
Sooner or later delicate death.
Praised be the fathomless universe,
For life and joy, and for objects and knowledge curious,
And for love, sweet love—but praise! praise! praise!
For the sure-enwinding arms of cool-enfolding death.
Dark mother, always gliding near with soft feet,
Have none chanted for thee a chant of fullest welcome?
Then I chant it for thee, I glorify thee above all,
I bring thee a song that when thou must indeed come, come unfalteringly.
Approach, strong deliveress,
When it is so, when thou hast taken them I joyously sing the dead,
Lost in the loving floating ocean of thee,
Laved in the flood of thy bliss, O death.
From me to thee glad serenades,
Dances for thee I propose saluting thee, adornments and feastings for thee,
And the sights of the open landscape and the high-spread sky are fitting,
And life and the fields, and the huge and thoughtful night.
The night in silence under many a star,
The ocean shore and the husky whispering wave whose voice I know,
And the soul turning to thee, O vast and well-veiled death,
And the body gratefully nestling close to thee.
Over the tree-tops I float thee a song,
Over the rising and sinking waves, over the myriad fields and the prairies wide,
Over the dense-packed cities all and the teeming wharves and ways,
I float this carol with joy, with joy to thee, O death!

To the tally of my soul,
Loud and strong kept up the gray-brown bird,
With pure deliberate notes, spreading, filling the night.
Loud in the pines and cedars dim,

Clear in the freshness moist and the swamp-perfume,
And I with my comrades there in the night.
While my sight that was bound in my eyes unclosed,
As to long panoramas of visions.
And I saw askant the armies,
I saw as in noiseless dreams hundreds of battle-flags,
Borne through the smoke of the battles and pierced with missiles I saw them,
And carried hither and yon through the smoke, and torn and bloody,
And at last but a few shreds left on the staffs, (and all in silence,)
And the staffs all splintered and broken.
I saw battle-corpses, myriads of them,
And the white skeletous of young men, I saw them,
I saw the debris and debris of all the slain soldiers of the war,
But I saw they were not as was thought,
They themselves were fully at rest, they suffered not,
The living remained and suffered, the mother suffered,
And the wife and the child and the musing comrade suffered,
And the armies that remained suffered.
Passing the visions, passing the night,
Passing, unloosing the hold of my comrades' hands,
Passing the song of the hermit bird and the tallying song of my soul,
Victorious song, death's outlet song, yet varying ever-altering song,
As low and wailing, yet clear the notes, rising and falling, flooding the night,
Sadly sinking and fainting, as warning and warning, and yet again bursting
    with joy,
Covering the earth and filling the spread of the heaven,
As that powerful psalm in the night I heard from recesses,
Passing, I leave thee, lilac with heart-shaped leaves,
I leave thee there in the dooryard, blooming, returning with spring.
I cease from my song for thee.
From my gaze on thee in the west, fronting the west, communing with thee,
O comrade, lustrous with silver face in the night!
Yet each to keep and all, retrievements out of the night,
The song, the wondrous chant of the gray-brown bird,
And the tallying chant, the echo aroused in my soul,
With the lustrous and drooping star with the countenance full of woe,
With the holders holding my hand, hearing the call of the bird,
Comrades mine and I in the midst, and their memory ever to keep, for the
    dead I loved so well,
For the sweetest, wisest soul of all my days and lands—and this for his
    dear sake,
Lilac and star and bird twined with the chant of my soul,
There in the fragrant pines and the cedars dusk and dim.

LINCOLN, THE MAN OF THE PEOPLE
EDWIN MARKHAM

When the Norn Mother saw the Whirlwind Hour
Greatening and darkening as it hurried on,
She left the Heaven of Heroes and came down
To make a man to meet the mortal need.
She took the tried clay of the common road—
Clay warm yet with the genial heat of Earth,
Dashed through it all a strain of prophecy;
Tempered the heap with thrill of human tears;
Then mixed a laughter with the serious stuff.
Into the shape she breathed a flame to light
That tender, tragic, ever-changing face;
And laid on him a sense of the Mystic Powers,
Moving—all hushed—behind the mortal veil.
Here was a man to hold against the world,
A man to match the mountains and the sea.
The color of the ground was in him, the red earth,
The smack and tang of elemental things:
The rectitude and patience of the cliff,
The good will of the rain that loves all leaves,
The friendly welcome of the wayside well,
The courage of the bird that dares the sea,
The gladness of the wind that shakes the corn,
The pity of the snow that hides all scars,
The secrecy of streams that make their way
Under the mountain to the lifted rock,
The tolerance and equity of light
That gives as freely to the shrinking flower
As to the great oak flaring to the wind—
To the grave's low hill as to the Matterhorn
That shoulders out the sky. Sprung from the West,
He drank the valorous youth of a new world.
The strength of virgin forests braced his mind,
The hush of spacious prairies stilled his soul,
His words were oaks in acorns; and his thoughts
Were roots that firmly gripped the granite truth.
Up from log cabin to the Capitol,
One fire was on his spirit, one resolve—
To send the keen ax to the root of wrong,
Clearing a free way for the feet of God,
The eyes of conscience testing every stroke,
To make his deed the measure of a man

He built the rail-pile as he built the State,
Pouring his splendid strength through every blow:
The grip that swung the ax in Illinois
Was on the pen that set a people free.
So came the Captain with the mighty heart;
And when the judgment thunders split the house,
Wrenching the rafters from their ancient rest,
He held the ridgepole up, and spiked again
The rafters of the Home. He held his place—
Held the long purpose like a growing tree—
Held on through blame and faltered not at praise—
Towering in calm rough-hewn sublimity.
And when he fell in whirlwind, he went down
As when a lordly cedar, green with boughs,
Goes down with a great shout upon the hills,
And leaves a lonesome place against the sky.

ON LINCOLN
By Noah Brooks

Noah Brooks describes Lincoln in his speech at Cooper Union, New York, in 1860, as follows:

"When Lincoln rose to speak, I was greatly disappointed. He was tall, tall—oh, how tall!—and so angular and awkward that I had, for an instant, a feeling of pity for so ungainly a man. His clothes were black and ill-fitting, badly wrinkled—as if they had been jammed carelessly into a small trunk. His bushy head, with stiff black hair thrown back, was balanced on a long and lean head-stalk, and when he raised his hands in an opening gesture, I noticed that they were very large. He began in a low tone of voice—as if he were used to speaking outdoors, and was afraid of speaking too loud. He said, 'Mr. Cheerman,' instead of 'Mr. Chairman,' and employed many other words with an old-fashioned pronunciation. I said to myself:

" 'Old fellow, you won't do; it's all very well for the wild West, but this will never go, down in New York.'

"But pretty soon he began to get into his subject; he straightened up, made regular and graceful gestures; his face lighted as with an inward fire; the whole man was transfigured. I forgot his clothes, his personal appearance, his individual peculiarities. Presently, forgetting myself, I was on my feet with the rest, yelling like a wild Indian, cheering this wonderful man. In the closing parts of his argument, you could hear the gentle sizzling of the gas-burners. When he reached a climax the thunders of applause were terrific. It was a great speech.

"When I came out of the hall, my face glowing with excitement and my frame all a-quiver, a friend, with his eyes aglow, asked me what I thought of Abe Lincoln, the rail-splitter. I said:

" 'He's the greatest man since St. Paul.' And I think so yet."

LETTER TO MRS. BIXBY
By Abraham Lincoln

November 21, 1864

Dear Madam:

I HAVE BEEN shown in the files of the War Department a statement of the Adjutant General of Massachusetts that you are the mother of five sons who have died gloriously on the field of battle. I feel how weak and fruitless must be any words of mine which should attempt to beguile you from the grief of a loss so overwhelming, but I cannot refrain from tendering to you the consolation that may be found in the thanks of the Republic that they died to save. I pray that the Heavenly Father may assuage the anguish of your bereavement, and leave you only the cherished memory of the loved and lost, and the solemn pride that must be yours to have laid so costly a sacrifice upon the altar of freedom.

Yours very sincerely and respectfully,

ABRAHAM LINCOLN

THE LINCOLN MEMORIAL*
By Ralph Henry Gabriel

. . . WHAT IS IT that Americans worship when they stand, uncovered, before that great, silent figure? For worship they do, more sincerely many of them, than when they occupy their pews in church. They do reverence, if one may hazard an analysis of those inarticulate emotions which put an end to loud talk and to boisterous conduct, to a personification of the American democratic faith. The phenomenon of Lincoln, Woodrow Wilson once remarked, makes it possible to believe in democracy. He rose, without the aid of a patron, from the poverty of the open-faced camp on Pidgeon Creek to more than the White House. He wielded such power as no previous President had ever known. Mighty armies of volunteers marched at his command to fight for the Union and for the freedom of men. He led his people to a righteous victory. But triumph did not make of him a Caesar. Through all the years in which he sat in the seats of the mighty he remained the sincere, humane, and humble democrat. His career was the fulfillment of the romantic democratic vision; it was Aladdin's dream come true. He founded his life on the Constitution and on its fundamental moral law. In striking the irons from the slave he gave new meaning to the doctrine of the free individual. He not only saved the Union; he expressed in unforgettable words the mission of democracy and of America. They are written on the walls of his temple: "With malice toward none; with charity for all; with firmness in the right as God gives us to see the right, let us strive to finish the work we are in; to bind up the nation's wounds; to care for him who shall have borne the battle and for his widow and his orphan, to do all which may achieve a just and lasting peace among ourselves, and with all nations."

The brooding Lincoln who sits in the Memorial in Washington is first among the folk heroes of the American people. He personifies that faith upon which the Republic rests.

* From "The Course of American Democratic Thought," by Ralph Henry Gabriel. Copyright, 1940, The Ronald Press Company.

ABRAHAM LINCOLN WALKS AT MIDNIGHT
VACHEL LINDSAY

It is portentous, and a thing of state
That here at midnight, in our little town
A mourning figure walks, and will not rest,
Near the old court-house, pacing up and down,

Or by his homestead, or in shadowed yards
He lingers where his children used to play,
Or through the market, on the well-worn stones
He stalks until the dawn-stars burn away.

A bronzed, lank man! His suit of ancient black,
A famous high top-hat and plain worn shawl
Make him the quaint great figure that men love,
The prairie-lawyer, master of us all.

He cannot sleep upon his hillside now.
He is among us—as in times before!
And we who toss and lie awake for long
Breathe deep, and start, to see him pass the door.

His head is bowed. He thinks on men and kings.
Yea, when the sick world cries, how can he sleep!
Too many peasants fight, they know not why,
Too many homesteads in black terror weep.

The sins of all the war-lords burn his heart.
He sees the dreadnaughts scouring every main.
He carries on his shawl-wrapped shoulders now
The bitterness, the folly and the pain.

He cannot rest until a spirit-dawn
Shall come—the shining hope of Europe free:
The league of sober folk, the Workers' Earth,
Bringing long peace to Cornland, Alp and Sea.

It breaks his heart that kings must murder still,
That all his hours of travail here for men
Seem yet in vain. And who will bring white peace
That he may sleep upon his hill again?

LINES FROM LINCOLN

THE MAN who can't make a mistake can't make anything.

IF I EVER GET a chance to hit that thing, I'll hit it hard! (On slavery)

As PRESIDENT, I have no eyes but constitutional eyes; I cannot see you.

"WE TRUST, SIR, that God is on our side." "It is more important to know that we are on God's side."

I DESIRE SO TO CONDUCT THE AFFAIRS of this administration that if at the end, when I come to lay down the reins of power, I have lost every other friend on earth, I shall at least have one friend left, and that friend shall be down inside of me.

IF I WERE TO TRY TO READ, MUCH LESS ANSWER, all the attacks made on me, this shop might as well be closed for any other business. I do the very best I know how and I mean to keep doing so until the end. If the end brings me out all right, what is said against me won't amount to anything. If the end brings me out wrong, ten angels swearing I was right would make no difference.

WE, ON OUR SIDE, are praying Him to give us victory, because we believe we are right; but those on the other side pray Him, too, for victory, believing they are right. What must He think of us?

I BELIEVE THIS GOVERNMENT cannot endure permanently half slave and half free. I do not expect the Union to be dissolved, but I do expect it will cease to be divided.

IN GIVING FREEDOM to the slave we assure freedom to the free, —honorable alike in what we give and what we preserve.

FORCE is all-conquering, but its victories are short-lived.

TRUTH is generally the best vindication against slander.

108

WORDS OF WALT WHITMAN

PEACE is always beautiful.

THE FUTURE is no more uncertain than the Present.

O AMERICA! Because you build for mankind, I build for you.

I WILL PUT in my poems that with you
   is heroism upon land and sea,
And I will report all heroism from an
   American point of view.

I SAY the real and permanent grandeur of these States
must be their religion.

THE UNITED STATES, themselves, are essentially the greatest poem . . . :
Here at last is something in the doings of man that corresponds with the
broadcast doings of the day and night.

BOOKS ARE TO BE CALLED FOR and supplied on the assumption
that the process of reading is not a half sleep, but in the
highest sense an exercise, a gymnastic struggle; that the reader
is to do something for himself.

THE WHOLE THEORY of the universe is
directed unerringly to one single individual—namely to you.

THE GREAT CITY is that which has the greatest
man or woman.

NOTHING can happen more beautiful than death.

NONE HAS BEGUN to think how
divine he himself is and how
certain the future is.

The Consul

By RICHARD HARDING DAVIS

$\mathcal{F}$OR OVER FORTY YEARS, in one part of the world or another, old man Marshall had served his country as a United States Consul. He had been appointed by Lincoln. For a quarter of a century that fact was his distinction. It was now his epitaph. But in former years, as each new administration succeeded the old, it had again and again saved his official head. When victorious and voracious place-hunters, searching the map of the world for spoils, dug out his hiding-place and demanded his consular sign as a reward for a younger and more aggressive party worker, the ghost of the dead President protected him. In the State Department, Marshall had become a tradition. "You can't touch *him!*" the State Department would say; "why, *he* was appointed by Lincoln!" Secretly, for this weapon against the hungry head-hunters, the department was infinitely grateful. Old man Marshall was a consul after its own heart. Like a soldier, he was obedient, disciplined. Wherever he was sent, there, without question, he would go. Never against exile, against ill-health, against climate did he make complaint. Nor when he was moved on and down to make way for some ne'er-do-well with influence, with a brother-in-law in the Senate, with a cousin owning a newspaper, with rich relatives who desired him to drink himself to death at the expense of the government rather than at their own, did old man Marshall point to his record as a claim for more just treatment.

And it had been an excellent record. His official reports, in a quaint, stately hand, were models of English; full of information, intelligent, valuable, well observed. And those few of his countrymen, who stumbled upon him in the out-of-the-world places to which of late he had been banished, wrote of him to the department in terms of admiration and awe. Never had he or his friends petitioned for promotion, until it was at last apparent that, save for his record and the memory of his dead patron, he had no friends. But, still in the department the tradition held and, though he was not advanced, he was not dismissed.

"If that old man's been feeding from the public trough ever since the Civil War," protested a practical politician, "it seems to me, Mr. Secretary, that he's about had his share. Ain't it time he give some one else a bite? Some of us that has done the work, that has borne the brunt——"

"This place he now holds," interrupted the Secretary of State suavely, "is one hardly commensurate with services like yours. I can't pronounce the name of it, and I'm not sure just where it is, but I see that, of the last six consuls we sent there, three resigned within a month and the other three died of yellow fever. Still, if you insist——"

The practical politician reconsidered hastily. "I'm not the sort," he protested, "to turn out a man appointed by our martyred President.

Besides, he's so old now, if the fever don't catch him, he'll die of old age, anyway."

The Secretary coughed uncomfortably. "And they say," he murmured, "republics are ungrateful."

"I don't quite get that," said the practical politician.

Of Porto Banos, of the Republic of Colombia, where as consul Mr. Marshall was upholding the dignity of the United States, little could be said except that it possessed a sure harbor. When driven from the Caribbean Sea by stress of weather, the largest of ocean tramps, and even battleships, could find in its protecting arms of coral a safe shelter. But, as young Mr. Aiken, the wireless operator, pointed out, unless driven by a hurricane and the fear of death, no one ever visited it. Back of the ancient wharfs, that dated from the days when Porto Banos was a receiver of stolen goods for buccaneers and pirates, were rows of thatched huts, streets, according to the season, of dust or mud, a few iron-barred, jail-like barracks, custom-houses, municipal buildings, and whitewashed adobe houses of the consuls. The back yard of the town was a swamp. Through this at five each morning a rusty engine pulled a train of flat cars to the base of the mountains, and, if meanwhile the rails had not disappeared into the swamp, at five in the evening brought back the flat cars laden with odorous coffee-sacks.

In the daily life of Porto Banos, waiting for the return of the train, and betting if it would return, was the chief interest. Each night the consuls, the foreign residents, the wireless operator, the manager of the rusty railroad met for dinner. There at the head of the long table, by virtue of his years, of his courtesy and dis-tinguished manner, of his office, Mr. Marshall presided. Of the little band of exiles he was the chosen ruler. His rule was gentle. By force of example he had made existence in Porto Banos more possible. For women and children Porto Banos was a death-trap, and before "old man Marshall" came there had been no influence to remind the enforced bachelors of other days. They had lost interest, had grown lax, irritable, morose. Their white duck was seldom white. Their cheeks were unshaven. When the sun shrank into the swamp and the heat still turned Porto Banos into a Turkish bath, they threw dice on the greasy tables of the Café Bolivar for drinks. The petty gambling led to petty quarrels; the drinks to fever. The coming of Mr. Marshall changed all that. His standards of life, his tact, his worldly wisdom, his cheerful courtesy, his fastidious personal neatness shamed the younger men; the desire to please him, to stand well in his good opinion, brought back pride and self-esteem.

The lieutenant of Her Majesty's gunboat *Plover* noted the change.

"Used to be," he exclaimed, "you couldn't get out of the Café Bolivar without some one sticking a knife in you; now it's a debating club. They all sit round a table and listen to an old gentleman talk world politics."

If Henry Marshall brought content to the exiles of Porto Banos, there was little in return that Porto Banos could give to him. Magazines and correspondents in six languages kept him in touch with those foreign lands in which he had represented his country, but of the country he had represented, newspapers and periodicals showed him only too clearly that in forty years it had grown away from him, changed beyond recognition.

111

When last he had called at the State Department, he had been made to feel he was a man without a country, and when he visited the home in Vermont, he was looked upon as a Rip Van Winkle. Those of his boyhood friends who were not dead had long thought of him as dead. And the sleepy, pretty village had become a bustling commercial center. In the lanes where, as a young man, he had walked among wheat-fields, trolley-cars whirled between rows of mills and factories. The children had grown to manhood with children of their own.

Like a ghost, he searched for house after house, where once he had been made welcome, only to find in its place a towering office building. "All had gone, the old familiar faces." In vain he scanned even the shop fronts for a friendly, home-like name. Whether the fault was his, whether he would better have served his own interests than those of his government, it now was too late to determine. In his own home, he was a stranger among strangers. In the service he had so faithfully followed, rank by rank, he had been dropped, until now he, who twice had been a consul-general, was an exile, banished to a fever swamp. The great Ship of State had dropped him overside, had "marooned" him, and sailed away.

Twice a day he walked along the shell road to the Café Bolivar, and back again to the consulate. There, as he entered the outer office, José, the Colombian clerk, would rise and bow profoundly.

"Any papers for me to sign, José?" the consul would ask.

"Not today, Excellency," the clerk would reply. Then José would return to writing a letter to his lady-love;

not that there was anything to tell her, but because writing on the official paper of the consulate gave him importance in his eyes, and in hers. And in the inner office the consul would continue to gaze at the empty harbor, the empty coral reefs, the empty, burning sky.

The little band of exiles were at second breakfast when the wireless man came in late to announce that a Red D. boat and the island of Curaçao had both reported a hurricane coming north. Also, that much concern was felt for the safety of the yacht *Serapis*. Three days before, in advance of her coming, she had sent a wireless to Wilhelmstad, asking the captain of the port to reserve a berth for her. She expected to arrive the following morning.

But for forty-eight hours nothing had been heard from her, and it was believed she had been overhauled by the hurricane. Owing to the presence on board of Senator Hanley, the closest friend of the new President, the man who had made him President, much concern was felt at Washington. To try to pick her up by wireless, the gunboat *Newark* had been ordered from Culebra, the cruiser *Raleigh*, with Admiral Hardy on board, from Colon. It was possible she would seek shelter at Porto Banos. The consul was ordered to report.

As Marshall wrote out his answer, the French consul exclaimed with interest:

"He is of importance, this Senator?" he asked. "Is it that in your country ships of war are at service of a senator?"

Aiken, the wireless operator, grinned derisively.

"At the service of *this* senator, they are!" he answered. "They call him

112

the 'king-maker,' the man behind the throne."

"But in your country," protested the Frenchman, "there is no throne. I thought your president was elected by the people?"

"That's what the people think," answered Aiken. "In God's country," he explained, "the trusts want a rich man in the Senate, with the same interests as their own, to represent them. They chose Hanley. He picked out of the candidates for the presidency the man he thought would help the interests. He nominated him, and the people voted for him. Hanley is what we call a boss."

The Frenchman looked inquiringly at Marshall.

"The position of the boss is the more dangerous," said Marshall gravely, "because it is unofficial, because there are no laws to curtail his powers. Men like Senator Hanley are a menace to good government. They s ee in public office only a reward for party workers."

"That's right," assented Aiken. "Your forty years' service, Mr. Consul, wouldn't count with Hanley. If he wanted your job, he'd throw you out as quick as he would a drunken cook."

Mr. Marshall flushed painfully, and the French consul hastened to interrupt.

"Then, let us pray," he exclaimed, with fervor, "that the hurricane has sunk the *Serapis*, and all on board."

Two hours later, the *Serapis*, showing she had met the hurricane and had come out second best, steamed into the harbor.

Her owner was young Herbert Livingstone, of Washington. He once had been in the diplomatic service, and, as minister to The Hague, wished to return to it. In order to bring this about he had subscribed liberally to the party campaign fund.

With him, among other distinguished persons, was the all-powerful Hanley. The kidnapping of Hanley for the cruise demonstrated the ability of Livingstone as a diplomat. It was the opinion of many that it would surely lead to his appointment as a minister plenipotentiary. Livingstone was of the same opinion. He had not lived long in the nation's capital without observing the value of propinquity. How many men he knew were now paymasters, and secretaries of legation, solely because those high in the government met them daily at the Metropolitan Club, and preferred them in almost any other place. And if, after three weeks, as his guest on board what the newspapers called his floating palace, the senator could refuse him even the prize legation of Europe, there was no value in modest merit. There was no need. To a statesman of Hanley's astuteness, the largeness of Livingstone's contribution to the campaign fund was self-explanatory.

After the wrestling-match with the hurricane, all those on board the *Serapis* seemed to find in land, even in the swamp land of Porto Banos, a compelling attraction. Before the anchors hit the water, they were in the launch. On reaching the shore, they made at once for the consulate. There were many cables they wished to start on their way by wireless; cables to friends, to newspapers, to the government.

José, the Colombian clerk, appalled by the unprecedented invasion of visitors, of visitors so distinguished, and Marshall, grateful for a chance to serve his fellow countrymen, and especially his countrywomen, were ubiquitous, eager, indispensable. At

113

José's desk the great senator, rolling his cigar between his teeth, was using, to José's ecstasy, José's own pen to write the reassuring message to the White House. At the consul's desk a beautiful creature, all in lace and pearls, was struggling to compress the very low opinion she had of a hurricane into ten words. On his knee, Henry Cairns, the banker, was inditing instructions to his Wall Street office, replying to the inquiries heaped upon Marshall's desk, from many newspapers.

It was just before sunset, and Marshall produced his tea things, and the young person in lace and pearls, who was Miss Cairns, made tea for the women, and the men mixed gin and limes with tepid water. The consul apologized for proposing a toast in which they could not join. He begged to drink to those who had escaped the perils of the sea. Had they been his oldest and nearest friends, his little speech could not have been more heartfelt and sincere. To his distress, it moved one of the ladies to tears, and in embarrassment he turned to the men.

"I regret there is no ice," he said, "but you know the rule of the tropics; as soon as a ship enters port, the ice-machine bursts."

"I'll tell the steward to send you some, sir," said Livingstone, "and as long as we're here——"

The senator showed his concern.

"As long as we're here?" he gasped.

"Not over two days," answered the owner nervously. "The chief says it will take all of that to get her in shape. As you ought to know, Senator, she was pretty badly mauled."

The senator gazed blankly out of the window. Beyond it lay the naked coral reefs, the empty sky, and the ragged palms of Porto Banos.

Livingstone felt that his legation was slipping from him.

"That wireless operator," he continued hastily, "tells me there is a most amusing place a few miles down the coast, Las Bocas, a sort of Coney Island, where the government people go for the summer. There's surf bathing and roulette and *cafés chantants*. He says there are some Spanish dancers——"

The guests of the *Serapis* exclaimed with interest; the senator smiled. To Marshall the general enthusiasm over the thought of a ride on a merry-go-round suggested that the friends of Mr. Livingstone had found their own society far from satisfying.

Greatly encouraged, Livingstone continued, with enthusiasm:

"And the wireless man said," he added, "that with the launch we can get there in half an hour. We might run down after dinner."

He turned to Mr. Marshall.

"Will you join us, Mr. Consul?" he asked, "and dine with us, first?"

Marshall accepted with genuine pleasure. It had been many months since he had sat at table with his own people. But he shook his head doubtfully.

"I was wondering about Las Bocas," he explained, "if your going there might get you in trouble at the next port. With a yacht, I think it is different, but Las Bocas is under quarantine——"

There was a chorus of exclamations.

"It's not serious," Marshall explained. "There was bubonic plague there, or something like it. You would be in no danger from that. It is only that you might be held up by the regulations. Passenger steamers can't land any one who has been there at any other port of the West

Indies. The English are especially strict. The *Royal Mail* won't even receive any one on board here without a certificate from the English Consul saying he has not visited Las Bocas. For an American they would require the same guarantee from me. But I don't think the regulations extend to yachts. I will inquire. I don't wish to deprive you of any of the many pleasures of Porto Banos," he added smiling, "but if you were refused a landing at your next port I would blame myself."

"It's all right," declared Livingstone decidedly. "It's just as you say; yachts and warships are exempt. Besides, I carry my own doctor, and if he won't give us a clean bill of health, I'll make him walk the plank. At eight, then, at dinner. I'll send the cutter for you. I can't give you a salute, Mr. Consul, but you shall have all the side boys I can muster."

Those from the yacht parted from their consul in the most friendly spirit.

"I think he's charming!" exclaimed Miss Cairns. "And did you notice his novels? They were in every language. It must be terribly lonely down here, for a man like that."

"He's the first of our consuls we've met on this trip," growled her father, "that we've caught sober."

"Sober!" exclaimed his wife indignantly. "He's one of the Marshalls of Vermont. I asked him."

"I wonder," mused Hanley, "how much the place is worth? Hamilton, one of the new senators, has been deviling the life out of me to send his son somewhere. Says if he stays in Washington he'll disgrace the family. I should think this place would drive any man to drink himself to death in three months, and young Hamilton, from what I've seen of him, ought to

be able to do it in a week. That would leave the place open for the next man."

"There's a postmaster in my State thinks he carried it." The senator smiled grimly. "He has consumption, and wants us to give him a consulship in the tropics. I'll tell him I've seen Porto Banos, and that it's just the place for him."

The senator's pleasantry was not well received. But Miss Cairns alone had the temerity to speak of what the others were thinking.

"What would become of Mr. Marshall?" she asked.

The senator smiled tolerantly.

"I don't know that I was thinking of Mr. Marshall," he said. "I can't recall anything he has done for this administration. You see, Miss Cairns," he explained, in the tone of one addressing a small child, "Marshall has been abroad now for forty years, at the expense of the taxpayers. Some of us think men who have lived that long on their fellow-countrymen had better come home and get to work."

Livingstone nodded solemnly in assent. He did not wish a post abroad at the expense of the taxpayers. He was willing to pay for it. And then, with "ex-minister" on his visiting cards, and a sense of duty well performed, for the rest of his life he could join the other expatriates in Paris.

Just before dinner, the cruiser *Raleigh*, having discovered the whereabouts of the *Serapis* by wireless, entered the harbor, and Admiral Hardy came to the yacht to call upon the senator, in whose behalf he had been scouring the Caribbean Seas. Having paid his respects to that personage, the admiral fell boisterously upon Marshall.

The two old gentlemen were friends of many years. They had

met, officially and unofficially, in many strange parts of the world. To each the chance reunion was a piece of tremendous good fortune. And throughout dinner the guests of Livingstone, already bored with each other, found in them and their talk of former days new and delightful entertainment. So much so that when, Marshall having assured them that the local quarantine did not extend to a yacht, the men departed for Las Bocas, the women insisted that he and the admiral remain behind.

It was for Marshall a wondrous evening. To foregather with his old friend, whom he had known since Hardy was a mad midshipman, to sit at the feet of his own charming countrywomen, to listen to their soft, modulated laughter, to note how quickly they saw that to him the evening was a great event, and with what tact each contributed to make it the more memorable; all served to wipe out the months of bitter loneliness, the stigma of failure, the sense of undeserved neglect. In the moonlight, on the cool quarter-deck, they sat, in a half-circle, each of the two friends telling tales out of school, tales of which the other was the hero or the victim, inside stories of great occasions, ceremonies, bombardments, unrecorded shirt-sleeve diplomacy.

Hardy had helped to open the Suez Canal. Marshall had assisted the Queen of Madagascar to escape from the French invaders. On the Barbary Coast Hardy had chased pirates. In Edinburgh Marshall had played chess with Carlyle. He had seen Paris in mourning in the days of the siege, Paris in terror in the days of the Commune; he had known Garibaldi, Gambetta, the younger Dumas, the creator of Pickwick.

"Do you remember that time in Tangier," the admiral urged, "when I was a midshipman, and got into the bashaw's harem?"

"Do you remember how I got you out?" Marshall replied grimly.

"And," demanded Hardy, "do you remember when Adelina Patti paid a visit to the *Kearsarge* at Marseilles in '65 (George Dewey was our second officer) and you were bowing and backing away from her, and you backed into an open hatch, and she said (my French isn't up to it) what was it she said?"

"I didn't hear it," said Marshall; "I was too far down the hatch."

"Do you mean the old *Kearsarge?*" asked Mrs. Cairns. "Were you in service then, Mr. Marshall?"

With loyal pride in his friend, the admiral answered for him:

"He was our consul-general at Marseilles!"

There was an uncomfortable moment. Even those denied imagination could not escape the contrast, could see in their mind's eye the great harbor of Marseilles, crowded with the shipping of the world, surrounding it the beautiful city, the rival of Paris to the north, and on the battleship the young consul-general making his bow to the young Empress of Song. And now, before their actual eyes, they saw the village of Porto Banos, a black streak in the night, a row of mud shacks, at the end of the wharf a single lantern in the clear moonlight.

Later in the evening Miss Cairns led the admiral to one side.

"Admiral," she began eagerly, "tell me about your friend. Why is he here? Why don't they give him a place worthy of him? I've seen many of our representatives abroad, and I know we cannot afford to waste men like that." The girl exclaimed indignantly: "He's one of the most interesting men I've ever met! He's lived everywhere, known every one. He's a distinguished man, a cultivated man; even I can see he knows his work, that he's a diplomat, born, trained, that he's——"

The admiral interrupted with a growl.

"You don't have to tell *me* about Henry," he protested. "I've known Henry twenty-five years. If Henry got his deserts," he exclaimed hotly, "he wouldn't be a consul on this coral reef; he'd be a minister in Europe. Look at me! We're the same age. We started together. When Lincoln sent him to Morocco as consul, he signed my commission as a midshipman. Now I'm an admiral. Henry has twice my brains and he's been a consul-general, and he's *here*, back at the foot of the ladder!"

"Why?" demanded the girl.

"Because the navy is a service and the consular service isn't a service. Men like Senator Hanley use it to pay their debts. While Henry's been serving his country abroad, he's lost his friends, lost his 'pull.' Those politicians up at Washington have no use for him. They don't consider that a consul like Henry can make a million dollars for his countrymen. He can keep them from shipping goods where there's no market, show them where there is a market." The admiral snorted contemptuously. "You don't have to tell *me* the value of a good consul. But those politicians don't consider that. They only see that he has a job worth a few hundred dollars, and they want it, and if he hasn't other politicians to protect him, they'll take it."

The girl raised her head.

"Why don't you speak to the senator?" she asked. "Tell him you've

known him for years that——"

"Glad to do it!" exclaimed the admiral heartily. "It won't be the first time. But Henry mustn't know. He's too touchy. He hates the *idea* of influence, hates men like Hanley, who abuse it. If he thought anything was given to him except on his own merit, he wouldn't take it."

"Then we won't tell him," said the girl. For a moment she hesitated. "If I spoke to Mr. Hanley," she asked, "told him what I learned tonight of Mr. Marshall, would it have any effect?"

"Don't know how it will affect Hanley," said the sailor, "but if you asked me to make anybody a consul-general, I'd make him an ambassador."

Later in the evening Hanley and Livingstone were seated alone on deck. The visit to Las Bocas had not proved amusing, but, much to Livingstone's relief, his honored guest was now in good-humor. He took his cigar from his lips, only to sip at a cool long drink. He was in a mood flatteringly confidential and communicative.

"People have the strangest idea of what I can do for them," he laughed. It was his pose to pretend he was without authority. "They believe I've only to wave a wand, and get them anything they want. I thought I'd be safe from them on board a yacht."

Livingstone, in ignorance of what was coming, squirmed apprehensively.

"But it seems," the senator went on, "I'm at the mercy of a conspiracy. The women folk want me to do something for this fellow Marshall. If they had their way, they'd send him to the Court of St. James's. And old Hardy, too, tackled me about him.

117

So did Miss Cairns. And then Marshall himself got me behind the wheel-house, and I thought he was going to tell me how good he was, too! He didn't."

As though the joke were on himself, the senator laughed appreciatively.

"Told me, instead, that Hardy ought to be a vice-admiral."

Livingstone, also, laughed, with the satisfied air of one who cannot be tricked.

"They fixed it up between them," he explained, "each was to put in a good word for the other." He nodded eagerly. "That's what *I* think."

There were moments during the cruise when Senator Hanley would have found relief in dropping his host overboard. With mock deference, the older man inclined his head.

"That's what *you* think, is it?" he asked. "Livingstone," he added, "you certainly are a good judge of men!"

The next morning, old man Marshall woke with a lightness at his heart that had long been absent. For a moment, conscious only that he was happy, he lay between sleep and waking, frowning up at his canopy of mosquito net, trying to realize what change had come to him. Then he remembered. His old friend had returned. New friends had come into his life and welcomed him kindly. He was no longer lonely. As eager as a boy, he ran to the window. He had not been dreaming. In the harbor lay the pretty yacht, the stately, white-hulled ship. The flag that dropped from the stern of each caused his throat to tighten, brought warm tears to his eyes, fresh resolve to his discouraged, troubled spirit. When he knelt down beside his bed, his heart poured out his thanks in gratitude and gladness.

While he was dressing, a blue-jacket brought a note from the admiral. It invited him to tea on board the warship, with the guests of the *Serapis*. His old friend added that he was coming to lunch with his consul, and wanted time reserved for a long talk. The consul agreed gladly. He was in holiday humor. The day promised to repeat the good moments of the night previous.

At nine o'clock, through the open door of the consulate, Marshall saw Aiken, the wireless operator, signaling from the wharf excitedly to the yacht, and a boat leave the ship and return. Almost immediately the launch, carrying several passengers, again made the trip shoreward.

Half an hour later, Senator Hanley, Miss Cairns, and Livingstone came up the water-front, and entering the consulate, seated themselves around Marshall's desk. Livingstone was sunk in melancholy. The senator, on the contrary, was smiling broadly. His manner was one of distinct relief. He greeted the consul with hearty good-humor.

"I'm ordered home!" he announced gleefully. Then, remembering the presence of Livingstone, he hastened to add: "I needn't say how sorry I am to give up my yachting trip, but orders are orders. The President," he explained to Marshall, "cables me this morning to come back and take my coat off."

The prospect, as a change from playing bridge on a pleasure boat, seemed far from depressing him.

"Those filibusters in the Senate," he continued genially, "are making trouble again. They think they've got me out of the way for another month, but they'll find they're wrong. When the bill comes up,

118

they'll find me at the old stand and ready for business!" Marshall did not attempt to conceal his personal disappointment.

"I am so sorry you are leaving," he said, "selfishly sorry, I mean. I'd hoped you all would be here for several days."

He looked inquiringly toward Livingstone.

"I understood the *Serapis* was disabled," he explained.

"She is," answered Hanley. "So's the *Raleigh*. At a pinch, the admiral might have stretched the regulations and carried me to Jamaica, but the *Raleigh's* engines are knocked about too. I've *got* to reach Kingston Thursday. The German boat leaves there Thursday for New York. At first it looked as though I couldn't do it, but we find that the *Royal Mail* is due today, and she can get to Kingston Wednesday night. It's a great piece of luck. I wouldn't bother you with my troubles," the senator explained pleasantly, "but the agent of the *Royal Mail* here won't sell me a ticket until you've put your seal to this."

He extended a piece of printed paper.

As Hanley had been talking, the face of the consul had grown grave. He accepted the paper, but did not look at it. Instead, he regarded the senator with troubled eyes. When he spoke, his tone was one of genuine concern.

"It is most unfortunate," he said, "but I am afraid the *Royal Mail* will not take you on board. Because of Las Bocas," he explained. "If we had only known!" he added, remorsefully. "It is *most* unfortunate."

"Because of Las Bocas?" echoed Hanley. "You don't mean they'll refuse to take me to Jamaica because I spent half an hour at the end of a wharf listening to a squeaky gramophone?"

"The trouble," explained Marshall, "is this: if they carried you, all the other passengers would be held in quarantine for ten days, and there are fines to pay, and there would be difficulties over the mails. But," he added hopefully, "maybe the regulations have been altered. I will see her captain, and tell him——"

"See her captain!" objected Hanley. "Why see the captain? He doesn't know I've been to that place. Why tell *him*? All I need is a clean bill of health from you. That's all *he* wants. You have only to sign that paper."

Marshall regarded the senator with surprise.

"But I can't," he said.

"You can't? Why not?"

"Because it certifies that you have not visited Las Bocas. Unfortunately, you have visited Las Bocas."

The senator had been walking up and down the room. Now he seated himself, and stared at Marshall curiously.

"It's like this, Mr. Marshall," he began quietly. "The President desires my presence in Washington, thinks I can be of some use to him there in helping carry out certain party measures—measures to which he pledged himself before his election. Down here, a British steamship line has laid down local rules which, in my case anyway, are ridiculous. The question is, are you going to be bound by the red tape of a ha'penny British colony, or by your oath to the President of the United States?"

The sophistry amused Marshall. He smiled good-naturedly and shook his head.

"I'm afraid, Senator," he said,

"that way of putting it is hardly fair. Unfortunately, the question is one of fact. I will explain to the captain ——"

"You will explain nothing to the captain!" interrupted Hanley. "This is a matter which concerns no one but our two selves. I am not asking favors of steamboat captains. I am asking an American consul to assist an American citizen in trouble, and," he added, with heavy sarcasm, "incidentally, to carry out the wishes of his President."

Marshall regarded the senator with an expression of both surprise and disbelief.

"Are you asking me to put my name to what is not so?" he said. "Are you serious?"

"That paper, Mr. Marshall," returned Hanley steadily, "is a mere form, a piece of red tape. There's no more danger of my carrying the plague to Jamaica than of my carrying a dynamite bomb. You *know* that."

"I *do* know that," assented Marshall heartily. "I appreciate your position, and I regret it exceedingly. You are the innocent victim of a regulation which is a wise regulation, but which is most unfair to you. My own position," he added, "is not important, but you can believe me, it is not easy. It is certainly no pleasure for me to be unable to help you."

Hanley was leaning forward, his hand on his knees, his eyes watching Marshall closely.

"Then you refuse?" he said. "Why?"

Marshall regarded the senator steadily. His manner was untroubled. The look he turned upon Hanley was one of grave disapproval.

"You know why," he answered quietly. "It is impossible."

In sudden anger Hanley rose. Marshall, who had been seated behind his desk, also rose. For a moment, in silence, the two men confronted each other. Then Hanley spoke; his tone was harsh and threatening.

"Then I am to understand," he exclaimed, "that you refuse to carry out the wishes of a United States Senator and of the President of the United States?"

In front of Marshall, on his desk, was the little iron stamp of the consulate. Protectingly, almost caressingly, he laid his hand upon it.

"I refuse," he corrected, "to place the seal of this consulate on a lie."

There was a moment's pause. Miss Cairns, unwilling to remain, and unable to withdraw, clasped her hands unhappily and stared at the floor. Livingstone exclaimed in indignant protest. Hanley moved a step nearer and, to emphasize what he said, tapped his knuckles on the desk. With the air of one confident of his advantage, he spoke slowly and softly.

"Do you appreciate," he asked, "that, while you may be of some importance down here in this fever swamp, in Washington I am supposed to carry some weight? Do you appreciate that I am a Senator from a State that numbers four millions of people and that you are preventing me from serving those people?"

Marshall inclined his head gravely and politely.

"And I want you to appreciate," he said, "that while I have no weight at Washington, in this fever swamp I have the honor to represent eighty millions of people, and as long as that consular sign is over my door I don't intend to prostitute it for *you*, or the President of the United States, or any one of those eighty millions."

Of the two men, the first to lower his eyes was Hanley. He laughed shortly, and walked to the door. There he turned, and indifferently, as though the incident no longer interested him, drew out his watch.

"Mr. Marshall," he said, "if the cable is working, I'll take your tin sign away from you by sunset."

For one of Marshall's traditions, to such a speech there was no answer save silence. He bowed, and, apparently serene and undismayed, resumed his seat. From the contest, judging from the manner of each, it was Marshall, not Hanley, who had emerged victorious.

But Miss Cairns was not deceived. Under the unexpected blow, Marshall had turned older. His clear blue eyes had grown less alert, his broad shoulders seemed to stoop. In sympathy, her own eyes filled with sudden tears.

"What will you do?" she whispered.

"I don't know what I shall do," said Marshall simply. "I should have liked to resign. It's a prettier finish. After forty years—to be dismissed by cable is—it's a poor way of ending it."

Miss Cairns rose and walked to the door. She turned there and looked back.

"I am sorry," she said. And both understood that in saying no more than that she had best shown her sympathy.

An hour later the sympathy of Admiral Hardy was expressed more directly.

"If he comes on board my ship," roared that gentleman, "I'll push him down an ammunition hoist and break his damned neck!"

Marshall laughed delightedly. The loyalty of his old friend was never so welcome.

"You'll treat him with every courtesy," he said. "The only satisfaction he gets out of this is to see that he has hurt me. We will not give him that satisfaction."

But Marshall found that to conceal his wound was more difficult than he had anticipated. When, at tea time, on the deck of the warship, he again met Senator Hanley and the guests of the *Serapis*, he could not forget that his career had come to an end. There was much to remind him that this was so. He was made aware of it by the sad, sympathetic glances of the women; by their tactful courtesies; by the fact that Livingstone, anxious to propitiate Hanley, treated him rudely; by the sight of the young officers, each just starting upon a career of honor, and possible glory, as his career ended in humiliation; and by the big warship herself, that recalled certain crises when he had only to press a button and warships had come at his bidding.

At five o'clock there was an awkward moment. The *Royal Mail*, having taken on her cargo, passed out of the harbor on her way to Jamaica, and dipped her colors. Senator Hanley, abandoned to his fate, observed her departure in silence.

Livingstone, hovering at his side, asked sympathetically:

"Have they answered your cable, sir?"

"They have," said Hanley gruffly.

"Was it—was it satisfactory?" pursued the diplomat.

"It *was*," said the senator, with emphasis.

Far from discouraged, Livingstone continued his inquiries.

"And when," he asked eagerly, "are you going to tell him?"

"Now!" said the senator.

The guests were leaving the ship. When all were seated in the admiral's steam launch, the admiral descended the accommodation ladder and himself picked up the tiller ropes.

"Mr. Marshall," he called, "when I bring the launch broadside to the ship and stop her, you will stand ready to receive the consul's salute."

Involuntarily, Marshall uttered an exclamation of protest. He had forgotten that on leaving the warship, as consul, he was entitled to seven guns. Had he remembered, he would have insisted that the ceremony be omitted. He knew that this admiral wished to show his loyalty, knew that his old friend was now paying him this honor only as a rebuke to Hanley. But the ceremony was no longer an honor. Hanley had made it a mockery. It served only to emphasize what had been taken from him. But, without a scene, it now was too late to avoid it. The first of the seven guns had roared from the bow, and, as often he had stood before, as never he would so stand again, Marshall took his place at the gangway of the launch. His eyes were fixed on the flag, his gray head was uncovered, his hat was pressed above his heart.

For the first time since Hanley had left the consulate, he fell into sudden terror lest he might give way to his emotions. Indignant at the thought, he held himself erect. His face was set like a mask, his eyes were untroubled. He was determined they should not see that he was suffering.

Another gun spat out a burst of white smoke, a stab of flame. There was an echoing roar. Another and another followed. Marshall counted seven, and then, with a bow to the admiral, backed from the gangway.

And then another gun shattered the hot, heavy silence. Marshall, confused, embarrassed, assuming he had counted wrong, returned to his place. But again before he could leave it, in savage haste a ninth gun roared out its greeting. He could not still be mistaken. He turned appealingly to his friend. The eyes of the admiral were fixed upon the warship. Again a gun shattered the silence. Was it a jest? Were they laughing at him? Marshall flushed miserably. He gave a swift glance toward the others. They were smiling. Then it *was* a jest. Behind his back, something of which they all were cognizant was going forward. The face of Livingstone alone betrayed a like bewilderment to his own. But the others, who knew, were mocking him.

For the thirteenth time a gun shook the brooding swamp land of Porto Banos. And then, and not until then, did the flag crawl slowly from the masthead. Mary Cairns broke the tenseness by bursting into tears. But Marshall saw that every one else, save she and Livingstone, was still smiling. Even the bluejackets in charge of the launch were grinning at him. He was beset by smiling faces. And then from the warship, unchecked, came, against all regulations, three long, splendid cheers.

Marshall felt his lips quivering, the warm tears forging their way to his eyes. He turned beseechingly to his friend. His voice trembled.

"Charles," he begged, "are they laughing at me?"

Eagerly, before the other could answer, Senator Hanley tossed his cigar into the water and, scrambling forward, seized Marshall by the hand.

"Mr. Marshall," he cried, "our President has great faith in Abraham Lincoln's judgment of men. And this salute means that this morning he appointed you our new minister to The Hague. I'm one of those politicians who keeps his word. I told you I'd take your tin sign away from you by sunset. I've done it!'"

THE TRUE GLORY OF A NATION
By E. P. WHIPPLE

THE TRUE GLORY of a nation is an intelligent, honest, industrious people. The civilization of a people depends on their individual character; and a constitution which is not the outgrowth of this character is not worth the parchment on which it is written. You look in vain in the past for a single instance where the people have preserved their liberties after their individual character was lost. It is not in the magnificence of its palaces, not in the beautiful creations of art lavished on its public edifices, not in costly libraries and galleries of pictures, not in the number or wealth of its cities, that we find a nation's glory.

The ruler may gather around him the treasures of the world, amid a brutalized people; the senate chamber may retain its faultless proportions long after the voice of patriotism is hushed within its walls; the monumental marble may commemorate a glory which has forever departed. Art and letters may bring no lesson to a people whose heart is dead.

The true glory of a nation is the living temple of a loyal, industrious, upright people. The busy click of machinery, the merry ring of the anvil, the lowing of the peaceful herds, and the song of the harvest home, are sweeter music than the paeans of departed glory or the songs of triumph in war. The vine-clad cottage on the hillside, the cabin of the woodsman, and the rural home of the farmer, are the true citadels of any country. There is a dignity in honest toil which belongs not to the display of wealth or the luxury of fashion. The man who drives the plow or swings his axe in the forest, or with cunning fingers plies the tools of his craft, is as truly the servant of his country as the statesman in the senate or the soldier in battle.

The safety of a nation depends not alone on the wisdom of the statesman or bravery of its generals . . .

Would you see the image of true national glory, I would show you villages where the crown and glory of the people are in common schools, where the voice of prayer goes heavenward, where the people have that most priceless gift, faith in God—for—

"Not gold, but only men can make
A people great and strong.
Men who for truth and honor's sake,
Stand fast and suffer long.
Brave men who work while others sleep,
Who dare while others fly—
They build a nation's pillars deep
And lift them to the sky."

WORDS OF GREAT AMERICANS:

RESISTANCE to tyrants is obedience to God.

THE PEOPLE are the only sure reliance for the
preservation of our liberty.

NEVER BUY what you do not want, because it is cheap;
it will be dear to you.

THE TIME TO GUARD against corruption and tyranny is before they shall have
gotten hold of us. It is better to keep the wolf out of the fold than to trust to
drawing his teeth and talons after he shall have entered.

INDEED, I tremble for my country when I reflect that God is just.

A LIVELY AND LASTING SENSE of filial duty is more effectually impressed on the
mind of a son or daughter by reading *King Lear*, than by all the dry volumes of
ethics, and divinity, that ever were written.

I WOULD RATHER be exposed to the inconveniences attending too much liberty
than to those attending too small a degree of it.

THE HAPPINESS of the domestic fireside is the first boon of mankind;
and it is well it is so, since it is that which is the lot, of the mass of mankind.

THE REPUBLICAN is the only form of government which is not eternally
at open or secret war with the rights of mankind.

HOW MUCH PAIN have cost us the evils which have never happened.

No PERSON will have occasion to complain of the want of time
who never loses any.

NEVER trouble another for what you can do yourself.

124

THOMAS JEFFERSON

WE NEVER REPENT of having eaten too little.

WHEN ANGRY, count ten before you speak;
if very angry, an hundred.

HISTORY, by apprising (men) of the past, will enable them
to judge of the future.

HE WHO RECEIVES an idea from me, receives instruction himself without les-
sening mine; as he who lights his taper at mine, receives light without darkening me.

I KNOW NO SAFE DEPOSITORY of the ultimate powers of society but the people
themselves; and if we think them not enlightened enough to exercise their control with a wholesome discretion, the remedy is not to take it from them, but
to inform their discretion by education.

CHERISH THE SPIRIT OF OUR PEOPLE and keep alive their attention. Do not be
too severe upon their errors, but reclaim them by enlightening them. If once
they become inattentive to public affairs, you and I, and Congress and assem-
blies, judges and governors, shall all become wolves.

HERE WAS BURIED Thomas Jefferson, author of the Declaration of American
Independence, of the statute of Virginia for religious freedom, and father of
the University of Virginia. (Self-written epitaph)

NOTHING GIVES one person so much advantage over another as to remain always
cool and unruffled under all circumstances.

THE GOD who gave us life, gave us liberty at the same time.

A LITTLE REBELLION now and then is a good thing. It is a medicine
necessary for the sound health of government.

NOTHING is troublesome that we do willingly.

Jerusalem

By LOUISE ANDREWS KENT

*The Appleyard family visit an old landmark of
New England and hear about an early American.*

*I*N AUGUST the Appleyards go to
Jerusalem: that is, if they can find it. You must choose the right day.
It should be so clear that every stone stands out on Catamountain.
Couching Lion must be cut out of larkspur-blue paper and pasted
against a sky that has clipper-ship
clouds sailing across it. On a hazy
day Jerusalem, that cup-shaped
green valley in the hills, vanishes
into the mist.

It should be easy enough to find it.
You follow the curves of the River
Road for a certain number of miles.
You cross by the second covered
bridge—or is it the third? Well, anyway, the one near where the watering
trough used to be. Then take the
third fork, and find the old sawmill.
The dam is still there, if you look
carefully, though the pond is gone.
There is still a trickle of water, and
maidenhair grows out between the
stones in a green waterfall. Another
turn, a yellow house in a field where
there are sheep feeding among the
boulders. If the stones quiver in the
haze so that you are not sure which
are stones and which are sheep, go
home: you will not find Jerusalem
that day.

If the stones stand still and the
sheep caper, keep on. There are only
one or two more turns before you
reach the road. It is only on the
wrong day that you do not see that
it is really a road. On the right day
it curves off into the woods so
obviously that you cannot see why
you missed it before. There is perhaps
a mile of it before you reach the first
gate. If your car has covered that
mile of rocks and bog holes without
losing any of its vital underparts, you
are a good driver and you had better
not demonstrate your skill any
further. Leave it in the next turnout.
It is just as well to walk, anyway,
because, while you are hugging the
steering wheel, either actually in the
front seat or mentally in the back
one, you may miss the place where
the hollow log used to be—the one
where Jonathan hid.

Walking, you can still see that the
shape of the log is still there, though
now it is only a bed of ferns and moss
and wood sorrel a little higher than
the ground around it. Unless he was
a short boy, Jonathan must have had
to pull in his feet, Stan says.

Stan lies down on the bed of moss
to prove this point. When he was
fourteen, it fitted him perfectly. Now
his five feet eleven extends out into
the rocks beyond. The soldiers would
certainly have seen Jonathan's feet,
unless he pulled his knees up to his
chin, if he was more than five feet
seven.

"What a whale of a pine it must
have been when it was standing to
have a hollow big enough to scrooch
your knees up in!" Hugh says, and

they move up the last steep pitch to the second gate.

Mrs. Appleyard begins to sound like a horse with the heaves. The family and assorted guests give her a series of helpful pushes, someone unfastens the gate so that she will not have to climb it, and they are in Jerusalem.

The Appleyards never find it without some of the sense of discovery that the first settlers must have felt. It is so green, so quiet, in its ring of dark, protecting hills. The air that moves softly through it seems cleaner and fresher than other air—even than other Vermont air! The gentians in the wet edge of the woods are bluer than other gentians. The sky has broken and fallen. You think: I must run and tell someone about this. The sheep need a trip to the cleaners less than most sheep. They have more resemblance to the toyshop lamb and less to potato sacks on burnt matches than the sheep of ordinary fields. You begin to see why sheep have nibbled their way into so much poetry. Even the suspicious bleat that comes from a clump of wild roses has something musical about it. You half-expect to hear a flute blown softly. Only the whispering of the white birches, the voice of pines, remembering that pines once stood by the sea, stops you from hearing it.

"Only it wouldn't be flutes," Mrs. Appleyard says. "Fiddles, perhaps. In the schoolhouse. It was over there. There were fifty children in the village school, you know, before the war."

"In 1914?" asks the visitor, looking around at the empty valley.

"In 1860," Mrs. Appleyard tells him; and he says, "Oh, that war," and adds, "Go on—you promised to tell me when we got here."

They all sit down on the closely nibbled turf in the shade of a twisted old apple tree. There is a spring that chuckles to itself a little way down the road. Weather and rain have worked on the road for eighty years, but you can still see where it ran.

For more than a hundred years people lived in Jerusalem. There are two men who fought in the Revolution buried under the old apple trees. You cannot see the graves, but you can feel them with your feet, and, when you have found them, see that the chunks of rough stone at the head and feet of the sunken oblongs were not always there. When men first came to the lonely valley, it was partly because it was a safe refuge from Indians, partly because even then it was a natural meadow where grass grew—a meadow that caught sunshine and held it, where the hills shut out the worst of the north wind. The soil was rocky, but it was fertile between the rocks and there were springs everywhere.

No one ever had a plough in Jerusalem. The women used hoes and scratched out places for vegetable gardens on the slopes back of their cabins. It was a pretty sight in the fall, people say, when the corn was tasselled out and the pumpkins were beginning to be bright on the ground and the maples were turning brighter than the pumpkins. The men went hunting. There was plenty of game back in the hills. They cut some of the biggest pines for timber, and when the March days were sunny and the nights freezing, they tapped the maples and boiled down the sap. They did not leave Jerusalem often. Their clothes came mostly from the wool of their own sheep. They grew the greater part of their own food. Sometimes a load of lumber went to

127

the world outside, and calico and boots and perhaps a long rifle came back, but, for the most part, the world and Jerusalem troubled each other very little.

It was on one of those autumn days, when the maples were burning on the hillsides, that the war came to Jerusalem. Suddenly there were horses galloping up the road. No one had horses in the valley. Oxen hauled their timber to market. The strange sound brought the whole village to the doors of the log cabins.

The soldiers—eight of them— stopped in front of the schoolhouse. To the children, many of whom had never been out of the valley, the horses, with their heaving sides, with mud on their flanks and foam on their bridles, must have been strange and exciting. Horses had been only pictures before. There was nothing in the pictures about the queer, hot, leathery, sweaty smell, or the creaking and the jingling and the thud of iron-shod feet.

The men who rode the horses were almost as strange as their mounts. Their fine blue coats with the sun winking on the buttons, their neatly shaven chins, their stiffly visored caps with the gold braid, were all something out of another world. In Jerusalem men melted into the landscape. Homespun was the color of tree-trunks. Whiskers and beards grew as the wind blows—where they listed. A partridge could hardly tell a man from a stump among dead ferns. If he had a hat at all, it was of fur or straw and, like the rest of him, was brought by sun and rain to the color of hay that has been left out all winter. The stiff visors of the soldiers' caps threw sharp shadows across their faces and made their eyes mysterious. One of them had a

bugle. With the sun on it, it looked like pure gold. When the bugler sounded it, the notes echoed from Little Wildcat to Owl's Head and back again. It brought everyone to the schoolhouse who was not there already. Almost before the last echoes died away, Jerusalem, though the women standing around the schoolhouse did not know it, was blown away.

That young recruiting officer knew his work. Every man in the valley who was fit to go enlisted.

Some of the women cried as the men marched off, but most of them were quiet, partly because they were brave, partly because silence was their way of meeting most things; but mostly, perhaps, because they could not yet know that with those shambling, shapeless, hairy men the life of the valley was pouring out of it.

It was never to flow back. Some of the men would be killed, others maimed. Others would like "outside" once they had seen it. The plains of the West would take some. The sea would call others. The South, wounded but unconquered, would take others and in its own good time make Southerners out of them. Jerusalem was finished.

Some of the women stayed through that first winter, managing somehow with the help of the boys and the old men to take care of the sheep and to feed their families. The second winter saw tallow candles still burning in a few cabin windows, but, one by one, the women gave up and went "outside." For a while they came back in the summer-time. Then slowly the little cabins began to leak and rot and heave with the frost. One by one they fell into the cellar holes that are still irregular dimples in the nibbled green turf of Jerusalem.

At last there was only Aunt Debby left. She never said what she thought of the women who gave up the struggle and left their town to fall to pieces, but her tongue was sharp enough with any well-meaning person who tried to get her to leave.

Why should she go "outside?" She had seen it and had a poor opinion of it which she expressed in crisp chirps. She was a small, brown, bright-eyed woman like a very old, wise chipping sparrow. She needed about as much as a sparrow to keep alive. She did so until she was a hundred years old or more.

That is her spring there under the apple tree. Her cabin was across the road. Those twisted lilacs, that clump of spirea, those stunted rosebushes, mark her cellar hole. Those two tiger lilies were on either side of her front door.

It was the herbs—yarbs she called them—that kept Aunt Debby alive so long, people in the village said. Armed with bottles, they used to tramp the three miles to the valley and get the yarb tea that she brewed. There were several kinds, good for various afflictions. One, if drunk in the dark of the moon, was a love philtre. A piece of calico or a pound of sugar would purchase half a pint: probably good value in most cases. Some claim that there were spells, procurable for tobacco, that made the brew even more potent. Unfortunately, they have been forgotten. The water from her spring is still good for keeping rheumatism away, though. Old women in the village still send their grandchildren for it as their grandmothers used to send them when they were children, in the days when they would find Aunt Debby sitting in her cabin door between the tiger lilies, smoking her pipe.

They say in the village that she still sits there on summer evenings. Not every evening and not for all eyes. An evening when the mist rises and the fireflies flash in the grass under the apple trees is best, but even in broad daylight small girls make a curious gesture as they pass the door that is no longer there between the tiger lilies. Village children no longer curtsey to their elders, but there is a suggestion of a curtsey in this curious duck and bob that they make toward the cellar hole.

Bowing to Aunt Debby, they call it . . .

She was sitting at her door, smoking her pipe, as the men went past on their way to the war. Jonathan Evans was with them, though he was only eighteen and small for his age. He was carrying the bundle of clothes that she had packed for him. There was a white shirt in it that had been his father's. Jonathan was an orphan. He lived with Aunt Debby, who was his great-aunt. She gave a wave of the pipe, as he passed, that made him know that she understood that he had to save the Union and free the slaves. They understood each other without speech. The wave of the pipe said that she'd hoe the garden and manage the sheep.

In his eighteen years Jonathan had never been out of Jerusalem except to go to the sawmill at the crossroads. He had always wanted to see "outside," and now was his chance. "Outside," however, proved disappointing. There was an emptiness about it. It had none of the sheltered cosiness of Jerusalem and none of the glitter and elegance that he had expected. Jonathan's notions of the world were based on a stray Currier and Ives print or two, *Uncle Tom's Cabin*, a tattered copy of *Godey's Ladies' Book*, and accounts by returned travellers who had been as far south as Montpelier or even Boston. His ideas included plush chairs, crimson curtains, marble-topped tables, striped candy, ladies in purple silk dresses big enough for a sheep to hide under, elegant gentlemen cracking whips over slaves, carpets with flowers on them, peacocks, and pink ice cream.

None of these things was anywhere to be seen.

The landscape had the same frost-nipped maples, the same clumps of fern turned orange and brown, hills not very different from his own hills, but arranged wrong. Perhaps the Winooski was the worst disappointment. They had to cross the river, the men said. To Jonathan a river meant the Mississippi, grand and vast, so wide that the opposite shore with its strange trees and runaway slaves faded into the mist. Great boats would float on it with black smoke in a plume behind them and music in the cabin and gamblers with grand waistcoats and diamond studs. Fur-trappers would go down on flatboats, singing. There would be buffalo and Indians and crocodiles and pink birds as tall as a young heifer . . .

The Winooski was too large for a brook. You couldn't wade across it, but had to go tramping through the dust to find a bridge. Considered as a brook, it was an annoyance. As a river, it was a complete failure. Not a flamingo in sight—not even a crocodile. Besides, his feet hurt him. He stopped to take off his boots. He had not worn them since the winter and they pinched his toes cruelly. He was just uncurling them when the voice of the sergeant cut into his moment of comfort.

What ugly voices they had "outside" . . .

He jammed his feet back into the boots and plodded on through the dust that the horses' feet raised. There was no dust in Jerusalem. It made tears run out of his eyes. It burned the inside of his nose and gritted between his teeth. He coughed and panted and sneezed and limped for fifteen miles.

Just when he decided to go back he probably could not have told. Perhaps it was when the sergeant shouted at him for lagging behind in Montpelier to gaze open-mouthed into a shop window. There was a lady in it as beautiful as any of the pictures in *Godey's*. She had braids of hair the color of a young chick and she was wearing a scarlet shawl with a border that had every color you could think of in it. She was looking just over his head with enormous blue eyes and holding out her hand with a pink rose in it. There was another rose in her hair and her dress was skyblue. He was still waiting to see if she would move when the sergeant bellowed at him.

"You're not a wax figure," was what he said, "though you'd make a good one."

This remark was wasted on Jonathan as wit, but it succeeded in making him feel if anything more unhappy than ever. Perhaps the final decision came when he learned that army fare did not include ice cream—that mysterious delicacy. At any rate, when the volunteers were ready to take the train at the Junction the next morning, Jonathan was missing.

Two of the troopers were sent after him.

"He's gone home, of course," the lieutenant said. "Where else would he go? You'll soon pick him up."

There was another troop train leaving that afternoon. They could travel by that, he said, and the troopers galloped off into the dust, not without exchanging a few remarks about homesick louts who deserted.

In his bare feet Jonathan had travelled fast. He followed the road at night, but when dawn came, he went 'cross-lots, wading brooks and splashing through swamps. Once he missed his way, but he had gone through the first gate and was plodding wearily up to Jerusalem when he heard horses behind him. A moment before he had been dragging his feet, wondering if he could take another step; now he ran, but though the trees began to move faster, the hoofbeats grew louder. They had to stop at the gate. He could hear the troopers cursing. The few moments while the gate was being opened were the ones he needed. He reached the hollow log just in time, shoved his boots and his bundle into it, crawled in himself, and lay there panting.

He heard the horses come scrabbling up the rocky slope, then their feet go *squelch, squelch,* in the soft spot, and the squeak of leather and a hoof ringing suddenly on a stone. He heard the trooper say: "Come up, you brute. I'll teach you to shy at your shadow," and the horses panting as they galloped through the mud. Then there was the pause at the upper gate and soon there was the sound of hoofs going *thud thock, thud thock,* on the firm turf.

Jonathan did not move after they were gone. He even slept a little while they were in the valley hunting for him. They gave it up after an hour or so. Aunt Debby was so evidently and honestly surprised by their visit, answered their questions with such frankness, fed them so generously on plain doughnuts and maple syrup and a partridge that she had shot herself, that they soon ceased to mistrust her. She prescribed some yarb tea for the discomfort that the fat trooper experienced after meals, and would not take a penny for it.

They asked at the other cabins, but no one had seen Jonathan. They got very muddy tramping through a swamp to get to a cave on Little Wildcat. It was the thin trooper's idea that there might be a cave and all the boys in the village were delighted to show it to the soldiers. The fat trooper was tired of this idea long before they reached the cave which was not much more than one rock leaning against another and as empty as a broken whiskey bottle.

This was what the fat trooper puffed out and he added that these folks had certainly not seen the boy and that he was of the opinion that the army was well rid of him.

"He's probably hiding in these woods somewhere, but we might as well hunt for a chipmunk in a stone wall. Wherever we'd be, he'd be somewhere else," the thin one said.

The fat one agreed, and added that the thing to do was to ride back to Montpelier and have dinner at the Pavilion. They must not miss that train, he said conscientiously, and if the boy had stopped for the night somewhere, as he probably had, they'd meet him on the road, wouldn't they?

So they set off. Jonathan, still in

131

the soft coolness of the log, heard the horses go past him down the hill. He lay there for a long time listening to make sure that they had really gone. At last he started to crawl out, but a noise in the woods set his heart beating hard. Could one of them be sneaking back to catch him? Then he heard a hen partridge talking to her chicks. The noise was only the covey among the leaves.

At last he was out, the blood singing in his ears, his eyes dazzled by the sun spattering through the maples, his knees stiff, pins and needles prickling in his feet.

Aunt Debby showed no surprise when his shadow cut off the sunlight from her door.

"Thought you might be back, Jonathan," was all she said. "I've got water hot. Guess you might like to wash your feet."

He soaked them in the hot suds, ate the food she brought him.

"It's big, outside," he said once; and later: "There was a shawl in a store window in the city. Red. Awful bright—and a lot of other colors in the edge of it. Like the leaves when they turn. You ought to have a shawl for winter."

"There's plenty of fine things outside," Aunt Debby said, in a tone of strict neutrality, "and there are those that like it there."

Jonathan went on pouring maple syrup into the holes of a doughnut. He got up after a while and walked out into the valley. He looked at the cabins with the traces of seed corn hanging beside the doors, at the gardens on the hillside with the corn in shocks and the pumpkins shining in the sunlight, at the place on Owl's Head where he shot the bear, at the children playing around the schoolhouse. He listened to the gurgle of

the spring and to the crows in the pines, to women turning spinning wheels and singing, to the sheep running on the turf, to the schoolbell calling the children in from their game. He took long breaths of air that smelled faintly of balsam and wood smoke and wet leaves.

He walked to the graveyard under the apple trees and leaned on the fence, looking down at the gray stones among the ground pine and myrtle. There was an apple at the top of the tree that the pickers had left.

"No, not left," Jonathan thought. "They couldn't reach it."

A gust of soft wind shook the tree and the apple fell at his feet. He picked it up and bit into its red cheek. No apples are so tart and sweet and juicy all at once as apples in Jerusalem.

With the taste of the apple still in his mouth and the picture of Jerusalem clear now in his mind beside the picture of the world outside it, he walked back to the cabin.

His aunt was sitting on the doorstep smoking. His bundle of clothes, his boots with the laces knotted together, the tin dinner pail that he used to carry to school, were beside her on the doorstep. He hung the boots around his neck, picked up the bundle and the pail, and stood for a moment looking down at his aunt's small brown figure.

At last he said, "Good-bye, Aunt Debby," and she nodded the way she did when she was pleased and said, "Good-bye," Jonathan."

Then he went back and fought all through the war.

"I see," says the visitor, eating raspberries from the tangle of bushes that are growing up among Aunt

Debby's lilacs—no raspberries distill sunshine into sweetness as raspberries do in Jerusalem—"he had to test the strange things by the familiar ones."

"He had to touch earth—his earth," says someone else, "you know, like that giant. We all have to, sometimes—to live."

"Did he come back?" asks the visitor, carefully lifting up a tiger-lily blossom to look into its freckled face. (Evidently the right sort of visitor to bring to Jerusalem. Once there was one who picked them. Mrs. Appleyard doesn't know where she is now.)

"Not to stay," Mrs. Appleyard says, "but I think he must have come to see her because one of the old women in the village—she used to come up here for water from the spring when she was a child—told me that she had often seen Aunt Debby sitting smoking and wearing her Paisley shawl. It was a Paisley with a scarlet centre, she said."

THE FLAG

ANONYMOUS

There's no coward stripe upon it,
And no shame is written on it,
All the blood that's in its crimson
Is the blood of manhood true;
There's no base and brutal glory
Woven sadly in its story.
It's a bright flag and a right flag,
And the flag for me and you.

It's the flag without a fetter;
It's the flag of manhood better;
It has never done a mean thing,
Never waved above a brute;
Greed and hate it never shielded,
Unto wrong it never yielded.
It's a fine flag, a divine flag
That in reverence we salute.

It's the flag of all the glory
That is written in man's story;
It's the emblem of his freedom
And the hope of men oppressed;
It asks no disgraceful duty,
Never stains with shame its beauty.
It's a pure flag, and a sure flag,
It is our flag and the best.

133

WORDS OF GREAT AMERICANS:

BE CIVIL to all; serviceable to many; friend to one; enemy to none.

THE EARLY morning has gold in its mouth.

HISTORY is full of the errors of states and princes.

DON'T SING your triumph before you have conquered.

AFTER CROSSES and losses, men grow humbler and wiser.

IF YOU WOULD not be forgotten as soon as you are dead, either write things worth reading or do things worth writing.

DOING AN INJURY puts you below your enemy; revenging one makes you even with him; forgiving it sets you above him.

HE THAT IDLY LOSES five shillings' worth of time, loses five shillings, and might as prudently throw five shillings into the sea.

BEING IGNORANT is not so much a shame as being unwilling to learn.

THE BIGGEST TREES do not always bear the most fruit.

IF YOUR RICHES are yours, why don't you take them with you to t'other world?

BEWARE of little expenses; a small leak will sink a great ship.

LOVE your neighbor; yet don't pull down your hedge.

GREAT talkers, little doers.

BENJAMIN FRANKLIN

FOREWARNED, forearmed.

MANY WORDS won't fill a bushel.

CONSTANT dropping wears away stones.

IF YOU WOULD keep your secret from an enemy,
tell it not to a friend.

ANGER is never without a reason, but seldom with a good one.

THE HONEST MAN takes pains, and then enjoys pleasures;
the knave takes pleasure, and then suffers pains.

IDLENESS AND PRIDE tax with a heavier hand than kings and parliaments. If
we can get rid of the former, we may easily bear the latter.

AFTER INDUSTRY AND FRUGALITY, nothing contributes more to the raising of
a young man in the world than punctuality and justice in all his dealings.

EXPERIENCE keeps a dear school, but fools will learn in no other.

BETTER is little with content, than much with contention.

HE THAT PURSUES two hares at once does not catch one
and lets t'other go.

HE THAT can compose himself is wiser than he that composes books.

CARELESSNESS does more harm than a want of knowledge.

BETTER slip with foot than tongue.

DANIEL BOONE*

ARTHUR GUITERMAN

Daniel Boone at twenty-one
Came with his tomahawk, knife and gun
Home from the French and Indian War
To North Carolina and the Yadkin shore.
He married his maid with a golden band,
Builded his house and cleared his land;
But the deep woods claimed their son again
And he turned his face from the homes of men.
Over the Blue Ridge, dark and lone,
The Mountains of Iron, the Hills of Stone,
Braving the Shawnee's jealous wrath,
He made his way on the Warrior's Path.
Alone he trod the shadowed trails;
But he was the lord of a thousand vales
As he roved Kentucky, far and near,
Hunting the buffalo, elk and deer.
What joy to see, what joy to win
So fair a land for his kith and kin,
Of streams unstained and woods unhewn!
"Elbowroom!" laughed Daniel Boone.

On the Wilderness Road that his axmen made
The settlers flocked to the first stockade;
The deerskin shirts and the coonskin caps
Filed through the glens and the mountain gaps;
And hearts were high in the fateful spring
When the land said "Nay!" to the stubborn king.
While the men of the East of farm and town
Strove with the troops of the British Crown,
Daniel Boone from a surge of hate
Guarded a nation's westward gate.
Down on the fort in a wave of flame
The Shawnee horde and the Mingo came,
And the stout logs shook in a storm of lead;
But Boone stood firm and the savage fled.
Peace! And the settlers flocked anew,
The farm lands spread, the town lands grew;
But Daniel Boone was ill at ease
When he saw the smoke in the forest trees.
"There'll be no game in the country soon.
Elbowroom!" cried Daniel Boone.

Straight as a pine at sixty-five—
Time enough for a man to thrive—
He launched his bateau on Ohio's breast
And his heart was glad as he oared it west;
There were kindly folk and his own true blood
Where great Missouri rolls his flood;
New woods, new streams and room to spare,
And Daniel Boone found comfort there.
Yet far he ranged toward the sunset still,
Where the Kansas runs and the Smoky Hill,
And the prairies toss, by the south wind blown;
And he killed his bear on the Yellowstone.
But ever he dreamed of new domains
With vaster woods and wider plains;
Ever he dreamed of a world-to-be
Where there are no bounds and the soul is free.
At four-score-five, still stout and hale,
He heard a call to a farther trail;
So he turned his face where the stars are strewn;
"Elbowroom!" sighed Daniel Boone.

Down the Milky Way in its banks of blue
Far he has paddled his white canoe
To the splendid quest of the tameless soul—
He has reached the goal where there is no goal.
Now he rides and rides an endless trail
On the Hippograff of the flaming tail
Or the Horse of the Stars with the golden mane,
As he rode the first of the blue-grass strain.
The joy that lies in the Search he seeks
On breathless hills with crystal peaks;
He makes his camp on heights untrod,
The steps of the shrine, alone with God.
Through the woods of the vast, on the plains of Space
He hunts the pride of the Mammoth race
And the Dinosaur of the triple horn,
The Manticore and the Unicorn,
As once by the broad Missouri's flow
He followed the elk and the buffalo,
East of the Sun and west of the Moon,
"Elbowroom!" laughs Daniel Boone.

*Taken from I SING THE PIONEER by Arthur Guiterman, published and copyright by E. P. DUTTON & CO., INC. New York. Copyright 1926.

The Pony Express

By SAMUEL CLEMENS

In this excerpt from Roughing It, *Samuel Clemens vividly presents the West that was.*

In a little while all interest was taken up in stretching our necks and watching for the pony-rider—the fleet messenger who sped across the continent from St. Joe to Sacramento, carrying letters nineteen hundred miles in eight days!

Think of that for perishable horse and human flesh and blood to do! The pony-rider was usually a little bit of a man, brimful of spirit and endurance. No matter what time of the day or night his watch came on, and no matter whether it was winter or summer, raining, snowing, hailing, or sleeting, or whether his beat was a level straight road or a crazy trail over mountain crags and precipices, or whether it led through peaceful regions or regions that swarmed with hostile Indians, he must be always ready to leap into the saddle and be off like the wind! There was no idling-time for a pony-rider on duty. He rode fifty miles without stopping, by daylight, moonlight, star-light, or through the blackness of darkness —just as it happened. He rode a splendid horse that was born for a racer and fed and lodged like a gentleman; kept him at his utmost speed for ten miles, and then, as he came crashing up to the station where stood two men holding fast a fresh, impatient steed, the transfer of rider and mail-bag was made in the twinkling of an eye, and away flew the eager pair and were out of sight before the spectator could get hardly the ghost of a look. Both rider and horse went flying light. The rider's dress was thin, and fitted close; he wore a roundabout, and a skull-cap, and tucked his pantaloons into his boot-tops like a race-rider. He carried no arms—he carried nothing that was not absolutely necessary, for even the postage on his literary freight was worth *five dollars a letter*. He got but little frivolous correspondence to carry— his bag had business letters in it, mostly. His horse was stripped of all unnecessary weight, too. He wore a little wafer of a racing-saddle, and no visible blanket. He wore light shoes, or none at all. The little flat mail-pockets strapped under the rider's thighs would each hold about the bulk of a child's primer. They held many and many an important business chapter and newspaper letter, but these were written on paper as airy and thin as gold-leaf, nearly, and thus bulk and weight were economized. The stage-coach traveled about a hundred to a hundred and twenty-five miles a day (twenty-four hours), the pony-rider about two hundred and fifty. There were about eighty pony-riders in the saddle all the time, night and day, stretching in a long, scattering procession from Missouri to California, forty flying eastward, and forty toward the west, and among them making four hundred gallant horses earn a stirring livelihood and see a deal of scenery every single day in the year.

We had had a consuming desire, from the beginning, to see a pony-rider, but somehow or other all that passed us and all that met us managed to streak by in the night, and so we heard only a whiz and a hail, and the swift phantom of the desert was gone before we could get our heads out of the windows. But now we were expecting one along every moment, and would see him in broad daylight. Presently the driver exclaims:

"HERE HE COMES!"

Every neck is stretched further, and every eye strained wider. Away across the endless dead level of the prairie a black speck appears against the sky, and it is plain that it moves. Well, I should think so! In a second or two it becomes a horse and rider, rising and falling, rising and falling—sweeping toward us nearer and nearer—growing more and more distinct, more and more sharply defined—nearer and still nearer, and the flutter of the hoofs comes faintly to the ear—another instant a whoop and a hurrah from our upper deck, a wave of the rider's hand, but no reply, and man and horse burst past our excited faces, and go swinging away like a belated fragment of a storm!

So sudden is it all, and so like a flash of unreal fancy, that but for the flake of white foam left quivering and perishing on a mail-sack after the vision had flashed by and disappeared, we might have doubted whether we had seen any actual horse and man at all, maybe.

We rattled through Scott's Bluffs Pass, by and by. It was along here somewhere that we first came across genuine and unmistakable alkali water in the road, and we cordially hailed it as a first-class curiosity, and a thing to be mentioned with *éclat* in letters to the ignorant at home. This water gave the road a soapy appearance, and in many places the ground looked as if it had been whitewashed. I think the strange alkali water excited us as much as any wonder we had come upon yet, and I know we felt very complacent and conceited, and better satisfied with life after we had added it to our list of things which *we* had seen and some other people had not. In a small way we were the same sort of simpletons as those who climb unnecessarily the perilous peaks of Mont Blanc and the Matterhorn, and derive no pleasure from it except the reflection that it isn't a common experience. But once in a while one of those parties trips and comes darting down the long mountain crags in a sitting posture, making the crusted snow smoke behind him, flitting from bench to bench, and from terrace to terrace, jarring the earth where he strikes, and still glancing and flitting on again, sticking an iceberg into himself every now and then, and tearing his clothes, snatching at things to save himself, taking hold of trees and fetching them along with him, roots and all, starting little rocks now and then, then big boulders, then acres of ice and snow and patches of forest, gathering and still gathering as he goes, and adding and still adding to his massed and sweeping grandeur as he nears a three-thousand-foot precipice, till at last he waves his hat magnificently and rides into eternity on the back of a raging and tossing avalanche!

This is all very fine, but let us not be carried away by excitement, but

139

ask calmly, how does this person feel about it in his cooler moments next day, with six or seven thousand feet of snow and stuff on top of him?

We crossed the sand-hills near the scene of the Indian mail robbery and massacre of 1856, wherein the driver and conductor perished, and also all the passengers but one, it was supposed; but this must have been a mistake, for at different times afterward on the Pacific coast I was personally acquainted with a hundred and thirty-three or four people who were wounded during that massacre, and barely escaped with their lives. There was no doubt of the truth of it—I had it from their own lips. One of these parties told me that he kept coming across arrow-heads in his system for nearly seven years after the massacre; and another of them told me that he was stuck so literally full of arrows that after the Indians were gone and he could raise up and examine himself, he could not restrain his tears, for his clothes were completely ruined.

The most trustworthy tradition avers, however, that only one man, a person named Babbitt, survived the massacre, and he was desperately wounded. He dragged himself on his hands and knee (for one leg was broken) to a station several miles away. He did it during portions of two nights, lying concealed one day and part of another, and for more than forty hours suffering unimaginable anguish from hunger, thirst, and bodily pain. The Indians robbed the coach of everything it contained, including quite an amount of treasure.

PRAIRIE

Carl Sandburg

I was born on the prairie and the milk of its wheat, the red of its clover, the eyes of its women, gave me a song and a slogan.

Here the water went down, the icebergs slid with gravel, the gaps and the valleys hissed, and the black loam came, and the yellow sandy loam.
Here between the sheds of the Rocky Mountains and the Appalachians, here now a morning star fixes a fire sign over the timber claims and cow pastures, the corn belt, the cotton belt, the cattle ranches.
Here the gray geese go five hundred miles and back with a wind under their wings honking the cry for a new home.
Here I know I will hanker after nothing so much as one more sunrise or a sky moon of fire doubled to a river moon of water.

The prairie sings to me in the forenoon and I know in the night I rest easy in the prairie arms, on the prairie heart.

After the sunburn of the day
handling a pitchfork at a hayrack,
after the eggs and biscuit and coffee,
the pearl-gray haystacks

in the gloaming
are cool prayers
to the harvest hands.

In the city among the walls the overland passenger train is choked and the
pistons hiss and the wheels curse.
On the prairie the overland flits on phantom wheels and the sky and the
soil between them muffle the pistons and cheer the wheels.

I am here when the cities are gone.
I am here before the cities come.
I nourished the lonely men on horses.
I will keep the laughing men who ride iron.
I am dust of men.

The running water babbled to the deer, the cottontail, the gopher.
You came in wagons, making streets and schools,
Kin of the ax and rifle, kin of the plow and horse,
Singing *Yankee Doodle, Old Dan Tucker, Turkey in the Straw,*
You in the coonskin cap at a log house door hearing a lone wolf howl,
You at a sod house door reading the blizzards and chinooks let loose from
Medicine Hat,
I am dust of your dust, as I am brother and mother
To the copper faces, the worker in flint and clay,
The singing women and their sons a thousand years ago
Marching single file the timber and the plain.

I hold the dust of these amid changing stars.
I last while old wars are fought, while peace broods mother-like,
While new wars arise and the fresh killings of young men.
I fed the boys who went to France in great dark days.
Appomattox is a beautiful word to me and so is Valley Forge and the Marne
and Verdun,
I who have seen the red births and the red deaths
Of sons and daughters, I take peace or war, I say nothing and wait.

Have you seen a red sunset drip over one of my cornfields, the shore of
night stars, the wave lines of dawn up a wheat valley?
Have you heard my threshing crews yelling in the chaff of a strawpile and
the running wheat of the wagon-boards, my cornhuskers, my harvest
hands hauling crops, singing dreams of women, worlds, horizons?

Rivers cut a path on flat lands.
The mountains stand up.
The salt oceans press in

141

And push on the coast lines.
The sun, the wind, bring rain
And I know what the rainbow writes across the east or
west in a half-circle:
A love-letter pledge to come again.

Towns on the Soo Line,
Towns on the Big Muddy,
Laugh at each other for cubs
And tease as children.

Omaha and Kansas City, Minneapolis and St. Paul, sisters in a house together, throwing slang, growing up.
Towns in the Ozarks, Dakota wheat towns, Wichita, Peoria, Buffalo, sisters
throwing slang, growing up.

Out of prairie-brown grass crossed with a streamer of wigwam smoke—out
of a smoke pillar, a blue promise—out of wild ducks woven in greens
and purples—
Here I saw a city rise and say to the people's round world: Listen, I am strong,
I know what I want.
Out of log houses and stumps—canoes stripped from tree-sides—flatboats
coaxed with an ax from the timber claims—in the years when the red
and the white men met—the houses and streets rose.

A thousand red men cried and went away to new places for corn and women:
a million white men came and put up skyscrapers, threw out rails and
wires, feelers to the salt sea: now the smokestacks bite the skyline with
stub teeth.

In an early year the call of a wild duck woven in greens and purples: now
the riveter's chatter, the police patrol, the song-whistle of the steamboat.

To a man across a thousand years I offer a handshake.
I say to him: Brother, make the story short, for the stretch of a thousand
years is short.

What brothers these in the dark?
What eaves of skyscrapers against a smoke moon?
These chimneys shaking on the lumber shanties
When the coal boats plow by on the river—
The hunched shoulders of the grain elevators—
The flame sprockets of the sheet steel mills
And the men in the rolling mills with their shirts off

Playing their flesh arms against the twisting wrists of steel:
>   what brothers these
>   in the dark
>   of a thousand years?

A headlight searches a snowstorm.
A funnel of white light shoots from over the pilot of the Pioneer Limited
    crossing Wisconsin.

In the morning hours, in the dawn,
The sun puts out the stars of the sky
And the headlight of the Limited train.

The fireman waves his hand to a country school teacher on a bobsled.
A boy, yellow hair, red scarf and mittens, on the bobsled, in his lunch box
    a pork chop sandwich and a V of gooseberry pie.

The horses fathom a snow to their knees.
Snow hats are on the rolling prairie hills.
The Mississippi bluffs wear snow hats.

Keep your hogs on changing corn and mashes of grain,
>   O farmerman.
>   Cram their insides till they waddle on short legs
>   Under the drums of bellies, hams of fat.
>   Kill your hogs with a knife slit under the ear.
>   Hack them with cleavers.
>   Hang them with hooks in the hind legs.

A wagonload of radishes on a summer morning.
Sprinkles of dew on the crimson-purple balls.
The farmer on the seat dangles the reins on the rumps of dapple-gray horses.
The farmer's daughter with a basket of eggs dreams of a new hat to wear to
    the county fair.

On the left- and right-hand side of the road,
>   Marching corn—
I saw it knee high weeks ago—now it is head high—tassels of red silk creep
    at the ends of the ears.

I am the prairie, mother of men, waiting.
They are mine, the threshing crews eating beefsteak, the farmboys driving
    steers to the railroad cattle pens.
They are mine, the crowds of people at a Fourth of July basket picnic,

listening to a lawyer read the Declaration of Independence, watching the pinwheels and Roman candles at night, the young men and women two by two hunting the bypaths and kissing bridges.

They are mine, the horses looking over a fence in the frost of late October saying good-morning to the horses hauling wagons of rutabaga to market.

They are mine, the old zigzag rail fences, the new barb wire.

The cornhuskers wear leather on their hands.
There is no let-up to the wind.
Blue bandannas are knotted at the ruddy chins.

Falltime and winter apples take on the smolder of the five-o'clock November sunset: falltime, leaves, bonfires, stubble, the old things go, and the earth is grizzled.

The land and the people hold memories, even among the anthills and the angleworms, among the toads and woodroaches—among gravestone writings rubbed out by the rain—they keep old things that never grow old.

The frost loosens corn husks.
The sun, the rain, the wind
          loosen corn husks.
The men and women are helpers.
They are all cornhuskers together.
I see them late in the western evening
          in a smoke-red dust.

The phantom of a yellow rooster flaunting a scarlet comb, on top of a dung pile crying hallelujah to the streaks of daylight,

The phantom of an old hunting dog nosing in the underbrush for muskrats, barking at a coon in a treetop at midnight, chewing a bone, chasing his tail round a corncrib,

The phantom of an old workhorse taking the steel point of a plow across a forty-acre field in spring, hitched to a harrow in summer, hitched to a wagon among cornshocks in fall,

These phantoms come into the talk and wonder of people on the front porch of a farmhouse late summer nights.

"The shapes that are gone are here," said an old man with a cob pipe in his teeth one night in Kansas with a hot wind on the alfalfa.

Look at six eggs
In a mockingbird's nest.

Listen to six mockingbird's

Flinging follies of O-be-joyful
Over the marshes and uplands.

Look at songs
Hidden in eggs.

When the morning sun is on the trumpet-vine blossoms, sing at the kitchen
    pans: *Shout All Over God's Heaven.*
When the rain slants on the potato hills and the sun plays a silver shaft on the
    last shower, sing to the bush at the backyard fence: *Mighty Lak a Rose.*
When the icy sleet pounds on the storm windows and the house lifts to a
    great breath, sing for the outside hills: *The Ole Sheep Done Know the Road,*
    the Young Lambs Must Find the Way.

Spring slips back with a girl face calling always: "Any new songs for me?
    Any new songs?"

O prairie girl, be lonely, singing, dreaming, waiting—your lover comes—
    your child comes—the years creep with toes of April rain on new-
    turned sod.
O prairie girl, whoever leaves you only crimson poppies to talk with, who-
    ever puts a good-bye kiss on your lips and never comes back—
There is a song deep as the falltime redhaws, long as the layer of black
    loam we go to, the shine of the morning star over the corn belt, the
    wave line of dawn up a wheat valley.

O prairie mother, I am one of your boys.
I have loved the prairie as a man with a heart shot full of pain over love.
Here I know I will hanker after nothing so much as one more sunrise or a
    sky moon of fire doubled to a river moon of water.

I speak of new cities and new people.
I tell you the past is a bucket of ashes.
I tell you yesterday is a wind gone down, a sun dropped in the west.
I tell you there is nothing in the world only an ocean of tomorrows, a
    sky of tomorrows.

I am a brother of the cornhuskers who say at sundown:
              Tomorrow is a day.

WORDS OF GREAT AMERICANS:

THAT MAN is free who is protected from injury.

CONFIDENCE is a thing that cannot be produced by compulsion.

WHEN TILLAGE BEGINS, other arts follow. The farmers therefore are the founders of human civilization.

HUMAN THOUGHT is the process by which human ends are ultimately answered.

I SHALL DEFER MY VISIT to Faneuil Hall, the cradle of American liberty, until its doors shall fly open on golden hinges to lovers of Union as well as lovers of liberty.

WE HAVE THE GOOD FORTUNE, under the blessing of a benign Providence, to live in a country which we are proud of for many things,—for its independence, for its public liberty, for its free institutions, for its public spirit, for its enlightened patriotism; but we are proud also,—and it is among those things we should be the most proud of,—we are proud of its public justice, of its sound faith, of its substantially correct morals in the administration of the Government, and the general conduct of the country, since she took her place among the nations of the world.

WASHINGTON—a fixed star in the firmament of great names, shining without twinkling or obscuration, with clear, beneficent light.

A SENSE OF DUTY pursues us ever. It is omnipresent, like the Deity. If we take to ourselves the wings of the morning, and dwell in the uttermost parts of the sea, duty performed or duty violated is still with us, for our happiness or our misery. If we say the darkness shall cover us, in the darkness as in the light our obligations are yet with us.

IT IS MY LIVING SENTIMENT, and, by the blessing of God, it shall be my dying sentiment,—INDEPENDENCE *now*, and INDEPENDENCE FOREVER!

KNOWLEDGE IS the only fountain both of the love and the principles of human liberty.

146

DANIEL WEBSTER

THANK GOD! I—also—am an American!

LIBERTY *and* Union, now and forever, one and inseparable!

A SOLEMN AND RELIGIOUS REGARD for spiritual and eternal things
is an indispensable element of all true greatness.

I WAS BORN an American; I will live an American; I shall die an American.

FOR OUR COUNTRY, she yet lives,—she ever dwells in our hearts, and it will, even
at that solemn moment, go up as our last aspiration to Heaven, that she may
be immortal!

WE WISH THAT THIS COLUMN, rising towards heaven among the pointed spires
of so many temples dedicated to God, may contribute also to produce in all
minds a pious feeling of dependence and gratitude. We wish, finally, that the
last object to the sight of him who leaves his native shore, and the first to gladden
his who revisits it, may be something which shall remind him of the liberty and
the glory of his country. Let it rise! Let it rise, till it meet the sun in his coming;
let the earliest light of the morning gild it, and parting day linger and play on
its summit!

LABOUR IN THIS COUNTRY is independent and proud. It has not to ask the patron-
age of capital, but capital solicits the aid of labour.

MEN HANG OUT THEIR SIGNS indicative of their respective trades: shoemakers
hang out a gigantic shoe; jewelers, a monster watch; and the dentist hangs
out a gold tooth; but up in the mountains of New Hampshire, God Almighty
has hung out a sign to show that there He makes men.

THERE IS NOTHING so powerful as truth,—and often nothing so strange.

JUSTICE, SIR, is the great interest of man on earth.

ONE COUNTRY, one constitution, one destiny.

From Life on the Mississippi

By SAMUEL CLEMENS

In this episode from one of his well-known books,
Samuel Clemens takes a lesson in piloting.

*W*HEN I RETURNED to the pilot-house St. Louis was gone, and I was lost. Here was a piece of river which was all down in my book, but I could make neither head nor tail of it: you understand, it was turned around. I had seen it when coming up-stream, but I had never faced about to see how it looked when it was behind me. My heart broke again, for it was plain that I had got to learn this troublesome river *both ways*.

The pilot-house was full of pilots, going down to "look at the river." What is called the "upper river" (the two hundred miles between St. Louis and Cairo, where the Ohio comes in) was low; and the Mississippi changes its channel so constantly that the pilots used to always find it necessary to run down to Cairo to take a fresh look, when their boats were to lie in port a week; that is, when the water was at a low stage. A deal of this "looking at the river" was done by poor fellows who seldom had a berth, and whose only hope of getting one lay in their being always freshly posted and therefore ready to drop into the shoes of some reputable pilot, for a single trip, on account of such a pilot's sudden illness, or some other necessity. And a good many of them constantly ran up and down inspecting the river, not because they ever really hoped to get a berth, but because (they being guests of the boat) it was cheaper to "look at the river" than stay ashore and pay board. In time these fellows grew dainty in their tastes, and only in-fested boats that had an established reputation for setting good tables. All visiting pilots were useful, for they were always ready and willing, winter or summer, night or day, to go out in the yawl and help buoy the channel or assist the boat's pilots in any way they could. They were like-wise welcomed because all pilots are tireless talkers, when gathered to-gether, and as they talk only about the river they are always understood and are always interesting. Your true pilot cares nothing about anything on earth but the river, and his pride in his occupation surpasses the pride of kings.

We had a fine company of these river inspectors along this trip. There were eight or ten, and there was abundance of room for them in our great pilot-house. Two or three of them wore polished silk hats, elab-orate shirtfronts, diamond breastpins, kid gloves, and patent-leather boots. They were choice in their English, and bore themselves with a dignity proper to men of solid means and prodigious reputation as pilots. The others were more or less loosely clad, and wore upon their heads tall felt cones that were suggestive of the days of the Commonwealth.

I was a cipher in this august com-

148

pany, and felt subdued, not to say torpid. I was not even of sufficient consequence to assist at the wheel when it was necessary to put the tiller hard down in a hurry; the guest that stood nearest did that when occasion required—and this was pretty much all the time, because of the crookedness of the channel and the scant water. I stood in a corner; and the talk I listened to took the hope all out of me. One visitor said to another:

"Jim, how did you run Plum Point, coming up?"

"It was in the night, there, and I ran it the way one of the boys on the *Diana* told me; started out about fifty yards above the wood-pile on the false point, and held on the cabin under Plum Point till I raised the reef-quarter less twain—then straightened up for the middle bar till I got well abreast the old one-limbed cottonwood in the bend, then got my stern on the cottonwood, and head on the low place above the point, and came through a-booming —nine and a half."

"Pretty square crossing, an't it!"

"Yes, but the upper bar's working down fast."

Another pilot spoke up and said:

"I had better water than that, and ran it lower down; started out from the false point—mark twain—raised the second reef abreast the big snag in the bend, and had quarter less twain."

One of the gorgeous ones remarked:

"I don't want to find fault with your leadsmen, but that's a good deal of water for Plum Point, it seems to me."

There was an approving nod all around as this quiet snub dropped on the boaster and "settled" him. And so they went on talk-talk-talk-ing. Meantime, the thing that was running in my mind was, "Now, if my ears hear aright, I have not only to get the names of all the towns and islands and bends, and so on, by heart, but I must even get up a warm personal acquaintanceship with every old snag and one-limbed cottonwood and obscure wood-pile that ornaments the banks of this river for twelve hundred miles; and more than that, I must actually know where these things are in the dark, unless these guests are gifted with eyes that can pierce through two miles of solid blackness. I wish the piloting business was in Jericho and I had never thought of it."

At dusk Mr. Bixby tapped the big bell three times (the signal to land), and the captain emerged from his drawing-room in the forward end of the "texas," and looked up inquiringly. Mr. Bixby said:

"We will lay up here all night, captain."

"Very well, sir."

That was all. The boat came to shore and was tied up for the night. It seemed to me a fine thing that the pilot could do as he pleased, without asking so grand a captain's permission. I took my supper and went immediately to bed, discouraged by my day's observations and experiences. My late voyage's notebooking was but a confusion of meaningless names. It had tangled me all up in a knot every time I had looked at it in the daytime. I now hoped for respite in sleep; but no, it reveled all through my head till sunrise again, a frantic and tireless nightmare.

Next morning I felt pretty rusty and low-spirited. We went booming along, taking a good many chances, for we were anxious to "get out of the river" (as getting out to Cairo

149

was called) before night should overtake us. But Mr. Bixby's partner, the other pilot, presently grounded the boat, and we lost so much time getting her off that it was plain the darkness would overtake us a good long way above the mouth. This was a great misfortune, especially to certain of our visiting pilots, whose boats would have to wait for their return, no matter how long that might be. It sobered the pilot-house talk a good deal. Coming up-stream, pilots did not mind low water or any kind of darkness; nothing stopped them but fog. But down-stream work was different; a boat was too nearly helpless, with a stiff current pushing behind her; so it was not customary to run down-stream at night in low water.

There seemed to be one small hope, however: if we could get through the intricate and dangerous Hat Island crossing before night, we could venture the rest, for we would have plainer sailing and better water. But it would be insanity to attempt Hat Island at night. So there was a deal of looking at watches all the rest of the day, and a constant ciphering upon the speed we were making; Hat Island was the eternal subject; sometimes hope was high and sometimes we were delayed in a bad crossing, and down it went again. For hours all hands lay under the burden of this suppressed excitement; it was even communicated to me, and I got to feeling so solicitous about Hat Island, and under such an awful pressure of responsibility, that I wished I might have five minutes on shore to draw a good, full, relieving breath, and start over again. We were standing no regular watches. Each of our pilots ran such portions of the river as he had run

when coming up-stream, because of his greater familiarity with it; but both remained in the pilot-house constantly.

An hour before sunset Mr. Bixby took the wheel, and Mr. W. stepped aside. For the next thirty minutes every man held his watch in his hand and was restless, silent, and uneasy. At last somebody said, with a doomful sigh:

"Well, yonder's Hat Island—and we can't make it."

All the watches closed with a snap, everybody sighed and muttered something about its being "too bad, too bad—ah, if we could *only* have got here half an hour sooner!" and the place was thick with the atmosphere of disappointment. Some started to go out, but loitered, hearing no bell-tap to land. The sun dipped behind the horizon, the boat went on. Inquiring looks passed from one guest to another; and one who had his hand on the door-knob and had turned it, waited, then presently took away his hand and let the knob turn back again. We bore steadily down the bend. More looks were exchanged, and nods of surprised admiration—but no words. Insensibly the men drew together behind Mr. Bixby, as the sky darkened and one or two dim stars came out. The dead silence and sense of waiting became oppressive. Mr. Bixby pulled the cord, and two deep, mellow notes from the big bell floated off on the night. Then a pause, and one more note was struck. The watchman's voice followed, from the hurricane-deck:

"Labboard lead, there! Stabboard lead!"

The cries of the leadsmen began to rise out of the distance, and were gruffly repeated by the word-passers on the hurricane-deck.

"M-a-r-k three! M-a-r-k three! Quarter-less-three! Half twain! Quarter twain! M-a-r-k twain! Quarter-less—"

Mr. Bixby pulled two bell-ropes, and was answered by faint jinglings far below in the engine-room, and our speed slackened. The steam began to whistle through the gauge-cocks. The cries of the leadsmen went on—and it is a weird sound, always, in the night. Every pilot in the lot was watching now, with fixed eyes, and talking under his breath. Nobody was calm and easy but Mr. Bixby. He would put his wheel down and stand on a spoke, and as the steamer swung into her (to me) utterly invisible marks—for we seemed to be in the midst of a wide and gloomy sea—he would meet and fasten her there. Out of the murmur of half-audible talk, one caught a coherent sentence now and then—such as:

"There; she's over the first reef all right!"

After a pause, another subdued voice:

"Her stern's coming down just *exactly* right, by *George!*"

"Now she's in the marks; over she goes!"

Somebody else muttered:

"Oh, it was done beautiful— *beautiful!*"

Now the engines were stopped altogether, and we drifted with the current. Not that I could see the boat drift, for I could not, the stars being all gone by this time. This drifting was the dismalest work; it held one's heart still. Presently I discovered a blacker gloom than that which surrounded us. It was the head of the island. We were closing right down upon it. We entered its deeper shadow, and so imminent seemed the peril that I was likely to suffocate; and I had the strongest impulse to do *something*, anything, to save the vessel. But still Mr. Bixby stood by his wheel, silent, intent as a cat, and all the pilots stood shoulder to shoulder at his back.

"She'll not make it!" somebody whispered.

The water grew shoaler and shoaler, by the leadsman's cries, till it was down to:

"Eight-and-a-half! E-i-g-h-t feet! E-i-g-h-t feet! Seven-and—"

Mr Bixby said warningly through his speaking-tube to the engineer:

"Stand by, now!"

"Ay, ay, sir!"

"Seven-and-a-half! Seven feet! *Six*-and—"

We touched bottom! Instantly Mr. Bixby set a lot of bells ringing, shouted through the tube, "*Now*, let her have it—every ounce you've got!" then to his partner, "Put her hard down! Snatch her! Snatch her!" The boat rasped and ground her way through the sand, hung upon the apex of disaster a single tremendous instant, and then over she went! And such a shout as went up at Mr. Bixby's back never loosened the roof of a pilot-house before!

There was no more trouble after that. Mr. Bixby was a hero that night; and it was some little time, too, before his exploit ceased to be talked about by river-men.

Fully to realize the marvelous precision required in laying the great steamer in her marks in that murky waste of water, one should know that not only must she pick her intricate way through snags and blind reefs, and then shave the head of the island so closely as to brush the overhanging foliage with her stern, but at one

151

place she must pass almost within arm's reach of a sunken and invisible wreck that would snatch the hull timbers from under her if she should strike it, and destroy a quarter of a million dollars' worth of steamboat and cargo in five minutes, and maybe a hundred and fifty human lives into the bargain.

The last remark I heard that night was a compliment to Mr. Bixby, uttered in soliloquy and with unction by one of our guests. He said:

"By the Shadow of Death, but he's a lightning pilot!"

AMERICA

SAMUEL FRANCIS SMITH

My country, 'tis of thee,
Sweet land of liberty,
    Of thee I sing;
Land where my fathers died,
Land of the pilgrim's pride,
From every mountain-side
    Let Freedom ring.

My native country, thee,
Land of the noble free,—
    Thy name I love;
I love thy rocks and rills,
Thy woods and templed hills:
My heart with rapture thrills
    Like that above.

Let music swell the breeze,
And ring from all the trees,
    Sweet Freedom's song:
Let mortal tongues awake,
Let all that breathe partake,
Let rocks their silence break,—
    The sound prolong.

Our fathers' God, to Thee,
Author of liberty,
    To Thee we sing;
Long may our land be bright
With Freedom's holy light;
Protect us by Thy might,
    Great God, our King.

O! SUSANNA

Stephen Foster

I came from Alabama
Wid my banjo on my knee;
I'm gwine to Louisiana,
My true love for to see.
It rained all night the day I left,
The weather it was dry,
The sun so hot I froze to death;
Susanna, don't you cry!

Chorus

> O! Susanna, O don't you cry for me;
> I've come from Alabama
> Wid my banjo on my knee!

I had a dream de odder night
When ebery t'ing was still;
I thought I saw Susanna
A-coming down the hill;
The buckwheat cake was in her mouth,
The tear was in her eye;
Says I, "I'm coming from the South,
Susanna, don't you cry!" (*Chorus.*)

I soon will be in New Orleans,
And den I'll look all round,
And when I find Susanna
I will fall upon the ground;
And if I do not find her
Dis darkie'll surely die,
And when I'm dead and buried,
Susanna, don't you cry!

Chorus

> O! Susanna, O don't you cry for me;
> I've come from Alabama
> Wid my banjo on my knee!

153

WORDS OF GREAT AMERICANS:

THIS WORLD is God's workshop for making men in.

HEAVEN will be inherited by every man who has heaven in his soul.

SUCCESS IS FULL of promise till men get it; and then it is a last year's nest, from which the bird has flown.

VICTORIES that are cheap are cheap. Those only are worth having, which come as the result of hard fighting.

IN THIS WORLD, it is not what we take up, but what we give up, that makes us rich.

A CONSERVATIVE YOUNG MAN has wound up his life before it was unreeled. We expect old men to be conservative; but when a nation's young men are so, its funeral bell is already rung.

IT IS TRIAL THAT PROVES one thing weak and another strong. A house built on the sand is, in fair weather, just as good as if builded on a rock. A cobweb is as good as the mightiest cable, when there is no strain upon it.

THERE IS no friendship, no love, like that of the parent for the child.

IN THE ORDINARY BUSINESS of life, industry can do anything which genius can do, and very many things which it cannot.

PRIVATE OPINION is weak, but public opinion is almost omnipotent.

THE HUMBLEST INDIVIDUAL exerts some influence, either for good or evil, upon others.

FAITH is nothing but spiritualized imagination.

GOOD HUMOR makes all things tolerable.

HENRY WARD BEECHER

No MAN is such a conqueror as the man
who has defeated himself.

No MAN is more cheated than the selfish man.

MEN must read for amusement as well as for knowledge.

IN THINGS pertaining to enthusiasm no man is sane who does not know how
to be insane on proper occasions.

A TOOL IS BUT THE EXTENSION of man's hand, and a machine is but a
complex tool. And he that invents a machine augments the power of
a man and the well-being of mankind.

IT IS NOT WORK THAT KILLS MEN; it is worry. Work is healthy; you can hardly
put more upon a man than he can bear. Worry is rust upon the blade. It is not
the revolution that destroys the machinery, but the friction. Fear secretes acids;
but love and trust are sweet juices.

WE ARE ALWAYS in the forge, or on the anvil; by trials, God is shaping
us for higher things.

GOD PLANTED FEAR IN THE SOUL as truly as He planted hope or
courage. Fear is a kind of bell, or gong, which rings the mind
into quick life and avoidance upon the approach of danger. It
is the soul's signal for rallying.

Now comes the mystery. (Henry Ward Beecher's dying words)

THE PHILOSOPHY of one century is the common sense of the next.

A MAN without mirth is like a wagon without springs.

CANT is the twin sister of hypocrisy.

An Ingenue of the Sierras

By BRET HARTE

$\mathcal{W}$E ALL HELD OUR BREATH as the coach rushed through the semidarkness of Galloper's Ridge. The vehicle itself was only a huge lumbering shadow; its side-lights were carefully extinguished, and Yuba Bill had just politely removed from the lips of an outside passenger even the cigar with which he had been ostentatiously exhibiting his coolness. For it had been rumored that the Ramon Martinez gang of road agents were laying for us on the second grade, and would time the passage of our lights across Galloper's in order to intercept us in the brush beyond. If we could cross the ridge without being seen, and so get through the brush before they reached it, we were safe. If they followed, it would only be a stern chase with the odds in our favor.

The huge vehicle swayed from side to side, rolled, dipped, and plunged, but Bill kept the track, as if, in the whispered words of the expressman, he could feel and smell the road he could no longer see. We knew that at times we hung perilously over the edge of slopes that eventually dropped a thousand feet sheer to the tops of the sugar-pines below, but we knew that Bill knew it also. The half visible heads of the horses, drawn wedge-wise together by the tightened reins, appeared to cleave the darkness like a ploughshare, held between his rigid hands. Even the hoofbeats of the six horses had fallen into a vague, monotonous, distant roll. Then the ridge was crossed, and we plunged into the still blacker obscurity of the brush. Rather we no longer seemed to move—it was only the phantom night that rushed by us.

The horses might have been submerged in some swift Lethean stream; nothing but the top of the coach and the rigid bulk of Yuba Bill rose above them. Yet even in that awful moment our speed was unslackened; it was as if Bill cared no longer to *guide* but only to drive, or as if the direction of his huge machine was determined by other hands than his. An incautious whisperer hazarded the paralyzing suggestion of our meeting another team. To our great astonishment Bill overheard it; to our greater astonishment he replied. "It 'ud be only a neck and neck race which would get to hell first," he said quietly. But we were relieved—for he had *spoken!* Almost simultaneously the wider turnpike began to glimmer faintly as a visible track before us; the wayside trees fell out of line, opened up, and dropped off one after another; we were on the broader tableland, out of danger, and apparently unperceived and unpursued.

Nevertheless, in the conversation that broke out again with the relighting of the lamps, and the comments, congratulations, and reminiscences that were freely exchanged, Yuba Bill preserved a dissatisfied and even resentful silence. The most generous praise of his skill and courage awoke no response. "I reckon the old man waz just spilin' for a fight, and

156

is feelin' disappointed," said a passenger. But those who knew that Bill had the true fighter's scorn for any purely purposeless conflict were more or less concerned and watchful of him. He would drive steadily for four or five minutes with thoughtfully knitted brows, but eyes still keenly observant under his slouched hat, and then, relaxing his strained attitude, would give way to a movement of impatience. "You ain't uneasy about anything, Bill, are you?" asked the expressman confidentially. Bill lifted his eyes with a slightly contemptuous surprise. "Not about anything ter *come*. It's what *hez* happened that I don't exactly *sabe*. I don't see no signs of Ramon's gang ever havin' been out at all, and ef they were out I don't see why they didn't go for us."

"The simple fact is that our ruse was successful," said an outside passenger. "They waited to see our lights on the ridge, and, not seeing them, missed us until we had passed. That's my opinion."

"You ain't puttin' any price on that opinion, air ye?" inquired Bill politely.

"No."

"'Cos thar's a comic paper in 'Frisco pays for them things, and I've seen worse things in it."

"Come off, Bill," retorted the passenger, slightly nettled by the tittering of his companions. "Then what did you put out the lights for?"

"Well," returned Bill grimly, "it mout have been because I didn't keer to hev you chaps blazin' away at the first bush you *thought* you saw move in your skeer, and bringin' down their fire on us."

The explanation, though unsatisfactory, was by no means an improbable one, and we thought it better to accept it with a laugh. Bill, however, resumed his abstracted manner.

"Who got in at the Summit?" he at last asked abruptly of the expressman.

"Derrick and Simpson of Cold Spring, and one of the Excelsior boys," responded the expressman.

"And that Pike County girl from Dow's Flat, with her bundles. Don't forget her," added the outside passenger ironically.

"Does anybody here know her?" continued Bill, ignoring the irony.

"You'd better ask Judge Thompson; he was mighty attentive to her; gettin' her a seat by the off window, and lookin' after her bundles and things."

"Gettin' her a seat by the *window*?" repeated Bill.

"Yes, she wanted to see everything, and wasn't afraid of the shooting."

"Yes," broke in a third passenger, "and he was so civil that when she dropped her ring in the straw, he struck a match agin all your rules, you know, and held it for her to find it. And it was just as we were crossin' through the brush, too. I saw the hull thing through the window, for I was hanging over the wheels with my gun ready for action. And it wasn't no fault of Judge Thompson's if his foolishness hadn't shown us up, and got us a shot from the gang."

Bill gave a short grunt, but drove steadily on without further comment or even turning his eyes to the speaker.

We were now not more than a mile from the station at the crossroads where we were to change horses. The lights already glimmered in the distance, and there was a faint suggestion of the coming dawn on the summits of the ridge to the west. We had

157

plunged into a belt of timber, when suddenly a horseman emerged at a sharp canter from a trail that seemed to be parallel with our own. We were all slightly startled; Yuba Bill alone preserving his moody calm.

"Hullo!" he said.

The stranger wheeled to our side as Bill slackened his speed. He seemed to be a packer or freight muleteer.

"Ye didn't get held up on the Divide?" continued Bill cheerfully.

"No," returned the packer, with a laugh. "*I* don't carry treasure. But I see you're all right, too. I saw you crossin' over Galloper's."

"*Saw* us?" said Bill sharply. "We had our lights out."

"Yes, but there was suthin' white —a handkerchief or woman's veil, I reckon—hangin' from the window. It was only a movin' spot agin the hillside, but ez I was lookin' out for ye I knew it was you by that. Goodnight!"

He cantered away. We tried to look at each other's faces, and at Bill's expression in the darkness, but he neither spoke nor stirred until he threw down the reins when we stopped before the station. The passengers quickly descended from the roof; the expressman was about to follow, but Bill plucked his sleeve.

"I'm goin' to take a look over this yer stage and these yer passengers with ye, afore we start."

"Why, what's up?"

"Well," said Bill, slowly disengaging himself from one of his enormous gloves, "when we waltzed down into the brush up there I saw a man, ez plain ez I see you, rise up from it. I thought our time had come and the band was goin' to play, when he sorter drew back, made a sign, and we just scooted past him."

"Well?"

"Well," said Bill, "it means that this yer coach was *passed through free* tonight."

"You don't object to *that*—surely? I think we were deucedly lucky."

Bill slowly drew off his other glove. "I've been riskin' my everlastin' life on this line three times a week," he said with mock humility, "and I'm allus thankful for small mercies. *But,*" he added grimly, "when it comes down to being passed free by some pal of a hoss thief, and thet called a speshal Providence, *I ain't in it!* No, sir, I ain't in it!"

It was with mixed emotions that the passengers heard that a delay of fifteen minutes to tighten certain screw-bolts had been ordered by the autocratic Bill. Some were anxious to get their breakfast at Sugar Pine, but others were not averse to linger for the daylight that promised greater safety on the road. The expressman, knowing the real cause of Bill's delay, was nevertheless at a loss to understand the object of it. The passengers were all well known; any idea of complicity with the road agents was wild and impossible, and, even if there was a confederate of the gang among them, he would have been more likely to precipitate a robbery than to check it. Again, the discovery of such a confederate—to whom they clearly owed their safety —and his arrest would have been quite against the Californian sense of justice, if not actually illegal. It seemed evident that Bill's quixotic sense of honor was leading him astray.

The station consisted of a stable, a wagon shed, and a building containing three rooms. The first was fitted up with bunks or sleeping berths for the employees; the second was the kitchen; and the third and larger apartment was dining-room or sitting-room, and was used as general waiting-room for the passengers. It was not a refreshment station, and there was no bar. But a mysterious command from the omnipotent Bill produced a demijohn of whiskey, with which he hospitably treated the company. The seductive influence of the liquor loosened the tongue of the gallant Judge Thompson. He admitted to having struck a match to enable the fair Pike Countian to find her ring, which, however, proved to have fallen in her lap. She was "a fine, healthy young woman— a type of the Far West, sir; in fact, quite a prairie blossom! Yet simple and guileless as a child." She was on her way to Marysville, he believed, "although she expected to meet friends—a friend, in fact—later on." It was her first visit to a large town— in fact, any civilized centre—since she crossed the plains three years ago. Her girlish curiosity was quite touching, and her innocence irresistible. In fact, in a country whose tendency was to produce "frivolity and forwardness in young girls, he found her a most interesting young person." She was even then out in the stableyard watching the horses being harnessed, "preferring to indulge a pardonable healthy young curiosity than to listen to the empty compliments of the younger passengers."

The figure which Bill saw thus engaged, without being otherwise distinguished, certainly seemed to justify the Judge's opinion. She appeared to be a well-matured country girl, whose frank gray eyes and large laughing mouth expressed a wholesome and abiding gratification in her life and surroundings. She was watching the replacing of luggage in the boot. A little feminine start, as one of her own parcels was thrown somewhat roughly on the roof, gave Bill his opportunity. "Now there," he growled to the helper, "ye ain't carting stone! Look out, will yer! Some of your things, miss?" he added, with gruff courtesy, turning to her. "These yer trunks, for instance?"

She smiled a pleasant assent, and Bill, pushing aside the helper, seized a large square trunk in his arms. But from excess of zeal, or some other mischance, his foot slipped, and he came down heavily, striking the corner of the trunk on the ground and loosening its hinges and fastenings. It was a cheap, common-looking affair, but the accident discovered in its yawning lid a quantity of white, lace-edged feminine apparel of an apparently superior quality. The young lady uttered another cry and came quickly forward, but Bill was profuse in his apologies, himself girded the broken box with a strap, and declared his intention of having the company "make it good" to her with a new one. Then he casually accompanied her to the door of the waiting-room, entered, made a place for her before the fire by simply lifting the nearest and most youthful passenger by the coat collar from the stool that he was occupying, and, having installed the lady in it, displaced another man who was standing before the chimney, and, drawing himself up to his full six feet of height in front of her, glanced down upon his fair passenger as he took his way-bill from his pocket.

"Your name is down here as Miss Mullins?" he said.

She looked up, became suddenly aware that she and her questioner were the centre of interest to the whole circle of passengers, and, with a slight rise of color, returned, "Yes."

"Well, Miss Mullins, I've got a question or two to ask ye. I ask it straight out afore this crowd. It's in my rights to take ye aside and ask it—but that ain't my style; I'm no detective. I needn't ask it at all, but act as ef I knowed the answer, or I might leave it to be asked by others. Ye needn't answer it ef ye don't like; ye've got a friend over there—Judge Thompson—who is a friend to ye, right or wrong, jest as any other man here is—as though ye'd packed your own jury. Well, the simple question I've got to ask ye is *this:* Did you signal to anybody from the coach when we passed Galloper's an hour ago?"

We all thought that Bill's courage and audacity had reached its climax here. To openly and publicly accuse a lady before a group of chivalrous Californians, and that lady possessing the further attractions of youth, good looks, and innocence, was little short of desperation. There was an evident movement of adhesion towards the fair stranger, a slight muttering broke out on the right, but the very boldness of the act held them in stupefied surprise. Judge Thompson, with a bland propriatory smile began: "Really, Bill, I must protest on behalf of this young lady"—when the fair accused, raising her eyes to her accuser, to the consternation of everybody answered with the slight but convincing hesitation of conscientious truthfulness:

"*I did.*"

"Ahem!" interposed the Judge hastily, "er—that is—er—you allowed your handkerchief to flutter from the window,—I noticed it myself—casually—one might say even playfully—

but without any particular significance."

The girl, regarding her apologist with a singular mingling of pride and impatience, returned briefly:

"I signaled."

"Who did you signal to?" asked Bill gravely.

"The young gentleman I'm going to marry."

A start, followed by a slight titter from the younger passengers, was instantly suppressed by a savage glance from Bill.

"What did you signal to him for?" he continued.

"To tell him I was here, and that it was all right," returned the young girl, with a steadily rising pride and color.

"Wot was all right?" demanded Bill.

"That I wasn't followed, and that he could meet me on the road beyond Cass's Ridge Station." She hesitated a moment, and then, with a still greater pride, in which a youthful defiance was still mingled, said: "I've run away from home to marry him. And I mean to! No one can stop me. Dad didn't like him just because he was poor, and Dad's got money. Dad wanted me to marry a man I hate, and got a lot of dresses and things to bribe me."

"And you're taking them in your trunk to the other feller?" said Bill grimly.

"Yes, he's poor," returned the girl defiantly.

"Then your father's name is Mullins?" asked Bill.

"It's not Mullins. I—I—took that name," she hesitated, with her first exhibition of self-consciousness.

"Wot *is* his name?"

"Eli Hemmings."

A smile of relief and significance

went round the circle. The fame of Eli or "Skinner" Hemmings, as a notorious miser and userer, had passed even beyond Galloper's Ridge.

"The step that you're taking, Miss Mullins, I need not tell you, is one of great gravity," said Judge Thompson, with a certain paternal seriousness of manner, in which, however, we were glad to detect a glaring affectation; "and I trust that you and your affianced have fully weighed it. Far be it from me to interfere with or question the natural affections of two young people, but may I ask you what you know of the—er—young gentleman for whom you are sacrificing so much, and, perhaps, imperiling your whole future? For instance, have you known him long?"

The slightly troubled air of trying to understand—not unlike the vague wonderment of childhood, with which Miss Mullins had received the beginning of this exordium, changed to a relieved smile of comprehension as she said quickly, "Oh, yes, nearly a whole year."

"And," said the Judge, smiling, "has he a vocation—is he in business?"

"Oh yes," she returned; "he's a collector."

"A collector?"

"Yes; he collects bills, you know, —money," she went on, with childish eagerness, "not for himself,—*he* never has any money, poor Charley,—but for his firm. It's dreadful hard work, too; keeps him out for days and nights, over bad roads and baddest weather. Sometimes, when he's stole over to the ranch just to see me, he's been so bad he could scarcely keep his seat in the saddle, much less stand. And he's got to take mighty big risks, too. Times the folks are cross with him and won't pay; once they

shot him in the arm, and he came to me, and I helped do it up for him. But he don't mind. He's real brave, jest as brave as he's good." There was such a wholesome ring of truth in this pretty praise that we were touched in sympathy with the speaker.

"What firm does he collect for?" asked the Judge gently.

"I don't know exactly—he won't tell me; but I think it's a Spanish firm. You see"—she took us all into her confidence with a sweeping smile of innocent yet half-mischievous artfulness—"I only know because I peeped over a letter he once got from his firm, telling him he must hustle up and be ready for the road the next day; but I think the name was Martinez—yes, Ramon Martinez."

In the dead silence that ensued—a silence so profound that we could hear the horses in the distant stable-yard rattling their harness—one of the younger Excelsior boys burst into a hysteric laugh, but the fierce eye of Yuba Bill was down upon him, and seemed to instantly stiffen him into a silent, grinning mask. The young girl, however, took no note of it. Following out, with lover-like diffusiveness, the reminiscences thus awakened, she went on:

"Yes, it's mighty hard work, but he says it's all for me, and as soon as we're married he'll quit it. He might have quit it before, but he won't take no money of me, nor what I told him I could get out of Dad! That ain't his style. He's mighty proud—if he is poor—is Charley. Why, thar's all Ma's money which she left me in the Savin's Bank that I wanted to draw out—for I had the right—and give it to him, but he wouldn't hear of it! Why, he wouldn't take one of the things I've got with me, if he knew it. And so he goes on ridin' and ridin',

161

here and there and everywhere, and gettin' more and more played out and sad, and thin and pale as a spirit, and always so uneasy about his business, and startin' up at times when we're meetin' out in the South Woods or in the far clearin', and sayin': 'I must be goin' now, Polly,' and yet always tryin' to be chiffle and chipper afore me. Why, he must have rid miles and miles to have watched for me thar in the brush at the foot of Galloper's tonight, jest to see if all was safe; and Lordy! I'd have given him the signal and showed a light if I'd died for it the next minit. There! That's what I know of Charley—that's what I'm running away from home for—that's what I'm running to him for, and I don't care who knows it! And I only wish I'd done it afore—and I would—if—if—if—he'd only *asked me!* There now!" She stopped, panted, and choked. Then one of the sudden transitions of youthful emotion overtook the eager, laughing face; it clouded up with the swift change of childhood, a lightning quiver of expression broke over it, and—then came the rain!

I think this simple act completed our utter demoralization! We smiled feebly at each other with that assumption of masculine superiority which is miserably conscious of its own helplessness at such moments. We looked out of the window, blew our noses, said: "Eh—what?" and "I say," vaguely to each other, and were greatly relieved, and yet apparently astonished, when Yuba Bill, who had turned his back upon the fair speaker, and was kicking the logs in the fireplace, suddenly swept down upon us and bundled us all into the road, leaving Miss Mullins alone. Then he walked aside with

Judge Thompson for a few moments; returned to us, autocratically demanded of the party a complete reticence towards Miss Mullins on the subject-matter under discussion, re-entered the station, reappeared with the young lady, suppressed a faint idiotic cheer which broke from us at the spectacle of her innocent face once more cleared and rosy, climbed the box, and in another moment we were under way.

"Then she don't know what her lover is yet?" asked the expressman eagerly.

"No."

"Are *you* certain it's one of the gang?"

"Can't say *for sure.* It mout be a young chap from Yolo who bucked agin the tiger at Sacramento, got regularly cleaned out and busted, and joined the gang for a flier. They say thar was a new hand in that job over at Keeley's—and a mighty game one, too; and ez there was some buckshot onloaded that trip, he might hev got his share, and that would tally with what the girl said about his arm. See! Ef that's the man, I've heered he was the son of some big preacher in the States, and a college sharp to boot, who ran wild in 'Frisco, and played himself for all he was worth. They're the wust kind to kick when they once get a foot over the traces. For stiddy, comf'ble kempany," added Bill reflectively, "give *me* the son of a man that was *hanged!*"

"But what are you going to do about this?"

"That depends upon the feller who comes to meet her."

"But you ain't going to try to take him? That would be playing it pretty low down on them both."

"Keep your hair on, Jimmy! The Judge and me are only going to

162

rastle with the sperrit of that gay young galoot, when he drops down for his girl—and exhort him pow'ful! Ef he allows he's convicted of sin and will find the Lord, we'll marry him and the gal offhand at the next station, and the Judge will officiate himself for nothin'. We're goin' to have this yer elopement done on the square—and our waybill clean—you bet!"

"But you don't suppose he'll trust himself in your hands?"

"Polly will signal to him that it's all square."

"Ah!" said the expressman. Nevertheless in those few moments the men seemed to have exchanged dispositions. The expressman looked doubtfully, critically, and even cynically before him. Bill's face had relaxed, and something like a bland smile beamed across it, as he drove confidently and unhesitatingly forward.

Day, meantime, although full blown and radiant on the mountain summits around us, was yet nebulous and uncertain in the valleys into which we were plunging. Lights still glimmered in the cabins and the few ranch buildings which began to indicate the thicker settlements. And the shadows were heaviest in a little copse, where a note from Judge Thompson in the coach was handed up to Yuba Bill, who at once slowly began to draw up his horses. The coach stopped finally near the junction of a small crossroad. At the same moment Miss Mullins slipped down from the vehicle, and, with a parting wave of her hand to the Judge, who had assisted her from the steps, tripped down the crossroad, and disappeared in its semiobscurity. To our surprise the stage waited, Bill holding the reins listlessly in his hands. Five minutes passed—an eternity of

expectation, and, as there was that in Yuba Bill's face which forbade idle questioning, an aching void of silence also! This was at last broken by a strange voice from the road:

"Go on—we'll follow."

The coach started forward. Presently we heard the sound of other wheels behind us. We all craned our necks backward to get a view of the unknown, but by the growing light we could only see that we were followed at a distance by a buggy with two figures in it. Evidently Polly Mullins and her lover! We hoped that they would pass us. But the vehicle, although drawn by a fast horse, preserved its distance always, and it was plain that its driver had no desire to satisfy our curiosity. The expressman had recourse to Bill.

"Is it the man you thought of?" he asked eagerly.

"I reckon," said Bill briefly.

"But," continued the expressman, returning to his former skepticism, "what's to keep them both from levanting together now?"

Bill jerked his hand towards the boot with a grim smile.

"Their baggage."

"Oh!" said the expressman.

"Yes," continued Bill. "We'll hang on to that gal's little frills and fixin's until this yer job's settled, and the ceremony's over, jest as ef we waz her own father. And, what's more, young man," he added, suddenly turning to the expressman, "*you'll* express them trunks of hers *through to Sacramento* with your kempany's labels, and hand her the receipts and checks for them, so she *can get 'em there.* That'll keep *him* outer temptation and the reach o' the gang, until they get away among white men and civilization again. When your hoary-headed ole grandfather, or, to speak

163

plainer, that partikler old whiskey-soaker known as Yuba Bill, wot sits on this box," he continued, with a diabolical wink at the expressman, "waltzes in to pervide for a young couple jest startin' in life, thar's nothin' mean about his style, you bet. He fills the bill every time! Speshul Providences take a back seat when he's around."

When the station hotel and straggling settlement of Sugar Pine, now distinct and clear in the growing light, at last rose within rifleshot on the plateau, the buggy suddenly darted swiftly by us, so swiftly that the faces of the two occupants were barely distinguishable as they passed, and keeping the lead by a dozen lengths, reached the door of the hotel. The young girl and her companion leaped down and vanished within as we drew up. They had evidently determined to elude our curiosity, and were successful.

But the material appetites of the passengers, sharpened by the keen mountain air, were more potent than their curiosity, and, as the breakfast-bell rang out at the moment the stage stopped, a majority of them rushed into the dining-room and scrambled for places without giving much heed to the vanished couple or to the Judge and Yuba Bill, who had disappeared also. The through coach to Marysville and Sacramento was likewise waiting, for Sugar Pine was the limit of Bill's ministration, and the coach which we had just left went no farther. In the course of twenty minutes, however, there was a slight and somewhat ceremonious bustling in the hall and on the veranda, and Yuba Bill and the Judge reappeared. The latter was leading, with some elaboration of manner and detail, the shapely figure of Miss Mullins,

and Yuba Bill was accompanying her companion to the buggy. We all rushed to the windows to get a good view of the mysterious stranger and probably ex-brigand whose life was now linked with our fair fellow-passenger. I am afraid, however, that we all participated in a certain impression of disappointment and doubt. Handsome and even cultivated-looking, he assuredly was—young and vigorous in appearance. But there was a certain half-shamed, half-defiant suggestion in his expression, yet coupled with a watchful lurking uneasiness which was not pleasant and hardly becoming in a bride-groom—and the possessor of such a bride. But the frank, joyous, innocent face of Polly Mullins, resplendent with a simple, happy confidence, melted our hearts again, and condoned the fellow's shortcomings. We waved our hands; I think we would have given three rousing cheers as they drove away if the omnipotent eye of Yuba Bill had not been upon us. It was well, for the next moment we were summoned to the presence of that soft-hearted autocrat.

We found him alone with the Judge in a private sitting-room, standing before a table on which there were a decanter and glasses. As we filed expectantly into the room and the door closed behind us, he cast a glance of hesitating tolerance over the group.

"Gentlemen," he said slowly, "you was all present at the beginnin' of a little game this mornin', and the Judge thar thinks that you oughter be let in at the finish. *I* don't see that it's any of *your* business—so to speak; but ez the Judge here allows you're all in the secret, I've called you in to take a partin' drink to the health of Mr. and Mrs. Charley Byng—ez is now comf'ably off on their bridal tower. What *you* know or what *you* suspects of the young galoot that's married the gal ain't worth shucks to anybody, and I wouldn't give it to a yaller pup to play with, but the Judge thinks you ought all to promise right here that you'll keep it dark. That's his opinion. Ez far as my opinion goes, gen'l'men," continued Bill, with greater blandness and apparent cordiality, "I wanter simply remark, in a keerless, offhand gin'ral way, that ef I ketch any God-forsaken, lop-eared, chuckleheaded, blatherin' idjet airin' *his* opinion"—

"One moment, Bill," interposed Judge Thompson with a grave smile; "let me explain. You understand, gentlemen," he said, turning to us, "the singular, and I may say affecting, situation which our good-hearted friend here has done so much to bring to what we hope will be a happy termination. I want to give here, as my professional opinion, that there is nothing in his request which, in your capacity as good citizens and law-abiding men, you may not grant. I want to tell you, also, that you are condoning no offense against the statutes; that there is not a particle of legal evidence before us of the criminal antecedents of Mr. Charles Byng, except that which has been told you by the innocent lips of his betrothed, which the law of the land has now sealed forever in the mouth of his wife, and that our own actual experience of his acts has been in the main exculpatory of any previous irregularity—if not incompatible with it. Briefly, no judge would charge, no jury convict, on such evidence. When I add that the young girl is of legal age, that there is no evidence of any previous undue influence, but rather of the reverse, on the part of the bridegroom, and that I was con-

tent, as a magistrate, to perform the ceremony, I think you will be satisfied to give your promise, for the sake of the bride, and drink a happy life to them both."

I need not say that we did this cheerfully, and even extorted from Bill a grunt of satisfaction. The majority of the company, however, who were going with the through coach to Sacramento, then took their leave, and, as we accompanied them to the veranda, we could see that Miss Polly Mullins's trunks were already transferred to the other vehicle under the protecting seals and labels of the all-potent Express Company. Then the whip cracked, the coach rolled away, and the last traces of the adventurous young couple disappeared in the hanging red dust of its wheels.

But Yuba Bill's grim satisfaction at the happy issue of the episode seemed to suffer no abatement. He even exceeded his usual deliberately regulated potations, and, standing comfortably with his back to the centre of the now deserted barroom, was more than usually loquacious with the expressman. "You see," he said, in bland reminiscence, "when your old Uncle Bill takes hold of a job like this, he puts it straight through without changin' hosses. Yet thar was a moment, young feller, when I thought I was stompt! It was when we'd made up our mind to make that chap tell the gal fust all what he was! Ef she'd rared or kicked in the traces, or hung back only ez much ez that, we'd hev given him jest five minits' law to get up and get and leave her, and we'd hev toted that gal and her fixin's back to her dad again! But she jest gave a little scream and start, and then went off inter hysterics, right on his buzzum, laughin' and cryin' and sayin' that nothin' should part 'em.

165

Gosh! if I didn't think *he* woz more cut up than she about it; a minit it looked as ef *he* didn't allow to marry her arter all, but that passed, and they was married hard and fast— you bet! I reckon he's had enough of stayin' out o' nights to last him, and ef the valley settlements hevn't got hold of a very shinin' member, at least the foothills hev got shut of one more of the Ramon Martinez gang."

"What's that about the Ramon Martinez gang?" said a quiet potential voice.

Bill turned quickly. It was the voice of the Divisional Superintendent of the Express Company,—a man of eccentric determination of character, and one of the few whom the autocratic Bill recognized as an equal,—who had just entered the barroom. His dusty pongee cloak and soft hat indicated that he had that morning arrived on a round of inspection.

"Don't care if I do, Bill," he continued, in response to Bill's invitatory gesture, walking to the bar. "It's a little raw out on the road. Well, what were you saying about Ramon Martinez' gang? You haven't come across one of 'em, have you?"

"No," said Bill, with a slight blinking of his eye, as he ostentatiously lifted his glass to the light.

"And you *won't*," added the Superintendent, leisurely sipping his liquor. "For the fact is, the gang is about played out. Not from want of a job now and then, but from the difficulty of disposing of the results of their work. Since the new instructions to the agents to identify and trace all dust and bullion offered to them went into force, you see, they can't get rid of their swag. All the gang are spotted at the offices, and it costs too much for them to pay a

fence or a middleman of any standing. Why, all that flaky river gold they took from the Excelsior Company can be identified as easy as if it was stamped with the company's mark. They can't melt it down themselves; they can't get others to do it for them; they can't ship it to the Mint or Assay Offices in Marysville and 'Frisco, for they won't take it without our certificate and seals; and *we* don't take any undeclared freight *within* the lines that we've drawn around their beat, except from people and agents known. Why, *you* know that well enough, Jim," he said, suddenly appealing to the expressman, "don't you?"

Possibly the suddenness of the appeal caused the expressman to swallow his liquor the wrong way, for he was overtaken with a fit of coughing, and stammered hastily as he laid down his glass, "Yes—of course—certainly."

"No, sir," resumed the Superintendent cheerfully, "they're pretty well played out. And the best proof of it is that they've lately been robbing ordinary passengers' trunks. There was a freight wagon held up near Dow's Flat the other day, and a lot of baggage gone through. I had to go down there to look into it. Darned if they hadn't lifted a lot o' woman's wedding things from that rich couple who got married the other day out at Marysville. Looks as if they were playing it rather low down, don't it? Coming down to hardpan and the bed rock—eh?"

The expressman's face was turned anxiously towards Bill, who, after a hurried gulp of his remaining liquor, still stood staring at the window. Then he slowly drew on one of his large gloves. "Ye didn't," he said, with a slow, drawling, but perfectly distinct, articulation, "happen to know old 'Skinner' Hemmings when you were over there?"

"Yes."

"And his daughter?"

"He hasn't got any."

"A sort o' mild, innocent, guileless child of nature?" persisted Bill, with a yellow face, a deadly calm, and Satanic deliberation.

"No. I tell you he *hasn't* any daughter. Old man Hemmings is a confirmed old bachelor. He's too mean to support more than one."

"And you didn't happen to know any o' that gang, did ye?" continued Bill, with infinite protraction.

"Yes. Knew 'em all. There was French Pete, Cherokee Bob, Kanaka Joe, One-eyed Stillson, Softy Brown, Spanish Jack, and two or three Greasers."

"And ye didn't know a man by the name of Charley Byng?"

"No," returned the Superintendent, with a slight suggestion of weariness and a distraught glance towards the door.

"A dark, stylish chap, with shifty black eyes and a curled-up mers-tache?" continued Bill, with dry, colorless persistence.

"No. Look here, Bill, I'm in a little bit of a hurry—but I suppose you must have your little joke before we part. Now, what *is* your little game?"

"Wot you mean?" demanded Bill, with sudden brusqueness.

"Mean? Well, old man, you know as well as I do. You're giving me the very description of Ramon Martinez himself, ha! ha! No— Bill! you didn't play me this time. You're mighty spry and clever, but you didn't catch on just then."

He nodded and moved away with a light laugh. Bill turned a stony face to the expressman. Suddenly a gleam of mirth came into his gloomy eyes. He bent over the young man, and said in a hoarse, chuckling whisper:

"But I got even after all!"

"How?"

"He's tied up to that lying little she-devil, hard and fast!"

DEAR LAND OF ALL MY LOVE

SIDNEY LANIER

Long as thine Art shall love true love,
Long as thy Science truth shall know,
Long as thine Eagle harms no Dove,
Long as thy Law by law shall grow,
Long as thy God is God above,
Thy brother every man below,
So long, dear Land of all my love,
Thy name shall shine, thy fame shall glow!

THE GHOST OF THE BUFFALOES
Vachel Lindsay

Last night at black midnight I woke with a cry,
The windows were shaking, there was thunder on high,
The floor was atremble, the door was ajar,
White fires, crimson fires, shone from afar.
I rushed to the dooryard. The city was gone.
My home was a hut without orchard or lawn.
It was mud-smear and logs near a whispering stream,
Nothing else built by man could I see in my dream . . .
Then . . .
Ghost-kings came headlong, row upon row,
Gods of the Indians, torches aglow.

They mounted the bear and the elk and the deer,
And eagles gigantic, aged and sere,
They rode long-horn cattle, they cried "A-la-la."
They lifted the knife, the bow, and the spear,
They lifted ghost-torches from dead fires below,
The midnight made grand with the cry "A-la-la."
The midnight made grand with a red-god charge,
A red-god show,
A red-god show,
"A-la-la, a-la-la, a-la-la, a-la-la."

With bodies like bronze, and terrible eyes
Came the rank and the file, with catamount cries,
Gibbering, yipping, with hollow-skull clacks,
Riding white bronchos with skeleton backs,
Scalp-hunters, beaded and spangled and bad,
Naked and lustful and foaming and mad,
Flashing primeval demoniac scorn,
Blood-thirst and pomp amid darkness reborn,
Power and glory that sleep in the grass
While the winds and the snows and the great rains pass.
They crossed the gray river, thousands abreast,
They rode in infinite lines to the west,
Tide upon tide of strange fury and foam,
Spirits and wraiths, the blue was their home,
The sky was their goal where the star-flags were furled,
And on past those far golden splendors they whirled.
They burned to dim meteors, lost in the deep.
And I turned in dazed wonder, thinking of sleep;

And the wind crept by
Alone, unkempt, unsatisfied,
The wind cried and cried—
Muttered of massacres long past,
Buffaloes in shambles vast . . .
An owl said: "Hark, what is a-wing?"
I heard a cricket caroling,
I heard a cricket caroling,
I heard a cricket caroling.

Then . . .
Snuffing the lightning that crashed from on high
Rose royal old buffaloes, row upon row.
The lords of the prairie came galloping by.
And I cried in my heart, "A-la-la, a-la-la,
A red-god show,
A red-god show,
A-la-la, a-la-la, a-la-la, a-la-la."

Buffaloes, buffaloes, thousands abreast,
A scourge and amazement, they swept to the west.
With black bobbing noses, with red rolling tongues,
Coughing forth steam from their leather-wrapped lungs,
Cows with their calves, bulls big and vain,
Goring the laggards, shaking the mane,
Stamping flint feet, flashing moon eyes.
Pompous and owlish, shaggy and wise.
Like sea-cliffs and caves resounded their ranks
With shoulders like waves, and undulant flanks.
Tide upon tide of strange fury and foam,
Spirits and wraiths, the blue was their home,
The sky was their goal where the star-flags are furled,
And on past those far golden splendors they whirled.
They burned to dim meteors, lost in the deep,
And I turned in dazed wonder, thinking of sleep.

I heard a cricket's cymbals play,
A scarecrow lightly flapped his rags,
And a pan that hung by his shoulder rang,
Rattled and thumped in a listless way,
And now the wind in the chimney sang,
The wind in the chimney,
The wind in the chimney,
The wind in the chimney,

Seemed to say:—
"Dream, boy, dream,
If you anywise can.
To dream is the work
Of beast or man.
Life is the west-going dream-storms' breath,
Life is a dream, the sign of the skies,
The breath of the stars, that nod on their pillows
With their golden hair mussed over their eyes."
The locust played on his musical wing,
Sang to his mate of love's delight.
I heard the whippoorwill's soft fret.
I heard a cricket caroling,
I heard a cricket caroling,
I heard a cricket say: "Good-night, good-night,
Good-night, good-night, . . . good-night."

. . . .

Would I might rouse the Lincoln in you all,
That which is gendered in the wilderness
From lonely prairies and God's tenderness.
Imperial soul, star of a weedy stream,
Born where the ghosts of the buffaloes still dream,
Whose spirit hoof-beats storm above his grave,
Above that breast of earth and prairie fire—
Fire, that freed the slave,
Fire, that freed the slave.

JOHNNY APPLESEED
EDGAR LEE MASTERS

When the air of October is sweet and cold as the wine of apples,
Hanging ungathered in frosted orchards along the Grand River,
I take the road that winds by the resting fields and wander
From Eastmanville to Nunica down to the Villa Crossing.

I look for old men to talk with, men as old as the orchards,
Men to tell me of ancient days, of those who built and planted,
Lichen gray, branch broken, bent and sighing,
Hobbling for warmth in the sun and for places to sit and smoke.

For there is a legend here, a tale of the croaking old ones,
That Johnny Appleseed came here, planted some orchards around here,
When nothing was here but the pine trees, oaks and the beeches,
And nothing was here but the marshes, lake and the river.

170

Peter Van Zylen is ninety and this he tells me:
My father talked with Johnny Appleseed there on the hillside,
There by the road on the way to Fruitport, saw him
Clearing pines and oaks for a place for an apple orchard.

Peter Van Zylen says: He got that name from the people
For carrying apple seed with him and planting orchards
All the way from Ohio, through Indiana across here,
Planting orchards, they say, as far as Illinois.

Johnny Appleseed said, so my father told me:
I go to a place forgotten, the orchards will thrive and be here
For children to come, who will gather and eat hereafter.
And few will know who planted, and none will understand.

I laugh, said Johnny Appleseed: Some fellow buys this timber
Five years, perhaps from today, begins to clear for barley.
And here in the midst of the timber is hidden an apple orchard.
How did it come here? Lord! Who was it here before me?

Yes, I was here before him, to make these places of worship,
Labor and laughter and gain in the late October.
Why did I do it, eh? Some folks say I am crazy.
Where do my labors end? Far west, God only knows!

Said Johnny Appleseed there on the hillside: Listen!
Beware the deceit of nurseries, sellers of seeds of the apple.
Think! You labor for years in trees not worth the raising.
You planted what you knew not, bitter or sour for sweet.

No luck more bitter than poor seed, but one as bitter:
The planting of perfect seed in soil that feeds and fails,
Nourishes for a little, and then goes spent forever.
Look to your seed, he said, and remember the soil.

And after that is the fight: the foe curled up at the root,
The scale that crumples and deadens, the moth in the blossoms
Becoming a life that coils at the core of a thing of beauty:
You bite your apple, a worm is crushed on your tongue!

And it's every bit the truth, said Peter Van Zylen.
So many things love an apple as well as ourselves.
A man must fight for the thing he loves, to possess it:
Apples, freedom, heaven, said Peter Van Zylen.

BEWARE OF RASHNESS, but with energy and sleepless vigilance go forward and give us victories.—*Lincoln*

OUR FEDERAL UNION! It must and shall be preserved!—*Jackson*

A POUND of pluck is worth a ton of luck.—*Garfield*

WHEN YOU DELIVER a matter, do it without passion and indiscretion, however mean the person may be you do it to.—*Washington*

I SHALL on all subjects have a policy to recommend, but none to enforce against the will of the people.—*Grant*

ALL FREE GOVERNMENTS are managed by the combined wisdom and folly of the people.—*Garfield*

NEVER WITH MY CONSENT shall an officer of the people, compensated for his services out of their pockets, become the pliant instrument of the Executive will.—*William Henry Harrison*

AS MUCH AS I CONVERSE with sages and heroes, they have very little of my love and admiration. I long for rural and domestic scenes, for the warbling of birds and the prattling of my children.—*John Adams*

NATIONAL HONOR is national property of the highest value.—*Monroe*

WE WANT NO MORE LAND. We do want to improve what we have, and want to see our neighbors improve and grow so strong that the design of any other country could not endanger them.—*Grant*

'TIS OUR TRUE POLICY to steer clear of permanent alliances with any portion of the foreign world.—*Washington*

WESTWARD the star of empire takes its way.—*John Quincy Adams*

THE WHITE HOUSE

BETTER TO REMAIN silent and be thought a fool than to speak
and to remove all doubt.—*Lincoln*

I BELIEVE in God, and I trust myself in His hands.—*Garfield*

ONE MAN with courage makes a majority.—*Jackson*

THE TIME IS NOW near at hand, which must probably determine whether
Americans are to be freemen or slaves.—*Washington*

A DECENT AND MANLY EXAMINATION of the acts of Government should be not
only tolerated, but encouraged.—*William Henry Harrison*

COMMERCE LINKS all mankind in one common brotherhood of
mutual dependence and interests.—*Garfield*

IF PARTIES IN A REPUBLIC are necessary to secure a degree of vigilance sufficient
to keep the public functionaries within the bounds of law and duty, at that
point their usefulness ends.—*William Henry Harrison*

THERE CAN BE no fifty-fifty Americanism in this country. There is room here
for only one-hundred per cent Americanism, only for those who are Americans
and nothing else.—*Theodore Roosevelt*

I PROPOSE to fight it out on this line if it takes all summer.—*Grant*

WE ADMIT OF NO GOVERNMENT by divine right . . . the only legitimate
right to govern is an express grant of power from the governed.
—*William Henry Harrison*

THINK of your forefathers! Think of your posterity!—*John Quincy Adams*

PUBLIC OFFICERS should owe their whole service to the government
and to the people.—*Hayes*

THE OREGON TRAIL*
ARTHUR GUITERMAN

Two hundred wagons, rolling out to Oregon
  Breaking through the gopher holes, lurching wide and free,
Crawling up the mountain pass, jolting, grumbling, rumbling on,
  Two hundred wagons, rolling to the sea.

From East and South and North they flock, to muster, row on row,
A fleet of ten-score prairie ships beside Missouri's flow.
The bullwhips crack, the oxen strain, the canvas-hooded files
Are off upon the long, long trail of sixteen hundred miles.
The women hold the guiding lines; beside the rocking steers
With goad and ready rifle walk the bearded pioneers
Through clouds of dust beneath the sun, through floods of sweeping rain
Across the Kansas prairie land, across Nebraska's plain.

Two hundred wagons, rolling out to Oregon,
  Curved around the campfire flame at halt when day is done,
Rest a while beneath the stars, yoke again and lumber on,
  Two hundred wagons, rolling with the sun.

Among the barren buttes they wind beneath the jealous view
Of Blackfoot, Pawnee, Omaha, Arapahoe, and Sioux.
No savage threat may check their course, no river deep and wide;
They swim the Platte, they ford the Snake, they cross the Great Divide.
They march as once from India's vales through Asia's mountain door
With shield and spear on Europe's plain their fathers marched before.
They march where leap the antelope and storm the buffalo
Still westward as their fathers marched ten thousand years ago.

Two hundred wagons, rolling out to Oregon
  Creeping down the dark defile below the mountain crest,
Surging through the brawling stream, lunging, plunging, forging on,
  Two hundred wagons, rolling toward the West.

Now toils the dusty caravan with swinging wagon poles
Where Walla Walla pours along, where broad Columbia rolls.
The long-haired trapper's face grows dark and scowls the painted brave;
Where now the beaver builds his dam the wheat and rye shall wave.
The British trader shakes his head and weighs his nation's loss,
For where those hardy settlers come the Stars and Stripes will toss.
Then block the wheels, unyoke the steers; the prize is his who dares;

*Taken from I SING THE PIONEER by Arthur Guiterman, published and copyright by E. P.
DUTTON & CO., INC., New York. Copyright 1926.

The cabins rise, the fields are sown, and Oregon is theirs!

They will take, they will hold,
By the spade in the mold,
By the seed in the soil,
By the sweat and the toil,
By the plow in the loam,
By the school and the home!

Two hundred wagons, rolling out to Oregon,
Two hundred wagons, ranging free and far,
Two hundred wagons, rumbling, grumbling, rolling on,
Two hundred wagons, following a star!

From *PIONEERS! O PIONEERS*
WALT WHITMAN

Come, my tan-faced children,
Follow well in order, get your weapons ready;
Have you your pistols? Have you your sharp-edged axes?
Pioneers! O pioneers!

For we cannot tarry here;
We must march, my darlings, we must bear the brunt of danger,
We, the youthful sinewy races, all the rest on us depend,
Pioneers! O pioneers!

O you youths, Western youths,
So impatient, full of action, full of manly pride and friendship,
Plain I see you, Western youths, see you tramping with the foremost,
Pioneers! O pioneers!

Have the elder races halted?
Do they droop and end their lesson, wearied over there beyond the seas?
We take up the task eternal, and the burden and the lesson,
Pioneers! O pioneers!

All the past we leave behind,
We debouch upon a newer mightier world, varied world;
Fresh and strong the world we seize, world of labor and the march,
Pioneers! O pioneers!

We detachments steady throwing,
Down the edges, through the passes, up the mountains steep,

Conquering, holding, daring, venturing as we go the unknown ways,
    Pioneers! O pioneers!

We primeval forests felling,
We the rivers stemming, vexing we and piercing deep the mines within,
We the surface broad surveying, we the virgin soil up-heaving,
    Pioneers! O pioneers!

Colorado men are we;
From the peaks gigantic, from the great Sierras and the high plateaus,
From the mine and from the gully, from the hunting trail, we come,
    Pioneers! O pioneers!

From Nebraska, from Arkansas,
Central inland race are we, from Missouri, with the continental blood
        interveined;
All the hands of comrades clasping, all the Southern, all the Northern,
    Pioneers! O pioneers!

O resistless restless race!
O beloved race in all! O my breast aches with tender love for all!
O I mourn and yet exult, I am rapt with love for all,
    Pioneers! O pioneers!

Raise the mighty mother mistress,
Waving high the delicate mistress, over all the starry mistress
        (bend your heads all),
Raise the fanged and warlike mistress, stern, impassive, weaponed mistress,
    Pioneers! O pioneers!

See, my children, resolute children,
By those swarms upon our rear we must never yield or falter,
Ages back in ghostly millions frowning there behind us urging,
    Pioneers! O pioneers!

On and on the compact ranks,
With accessions ever waiting, with the places of the dead quickly filled,
Through the battle, through defeat, moving yet and never stopping,
    Pioneers! O pioneers!

O to die advancing on!
Are there some of us to droop and die? Has the hour come?
Then upon the march we fittest die, soon and sure the gap is filled,
    Pioneers! O pioneers!

All the pulses of the world,
Falling in they beat for us, with the Western movement beat,
Holding single or together, steady moving to the front, all for us,
      Pioneers! O pioneers!

Life's involved and varied pageants,
All the forms and shows, all the workmen at their work,
All the seamen and the landsmen, all the masters with their slaves,
      Pioneers! O pioneers!

All the hapless silent lovers,
All the prisoners in the prisons, all the righteous and the wicked,
All the joyous, all the sorrowing, all the living, all the dying,
      Pioneers! O pioneers!

I too with my soul and body,
We, a curious trio, picking, wandering on our way,
Through these shores amid the shadows, with the apparitions pressing,
      Pioneers! O pioneers!

Lo, the darting bowling orb!
Lo, the brother orbs around, all the clustering suns and planets,
All the dazzling days, all the mystic nights with dreams,
      Pioneers! O pioneers!

These are of us, they are with us,
All for primal needed work, while the followers there in embryo wait behind;
We today's procession heading, we the route for travel clearing,
      Pioneers! O pioneers!

O you daughters of the West!
O you young and elder daughters! O you mothers and you wives!
Never must you be divided, in our ranks you move united,
      Pioneers! O pioneers!

Minstrels latent on the prairies
(Shrouded bards of other lands, you may rest, you have done your work),
Soon I hear you coming warbling, soon you rise and tramp amid us,
      Pioneers! O pioneers!

Not for delectations sweet,
Not the cushion and the slipper, not the peaceful and the studious,
Not the riches safe and palling, not for us the tame enjoyment,
      Pioneers! O pioneers!

Do the feasters gluttonous feast?
Do the corpulent sleepers sleep? Have they locked and bolted doors?
Still be ours the diet hard, and the blanket on the ground,
    Pioneers! O pioneers!

Has the night descended?
Was the road of late so toilsome? Did we stop discouraged nodding on our way?
Yet a passing hour I yield you in your tracks to pause oblivious,
    Pioneers! O pioneers!

Till with sound of trumpet,
Far, far off the daybreak call—hark! How loud and clear I hear it wind!
Swift! To the head of the army! Swift! Spring to your places,
    Pioneers! O pioneers!

COLUMBIA, THE GEM OF THE OCEAN
THOMAS À BECKET

O Columbia, the gem of the ocean, the home of the brave and the free,
The shrine of each patriot's devotion, a world offers homage to thee!
Thy mandates make heroes assemble, when Liberty's form stands in view;
Thy banners make tyranny tremble, when borne by the red, white, and blue!

Chorus

When borne by the red, white, and blue!
When borne by the red, white, and blue!
Thy banners make tyranny tremble,
When borne by the red, white, and blue!

When war winged its wide desolation, and threatened the land to deform,
The ark then of freedom's foundation, Columbia rode safe through the
    storm;
With her garlands of vict'ry around her, when so proudly she bore her brave
    crew;
With her flag proudly floating before her, the boast of the red, white, and
    blue.

The star-spangled banner bring hither, o'er Columbia's true sons let it wave;
May the wreaths they have won never wither, nor its stars cease to shine on
    the brave:
May thy service, united, ne'er sever, but hold to their colors so true;
The army and navy forever, three cheers for the red, white, and blue!

178

Rip Van Winkle

By WASHINGTON IRVING

$\mathcal{W}$HOEVER has made a voyage up the Hudson must remember the Catskill Mountains. They are a dismembered branch of the great Appalachian family, and are seen away to the west of the river, swelling up to a noble height, and lording it over the surrounding country.

Every change of season, every change of weather, indeed, every hour of the day, produces some change in the magical hues and shapes of these mountains, and they are regarded by all the good wives, far and near, as perfect barometers. When the weather is fair and settled, they are clothed in blue and purple, and print their bold outlines on the clear evening sky; but sometimes, when the rest of the landscape is cloudless, they will gather a hood of gray vapors about their summits, which, in the last rays of the setting sun, will glow and light up like a crown of glory.

At the foot of these fairy mountains the voyager may have described the light smoke curling up from a village, whose shingle roofs gleam among the trees, just where the blue tints of the upland melt away into the fresh green of the nearer landscape. It is a little village of great antiquity, having been founded by some of the Dutch colonists, in the early times of the province, just about the beginning of the government of the good Peter Stuyvesant (may he rest in peace!), and there were some of the houses of the original settlers standing within a few years, with lattice windows, gable fronts surmounted with weathercocks, and built of small yellow bricks brought from Holland.

In that same village, and in one of these very houses (which, to tell the precise truth, was sadly timeworn and weather-beaten), there lived many years since, while the country was yet a province of Great Britain, a simple, good-natured fellow, of the name of Rip Van Winkle. He was a descendant of the Van Winkles who figured so gallantly in the chivalrous days of Peter Stuyvesant, and accompanied him to the siege of Fort Christina. He inherited, however, but little of the martial character of his ancestors. I have observed that he was a simple, good-natured man; he was, moreover, a kind neighbor and an obedient, henpecked husband. Indeed, to the latter circumstance might be owing that meekness of spirit which gained him such universal popularity; for those men are most apt to be obsequious and conciliating abroad, who are under the discipline of shrews at home. Their tempers, doubtless, are rendered pliant and malleable in the fiery furnace of domestic tribulation; and a curtain lecture is worth all the sermons in the world for teaching the virtues of patience and long-suffering. A termagant wife may, therefore, in some respects, be considered a tolerable blessing; and if so, Rip Van Winkle was thrice blessed.

Certain it is that he was a great

favorite among all the good wives of the village, who, as usual with the amiable sex, took his part in all family squabbles, and never failed, whenever they talked those matters over in their evening gossipings, to lay all the blame on Dame Van Winkle. The children of the village, too, would shout with joy whenever he approached. He assisted at their sports, made their playthings, taught them to fly kites and shoot marbles, and told them long stories of ghosts, witches, and Indians. Whenever he went dodging about the village, he was surrounded by a troop of them, hanging on his skirts, clambering on his back, and playing a thousand tricks on him with impunity; and not a dog would bark at him throughout the neighborhood.

The great error in Rip's composition was an insuperable aversion to all kinds of profitable labor. It could not be from the want of assiduity or perseverance; for he would sit on a wet rock, with a rod as long and heavy as a Tartar's lance, and fish all day without a murmur, even though he should not be encouraged by a single nibble. He would carry a fowling piece on his shoulder, for hours together, trudging through woods and swamps, and up hill and down dale, to shoot a few squirrels or wild pigeons. He would never refuse to assist a neighbor, even in the roughest toil, and was a foremost man at all country frolics for husking Indian corn, or building stone fences. The women of the village, too, used to employ him to run their errands, and to do such little odd jobs as their less obliging husbands would not do for them; in a word, Rip was ready to attend to anybody's business but his own; but as to doing family duty,

and keeping his farm in order, it was impossible.

In fact, he declared it was of no use to work on his farm; it was the most pestilent little piece of ground in the whole country; everything about it went wrong, and would go wrong, in spite of him. His fences were continually falling to pieces; his cow would either go astray or get among the cabbages; weeds were sure to grow quicker in his fields than anywhere else; the rain always made a point of setting in just as he had some outdoor work to do; so that though his patrimonial estate had dwindled away under his management, acre by acre, until there was little more left than a mere patch of Indian corn and potatoes, yet it was the worst-conditioned farm in the neighborhood.

His children, too, were as ragged and wild as if they belonged to nobody. His son Rip, an urchin begotten in his own likeness, promised to inherit the habits, with the old clothes of his father. He was generally seen trooping like a colt at his mother's heels, equipped in a pair of his father's cast-off galligaskins, which he had much ado to hold up with one hand, as a fine lady does her train in bad weather.

Rip Van Winkle, however, was one of those happy mortals, of foolish, well-oiled dispositions, who take the world easy, eat white bread or brown, whichever can be got with least thought or trouble, and would rather starve on a penny than work for a pound. If left to himself, he would have whistled life away, in perfect contentment; but his wife kept continually dinning in his ears about his idleness, his carelessness, and the ruin he was bringing on his family. Morning, noon, and night, her tongue was incessantly going, and everything he said or did was sure to produce a torrent of household eloquence. Rip had but one way of replying to all lectures of the kind, and that, by frequent use, had grown into a habit. He shrugged his shoulders, shook his head, cast up his eyes, but said nothing. This, however, always provoked a fresh volley from his wife, so that he was fain to draw off his forces, and take to the outside of the house—the only side which, in truth, belongs to a henpecked husband.

Rip's sole domestic adherent was his dog Wolf, who was as much henpecked as his master; for Dame Van Winkle regarded them as companions in idleness, and even looked upon Wolf with an evil eye, as the cause of his master's so often going astray. True it is, in all points of spirit befitting an honorable dog, he was as courageous an animal as ever scoured the woods—but what courage can withstand the ever-during and all-besetting terrors of a woman's tongue? The moment Wolf entered the house his crest fell, his tail drooped to the ground, or curled between his legs; he sneaked about with a gallows air, casting many a sidelong glance at Dame Van Winkle, and at the least flourish of a broomstick or ladle would fly to the door with yelping precipitation.

Times grew worse and worse with Rip Van Winkle as years of matrimony rolled on; a tart temper never mellows with age, and a sharp tongue is the only edged tool that grows keener by constant use. For a long while he used to console himself, when driven from home, by frequenting a kind of perpetual club of the sages, philosophers, and other idle personages of the village, which held its sessions on a bench before a small inn, designated by a rubicund portrait of his majesty George the Third. Here they used to sit in the shade, of a long lazy summer's day, talking listlessly over village gossip, or telling endless sleepy stories about nothing. But it would have been worth any statesman's money to have heard the profound discussions which sometimes took place, when by chance an old newspaper fell into their hands, from some passing traveler. How solemnly they would listen to the contents, as drawled out by Derrick Van Bummel, the schoolmaster, a dapper, learned little man, who was not to be daunted by the most gigantic word in the dictionary; and how sagely they would deliberate upon public events some months after they had taken place.

The opinions of this junto were completely controlled by Nicholas Vedder, a patriarch of the village, and landlord of the inn, at the door of which he took his seat from morning till night, just moving sufficiently to avoid the sun, and keep in the shade of a large tree; so that the neighbors could tell the hour by his movements as accurately as by a sundial. It is true, he was rarely heard to speak, but smoked his pipe incessantly. His adherents, however (for every great man has his adherents), perfectly understood him, and knew how to gather his opinions. When anything that was read or related displeased him, he was observed to smoke his pipe vehemently, and send forth short, frequent, and angry puffs; but when pleased, he would inhale the smoke slowly and tranquilly, and emit it in light and placid clouds, and sometimes taking the pipe from his mouth, and letting the fragrant vapor curl about his nose, would gravely nod his head in token of perfect approbation.

From even this stronghold the unlucky Rip was at length routed by his termagant wife, who would suddenly break in upon the tranquility of the assemblage, and call the members all to naught; nor was that august personage, Nicholas Vedder himself, sacred from the daring tongue of this terrible virago, who charged him outright with encouraging her husband in habits of idleness.

Poor Rip was at last reduced almost to despair; and his only alternative, to escape from the labor of the farm and clamor of his wife, was to take gun in hand and stroll away into the woods. Here he would sometimes seat himself at the foot of a tree, and share the contents of his wallet with Wolf, with whom he sympathized as a fellow-sufferer in persecution. "Poor Wolf," he would say, "thy mistress leads thee a dog's life of it; but never mind, my lad, while I live thou shalt never want a friend to stand by thee!" Wolf would wag his tail, look wistfully in his master's face, and if dogs can feel pity, I verily believe he reciprocated the sentiment with all his heart.

In a long ramble of the kind on a fine autumnal day, Rip had unconsciously scrambled to one of the highest parts of the Catskill Mountains. He was after his favorite sport of squirrel shooting, and the still solitudes had echoed and reechoed with the reports of his gun. Panting and fatigued, he threw himself, late in the afternoon, on a green knoll, covered with mountain herbage, that crowned the brow of the precipice. From an opening between the trees he could overlook all the lower country for many a mile of rich woodland. He saw at a distance the lordly Hudson, far, far below him, moving on its silent but majestic course, the reflection of a purple cloud, or the sail of a lagging bark, here and there sleeping on its glassy bosom, and at last losing itself in the blue highlands.

On the other side he looked down into a deep mountain glen, wild, lonely, and shagged, the bottom filled with fragments from the impending cliffs, and scarcely lighted by the reflected rays of the setting sun. For some time Rip lay musing on this scene; evening was gradually advancing; the mountains began to throw their long blue shadows over the valleys; he saw that it would be dark long before he could reach the village, and he heaved a heavy sigh when he thought of encountering the terrors of Dame Van Winkle.

As he was about to descend, he heard a voice from a distance, hallooing, "Rip Van Winkle! Rip Van Winkle!" He looked around, but could see nothing but a crow winging its solitary flight across the mountain. He thought his fancy must have deceived him, and turned again to descend, when he heard the same cry ring through the still evening air: "Rip Van Winkle! Rip Van Winkle!" At the same time Wolf bristled up his back, and giving a low growl, skulked to his master's side, looking fearfully down into the glen. Rip now felt a vague apprehension stealing over him; he looked anxiously in the same direction, and perceived a strange figure slowly toiling up the rocks, and bending under the weight of something he carried on his back. He was surprised to see any human being in this lonely and unfrequented place, but supposing it to be some one of the neighborhood in need of assistance, he hastened down to yield it.

On nearer approach, he was still more surprised at the singularity of the stranger's appearance. He was a short, square-built old fellow, with thick bushy hair, and a grizzled beard. His dress was of the antique Dutch fashion—a cloth jerkin strapped around the waist—several pair of breeches, the outer one of ample volume, decorated with rows of buttons down the sides, and bunches at the knees. He bore on his shoulders a stout keg, that seemed full of liquor, and made signs for Rip to approach and assist him with the load. Though rather shy and distrustful of this new acquaintance, Rip complied with his usual alacrity, and mutually relieving one another, they clambered up a narrow gully, apparently the dry bed of a mountain torrent. As they ascended, Rip every now and then heard long rolling peals, like distant thunder, that seemed to issue out of a deep ravine, or rather cleft between lofty rocks, toward which their rugged path conducted. He paused for an instant, but supposing it to be the muttering of one of those transient thunder showers which often take place in mountain heights, he proceeded. Passing through the ravine, they came to a hollow, like a small amphitheater, surrounded by perpendicular precipices, over the brinks of which impending trees shot their branches, so that you only caught glimpses of the azure sky and the bright evening cloud. During the whole time, Rip and his companion had labored on in silence, for though the former marveled greatly what could be the object of carrying a keg of liquor up this wild mountain, yet there was something strange and incomprehensible about the unknown that inspired awe and checked familiarity.

On entering the amphitheater, new objects of wonder presented themselves. On a level spot in the center was a company of odd-looking personages playing at ninepins. They were dressed in a quaint, outlandish fashion: some wore short doublets, others jerkins, with long knives in their belts, and most had enormous breeches, of similar style with that of the guide's. Their visages, too, were peculiar: one had a large head, broad face, and small, piggish eyes; the face of another seemed to consist entirely of nose, and was surmounted by a white sugar-loaf hat set off with a little red cock's tail. They all had beards, of various shapes and colors. There was one who seemed to be the commander. He was a stout old gentleman, with a weatherbeaten countenance; he wore a laced doublet, broad belt and hanger, high-crowned hat and feather, red stockings, and high-heeled shoes, with roses in them. The whole group reminded Rip of the figures in an old Flemish painting, in the parlor of Dominie Van Shaick, the village parson, and which had been brought over from Holland at the time of the settlement.

What seemed particularly odd to Rip, was that though these folks were evidently amusing themselves, yet they maintained the gravest faces, the most mysterious silence, and were, withal, the most melancholy party of pleasure he had ever witnessed. Nothing interrupted the stillness of the scene but the noise of the balls, which, whenever they were rolled, echoed along the mountains like rumbling peals of thunder.

As Rip and his companion approached them, they suddenly desisted from their play, and stared at him with such fixed statue-like gaze, and such strange, uncouth, lack-luster countenances, that his heart turned within him, and his knees smote together. His companions now emptied the contents of the keg into large flagons, and made signs to him to wait upon the company. He obeyed with fear and trembling; they quaffed the liquor in profound silence, and then returned to their game.

By degrees, Rip's awe and appre-hension subsided. He even ventured, when no eye was fixed upon him, to taste the beverage, which he found had much of the flavor of excellent Hollands. He was naturally a thirsty soul, and was soon tempted to repeat the draught. One taste provoked another, and he reiterated his visits to the flagon so often, that at length his senses were overpowered, his eyes swam in his head, his head gradually declined, and he fell into a deep sleep.

On awakening, he found himself on the green knoll from whence he had first seen the old man of the glen. He rubbed his eyes—it was a bright sunny morning. The birds were hopping and twittering among the bushes, and the eagle was wheel-ing aloft and breasting the pure mountain breeze. "Surely," thought Rip, "I have not slept here all night." He recalled the occurrences before he fell asleep. The strange man with a keg of liquor—the moun-tain ravine—the wild retreat among the rocks—the woe-begone party at ninepins—the flagon—"Oh! that flagon! that wicked flagon!" thought Rip—"what excuse shall I make to Dame Van Winkle?"

He looked round for his gun, but in place of the clean, well-oiled fowling piece, he found an old firelock lying by him, the barrel incrusted with rust, the lock falling off, and the stock worm-eaten. He now suspected that the grave roysters of the mountain had put a trick upon him, and having dosed him with liquor, had robbed him of his gun. Wolf, too, had dis-appeared, but he might have strayed away after a squirrel or partridge. He whistled after him, shouted his name, but all in vain; the echoes re-peated his whistle and shout, but no dog was to be seen.

He determined to revisit the scene of the last evening's gambol, and if he met with any of the party, to demand his dog and gun. As he rose to walk, he found himself stiff in the joints, and wanting in his usual activity. "These mountain beds do not agree with me," thought Rip, "and if this frolic should lay me up with a fit of the rheumatism, I shall have a blessed time with Dame Van Winkle." With some difficulty he got down into the glen; he found the gully up which he and his com-panion had ascended the preceding evening; but to his astonishment a mountain stream was now foaming down it, leaping from rock to rock, and filling the glen with babbling murmurs. He, however, made shift to scramble up its sides, working his toilsome way through thickets of birch, sassafras, and witch-hazel, and sometimes tripped up or entangled by the wild grape vines that twisted their coils and tendrils from tree to tree, and spread a kind of network in his path.

At length he reached to where the ravine had opened through the cliffs to the amphitheater; but no traces of such opening remained. The rocks presented a high, impenetrable wall, over which the torrent came tumbling in a sheet of feathery foam, and fell into a broad, deep basin, black from the shadows of the surrounding forest. Here, then, poor Rip was brought to a stand. He again called and whistled after his dog; he was only answered by the cawing of a flock of idle crows, sporting high in air about a dry tree that overhung a sunny precipice; and who, secure in their elevation, seemed to look down and scoff at the poor man's perplexities. What was to be done? The morning was passing away, and Rip felt famished for want of his breakfast. He grieved to give up his dog and gun; he dreaded to meet his wife; but it would not do to starve among the mountains. He shook his head, shouldered the rusty firelock, and, with a heart full of trouble and anxiety, turned his steps homeward.

As he approached the village, he met a number of people, but none whom he knew, which somewhat surprised him, for he had thought himself acquainted with everyone in the country round. Their dress, too, was of a different fashion from that to which he was accustomed. They all stared at him with equal marks of surprise, and whenever they cast their eyes upon him, invariably stroked their chins. The constant recurrence of this gesture induced Rip, involuntarily, to do the same, when, to his astonishment, he found his beard had grown a foot long!

He had now entered the skirts of the village. A troop of strange children ran at his heels, hooting after him, and pointing at his gray beard. The dogs, too, none of which he recognized for his old acquaintances, barked at him as he passed. The very village was altered: it was larger and more populous. There were rows of houses which he had never seen before, and those which had been his familiar haunts had disappeared. Strange names were over the doors—strange faces at the windows—everything was strange. His mind now misgave him; he doubted whether both he and the world around him were not bewitched. Surely this was his native village, which he had left but the day before. There stood the Catskill Mountains—there ran the silver Hudson at a distance—there was every hill and dale precisely as it had always been—Rip was sorely perplexed—"That flagon last night," thought he, "has addled my poor head sadly!"

It was with some difficulty he found the way to his own house, which he approached with silent awe, expecting every moment to hear the shrill voice of Dame Van Winkle. He found the house gone to decay—the roof fallen in, the windows shattered, and the doors off the hinges. A half-starved dog, that looked like Wolf, was skulking about it. Rip called him by name, but the cur snarled, showed his teeth, and passed on. This was an unkind cut, indeed—"My very dog," sighed poor Rip, "has forgotten me!"

He entered the house, which, to tell the truth, Dame Van Winkle had always kept in neat order. It was empty, forlorn, and apparently abandoned. This desolateness overcame all his connubial fears—he called loudly for his wife and children—the lonely chambers rang for a moment with his voice, and then all again was silence.

He now hurried forth, and hastened to his old resort, the little village inn—but it too was gone. A large rickety wooden building stood in its place, with great gaping windows, some of them broken, and mended with old hats and petticoats, and over the door was painted, "The Union Hotel, by Jonathan Doolittle." Instead of the great tree which used to shelter the quiet little Dutch inn of yore, there now was reared a tall naked pole, with something on the top that looked like a red nightcap, and from it was fluttering a flag, on which was a singular assemblage of stars and stripes—all this was strange and incomprehensible. He recognized on the sign, however, the ruby face of King George, under which he had smoked so many a peaceful pipe, but even this was singularly metamorphosed. The red coat was changed for one of blue and buff, a sword was stuck in the hand instead of a scepter, the head was decorated with a cocked hat, and underneath was painted in large characters, GENERAL WASHINGTON.

There was, as usual, a crowd of folk about the door, but none whom Rip recollected. The very character of the people seemed changed. There was a busy, bustling, disputatious tone about it, instead of the accustomed phlegm and drowsy tranquility. He looked in vain for the sage Nicholas Vedder, with his broad face, double chin, and fair long pipe, uttering clouds of tobacco smoke instead of idle speeches; or Van Bummel, the schoolmaster, doling forth the contents of an ancient newspaper. In place of these, a lean, bilious-looking fellow, with his pockets full of hand-bills, was haranguing vehemently about rights of citizens—election—members of Congress—liberty—Bunker's Hill—heroes of '76 —and other words, that were a perfect Babylonish jargon to the bewildered Van Winkle.

The appearance of Rip, with his long grizzled beard, his rusty fowling piece, his uncouth dress, and the army of women and children that had gathered at his heels, soon attracted the attention of the tavern politicians. They crowded around him, eyeing him from head to foot, with great curiosity. The orator bustled up to him, and drawing him partly aside, inquired "on which side he voted?" Rip stared in vacant stupidity. Another short but busy little fellow pulled him by the arm, and rising on tiptoe, inquired in his ear, "whether he was Federal or Democrat." Rip was equally at a loss to comprehend the questions; when a knowing, self-important old gentleman, in a sharp cocked hat, made his way through the crowd, putting them to the right and left with his elbows as he passed, and planting himself before Van Winkle, with one arm akimbo, the other resting on his cane, his keen eyes and sharp hat penetrating, as it were, into his very soul, demanded, in an austere tone, "what brought him to the election with a gun on his shoulder, and a mob at his heels, and whether he meant to breed a riot in the village?" "Alas! gentlemen," cried Rip, somewhat dismayed, "I am a poor quiet man, a native of the place, and a loyal subject of the King, God bless him!"

Here a general shout burst from the bystanders—"A Tory! a Tory! a spy! a refugee! hustle him! away with him!" It was with great difficulty that the self-important man in the cocked hat restored order; and having assumed a tenfold austerity of brow, demanded again of the unknown culprit, what he came there for, and whom he was seeking. The poor man humbly assured him that he meant no harm; but merely came in search of some neighbors, who used to keep about the tavern.

"Well—who are they?—name them."

Rip bethought himself a moment, and then inquired, "Where's Nicholas Vedder?"

There was silence for a little while, when an old man replied in a thin, piping voice, "Nicholas Vedder? why, he is dead and gone these eighteen years! There was a wooden tombstone in the churchyard that used to tell all about him, but that's all rotted and gone, too."

"Where's Brom Dutcher?"

"Oh, he went off to the army in the beginning of the war; some say he was killed at the battle of Stony Point—others say he was drowned in a squall, at the foot of Antony's Nose. I don't know—he never came back again."

"Where's Van Bummel, the schoolmaster?"

"He went off to the wars, too, was a great militia general, and is now in Congress."

Rip's heart died away, at hearing of these sad changes in his home and friends, and finding himself thus alone in the world. Every answer puzzled him, too, by treating of such enormous lapses of time, and of matters which he could not understand: war—Congress—Stony Point! —he had no courage to ask after any more friends, but cried out in despair, "Does nobody here know Rip Van Winkle?"

"Oh, Rip Van Winkle!" exclaimed two or three, "Oh, to be sure! that's Rip Van Winkle yonder, leaning against the tree."

Rip looked, and beheld a precise counterpart of himself, as he went up the mountain: apparently as lazy, and certainly as ragged. The poor fellow was now completely confounded. He doubted his own identity, and whether he was himself or another man. In the midst of his bewilderment, the man in the cocked hat demanded who he was, and what was his name?

"God knows," exclaimed he, at his wit's end; "I'm not myself—I'm somebody else—that's me yonder—no—that's somebody else, got into my shoes—I was myself last night, but I fell asleep on the mountain, and they've changed my gun, and everything's changed, and I'm changed, and I can't tell what's my name, or who I am!"

The bystanders began now to look at each other, nod, wink significantly, and tap their fingers against their foreheads. There was a whisper, also, about securing the gun, and keeping the old fellow from doing mischief; at the very suggestion of which, the self-important man in the cocked hat retired with some precipitation. At this critical moment a fresh, likely woman pressed through the throng to get a peep at the gray-bearded man. She had a chubby child in her arms, which, frightened at his looks, began to cry. "Hush, Rip," cried she, "hush, you little fool, the old man won't hurt you." The name of the child, the air of the mother, the tone of her voice, all awakened a train of recollections in his mind. "What is your name, my good woman?" asked he.

"Judith Gardenier."

"And your father's name?"

"Ah, poor man, his name was Rip Van Winkle; it's twenty years since he went away from home with his gun, and never has been heard of since—his dog came home without him; but whether he shot himself, or was carried away by the Indians, nobody can tell. I was then but a little girl."

Rip had but one question more to ask; but he put it with a faltering voice:—

"Where's your mother?"

"Oh, she too had died but a short time since; she broke a blood vessel in a fit of passion at a New England peddler."

There was a drop of comfort, at least, in this intelligence. The honest man could contain himself no longer. —He caught his daughter and her child in his arms. "I am your father!" cried he—"Young Rip Van Winkle once—old Rip Van Winkle now!— Does nobody know poor Rip Van Winkle!"

All stood amazed, until an old woman, tottering out from among the crowd, put her hand to her brow, and peering under it in his face for a moment, exclaimed, "Sure enough! it is Rip Van Winkle—it is himself! Welcome home again, old neighbor. —Why, where have you been these twenty long years?"

Rip's story was soon told, for the whole twenty years had been to him but as one night. The neighbors stared when they heard it; some were seen to wink at each other, and put their tongues in their cheeks; and the self-important man in the cocked hat, who, when the alarm was over, had returned to the field, screwed down the corners of his mouth, and shook his head—upon which there was a general shaking of the head throughout the assemblage.

It was determined, however, to take the opinion of old Peter Vanderdonk, who was seen slowly advancing up the road. He was a descendant of the historian of that name, who wrote one of the earliest accounts of the province. Peter was the most ancient inhabitant of the village and well versed in all the wonderful events and traditions of the neighborhood. He recollected Rip at once, and corroborated his story in the most satisfactory manner. He assured the company that it was a fact, handed down from his ancestor the historian, that the Catskill Mountains had always been haunted by strange beings. That it was affirmed that the great Hendrick Hudson, the first discoverer of the river and country, kept a kind of vigil there every twenty years, with his crew of the *Half-Moon*, being permitted in this way to revisit the scenes of his enterprise, and keep a guardian eye upon the river, and the great city called by his name. That his father had once seen them in their old Dutch dresses playing at ninepins in a hollow of the mountain; and that he himself had heard, one summer afternoon, the sound of their balls, like long peals of thunder.

To make a long story short, the company broke up, and returned to the more important concerns of the election. Rip's daughter took him home to live with her; she had a snug, well-furnished house, and a stout cheery farmer for a husband, whom Rip recollected for one of the urchins that used to climb upon his back. As to Rip's son and heir, who was the ditto of himself, seen leaning against the tree, he was employed to work on the farm; but evinced an hereditary disposition to attend to anything else but his business.

Rip now resumed his old walks and habits; he soon found many of his former cronies, though all rather the worse for the wear and tear of time; and preferred making friends among the rising generation, with whom he soon grew into great favor.

Having nothing to do at home and being arrived at that happy age when a man can do nothing with impunity, he took his place once more on the bench, at the inn door, and was reverenced as one of the patriarchs of the village, and a chronicle of the old times "before the war." It was some time before he could get into the regular track of gossip, or could be made to comprehend the strange events that had taken place during his torpor. How that there had been a revolutionary war—that the country had thrown off the yoke of old England—and that, instead of being a subject of his majesty, George III, he was now a free citizen of the United States. Rip, in fact, was no politician; the changes of states and empires made but little impression on him; but there was one species of despotism under which he had long groaned, and that was— petticoat government; happily, that was at an end; he had got his neck out of the yoke of matrimony, and could go in and out whenever he pleased, without dreading the tyranny of Dame Van Winkle. Whenever her name was mentioned, however, he shook his head, shrugged his shoulders, and cast up his eyes; which might pass either for an expression of resignation to his fate, or joy at his deliverance.

He used to tell his story to every stranger that arrived at Mr. Doolittle's hotel. He was observed, at first, to vary on some points every time he told it, which was, doubtless, owing to his having so recently awakened. It at last settled down precisely to the tale I have related, and not a man, woman or child in the neighborhood but knew it by heart. Some always pretended to doubt the reality of it, and insisted that Rip had been out of his head, and that was one point on which he always remained flighty. The old Dutch inhabitants, however, almost universally gave it full credit. Even to this day they never hear a thunderstorm of a summer afternoon, about the Catskills, but they say Hendrick Hudson and his crew are at their game of ninepins; and it is a common wish of all henpecked husbands in the neighborhood, when life hangs heavy on their hands, that they might have a quieting draught out of Rip Van Winkle's flagon.

❋ ❋ ❋

FREEDOM NEVER SLEEPS
WILLIAM CULLEN BRYANT

Oh! not yet
May'st thou unbrace thy corselet, nor lay by
Thy sword, nor yet, O Freedom! close thy lids
In slumber; for thine enemy never sleeps.
And thou must watch and combat, till the day
Of the new Earth and Heaven.

189

FREEDOM's soil hath only place
For a free and fearless race!
—*Whittier*

ART is the child of Nature.—*Longfellow*

LOOK, then, into thine heart, and write!—*Longfellow*

IF WE LOVE one another, nothing, in truth, can harm us, whatever mischances
may happen.—*Longfellow*

THE ONLY FAITH that wears well and holds its color in all weathers
is that which is woven of conviction and set with the sharp mordant
of experience.—*Lowell*

PURITANISM, believing itself quick with the seed of religious liberty, laid, without knowing it, the egg of democracy.—*Lowell*

WHO LOVES a garden still his Eden keeps, perennial pleasures plants,
and wholesome harvest reaps.—*Bronson Alcott*

SOME FALSEHOOD mingles with all truth.—*Longfellow*

THE LOWEST EBB is the turn of the tide.—*Longfellow*

CONSULT THE DEAD upon the things that were,
But the living only on things that are.
—*Longfellow*

BE NOBLE in every thought and in every deed!—*Longfellow*

FREEDOM IS re-created year by year,
In hearts wide open on the Godward side.
—*Lowell*

WISDOM OF LONGFELLOW

INTO EACH LIFE some rain must fall,
Some days must be dark and dreary.

ALL THINGS COME to him who will but wait.

FAME COMES ONLY when deserved, and then is as inevitable as destiny,
for it is destiny.

WE JUDGE OURSELVES by what we feel capable of doing, while others judge us
by what we have already done.

A SINGLE CONVERSATION across the table with a wise man is better than ten years'
study of books.

GLORIOUS INDEED IS THE WORLD of God around us, but more glorious
the world of God within us. There lies the land of song; there lies
the poet's native land.

IF WE COULD READ the secret history of our enemies we should find in each man's
life sorrow and suffering enough to disarm all hostility.

THE SETTING of a great hope is like the setting of the sun. The
brightness of our life is gone.

IF SPRING CAME BUT ONCE in a century instead of once a year, or
burst forth with the sound of an earthquake and not in silence,
what wonder and expectation there would be in all hearts, to behold the miraculous change.

ALL THAT I HAVE is the Lord's; not mine to give or withhold it;
His, not mine, are the gifts, and only so far can I make them
Mine, as in giving I add my heart to whatever is given.

FOR TIME WILL TEACH thee soon the truth,
There are no birds in last year's nest!

The Gray Champion

By NATHANIEL HAWTHORNE

In this American legend, one of America's great writers shows how the spirit of resistance to oppression has always appeared at times of crisis in American history.

THERE WAS ONCE A TIME (in 1689) when New England groaned under the actual pressure of heavier wrongs than those threatened ones which brought on the Revolution. James II, the bigoted successor of Charles the Voluptuous, had annulled the charters of all the colonies, and sent a harsh and unprincipled soldier to take away our liberties and endanger our religion. The administration of Sir Edmund Andros lacked scarcely a single characteristic of tyranny: a governor and council, holding office from the king, and wholly independent of the country; laws made and taxes levied without concurrence of the people immediate or by their representatives; the rights of private citizens violated, and the titles of all landed property declared void; the voice of complaint stifled by restrictions on the press; and, finally, disaffection overawed by the first band of mercenary troops that ever marched on our free soil. For two years our ancestors were kept in sullen submission by that filial love which had invariably secured their allegiance to the mother country, whether its head chanced to be a Parliament, Protector, or Monarch. Till these evil times, however, such allegiance had been merely nominal, and the colonists had ruled themselves, enjoying far more freedom than is even yet the privilege of the native subjects of Great Britain.

At length a rumor reached our shores that the Prince of Orange had ventured on an enterprise the success of which would be the triumph of civil and religious rights and the salvation of New England. It was but a doubtful whisper; it might be false, or the attempt might fail; and, in either case, the man that stirred against King James would lose his head. Still the intelligence produced a marked effect. The people smiled mysteriously in the streets, and threw bold glances at their oppressors; while far and wide there was a subdued and silent agitation, as if the slightest signal would rouse the whole land from its sluggish despondency. Aware of their danger, the rulers resolved to avert it by an imposing display of strength, and perhaps to confirm their despotism by yet harsher measures. One afternoon in April, 1689, Sir Edmund Andros and his favorite councillors, being warm with wine, assembled the redcoats of the Governor's Guard, and made their appearance in the streets of Boston. The sun was near setting when the march commenced.

The roll of the drum at that unquiet crisis seemed to go through the streets, less as the martial music of the soldiers than as a muster-call to the inhabitants themselves. A multitude, by various avenues, assembled in King Street, which was destined to be the scene, nearly a century afterward, of another encounter between the troops of Britain and a people struggling against her tyranny. Though more than sixty years had elapsed since the Pilgrims came, this crowd of their descendants still showed the strong and somber features of their character, perhaps more strikingly in such a stern emergency than on happier occasions. There was the sober garb, the general severity of mien, the gloomy but undismayed expression, the Scriptural forms of speech, and the confidence in Heaven's blessing on a righteous cause, which would have marked a band of the original Puritans, when threatened by some peril of the wilderness. Indeed, it was not yet time for the old spirit to be extinct; since there were men in the street that day who had worshipped there beneath the trees, before a house was reared to the God for whom they had become exiles. Old soldiers of the Parliament were here, too, smiling grimly at the thought, that their aged arms might strike another blow against the House of Stuart. Here, also, were the veterans of King Philip's War, who had burned villages and slaughtered young and old, with pious fierceness, while the godly souls throughout the land were helping them with prayer. Several ministers were scattered among the crowd, which, unlike all other mobs, regarded them with such reverence, as if there were sanctity in their very garments. These holy men exerted their influence to quiet the people, but not to disperse them. Meantime, the purpose of the Governor, in disturbing the peace of the town at a period when the slightest commotion might throw the country into a ferment, was almost the universal subject of inquiry, and variously explained.

"Satan will strike his master-stroke presently," cried some, "because he knoweth that his time is short. All our godly pastors are to be dragged to prison! We shall see them at a Smithfield fire in King Street!"

Hereupon the people of each parish gathered closer round their minister, who looked calmly upward and assumed a more apostolic dignity, as well befitted a candidate for the highest honor of his profession, the crown of martyrdom. It was actually fancied, at that period, that New England might have a John Rogers of her own, to take the place of that worthy in the Primer.

"The Pope of Rome has given orders for a new St. Bartholomew!" cried others. "We are to be massacred, man and male child!"

Neither was this rumor wholly discredited, although the wiser class believed the Governor's object somewhat less atrocious. His predecessor under the old charter, Bradstreet, a venerable companion of the first settlers, was known to be in town. There were grounds for conjecturing that Sir Edmund Andros intended at once to strike terror by a parade of military force, and to confound the opposite faction by possessing himself of their chief.

"Stand firm for the old charter, Governor!" shouted the crowd, seizing upon the idea. "The good old Governor Bradstreet!"

While this cry was at the loudest, the people were surprised by the well-known figure of Governor Bradstreet himself, a patriarch of nearly ninety, who appeared on the elevated steps of a door, and, with characteristic mildness, besought them to submit to the constituted authorities.

"My children," concluded this venerable person, "do nothing rashly. Cry not aloud, but pray for the welfare of New England, and expect patiently what the Lord will do in this matter!"

The event was soon to be decided. All this time the roll of the drum had been approaching through Cornhill, louder and deeper, till with reverberations from house to house, and the regular tramp of martial footsteps, it burst into the street. A double rank of soldiers made their appearance, occupying the whole breadth of the passage, with shouldered matchlocks, and matches burning, so as to present a row of fires in the dusk. Their steady march was like the progress of a machine that would roll irresistibly over everything in its way. Next, moving slowly, with a confused clatter of hoofs on the pavement, rode a party of mounted gentlemen, the central figure being Sir Edmund Andros, elderly, but erect and soldier-like. Those around him were his favorite councillors, and the bitterest foes of New England. At his right hand rose Edward Randolph, our arch-enemy, that "blasted wretch," as Cotton Mather calls him, who achieved the downfall of our ancient government, and was followed with a sensible curse, through life and to his grave. On the other side was Bullivant, scattering jests and mockery as he rode along. Dudley came behind, with a downcast look, dreading, as well he might. to meet the indignant gaze of the people, who beheld him, their only countryman by birth, among the oppressors of his native land. The captain of a

frigate in the harbor, and two or three civil officers under the Crown, were also there. But the figure which most attracted the public eye, and stirred up the deepest feeling, was the Episcopal clergyman of King's Chapel, riding haughtily among the magistrates in his priestly vestments, the fitting representative of prelacy and persecution, the union of Church and State, and all those abominations which had driven the Puritans to the wilderness. Another guard of soldiers, in double rank, brought up the rear.

The whole scene was a picture of the condition of New England, and its moral was the deformity of any government that does not grow out of the nature of things and the character of the people. On one side the religious multitude, with their sad visages and dark attire, and on the other, the group of despotic rulers, with the high churchman in the midst, and here and there a crucifix at their bosoms. all magnificently clad, flushed with wine, proud of unjust authority and scoffing at the universal groan. And the mercenary soldiers, waiting but the word to deluge the street with blood, showed the only means by which obedience could be secured.

"O Lord of Hosts," cried a voice among the crowd, "provide a Champion for thy people!"

This ejaculation was loudly uttered, and served as a herald's cry. to introduce a remarkable personage. The crowd had rolled back, and were now huddled together nearly at the extremity of the street, while the soldiers had advanced no more than a third of its length. The intervening space was empty—a paved solitude, between lofty edifices, which

194

threw almost a twilight shadow over it. Suddenly, there was seen the figure of an ancient man, who seemed to have emerged from among the people, and was walking by himself along the centre of the street, to confront the armed band. He wore the old Puritan dress, a dark cloak and a steeple-crowned hat, in the fashion of at least fifty years before, with a heavy sword upon his thigh, but a staff in his hand to assist the tremulous gait of age.

When at some distance from the multitude, the old man turned slowly round, displaying a face of antique majesty, rendered doubly venerable by the hoary beard that descended on his breast. He made a gesture at once of encouragement and warning, then turned again, and resumed his way.

"Who is this gray patriarch?" asked the young men of their sires.

"Who is this venerable brother?" asked the old men among themselves.

But none could make reply. The fathers of the people, those of fourscore years and upward, were disturbed, deeming it strange that they should forget one of such evident authority, whom they must have known in their early days, the associate of Winthrop, and all the old councillors, giving laws, and making prayers, and leading them against the savage. The elderly men ought to have remembered him, too, with locks as gray in their youth as their own were now. And the young! How could he have passed so utterly from their memories—that hoary sire, the relic of long-departed times, whose awful benediction had surely been bestowed on their uncovered heads in childhood?

"Whence did he come? What is his purpose? Who can this old man be?" whispered the wondering crowd.

Meanwhile, the venerable stranger, staff in hand, was pursuing his solitary walk along the center of the street. As he drew near the advancing soldiers, and as the roll of their drum came full upon his ear, the old man raised himself to a loftier mien, while the decrepitude of age seemed to fall from his shoulders, leaving him in gray but unbroken dignity. Now, he marched onward with a warrior's step, keeping time to the military music. Thus the aged form advanced on one side, and the whole parade of soldiers and magistrates on the other, till, when scarcely twenty yards remained between, the old man grasped his staff by the middle, and held it before him like a leader's truncheon.

"Stand!" cried he.

The eye, the face, and attitude of command; the solemn, yet warlike peal of that voice, fit either to rule a host in the battlefield or be raised to God in prayer, were irresistible. At the old man's word and outstretched arm, the roll of the drum was hushed at once, and the advancing line stood still. A tremulous enthusiasm seized upon the multitude. That stately form, combining the leader and the saint, so gray, so dimly seen, in such an ancient garb, could only belong to some old champion of the righteous cause, whom the oppressor's drum had summoned from his grave. They raised a shout of awe and exultation, and looked for the deliverance of New England.

The Governor and the gentlemen of his party, perceiving themselves brought to an unexpected stand, rode hastily forward, as if they would have pressed their snorting and affrighted horses right against the hoary apparition. He, however, blenched not a step, but glancing his severe eye round the group, which half encompassed him, at last bent it sternly on Sir Edmund Andros. One would have thought that the dark old man was chief ruler there, and that the Governor and Council, with soldiers at their back, representing the whole power and authority of the Crown, had no alternative but obedience.

"What does this old fellow here?" cried Edward Randolph, fiercely. "On, Sir Edmund! Bid the soldiers forward, and give the dotard the same choice that you give all his countrymen—to stand aside or be trampled on!"

"Nay, nay, let us show respect to the good grandsire," said Bullivant, laughing. "See you not, he is some old roundheaded dignitary, who hath lain asleep these thirty years, and knows nothing of the change of times? Doubtless, he thinks to put us down with a proclamation in Old Noll's name!"

"Are you mad, old man?" demanded Sir Edmund Andros in loud and harsh tones. "How dare you stay the march of King James's Governor?"

"I have stayed the march of the king himself, ere now," replied the gray figure, with stern composure. "I am here, Sir Governor, because the cry of an oppressed people hath disturbed me in my secret place; and beseeching this favor earnestly of the Lord, it was vouchsafed me to appear once again on earth, in the good old cause of his saints. And what speak ye of James? There is no longer a tyrant on the throne of England, and by tomorrow noon his name shall be a byword in this very street, where ye would make it a word of terror.

Back, thou that wast a Governor, back! With this night thy power is ended—tomorrow, the prison!— Back, lest I foretell the scaffold!"

The people had been drawing nearer and nearer, and drinking in the words of their champion, who spoke in accents long disused, like one unaccustomed to converse, except with the dead of many years ago. But his voice stirred their souls. They confronted the soldiers, not wholly without arms, and ready to convert the very stones of the street into deadly weapons. Sir Edmund Andros looked at the old man; then he cast his hard and cruel eye over the multitude, and beheld them burning with that lurid wrath, so difficult to kindle or to quench; and again he fixed his gaze on the aged form, which stood obscurely in an open space, where neither friend nor foe had thrust himself. What were his thoughts, he uttered no word which might discover. But whether the oppressor were overawed by the Gray Champion's look, or perceived his peril in the threatening attitude of the people, it is certain that he gave back, and ordered his soldiers to commence a slow and guarded retreat. Before another sunset, the Governor, and all that rode so proudly with him, were prisoners, and long ere it was known that James had abdicated, King William was proclaimed throughout New England.

But where was the Gray Champion? Some reported that, when the troops had gone from King Street, and the people were thronging tumultuously in their rear, Bradstreet, the aged Governor, was seen to embrace a form more aged than his own. Others soberly affirmed that, while they marvelled at the venerable grandeur of his aspect, the old man had faded from their eyes, melting slowly into the hues of twilight, till, where he stood, there was an empty space. But all agreed that the hoary shape was gone. The men of that generation watched for his reappearance, in sunshine and in twilight, but never saw him more, nor knew when his funeral passed, nor where his gravestone was.

And who was the Gray Champion? Perhaps his name might be found in the records of that stern Court of Justice, which passed a sentence, too mighty for the age, but glorious in all aftertimes, for its humbling lesson to the monarch and its high example to the subject. I have heard that whenever the descendants of the Puritans are to show the spirit of their sires the old man appears again. When eighty years had passed, he walked once more in King Street. Five years later, in the twilight of an April morning, he stood on the green beside the meeting-house at Lexington, where now the obelisk of granite, with a slab of slate inlaid, commemorates the first fallen of the Revolution. And when our fathers were toiling at the breastwork on Bunker Hill, all through that night the old warrior walked his rounds. Long, long may it be, ere he comes again! His hour is one of darkness, and adversity, and peril. But should domestic tyranny oppress us or the invader's step pollute our soil, still may the Gray Champion come, for he is the type of New England's hereditary spirit; and his shadowy march, on the eve of danger, must ever be the pledge that New England's sons will vindicate their ancestry.

GIVE ME THE SPLENDID SILENT SUN
WALT WHITMAN

Give me the splendid silent sun with all his beams full-dazzling,
Give me juicy autumnal fruit, ripe and red from the orchard,
Give me a field where the unmowed grass grows,
Give me an arbor, give me the trellised grape,
Give me fresh corn and wheat, give me serene-moving animals teaching
    content,
Give me nights perfectly quiet as on high plateaus west of the Mississippi,
    and I looking up at the stars,
Give me odorous at sunrise a garden of beautiful flowers where I can
    walk undisturbed,
Give me for marriage a sweet-breathed woman of whom I should never tire,
Give me a perfect child, give me, away aside from the noise of the
    world, a rural domestic life,
Give me to warble spontaneous songs recluse by myself, for my own ears
    only,
Give me solitude, give me Nature, give me again, O Nature, your primal
    sanities!

AS POOR RICHARD SAYS

BE INDUSTRIOUS and free; be frugal and free!

FOND PRIDE OF DRESS is, sure, a very curse;
Ere fancy you consult, consult your purse.

GREAT GOOD NATURE, without prudence, is a great misfortune.

GREAT BEAUTY, GREAT STRENGTH, and great riches are really and truly
of no great use; a right heart exceeds all.

ALL MANKIND are beholden to him that is kind to the good.

IN THE AFFAIRS of this world men are saved, not by faith,
but by the want of it.

IF YOU WOULD have a faithful servant, and one that you like, serve yourself.

BUY WHAT thou hast no need of, and ere long thou shalt sell thy necessaries.

HE THAT HATH A TRADE hath an estate, and he that hath a calling
hath an office of profit and honor.

BY DILIGENCE and patience the mouse ate the cable in two.

EMPLOY thy time well, if thou meanest to gain leisure.

FOR ONE POOR person there are a hundred *indigent*.

BUT DOST THOU love life? Then do not squander time,
for that's the stuff life is made of.

A GOOD EXAMPLE is the best sermon.

198

. . . . *BENJAMIN FRANKLIN*

BE ASHAMED to catch yourself idle!

CREDITORS have better memories than debtors.

THE EYE of the master will do more work than both his hands.

'TIS EASIER to suppress the first desire, than to satisfy all
that follow it.

TROUBLE springs from idleness, and grievous toil from needless ease.

WHEN I SEE A MERCHANT overpolite to his customers, begging them to take
a little brandy, and throwing his goods on the counter, thinks I, that man has
an ax to grind.

DILIGENCE is the mother of good luck, and God gives all things to industry.

LET OUR FATHERS and grandfathers be valued for *their* goodness,
ourselves for *our* own.

IF YOU WILL not hear reason, she'll surely rap your knuckles.

RATHER go to bed supperless than rise in debt.

PRIDE IS as loud to a beggar as Want,
and a great deal more saucy.

THERE are no gains without pains; then help, hands!

THEY THAT won't be counselled, can't be helped.

DRIVE thy business! Let not that drive thee!

Brer Rabbit Grossly Deceives Mr. Fox

By JOEL CHANDLER HARRIS

Here is another type of American legend—plantation folklore of the Old South, drawn from the boyhood memories of Joel Chandler Harris. Wise old Uncle Remus, who explains the mysteries of life through the actions of his amusing animals, has the simplicity of greatness.

ONE EVENING when the little boy, whose nights with Uncle Remus were as entertaining as those Arabian ones of blessed memory, had finished supper and hurried out to sit with his venerable patron, he found the old man in great glee. Indeed, Uncle Remus was talking and laughing to himself at such a rate that the little boy was afraid he had company. The truth is, Uncle Remus had heard the child coming and, when the rosy-cheeked chap put his head in at the door, was engaged in a monologue, the burden of which seemed to be—

> Ole Molly Har'
> W'at you doin' dar,
> Settin' in de cornder
> Smokin' yo' seegyar?

As a matter of course this vague allusion reminded the little boy of the fact that the wicked Fox was still in pursuit of the Rabbit, and he immediately put his curiosity in the shape of a question.

"Uncle Remus, did the Rabbit have to go clean away when he got loose from the Tar-Baby?"

"Bless grashus, honey, dat he didn't. Who? Him? You dunno nuthin' 'tall 'bout Brer Rabbit ef dat's de way you puttin' 'im down. W'at he gwine 'way fer? He moughter stayed sorter close twel de pitch rub off'n his ha'r, but twern't menny days 'fo' he was lopin' up en down de neighborhood same ez ever, en I dunno ef he wern't mo' sassier dan befo'.

"Seem like dat de tale 'bout how he got mixt up wid' de Tar-Baby got 'roun' 'mongst de nabers. Leas'-ways, Miss Meadows en de gals got win' un' it, en de nex' time Brer Rabbit paid 'um a visit Miss Meadows tackled 'im 'bout it, en de gals sot up a monstus gigglement. Brer Rabbit, he sot up des ez cool ez a cowcumber, he did, en let 'em run on."

"Who was Miss Meadows, Uncle Remus?" inquired the little boy.

"Don't ax me, honey. She wuz in de tale, Miss Meadows en de gals wuz, en de tale I give you like hi't wer' gun ter me. Brer Rabbit, he sot dar, he did, sorter lam' like, en den bimeby he cross his legs, he did, and wink his eye slow, en up and say, sezee:

"'Ladies, Brer Fox wuz my daddy's ridin'-hoss for thirty year; maybe mo', but thirty year dat I knows un,' sezee; en den he paid 'um his

200

'specks, en tip his beaver, en march off, he did, des ez stiff en ez stuck up ez a fire stick.

"Nex' day, Brer Fox cum a callin', and w'en he gun fer ter laugh 'bout Brer Rabbit, Miss Meadows en de gals, dey ups en tells 'im 'bout w'at Brer Rabbit say. Den Brer Fox grit his tushes sho' nuff, he did, en he look mighty dumpy, but w'en he riz fer ter go he up and say, sezee:

" 'Ladies, I ain't 'sputin' w'at you say, but I'll make Brer Rabbit chaw up his words en spit 'um out right yer whar you kin see 'im,' sezee, en wid dat off Brer Fox put.

"En w'en he gor in de big road, he shuck de dew off'n his tail, en made a straight shoot fer Brer Rabbit's house. W'en he got dar, Brer Rabbit wuz spectin' un 'im, en de do' wuz shet fas'. Brer Fox knock. Nobody ans'er. Brer Fox knock. Nobody ans'er. Den he knock agin—blam! blam! Den Brer Rabbit holler out mighty weak:

" 'Is dat you, Brer Fox? I want you ter run en fetch de doctor. Dat bait er pusly w'at I e't this mawnin' is gittin' 'way wid me. Do, please, Brer Fox, run quick,' sez Brer Rabbit, sezee.

" 'I come after you, Brer Rabbit,' sez Brer Fox, sezee. 'Dar's gwineter be a party up at Miss Meadows's,' sezee. 'All de gals'll be dere, en I promus' dat I'd fetch you. De gals, dey 'lowed dat hit wouldn't be no party 'ceppin' I fotch you,' sez Brer Fox, sezee.

"Den Brer Rabbit say he wuz too sick, en Brer Fox say he wuzzent, en dar dey had it up and down, 'sputin' en contendin'. Brer Rabbit say he can't walk. Brer Fox say he tote 'im. Brer Rabbit say how? Brer Fox say in his arms. Brer Rabbit say he drap 'im. Brer Fox 'low he won't. Bimeby Brer Rabbit say he go ef Brer Fox tote 'im on his back. Brer Fox say he would. Brer Rabbit say he can't ride widout a saddle. Brer Fox say he git de saddle. Brer Rabbit say he can't set in saddle less he have bridle fer ter hol' by. Brer Fox say he git de bridle. Brer Rabbit say he can't ride widout bline bridle, kaze Brer Fox be shyin' at stumps 'long de road, en fling 'im off. Brer Fox say he git bline bridle. Den Brer Rabbit say he go. Den Brer Fox say he ride Brer Rabbit mos' up ter Miss Meadows's, en den he could get down en walk de balance er de way. Brer Rabbit 'greed, en den Brer Fox lipt out atter de saddle en de bridle.

"Co'se Brer Rabbit know de game dat Brer Fox wuz fixin' fer ter play, en he 'termin' fer ter outdo 'im, en by de time he koam his ha'r en twis' his mustarch, en sorter rig up, yer come Brer Fox, saddle en bridle on, en lookin' ez peart ez a circus pony. He trot up ter de do' en stan' dar pawin' de ground en chompin' de bit same like sho 'nuff hoss, en Brer Rabbit he mount, he did, en dey amble off. Brer Fox can't see behime wid de bline bridle on, but bimeby he feels Brer Rabbit raise one er his foots.

" 'W'at you doin' now, Brer Rabbit?' sezee.

" 'Short'nin' de lef' stir'p, Brer Fox,' sezee.

"Bimeby Brer Rabbit raise up de udder foot.

" 'W'at you doin' now, Brer Rabbit?'' sezee.

" 'Pullin' down my pants, Brer Fox,' sezee.

"All de time, bless grashus, honey, Brer Rabbit wer' puttin' on his spurrers, en w'en dey got close to Miss Meadows's, whar Brer Rabbit wuz to git off, en Brer Fox made a motion fer ter stan' still, Brer Rabbit slap de spurrers inter Brer Fox flanks, en you better b'leeve he got over groun'. W'en dey got ter de house, Miss Meadows en all de gals wuz settin' on de peazzer, en stidder stoppin' at de gate, Brer Rabbit rid on by, he did, en den come gallopin' down de road en up ter de hossrack, w'ich he hitch Brer Fox at, en den he santer inter de house, he did, en shake han's wid de gals, en set dar, smokin' his seegyar same ez a town man. Bimeby he draw in a long puff, en den let hit out in a cloud, en squar hisse'f back en holler out, he did:

" 'Ladies, ain't I done tell you Brer Fox wuz de ridin'-hoss fer our fambly? He sorter losin' his gait now, but I speck I kin fotch 'im all right in a mont' er so,' sezee.

"En den Brer Rabbit sorter grin, he did, en de gals giggle, en Miss Meadows, she praise up de pony, en dar wuz Brer Fox hitch fas' ter de rack, en couldn't he'p hisse'f."

"Is that all, Uncle Remus?" asked the little boy as the old man paused.

"Dat ain't all, honey, but 'twon't do fer ter give out too much cloff fer ter cut one pa'r pants," replied the old man sententiously.

OUR LEGENDARY HEROES
By GEORGE EATON

PAUL BUNYAN, idol of our northern lumber camps . . . Pecos Bill, cow-punchin' king of the cowboys . . . Old Stormalong, rambunctious New England sailorman . . . Johnny Appleseed, the man Jonathan Chapman who became a legend . . . John Henry, giant Negro stevedore and railroad laborer . . . and Joe Magarac, Colossus of the steel workers . . . all are strictly American in the boundless courage and optimism with which they overcame every difficulty. Their gigantic achievements have been magnified from group to group, camp to camp, generation to generation until they have become enlarged images of the American *ideal*. Proof that great legends need not necessarily be tales from distant ages are these strong, courageous, fun-loving, vital personalities who will live on and grow with our country.

OBLIGATION
GAIL BROOK BURKET

Great men have gone before us.
Great men will follow after.
Time's vaulted arches echo
With their brave-hearted laughter.
The valiant men before us
Left all mankind their debtor.
They found life good in living
And sought to leave it better.

The men who follow after
Loom like a gleaming tower.
Can we be less than heroes
In our appointed hour?

THE WILDERNESS IS TAMED
Elizabeth Coatsworth

The ax has cut the forest down,
The laboring ox has smoothed all clear,
Apples now grow where pine trees stood,
And slow cows graze instead of deer.

Where Indian fires once raised their smoke
The chimneys of a farmhouse stand,
And cocks crow barnyard challenges
To dawns that once saw savage land.

The ax, the plow, the binding wall,
By these the wilderness is tamed,
By these the white man's will is wrought,
The rivers bridged, the new towns named.

I HEAR PAUL BUNYAN
Louise Leighton

When the night is still and the wind, that ancient squatter
Claiming the timeless land of the sky-blue water,
Sleeps in his weathered wigwam of birch bark,
I hear Paul Bunyan tramping through the dark.
I hear the sibilance of aspens quaking,
I feel the tremor his mighty feet are making,
I can almost see him striding by,
Parting the Norway pines to clear the sky.
Between the boughs the star-combed waters glisten,
And vibrant, breathing forests pause to listen,
As throb, throb, throbbing through the night,
Paul Bunyan haunts the land of his delight.

The Great Hunter of the Woods

By JAMES STEVENS

We now introduce the great Paul Bunyan,
legendary hero of American lumbermen.

"$\mathcal{I}$ WAS THINKIN' of the most famous hunt of history," said old Larrity the bull cook. "That was when Paul Bunyan, the first great hunter of the woods, shouldered his scatter-cannon to bring down the wing-tailed turkey that had ravaged the Round River country of its game. A terrible turkey that was, indade, for even such hunters as Paul Bunyan and Dublin, the wire-haired terror who was tall as any tree. Such huntin' there was in that time long ago, a time too far away for even mention in the history books."

The old logger stopped there for a shrewd glance at the two by his side. They were Jeff Gavin, whose grandfather was the owner of the logging camp, and Mike, the boy's wire-haired terrier pup. Both were staring mournfully at the flaming leaves of dogwood thickets up the creek. There three men in red caps and brown coats with big spotted dogs sniffing and scampering at their heels, had vanished a few moments before.

"Whist, now, and you should be glad your grandpa left you with me. Pheasants they will be shootin'," said Larrity scornfully. "And the huntin' of chickens is too triflin' for the bother of old woodsmen like us, so it is. How much better, Jeff, to sun ourselves here on the creek bank and talk of the days of real huntin'."

Curiosity lightened the boy's eyes. On other Saturday afternoons he had listened to stories of Paul Bunyan from old Larrity, who had learned them many years ago in the faraway Michigan woods. Here in the Oregon timber the stories would come to life. The Gavin grandson forgot his grief at being left in camp by the hunters. Mike, the terrier pup, also seemed resigned, as he stretched himself out in the rusty grass of the creek bank, crossed his paws, rested his chin on them and shut his eyes.

Old Larrity was telling of the great hunter of the woods. As his voice drawled on, the boy saw a mighty figure rising dimly among the shadows of the trees . . . . Paul Bunyan, whose curly black beard brushed the tree tops . . . and at his heels trotted Dublin, wire-haired terror of the hunting trails. . . .

On the first day of a certain Christmas week (said old Larrity) the great hunter of the woods and his dog, Dublin, marched into the Round River country. This was the game country in the time when Ameriky was all one big timberland, and Paul Bunyan was the ruler of it and all the rest. In the black wild woods circled by Round River the famous logger always did his Christmas huntin'. That was only to provide rare holiday dinners for his seven hun'erd bully men. This huntin' season the reg'lar game was ruined. And all because the terrible turkey, the most ferocious fowl of the tall timber, had at last migrated to Round River from the mountains of the North.

Paul Bunyan had no hint of the trouble and grief ahead as he tramped through the autumn woods for Round River. He saw nothin' but a promise of cheer in the keen, bright mornin'. Above him shone the clean blue sky and about him blazed the fire colors of leaves. The frost made his breath steam till white clouds trailed him. Sunlight glinted from the forty-seven barrels of his scatter-cannon. At his heels the tremendous terror was a gay dog, ever waggin' his tree of a tail.

For Paul Bunyan talked to Dublin, even as you talk to your Mike when the two of you walk together. It was all gladness in the mighty voice, for Paul Bunyan spoke of the men in the camp behind. Of Johnny Inkslinger Paul spoke, that timekeeper who was such a big figger that his pens were made of peeled trees. He had kind words also for the Big Swede, his foreman, and a man with legs so much like sawlogs that the reg'lar sized loggers were forever goin' after them with crosscuts and axes. Paul Bunyan spoke fondly to Dublin of Babe the Blue Ox, a beast that was even bigger than the dog, measurin' forty-two ax handles and a barrel of pickles betwixt the horns.

Of all these big figgers Paul Bunyan spoke kindly and well, but his best words were for his seven hun'erd men, who were no bigger than me or your grandfather. Never had his men done such fine loggin' as in this season. And for a reward they should have the grandest Christmas dinner ever heard of at all.

"What game shall it be for such a dinner?" said Paul Bunyan to Dublin, when they were to the bank of Round River. "The best meat will be none too good for my loggers' Christmas dinner, no sir! Should we bag some fat bucks for rabbit stews, Dublin? Or deer, to make a great steak dinner? Or cinnamon bears for the spicy roasts the loggers like so well? What do you say, you wire-haired terror, you?"

Dublin acted for all the world like he understood every one of Paul Bunyan's words. He sat down, and slowly scratched his ear with his left foot, seemin' to be in the deepest thought.

"I know what you want to be huntin', first, last and all the time, Dublin, I do." Paul Bunyan smiled down through his beard. "Yes, sir, mince-hunter that you are. You would have us go back with nothin' but mince meat for the Christmas pies, you would. But we must hunt other game than minces."

Sayin' that, he leaned restfully on his scatter-cannon and gazed into the black wild woods across the river. Now he began to notice that they were silent, almost. Every other autumn the woods had been roarin' with sounds of wild life. The game of the country had never migrated beyond the river that circled their home.

We would think such a stream as Round River most peculiar nowadays, but sure, in the time of Paul Bunyan rivers were young and wild, and each one would run to suit itself. It suited this river to run always in a circle, bein' too proud, no doubt, to run into another river, or even into the great salt ocean.

Whatever the reason, I'm telling you now, that river was round. In its circle lived timber beasts like the hodag and sauger, which are remembered only by old loggers. And there were creatures like our deer, rabbits, bobcats and bears, only, mind you, they all had tails in those times when the timberlands were young.

Fine and flourishin' tails were on all of them. The roarin' rabbit of the Round River woods was no such timorious, cowerin' and cringin' beastie as the rabbit of our time. Before he lost his tail the Round River rabbit would tackle a panther, he would, noosin' his powerful, long tail about the beast's neck, jerkin' him down, then kickin' the life out of the panther with both hind feet. In them days the blood-curdlin' roar of a rabbit was the most awful of all the wild wood sounds. The rabbits had run all the panthers out of the woods when the terrible turkey came to Round River.

The deer of them woods also had a fine tail for himself, one like a plume and the brightest spot of beauty in the forest. The bobcat's tail was more of a fightin' kind, like you'd expect. It was a fang tail, with sharp teeth in the tip, and with them the bobcat would strike like a snake at birds and small beasts for his prey. The black and cinnamon bears had stiff brushy tails which they used mostly for the sweepin' of their caves. There were never cleaner creatures than the cave bears of Paul Bunyan's time; always hustlin' and bustlin' in every nook and cranny, keepin' everything spick and span.

Paul Bunyan did not dream that such a course had befallen the timber beasts as the loss of their tails. He had never even heard of the wing-tailed terrible turkey, so of course he did not know how this ferocious fowl made its meals. The dismal quiet of the black wild woods was all a mystery to Paul Bunyan, a quiet broken only by a whispering moan

like the rustle of wind in trees at night. But this was no wind, indade; it was the timber beasts of Round River, hidin' away, and sighin' in sorrow and sadness for the lost tails of them.

Paul Bunyan wondered and worried, as he forded the river. Not even the mutter of a mince was heard, for that little beast, whose meat was so good for pies, was entirely gone. On no other huntin' trip had Paul Bunyan and Dublin come into the woods without hearin' minces mutterin' from their lairs. For the minces of Round River always muttered, so they did, just as the rabbits roared and the bears bellowed and growled. That mutter was the sweetest of music to the wire-haired terror's ears.

At last Dublin thought he heard it, when they had reached the inside bank of Round River. Paul Bunyan leaned on his scatter-cannon again, and wondered and worried still more about the dismal quiet of the black wild woods, with only that whisperin' moan to break it at all. But something else was soundin' in the terror's ears. He perked them up and made himself believe that this was a mince mutterin' out of the woods. So he came to a point, with the blunt muzzle of himself stuck out, and his tail wavin' and waggin' in the wind. For Dublin could never point a mince without h'istin' and waggin' his fine tail, such a gay dog he was when huntin' his favorite game.

Then it happened. What Dublin thought was the mutter of a mince suddenly growed into growlin' thunder. Paul Bunyan stiffened up, but before he could bring the scatter-cannon to his shoulder a coppery streak touched with red at the head of it and with a whirlin' blur behind, flashed from sight along the circle of the river. In the same instant there rose a fearful howl of grief from the wire-haired terror.

Pore dog, indeed pore Dublin, sure he had a right to howl, for all but a stub of his tail was gone, clipped clean away before he could wink an eye. Now he was a sad dog, with tears tricklin' from his eyes as he looked up at Paul Bunyan. He whimpered and moaned with a sound which melted into that whisperin' from the forest, and now that was a mystery no longer to Paul Bunyan. He knew the reason for the sorrowful sound. Certainly all the timber beasts had been denuded of their tails, and like Dublin all were bemoanin' their loss. And the robber of all was none other than this red-headed thunderbolt in coppery feathers, this ferocious fowl who drove like lightnin' through the air by the power of his whirlin' wing tail.

Paul Bunyan figgered that out as he doctored Dublin's hurt with arnicky, stanched it and bound it. Then with kind words he comforted the grievin' terror. As he did so, he again heard that sound like the mutter of a mince from its lair; and it soon growed into rolls of thunder.

The great hunter of the woods stared up at the sound, his head turnin' back till the tip of his curly black beard waved at the sky. And here was the roar and the rush again; but now it was Paul Bunyan's time to howl; for all of his beard was gone, so it was, nipped and clipped slick away from his chin.

But Paul Bunyan did not howl with grief, nor did he roar with rage or sigh with sorrow or anything like that at all. Paul Bunyan was not that kind of a man. Enough had happened, indade, to drive anybody distracted—the ruin of the game, the loss of the grand Christmas dinner he had planned for his men, the thievery of Dublin's fine tail, and the snippin' and pluckin' away of his famous beard. Disaster and disgrace it all was, enough to make even a hero like Paul Bunyan despair.

But sure the great hunter would not give up, not even when he realized that he could do no thinkin' until his beard growed out again. Paul Bunyan could think only when he brushed his beard with a young pine tree. Now he had no beard to brush at all.

"If I cannot think, then I must act," said Paul Bunyan, makin' the best of things. "And I'll do that soon and sudden."

What to do was plain enough. Paul Bunyan could see it all without thinkin'. Both times the wing-tailed terrible turkey had flown in a perfect circle, follyin' the course of Round River. To get the feathered thunderbolt on the wing, he must shoot in a circle. So Paul Bunyan first bent the forty-seven barrels of his scatter-cannon so that they would do just that—shoot their loads of cannon balls in an in-curve that would exactly folly the course of Round River.

Next, it was plain that he must set up a lure, to bring the ferocious fowl swoopin' down again. Paul Bunyan fixed a lure by pluckin' a colossyal cattail from the riverbank and bindin' it to the pore stump left to Dublin. The dog whimpered, and he shed more tears at such a fake of a tail; he felt disgraced, indade, to have a cattail foisted on such a tremenjus dog as himself, and would have stuck it betwixt his hind legs and crept off in shame. But Paul

Bunyan spoke to him stern-like, and Dublin, obejient wire-haired terror that he was, set up and took notice, flourishin' the shameful fake of a tail to please his master.

Well, the fake fooled the terrible turkey, who had no more brains than the small gobblers of our own time. Soon there was the mutter again, and then the thunder. A coppery streak bolted down from the blue sky, and the false tail was snipped up like lightnin'. So fast was it grabbed and gobbled that Paul Bunyan's scatter-cannon would have been no use at all, had not the terrible turkey gone red with wrath over the deceit played on him. He stopped in mid air to spit the cattail out of his beak, and also to strut and pout—and that was the chance for the great hunter to bring him down.

For two seconds Paul Bunyan took careful aim. The terrible turkey hovered low, and so was on a level with Paul Bunyan's shoulders. While he hovered, he puffed and swelled, the terrible turkey did, till only his wattles showed like flames from his ruffle of coppery feathers. His wrathy gobbles sounded like the stormiest thunder now. The wing tail of him, spread like a windmill, whirled slow, just holdin' him above the trees.

Paul Bunyan's aim was set. He squeezed the trigger, and the forty-seven barrels roared as one cannon. The balls whistled and screamed, powder smoke fogged up like a storm cloud, the earth shook, the timber shivered, and waves rolled over the river from the mighty blast of Paul Bunyan's scatter-cannon. The terrible turkey took alarm in the instant of an instant, so he did.

The cloud of balls was hardly out of the muzzles before he was off at full speed, his side wings spread, his wing tail a whirlin' blur again, his body a red-headed coppery streak.

"A second too late," groaned Paul Bunyan. "He is out-flyin' my cannon balls, a curse on me now for bein' too careful and slow!"

The terrible turkey was gone. The streak and blur of him disappeared around the curve of the river. The cloud of cannon balls curved after him, but slower, and they were soon left behind.

Paul Bunyan was like to give up at that. He was minded to turn his back on the huntin' woods at once and return to his loggers with an empty bag. Never had he been so grieved, to know that this year he could give his loggers no fine Christmas dinner. Dublin stood by him and licked his hand, tryin' also, pore dog, to wag the stub of a tail which was left to him.

"So we must go back, Dublin," said Paul Bunyan sadly, "without even a mince for the loggers. Dear, oh, dear, and such a curse!"

He swung his gun over his shoulder to go. Just then the terrible turkey thundered down the river again. It was roarin' thunder indade this trip, for the fowl had his wing tail whirlin' at the speed limit. Down the river he curved, and was gone. And now, from away back up the river, sounded the whistle and screech of the cannon balls, too slow indade for that feathered thunderbolt. Paul Bunyan blushed with shame to see them so far behind.

Now they were beginnin' to fall. White spouts of water and foam gushed up from the river as spent cannon balls dropped, the spray flashin' in the sunlight, makin' rainbows bright to see. But Paul Bunyan took no joy in the sight. He was ashamed to think that his cannon balls were so slow that the terrible turkey might catch 'em from behind in the great circle of the river.

Paul Bunyan raised his eyes, to look behind the cannon balls which still whistled and whined down the river. And now Paul Bunyan got a hope, a flimsy and scrawny hope, but he needed no more. Paul Bunyan was that kind of a man.

"Up and ready, Dublin!" he roared. "Sic 'em, boy! *Up* the river!"

That was enough for Dublin. What was up the wire-haired terror didn't know, but he lepped up river. And with that Paul Bunyan threw up his scatter-cannon with the forty-seven barrels of it curved like a hoop; and he let fly. After the terrible turkey? Not at all. Sure, he'd tried that once. The bird was too fast for that. Paul Bunyan turned his back and fired in the opposite direction. For when he said to Dublin, "*Up* the river, boy," he'd bent the forty-seven barrels to the other side. Down the river curved the big bird and was gone. So *up* the river curved the shot, whistling and screeching. And Dublin after them.

There was a great sound as the terrible turkey flew head on into them new cannon balls. Feathers flew in clouds, and the river boiled and foamed as the cannon balls splashed down. The terrible turkey fell, but in a great rainbow curve, for his speed carried him on, turnin' him over and over, while the dog lepped in frantic chase of him.

Paul Bunyan runnin' after both, saw the terrible turkey sail down like a coppery cloud, while Dublin lunged up like a black-spotted white cloud to meet him. The great hunter reached the death-grapple just in time. With one snap Dublin had taken off the terrible turkey's head in return for

his tail and was goin' after the rest of him. Paul Bunyan had to grope his way to the dog through a snowstorm of feathers, but he got there in time.

Dublin soon had the terrible turkey well plucked. And when Paul Bunyan saw the royal drumsticks of the fowl, the rich meat of his breast, the grandeur of his giblets, and all the rest, his gladness was so great that he was like to sheddin' tears of joy.

"Would you but look at the drumsticks of him, Dublin!" cried Paul Bunyan. "What logger would ask for a rabbit stew, deer steak or cinnamon bear roast, when he can have such fine eatin' as this for his Christmas dinner? Tender and plump, juicy and drippin', crisped to a fine golden brown, stuffed till he bulges, this behemoth of a bird will be enough for twice seven hun'erd men. Here is the meat for the finest Christmas dinner ever heard of; yes, sir!"

Yet the Dublin dog looked troubled. And Paul Bunyan knew why.

"Never mind," said the great logger cheerily. "I'll invent a recipe for mince meat which will beat that from the mutterin' minces of the Round River woods. You leave it to me, Dublin."

And so Paul Bunyan did. He invented such fine mince meat that cooks have used it ever since, and minces are never hunted any more for their meat at all. And the dinner from the terrible turkey was so ravishin' to Paul Bunyan's seven hun'erd men that they took his breast bone and made a mountain out of it, to stand as a moniment to the first Christmas turkey dinner.

And so we have had turkey dinners for Christmas ever since. To be sure, they are not terrible turkeys nowadays, for Paul Bunyan glued up the tails of all the young ones of the turkey tribe, and soon they had forgot how to fly with any but their side wings. But even our tame turkeys of today will pout and strut and spread their stiff tails, just like the terrible turkey of old. And their tails look like windmills, but never can they twist and turn, to make turkeys fly like lightnin' and thunder. Nor can our tame turkeys bite off dogs' tails, but they will peck at them every chance, in memory of what the daddy of 'em all used to do.

There is a bit of sadness to remember, too. For the rabbit was made a coward by the loss of the tail with which he choked panthers in the old times, and the rabbit roars no more. Nor did deer, bobcats and bears ever grow fine tails again. Neither do you see tails worth the mention on wire-haired terrors, these tiny descendants of Dublin, the tremendous terror who follied the first great hunter of the woods.

But sure it was worth it all to discover the glory of turkey for Christmas dinner. For that you must ever remember Paul Bunyan.

Old Larrity was silent. Jeff stroked his dog's head and stared out into the timber. Now, here in the autumn woods, he could imagine that he was Paul Bunyan and that Mike the pup was Dublin, a wire-haired terrier as tall as a tree.

THE CONCORD HYMN
Ralph Waldo Emerson

By the rude bridge that arched the flood,
Their flag to April's breeze unfurled,
Here once the embattled farmers stood,
And fired the shot heard round the world.

The foe long since in silence slept;
Alike the conqueror silent sleeps;
And Time the ruined bridge has swept
Down the dark stream which seaward creeps.

On this green bank, by this soft stream,
We set today a votive stone;
That memory may their deed redeem,
When, like our sires, our sons are gone.

Spirit, that made those spirits dare
To die, and leave their children free,
Bid Time and Nature gently spare
The shaft we raise to them and thee.

210

CENTENNIAL HYMN

JOHN GREENLEAF WHITTIER

Our fathers' God! From out whose hand
The centuries fall like grains of sand,
We meet today, united, free,
And loyal to our land and Thee,
To thank Thee for the era done,
And trust Thee for the opening one.

Here, where of old, by Thy design,
The fathers spake that word of Thine
Whose echo is the glad refrain
Of rended bolt and falling chain,
To grace our festal time, from all
The zones of earth our guests we call.

Be with us while the New World greets
The Old World thronging all its streets,
Unveiling all the triumphs won
By art or toil beneath the sun;
And unto common good ordain
This rivalship of hand and brain.

Thou, who hast here in concord furled
The war flags of a gathered world,
Beneath our Western skies fulfil
The Orient's mission of good will,
And, freighted with love's Golden Fleece,
Send back its Argonauts of peace.

For art and labor met in truce,
For beauty made the bride of use,
We thank Thee; but, withal, we crave
The austere virtues strong to save,
The honor proof to place or gold,
The manhood never bought nor sold!

Oh make Thou us, through centuries long,
In peace secure, in justice strong;
Around our gift of freedom draw
The safeguards of Thy righteous law:
And, cast in some diviner mould,
Let the new cycle shame the old!

211

WORDS OF GREAT AMERICANS:

New occasions teach new duties.

Talent is that which is in a man's power;
Genius is that in whose power a man is!

Not suffering, but faint heart, is worst of woes.

The soil out of which such men as he are made is good to be born on,
good to live on, good to die for and to be buried in.

In the scale of the destinies, brawn will never weigh so much as brain.

It was in making education not only common to all, but in some sense compulsory on all, that the destiny of the free republics of America was practically settled.

Don't print too much and too soon; don't get married in a hurry; read what will make you think, not dream; hold yourself dear, and more power to your elbow. (to William Dean Howells)

There is no work of genius which has not been the delight of mankind, no word of genius to which the human heart and soul have not sooner or later responded.

The devil loves nothing better than the intolerance of reformers, and dreads nothing so much as their charity and patience.

It is by presence of mind in untried emergencies, that the native metal of a man is tested.

He gives nothing but worthless gold
Who gives from a sense of duty.

Democracy gives every man the right to be his own oppressor:

212

JAMES RUSSELL LOWELL

NOT FAILURE, but low aim, is crime.

I DO NOT FEAR to follow out the truth,
Albeit along the precipice's edge . . . .

BEFORE MAN made us citizens, great Nature made us men.

THERE IS NO GOOD in arguing with the inevitable. The only argument
available with an east wind is to put on your overcoat.

DEMOCRACY means not "I am equal to you" but "you are equal to me."

THE SECRET OF FORCE in writing lies not so much in the pedigree of nouns and
adjectives and verbs, as in having something that you believe in to say, and
making the parts of speech vividly conscious of it.

PRESIDENT LINCOLN DEFINED democracy to be "the government of the people,
by the people, for the people." This is a sufficiently compact statement of it as
a political arrangement. Theodore Parker said that "Democracy meant not
'I'm as good as you are,' but 'You're as good as I am'." And this is the ethical
conception of it, necessary as a complement of the other.

TRUTH IS QUITE BEYOND the reach of satire. There is so brave a
simplicity in her that she can have no more to be made ridiculous than an oak or a pine.

ONCE TO EVERY MAN and nation comes the moment to decide,
In the strife of Truth with Falsehood, for the good or evil side.

BUT THE TUFT OF MOSS before him
Opened while he waited yet,
And, from out the rock's hard bosom,
Sprang a tender violet.

THEY WHO LOVE are but one step from Heaven.

The Fleet Goes By

By MARY SYNON

*P*OISED like some watcher on a tower, Alida Cushing, known to her public as Mademoiselle Alvidua, of the Milan Opera, stood at the prow of the liner, which was bringing her again to Malta, the scene of her first triumph.

Nine years before she had won it, she had left San Francisco, an adventuring girl of nineteen, in the company of her Spanish grandmother, the Señora Alvidua. She had gone to Malta, an unknown singer, and had there been given an eleventh-hour chance, in the rôle of *Tosca*. She had scaled the heights in the presence of the prince who was soon to be King of England. Now, after five years of Continental successes had established her position, she was going back to Malta to receive the decoration that the governor of the island was to give her in token of his majesty's remembrance of the night when Fame had found her.

One of the passengers, distinctively American, stood watching the singer intently. At last he rose and went to where she stood looking out on the stone walls of the harbor into which the liner was sliding. "Looks a little like our old San Francisco, doesn't it, greaser?" he asked.

Alida Cushing flashed toward him, her eyes blazing rebuke of the stranger's impertinence even before she realized the import of his words. His white hat came off with a flourish as he faced her in amused appraisal. "I am," he said, "at the service of Mademoiselle Alvidua, if Alida Cushing doesn't remember her old friends."

"Billy Corse!" she cried. "Where did you come from? What are you doing here? How did you know me?

Oh, but I am most happy to see you!"

"Not half so glad as I am to see you," he declared fervently. "I've come from New York by way of Havre. You came aboard at Tunis?"

"I sing at Malta tonight," she explained. "A command performance. Can you stay over? Or are you on a cruise?"

"I shall stay in Malta," said Billy Corse, "if all the fleets in the world change course today. To hear you sing again I should mutiny from heaven."

"What do you here?"

Billy Corse laughed at the little foreign idiom. "I do here begin to labor," he told her. "I am of the wicked who never cease from troubling. I am a day laborer for the United Press, and I've come to meet the fleet, or that part of it that passes here today. You see, we've a war on tap with Mexico, and I've orders to swing in on the chance that our ships will go right into the Gulf."

"With Mexico? Is it so?"

Billy Corse stared at her frowningly. "You're the first American I've met since I left New York who wasn't half-mad with excitement over the mere idea."

"They haven't lived over here long," she said. "I know very little of America any more, I haven't been there in years."

"Aren't you ever going home again?"

"Our home is in Paris."

"Honestly?" Billy Corse shoved his hands into his pockets and stood looking down at her. "I suppose," he said, "that it's all right, but, you see, I remember the Alida Cushing who used to carry the flag up Nob Hill in front of a crowd of us young ruffians. She was a girl who wanted to lead a raid on Chinatown because it was a foreign menace."

"How very funny she must have been!"

"Don't you want to see the landing?" he asked Alida. As she turned to go with him the *señora* admonished her not to forget that Sir William was to meet them at the dock.

"Who is Sir William?" Corse asked directly.

"Sir William Price-Cherrill," Alida told him. "He's a special commissioner of the British Government to Malta, and he has brought the decoration that the girl who used to carry the flag up Nob Hill will be given tonight."

"I've heard of him," said Billy Corse. "He's a wonderful chap they say; one of the fellows who look like Christmas trees when they wear their service medals. Know him well?"

"Very well," Alida said. She was looking toward the landing-stage with the gaze of one who sees beyond the scene into great vistas, the look that Billy Corse had glimpsed while she stood at the prow.

He sighed suddenly. "I suppose," he said, "that life over here has fascinations, especially for a woman with a gift like yours. And yet it hurts me a little that a real American girl turns her back on the stars and stripes. Out there on the coast we had to fight harder to *be* Americans than the folks back East did. Sometimes the mountains made it seem another country. But we proved up, didn't we? And now one of the girls we want to keep ours chooses to be an expatriate."

"You don't understand," she told him. "I'm not unpatriotic, Billy, but I have no interests in America any more. All the beauty, all the opportunity, all the inspiration of my life have come to me over here. And since father died I've no tie to take me back."

"It's your country," said Billy Corse.

"You do not grow up, do you?" She smiled in deprecation of her words as she felt his rising irritation. Billy Corse had been one of her most joyous playmates in the days before Doña Alvidua had found her granddaughter's gift. She was very glad to find Billy Corse so little changed. "You will come to the opera tonight?" she asked him.

"If I have to kill a king to get there," he promised.

Their handclasp made the promise binding, and Billy Corse, old enough to know better, thrilled under it boyishly. But when he saw her meeting the big Englishman, whose visible importance had brought him first over the gangplank, Billy Corse clenched his fist.

At the landing and all about the hotel there was an atmosphere of excitement. So vividly alert were the officers, whose brilliant uniforms blazed through the dining-hall, that the singer demanded of Sir William: "What's happening here? Or what is about to happen?"

"Oh, didn't you know?" he asked. "Your fleet comes here today."

"The American fleet?"

215

"And isn't that yours?" he inquired.

"I haven't been in America for nearly fourteen years," she said.

"That's of no consequence," he said lightly. "I was away from home for eleven years once. But England's England, no matter where I am. Your country's born into you, you know, like your eyes, or your hair, or your voice."

Then he fell into talk of other things, but two hours later, after she had been able to retreat in preparation for her appearance at the opera, Alida Cushing remembered Sir William's words.

The beauty of Malta, the softened, dream-making loveliness of the island, drew her from her room to the balcony from which she might see afar across the city of Valetta to the open sea. Looking upon it, Alida Cushing drew a sharp breath of triumphant appreciation that she, too, was a conqueror of Malta. Then, as the tide turned back, her triumph went out in the thought that, like every other conqueror, she was alien to the land she had won. To the men and women of the official world of the island, Malta was but a place of service, of exile. "England was England" to them. The *señora* had carried Spain in her heart through forty years of life in another land. Billy Corse, scouting the world, held his country as sword and shield. Only she, Alida Cushing, born in San Francisco and "one of the Massachusetts Cushings," was an expatriate.

Below her, past the grim walls of fortifications, beyond the gay sails of polyglot craft near the shore, four battleships lay at anchor. Something in their line, their color, brought to Alida Cushing the certainty that these were the ships that Billy Corse had come to meet, that these were the warships of the American fleet.

Into the picture there shifted poignant memories of her old home, and of that ship that had lain in San Francisco harbor on the day when the boys of the First California had come home from the Philippines. With the eyes of memory she looked through the years to that most vivid scene of her last days in her father's house. She was standing on its balcony, straining her eyes as up Van Ness Avenue came the regiment, marching slowly behind the long line of ambulances. No cheer greeted them. For the watchers remembered how the boys of the First had gone out to the East, one thousand and six of them. And not five hundred had come back.

The gloom of that procession, wending its way toward the Presidio, had clutched at the heart of the watching girl till she felt that she must cry out a tocsin of courage, of gratitude, to the men who had come back from the war. They had fought. They had suffered. They had been ready to die as their comrades had died. Would no one tell them that they had not fought in vain? Alida Cushing had reached above her, snatching down the flag that her father had raised that morning, and, waving it on high, the girl had cried out in that glorious voice that was to thrill kings and emperors in after years: "Well, anyhow, boys, you won!" One white-faced boy in the ranks had shouted back to her: "You bet we did win, kid!" And her father had caught her to him with such a look of pride and glory on his face as she never saw before and never saw again. "Thank God," he had said, "you're an American!"

Darkness came over the sea before Alida Cushing moved from the place of her vision. Then she took her way to the Royal Opera House.

When the curtain had gone down on the last act of *Louise*, the governor of Malta, between the cheers of an audience that filled the building, gave to Alida Cushing, of the Milan opera, the decoration sent to her by his Most Gracious Majesty, George the Fifth, King of Great Britain and Ireland, and Emperor of India. Billy Corse, standing in the wings, saw the tears that filled the singer's eyes. The orchestra leader waited her final obeisance before he struck up the notes of "God Save the King." But Alida Cushing did not bow herself toward the wings, but pushed her way through the masses of flowers till she stood at the footlights.

Her gaze, intent and eager, went past the royal box and over the heads of the splendidly gowned women and the gorgeously red-coated men who had come to give her tribute. It glanced in its way upon the white-uniformed officers of the American ships. It rose higher and higher till it found the blue-clad sailors, the jackies of the fleet, sitting in the high tiers of the gallery. And it was to them she spoke.

"Every one has always been good to me over here," she said, "and I can never say how wonderful tonight has been. I'm grateful, oh, so grateful, and I hope that all those who have been so good to me will understand why I must ask their patience for just one favor more. I'm an American, one of you. And I know that our friends here would wish me to sing you an American song."

The orchestra leader raised his baton, looking upward inquiringly to catch her signal. But without orchestra she began:

Oh, say, can you see—

A shuffling surge, as when the sea strikes cliffs, swept through the opera-house. White-uniformed officers, blue-uniformed men rose to their feet, standing at attention, every man's face alight. Breathless, red-coated men and the bejeweled women beside them watched the governor of Malta. A moment he frowned, as if puzzled by the meaning of the song. Then he arose. And every red-coated man at the opera that night arose with him.

It was the jackies who joined in the last chorus. It was the jackies who led the maddest cheers that had ever shaken Valetta's opera house. They were still cheering when Alida Cushing came back to the wings where Sir William Price-Cherrill stood beside Billy Corse. The Englishman spoke to her first.

"We all hear the call," he said, "when our fleets go by, do we not?"

"Yes," she said, "we hear it."

Then she turned to Billy Corse. "I'm going home, Billy," she said. "If you happen to be in New York, and there shouldn't be a war in Mexico, will you come to hear me again?"

⚓ ⚓ ⚓

217

EXCERPT FROM A SPEECH AT A DINNER OF THE HARVARD LAW SCHOOL ASSOCIATION OF NEW YORK ON FEBRUARY 15, 1913

By OLIVER WENDELL HOLMES, JR.

IF I AM RIGHT it will be a slow business for our people to reach rational views, assuming that we are allowed to work peaceably to that end. But as I grow older I grow calm. If I feel what are perhaps an old man's apprehensions, that competition from new races will cut deeper than working men's disputes and will test whether we can hang together and can fight; if I fear that we are running through the world's resources at a pace that we cannot keep; I do not lose my hopes. I do not pin my dreams for the future to my country or even to my race. I think it probable that civilization somehow will last as long as I care to look ahead—perhaps with smaller numbers, but perhaps also bred to greatness and splendor by science. I think it not improbable that man, like the grub that prepares a chamber for the winged thing it never has seen but is to be—that man may have cosmic destinies that he does not understand. And so beyond the vision of battling races and an impoverished earth I catch a dreaming glimpse of peace.

The other day my dream was pictured to my mind. It was evening. I was walking homeward on Pennsylvania Avenue near the Treasury, and as I looked beyond Sherman's Statue to the west the sky was aflame with scarlet and crimson from the setting sun. But, like the note of downfall in Wagner's opera, below the sky line there came from little globes the pallid discord of the electric lights. And I thought to myself the *Götterdämmerung* will end, and from those globes clustered like evil eggs will come the new masters of the sky. It is like the time in which we live. But then I remembered the faith that I partly have expressed, faith in a universe not measured by our fears, a universe that has thought and more than thought inside of it, and as I gazed, after the sunset and above the electric lights, there shone the stars.

THIS GREAT MELTING POT

By ISRAEL ZANGWILL

AMERICA is God's crucible, the Great Melting Pot, where all the races of Europe are reforming. Here you stand, goodfolk, think I, when I see them at Ellis Island, here you stand in your fifty groups with your fifty languages and histories and your fifty blood-hatreds and rivalries. But you won't long be like that, brothers, for these are the fires of God you've come to—these are the fires of God. A fig for your feuds and vendettas. Germans and Frenchmen, Irishmen and Englishmen, Jews and Russians, into the crucible with you all. God is making the American.

THE CORN SONG

John Greenleaf Whittier

Heap high the farmer's wintry hoard!
   Heap high the golden corn!
No richer gift has Autumn poured
   From out her lavish horn!

Let other lands, exulting, glean
   The apple from the pine,
The orange from its glossy green,
   The cluster from the vine;

We better love the hardy gift
   Our rugged vales bestow,
To cheer us when the storm shall drift
   Our harvest-fields with snow.

Through vales of grass and meads of flowers
   Our ploughs their furrows made,
While on the hills the sun and showers
   Of changeful April played.

We dropped the seed o'er hill and plain
   Beneath the sun of May,
And frightened from our sprouting grain
   The robber crows away.

All through the long, bright days of June
   Its leaves grew green and fair,
And waved in hot midsummer's noon
   Its soft and yellow hair.

And now, with autumn's moonlit eves,
   Its harvest-time has come,
We pluck away the frosted leaves,
   And bear the treasure home.

. . . .

But let the good old crop adorn
   The hills our fathers trod;
Still let us, for His golden corn,
   Send up our thanks to God!

THE ADMINISTRATION of justice is the firmest pillar
of government.—*Washington*

IT HAS BEEN my experience that folks who have no vices
have very few virtues.—*Lincoln*

NOTHING HAS EVER been decided by war that could not be decided
without it; and if decided after war, why not before?—*Grant*

THE DELICATE DUTY of devising schemes of revenue should be left where the
Constitution has placed it—with the immediate representatives of the people.—
William Henry Harrison

SICKLES, THEY CHARGE YOU with bringing on the battle. They say that you pushed
out with your men too near the enemy and began to fight just as that council
of war met. I am afraid that what they say of you is true, and God bless you for
it!—*Lincoln*

THERE IS A POINT, of course, where a man must take the isolated peak and break
with all his associates for clear principle; but until that time comes he must work,
if he would be of use, with men as they are. As long as the good in them over-
balances the evil, let him work with them for the best that can be obtained.—
Theodore Roosevelt

LET US, THEN, RELY on the goodness of our cause, and the aid of the
Supreme Being, in whose hands victory is, to animate and encourage
us to great and noble actions.—*Washington*

LABOR DISGRACES NO MAN; unfortunately, you occasionally find men
disgrace labor.—*Grant*

I DON'T KNOW who my grandfather was; I am much more concerned
to know what his grandson will be.—*Lincoln*

GENTLEMEN, this is a land where freedom of speech
is guaranteed.—*Lincoln*

THE WHITE HOUSE

No PERSONAL CONSIDERATION should stand in the way
of performing a public duty.—*Grant*

To BE PREPARED for war is one of the most effectual means
of preserving peace.—*Washington*

THEY CULTIVATED INDUSTRY and frugality at the same time—which is
the real foundation of the greatness of the Pilgrims.—*Grant*

As THE HAPPINESS OF THE PEOPLE is the sole end of government, so the consent
of the people is the only foundation of it, in reason, morality, and the natural
fitness of things.—*John Adams*

THIS COUNTRY, WITH ITS INSTITUTIONS, belongs to the people who inhabit it. Whenever they shall grow weary of the existing government they can exercise their
constitutional right of amending it, or their revolutionary right to dismember
or overthrow it.—*Lincoln*

YESTERDAY THE GREATEST QUESTION was decided which ever was
debated in America; and a greater perhaps never was, nor will be
decided among men. A resolution was passed without one dissenting
colony, that those United Colonies are, and of right ought to be,
free and independent States.—*John Adams*

I SHALL TRY TO CORRECT errors when shown to be errors, and I shall adopt new
views so fast as they shall appear to be true views.—*Lincoln*

LET US REMEMBER that revolutions do not always establish freedom.—*Fillmore*

I ALWAYS talk better lying down. (Last words.)—*Madison*

THIS HAND, TO TYRANTS ever sworn the foe,
For Freedom only deals the deadly blow;
Then sheathes in calm repose the vengeful blade,
For gentle peace in Freedom's hallowed shade.
                    —*John Quincy Adams*

221

A New Englander

By DOROTHY CANFIELD FISHER

*H*E WAS BORN so long ago, my Great-Uncle Zadok Canfield, that he could remember the War of 1812. I never pass a certain grassy bank near our house without seeing a flash of scarlet, for it was there that Uncle Zed saw enemy soldiers who had crossed the ocean and invaded our country. They were prisoners, being marched down the rough Vermont roads; and had stopped for an hour's rest. While they sat there a sharp-eyed little American boy gazed at them, and began a lifelong effort not only to know what was happening in our country but to understand why it happened.

Uncle Zed could even remember what happened before he was born, for the older people in his family had lived through the uncertain, wavering struggles to make one new nation out of the thirteen colonies. The desperate uncertainties of those floundering early days were all part of the story of America he painted to his small great-niece. He did not take this federation of our states for granted, as most of us do. He had an absorbing concern with its fate; he leaned over it, fascinated as by a serial story of adventure, to see whether it was really going to work or not.

"It was nip and tuck," he would say, "whether folks would give in and let themselves be bossed by the Congress, so far away. It was nip and tuck whether the federal idea would really stand or not, and don't you forget it!"

For it was not just defeated, scarlet-coated soldiers he showed you when he pulled up his aged roan at that grassy bank. He went on to tell you how foolishly, only four or five years before that, many people of our state had done their best to loosen that national unity which is our only strength. Potash was the great cash crop of Vermont at that time—potash made from the ashes of the trees cut to clear the land. Potash was sold to England, through Canada. Vermont was glad enough to be one of the United States, yet the very first time that national unity *cost* Vermonters anything—when President Jefferson laid on the Embargo Act and they could not sell their potash —what happened?

"Did they stop to think that you can't get something for nothing in national life, any more than in any other kind of life?" Uncle Zed would ask. "No, sir, they laid back their ears and all but kicked the harness to pieces, smuggling potash up Lake Champlain with armed forces defending the boats. And proud of it, every darned fool of them! You'll hear a lot of hollering," he would go on, "about the way our Vermonters riz up with pitchforks and scythes to drive back the British. Ready to knock 'em galley west, wa'n't we, to save the country? I swanny! Wa'n't one of 'em had headpiece enough to see you're *in* a federation and don't abide by its laws, that ain't exactly saving the nation, is it? Fight? They'd fight all right. But have a mite of sense? No, sir, that'd be too hard work."

Sense was what Uncle Zed wanted people to have, just ordinary sense. To accept sound evidence even when it went against your wishes, and to reject unsound evidence even when it "looked pretty," that was his religion. His most frequent text was "Experience is a hard school, but fools will learn in no other." I imagine that he talked so much to me because he did not exclude my sex from his demand for good sense. "I never could abide a fool," I have heard him say a hundred times. "And I don't like a fool any better for being a woman."

Uncle Zed used to sit on the front porch to keep track of what was going on in the serial life stories of the people of our town. His comments are part of our communal inheritance. One day he saw a young mother leading her eight-year-old past the house. She explained indignantly that the teacher had spoken harshly to young Fred, although he was a high-spirited boy of one of the three best families in town. (At this phrase Uncle Zed snorted ominously.) Fred had run home to tell his mother. "I went right back with him and gave the teacher a piece of my mind," the mother cried. "I told her I would never allow Fred to set foot in the schoolhouse again. I'll make his father have a tutor for him at home."

Uncle Zed leaned back in his chair and told her equably, "Millie, advice is cheap and worth just what it costs, so I'll give you a piece. You tie a stone around that boy's neck right *now*, and throw him in the river. You might's well. You've done for him!"

That mother wore crinoline, but the lesson in parent education given her so long ago is to this day vividly fresh in our collective town mind.

There is scarcely a corner of our much-loved home valley which does not suggest one of Uncle Zed's marrowy stories, rich with human significance. At a certain turn of the road he used to stop old Dick and point with his whip. "Right *there* was where Eli and I saw the bear." Eli was my grandfather, Uncle Zed's little brother. The two small boys had been sent on an errand. As they trotted around the turn of the road, there stood a great bear. The little boys froze. The bear, after a long moment's stare, scrambled off into the bushes. Uncle Zed always spoke of the incident with pride. He and his little brother did not run home to their mother. They clenched their trembling hands to fists, and went on to do their errand. "That kind of thing's good growing weather," Uncle Zed would tell me. "A young 'un turns a corner he'll never have to turn again, once he's had a chance to find out he can go on and get his business done, even if he is scared."

He was always thinking about how to defend his country from its foes inside and out. And his country began right at home at Town Meeting. The most dramatic episode in our valley, after Revolutionary times, was the proposition to bond the towns to pay for the first railroad. In the excitement our small, poor, rural towns got sold down the river by slick operators far too smart for our country brains.

But not for Uncle Zed's. He fought the bonding tooth and nail, with one of his favorite axioms, "Everybody's got to learn how to say 'No!' You're a goner if you don't. Just because a proposition looks good, you don't *have* to say 'Yes.' Let's look into this.

223

There's no hurry."

But the expansion fever was running high and his solitary voice did not prevail. Our town and those to the north and the south did bond themselves for sums out of all proportion to their resources. The vote was carried triumphantly in an excited Town Meeting.

When the proposition turned out to be an exploitation of the guileless towns, Uncle Zed came back to Town Meeting with one idea, repeated as often as old Cato's about Carthage. "We've got to pay off that bond."

"But gosh, Mr. Zadok, those fellows just skinned us alive."

"Never mind about all that. And it isn't them we owe. They've got from under. It's other people who paid good money for our bonds. When you owe money, there's just one thing to do—*pay* it!"

It was sour, unpalatable advice. The more people made faces over its sourness, the louder Uncle Zed shouted at Town Meeting. And presently our town began painfully to pay off those thousands of dollars. Year by year, hill-farmers in patched clothes took out of their lean pocketbooks sweat-earned dollars to put them into the well-tailored pockets of people who did not need them. Other towns paid only the interest on the bonded debt. Some even let interest pile up. Our town groaningly paid interest and capital. People were in a perpetual rage about it.

Presently the town saw light ahead. The debt was actually less. And then less again. And one glorious day it was paid, gone from our burdens. Other towns were still raising money to pay interest. Our town could put money into a new school. Nothing so very important had happened, only

that a group of country folk had accepted, like men, the consequences of their own action. "How do you feel *now*, Mr. Zadok?" they asked the old man, for he was old before the debt was paid off.

"*Pretty* good," he said moderately.

In one of the houses Uncle Zed owned, Colonel Shays had lived for a while, after the years he had hidden from justice in the woods. Whoever drove with Uncle to collect the monthly rent from the people who then lived in the old Shays house, heard a good deal about Shays' Rebellion. You won't find much about it unless you look in a very big history book: just that it was an abortive rising by tax-ridden, debt-pinched Massachusetts dirt farmers a few years after the Revolution. But Uncle Zed knew all the details of the muster, rioting, and shooting. He had heard them as a boy from the village elders. And they had heard them from men who had fought on one side or the other, wondering as they heard whether all that the Revolution had won might not be in danger.

Uncle Zed saw in Shays' Rebellion something more than one of the first attacks on the new government. To him it was a case of rich people bearing down too hard on poor people. "There ain't but one trough for us all to feed out of," he used to tell me, "and when a few crowd out the rest, well, there's no fence can be built that'll hold in that fight when it gets going. Thing to do is not to *let* it get going!"

"But, Uncle Zed, Colonel Shays' Rebellion failed."

"Maybe it failed for *him*. But the rich folks down Massachusetts-way let up on the poor folks after that. They had learned they couldn't go

224

but just so far—not on *this* side the ocean."

It was not from any soft-hearted philanthropy that Uncle Zed spoke, but from long observation of the stresses and strains in national life. Mr. Zadok (as he was always called, because there were so many Canfields in Arlington they could be distinguished only by using their Christian names) was, as a matter of fact, not considered to be very kind to poor people. Especially the thriftless ones. He was feared and sometimes hated for his ruthless analysis of the reasons brought forward by self-pity to explain failures. People in our town said ruefully, "My! Mr. Zadok has a *nawful* sharp tongue. He don't make *allowances* for folks!"

But as he lived on and on, sturdy, keen-eyed, razor-tongued, passionately concerned with every detail of the life of our country, he became a sort of institution. Everybody realized that, hard though he might be, he had helped keep up the standard of intelligence and self-respecting independence of the town. Men would come to lean on the railing of the front porch where Uncle Zed sat, to ask him, "Say, Mr. Zadok, what d'ye think of the election this year?" And then stand, their eyes thoughtfully fixed on a distant mountain while the old man set forth what he thought of the election, in a perspective which reached from the Declaration of Independence to that year. He liked to have other people tell him what *they* thought of the election too; but he listened, watchful as a cat before a mousehole, for any sign of muddled thinking, and pounced with a snort on any foolish or inconsequential reason for a political opinion.

At a great old age he went to bed and never got up. It seemed incredible. Mr. Zadok had been there as long as Red Mountain—so it seemed to us younger people. We realized with a shock that now we must find out for ourselves what this year's election meant. We must now try to do what he did, pore over American life, seeking to understand each event in its relation to the whole.

After the funeral my aunts put away in the attic the fine linen shirts with the collars that thrust up a long point beside the cheek, like those of Daniel Webster. The clothes and shoes were passed on to the poor. And the lawyer went through the iron box in which Uncle Zed had always kept his papers. He found notes and notes and notes, representing loans made to the needy. Some had a few small payments marked on the back. Most were not paid at all— money which he had loaned to keep a farm from being sold away from elderly owners, to help a bright boy through college, to pay the doctor's bills for somebody whose wife was an invalid. Those, and not stocks and bonds, were what filled Uncle Zed's strong box.

IMMIGRANTS

ROBERT FROST

No ship of all that under sail or steam
Have gathered people to us more and more
But Pilgrim-manned the Mayflower in a dream
Has been her anxious convoy in to shore.

225

AMERICA
EDGAR A. GUEST

God has been good to men. He gave
His Only Son their souls to save,
And then he made a second gift,
Which from their dreary lives should lift
The tyrant's yoke and set them free
From all who'd throttle liberty.
He gave America to men—
Fashioned this land we love, and then
Deep in her forests sowed the seed
Which was to serve man's earthly need.
When wisps of smoke first upwards curled
From pilgrim fires, upon the world
Unnoticed and unseen, began
God's second work of grace for man.
Here where the savage roamed and fought,
God sowed the seed of nobler thought;
Here to the land we love to claim,
The pioneers of freedom came;
Here has been cradled all that's best
In every human mind and breast.

For full four hundred years and more
Our land has stretched her welcoming shore
To weary feet from soils afar;
Soul-shackled serfs of king and czar
Have journeyed here and toiled and sung
And talked of freedom to their young,
And God above has smiled to see
This precious work of liberty,
And watched this second gift He gave
The dreary lives of men to save.
And now, when liberty's at bay,
And blood-stained tyrants force the fray,
Worn warriors, battling for the right,
Crushed by oppression's cruel might,
Hear in the dark through which they grope
America's glad cry of hope:
Man's liberty is not to die!
America is standing by!
World-wide shall human lives be free:
America has crossed the sea!

226

America! The land we love!
God's second gift from Heaven above,
Builded and fashioned out of truth,
Sinewed by Him with splendid youth
For that glad day when shall be furled
All tyrant flags throughout the world.
For this our banner holds the sky:
That liberty shall never die.
For this, America began:
To make a brotherhood of man.

THE HOME AND THE REPUBLIC
By HENRY W. GRADY

I WENT to Washington the other day, and as I stood on Capitol Hill my heart beat quickly as I looked at the towering marble of my Country's Capitol, and the mist gathered in my eyes as I thought of its tremendous significance, the armies, and the Treasury, and the Courts, and Congress and the President, and all that was gathered there. And I felt that the sun in all its course could not look down upon a better sight than that majestic home of the Republic that had taught the world its best lessons in liberty.

Two days afterwards I went to visit a friend in the country, a modest man, with a quiet country home. It was just a simple, unpretentious house, set about with great trees, encircled in meadow and fields rich with the promise of harvest. The fragrance of pink and hollyhock in the front yard was mingled with the aroma of the orchard and of the garden, and resonant with the cluck of poultry and the hum of bees. Inside was quiet, cleanliness, thrift and comfort. Outside there stood my friend—master of his land and master of himself. There was his old father, an aged, trembling man, happy in the heart and home of his son. And as they started to their home the hands of the old man went down on the young man's shoulders, laying there the unspeakable blessing of an honored and grateful father, and ennobling it with the knighthood of the fifth commandment.

And I saw the night come down on that home, falling gently as from the wings of an unseen dove, and the old man, while a startled bird called from the forest, and the trees shrilled with the cricket's cry, and the stars were swarming in the sky, got the family around him, and taking the old Bible from the table, called them to their knees, while he closed the record of that simple day by calling down God's blessing on that family and that home. And while I gazed, the vision of the marble Capitol faded. Forgotten were its treasures and its majesty, and I said: "O surely, here in the hearts of the people, at least are lodged the strength and responsibilities of this government, the hope and promise of this Republic."

WORDS OF THEODORE ROOSEVELT

THE COUNTRY'S HONOR must be upheld at home and abroad.

PERFORMANCE should be made square with promise.

NINE-TENTHS OF WISDOM consists of being wise in time.

I WISH TO PREACH not the doctrine of ignoble ease, but the doctrine of the strenuous life.

ONLY THOSE are fit to live who do not fear to die; and none are fit to die who have shrunk from the joy of life and the duty of life.

IT IS ONLY THROUGH LABOR and painful effort, by grim energy, and resolute courage, that we move on to better things.

THERE IS A HOMELY OLD ADAGE which runs: "Speak softly and carry a big stick; you will go far." If the American nation will speak softly and yet build and keep at a pitch of the highest training a thoroughly efficient navy, the Monroe Doctrine will go far.

IS IT COMPULSORY to obey oral orders? If not, I will remain to die by the American flag, if I die alone.

WE HAVE ROOM in this country for but one flag, the Stars and Stripes. . . . We have room for but one loyalty, loyalty to the United States.

I CARE NOTHING for a man's creed or his birthplace, or descent—but I regard him as an unworthy citizen unless he is an American and nothing else.

THE DOER IS BETTER than the critic, and the man who strives stands far above the man who stands aloof.

LET ME URGE that we keep clear of two besetting sins —hardness of heart and softness of heart.

THE AMERICAN CONTINENTS . . . are henceforth not to be considered as subjects for future colonization by any European powers.—*Monroe*

PEACE, ABOVE ALL THINGS, is to be desired, but blood must sometimes be spilled to obtain it on equable and lasting terms.—*Jackson*

FELLOW CITIZENS! God reigns, and the Government at Washington lives! (After Lincoln's death was reported)—*Garfield*

NO TERMS OTHER than immediate and unconditional surrender can be accepted. I propose to move immediately upon your works.—*Grant*

WE OWE IT, THEREFORE, TO CANDOR, and to the amicable relations existing between the United States and those powers, to declare that we should consider any attempt on their part to extend their system to any portion of this hemisphere as dangerous to our peace and safety. With the existing colonies or dependencies of any European power, we . . . shall not interfere. But with the governments . . . whose independence we have . . . acknowledged, we could not view any interposition for the purpose of oppressing, or controlling, in any other manner, their destiny, by any European power, in any other light than as a manifestation of an unfriendly disposition towards the United States. —*Monroe*

AS LONG AS OUR GOVERNMENT is administered for the good of the people, and is regulated by their will; as long as it secures to us the rights of persons and of property, liberty of conscience and of the press, it will be worth defending.—*Jackson*

I TREAD IN THE FOOTSTEPS of illustrious men . . . in receiving from the people the sacred trust confided to my illustrious predecessor.—*Van Buren*

THE DIE WAS NOW CAST; I had passed the Rubicon. Swim or sink, live or die, survive or perish with my country was my unalterable determination.—*John Adams*

COLUMBUS

CHARLES BUXTON GOING

The night air brings strange whisperings—vague scents—
Over the unknown ocean, which his dreams
Had spanned with visions of new continents;
Fragrance of clove and cedar, and the balms
With which the heavy tropic forest teems,
And murmur as of wind among the palms.

They breathe across the high deck where he stands
With far-set eyes, as one who dreams awake
Waiting sure dawn of undiscovered lands;
Till, on the slow lift of the purple swells,
The golden radiances of morning break
Lighting the emblazoned sails of caravels.

Then from the foremost sounds a sudden cry—
The Old World's startled greeting to the New—
For lo! the land, across the western sky!
The exultant land! Oh, long-starved hopes, black fears,
Gibings of courtiers, mutinies of crew—
Answered forever, as that shore appears!

Great Master Dreamer! Grander than Cathay,
Richer than India, that new Western World
Shall flourish when Castile has passed away.
Not even thy gigantic vision spanned
Its future, as with Cross and flag unfurled,
Thy deep Te Deum sounded on the strand.

By this small outpost of the unbounded shore—
This small, bright island, slumbering in the sea—
A long, resistless tide of life shall pour;
Loosed from its long-worn fetters, joyous, free,
Leaping to heights none ever touched before
And hurrying on to greater things to be.

The end is larger than thy largest plan;
Nobler than golden fleets of argosies
The land and life new-opening to man.
Within the womb of this mysterious morn
Quicken vast cities, mighty destinies,
Ideals and empires, waiting to be born.

But yet—there are but three small caravels,
Wrapped in the magic radiance of the seas,
Slow-moved, slow heaving on low-bosomed swells.

From *OUT OF THE CRADLE ENDLESSLY ROCKING*
Walt Whitman

Loud! Loud! Loud!
Loud I call to you, my love!
High and clear I shoot my voice over the waves;
Surely you must know who is here, is here,
You must know who I am, my love.

Low-hanging moon!
What is that dusky spot in your brown yellow?
O it is the shape, the shape of my mate!
O moon, do not keep her from me any longer.

Land! Land! Land!
Whichever way I turn, O I think you could give me my mate back again
    if you only would,
For am I almost sure I see her dimly whichever way I look.

O rising stars!
Perhaps the one I want so much will rise, will rise with some of you.

O throat! O trembling throat!
Sound clearer through the atmosphere!
Pierce the woods, the earth;
Somewhere listening to catch you must be the one I want.

But soft! Sink low!
Soft! let me just murmur,
And do you wait a moment, you husky-noised sea,
For somewhere I believe I heard my mate responding to me,
So faint, I must be still, be still to listen,
But not altogether still for then she might not come immediately
    to me.

Hither my love!
Here I am! Here!
With this just-sustained note I announce myself to you,
This gentle call is for you my love, for you.

231

DISCOVERING AMERICA
EDGAR LEE MASTERS

Would you know the American spirit, faith and destiny?
Would you see that they have no need of the faith of any other land?
Then take wings of steel and cross the Appalachian Plateau,
Look down upon the Ohio Valley and the cornlands,
And the drumlins and moraines of Wisconsin,
And the mines of copper and salt,
And fields of wheat, and lands of fruits and vegetables in Texas.
Go out to the desert where Phoenix stands amid peach trees,
And to the Columbia Basin, green with apple trees,
And vineyards purpling to the golden air.

This is the country that Cabot, Hudson, Raleigh, Smith,
Coronado, Cabrillo, De Soto stared at with blinded eyes,
Doing all that they could to understand its meaning.

This land is not for mathematics devouring labor,
It is not for Caesarisms seizing the cities.
Ponce de Leon is not its spirit,
Nor Americus the grocerman.
Its symbol is not the sickle rusted with the blood of insurrection,
Nor the fasces borne in a procession of despots.
Its symbols are the plow, the axe.
The myths by which it will live
Are tales of the heroes who searched for light,
For beauty and justice, who fought hunger the destroyer,
Poverty the waster, and war the killer of men,
Who loved the land and strove to preserve it
Against the spirochaetae of corruption,
The contagion of alien dreams,
The sneers of supercilious charlatans,
The rootless springs of the pavements,
The hate and conceit of gabs and scribblers,
All the wanderers and adventurers who ignored the land hastening for gold.
As Washington rapped with his sword
On the door of Fort Duquesne,
Leaving it to another day, to other hands
To lift the bars,
So we must knock on the portals of today,
And pass the frontiers in the forward march,
Using today for the search for wisdom,
Remembering what Drake and Coronado,
Cabrillo and de Vaca did not do.

THE LANDING OF THE PILGRIM FATHERS

FELICIA DOROTHEA HEMANS

The breaking waves dashed high
  On a stern and rock-bound coast,
And the woods against a stormy sky
  Their giant branches tossed;

And the heavy night hung dark,
  The hills and waters o'er,
When a band of exiles moored their bark
  On the wild New England shore.

Not as the conqueror comes,
  They, the true-hearted, came;
Not with the roll of the stirring drums,
  And the trumpet that sings of fame;

Not as the flying come,
  In silence and in fear;
They shook the depths of the desert gloom
  With their hymns of lofty cheer.

Amidst the storm they sang,
  And the stars heard, and the sea;
And the sounding aisles of the dim woods rang
  To the anthem of the free.

The ocean eagle soared
  From his nest by the white wave's foam,
And the rocking pines of the forest roared—
  This was their welcome home.

There were men with hoary hair
  Amidst that pilgrim band:
Why had they come to wither there,
  Away from their childhood's land?

There was woman's fearless eye,
  Lit by her deep love's truth;
There was manhood's brow serenely high,
  And the fiery heart of youth.

What sought they thus afar?
  Bright jewels of the mine?

The wealth of seas, the spoils of war?
  They sought a faith's pure shrine!

Ay, call it holy ground,
  The soil where first they trod;
They have left unstained what there they found—
  Freedom to worship God.

AMERICA
William Cullen Bryant

O Mother of a mighty race,
Yet lovely in thy youthful grace!
The elder dames, thy haughty peers,
Admire and hate thy blooming years;
            With words of shame
And taunts of scorn they join thy name.

For on thy cheeks the glow is spread
That tints thy morning hills with red;
Thy step,—the wild deer's rustling feet
Within thy woods are not more fleet;
            Thy hopeful eye
Is bright as thine own sunny sky.

Ay, let them rail, those haughty ones,
While safe thou dwellest with thy sons.
They do not know how loved thou art,
How many a fond and fearless heart
            Would rise to throw
Its life between thee and the foe.

They know not, in their hate and pride,
What virtues with thy children bide,—
How true, how good, thy graceful maids
Make bright, like flowers, the valley shades;
            What generous men
Spring, like thine oaks, by hill and glen;

What cordial welcomes greet the guest
By thy lone rivers of the West;
How faith is kept, and truth revered,
And man is loved, and God is feared,

234

In woodland homes,
And where the ocean border foams!

There's freedom at thy gates, and rest
For earth's down-trodden and opprest,
A shelter for the hunted head,
For the starved laborer toil and bread.
Power, at thy bounds,
Stops, and calls back his baffled hounds.

O fair young mother! On thy brow
Shall sit a nobler grace than now.
Deep in the brightness of thy skies,
The thronging years in glory rise,
And, as they fleet,
Drop strength and riches at thy feet.

Thine eye, with every coming hour,
Shall brighten, and thy form shall tower;
And when thy sisters, elder born,
Would brand thy name with words of scorn,
Before thine eye
Upon their lips the taunt shall die.

LIBERTY

John Howard Bryant

Bright cloud of Liberty! full soon,
    Far stretching from the ocean strand,
Thy glorious folds shall spread abroad,
    Encircling our beloved land.
Like the sweet rain on Judah's hills,
    The glorious boon of love shall fall,
And our bond millions shall arise,
    As at an angel's trumpet-call.
Then shall a shout of joy go up,
    The wild, glad cry of freedom come
From hearts long crushed by cruel hands,
    And songs from lips long sealed and dumb.
And every bondman's chain be broke,
    And every soul that moves abroad
In this wide realm shall know and feel
    The blessed Liberty of God.

AS POOR RICHARD SAYS

HE THAT goes a borrowing, goes a sorrowing.

IT IS HARD for an empty sack to stand upright.

MANY have been ruined by buying good pennyworths.

SILKS and satins, scarlets and velvets, put out the kitchen fire.

THERE is no man so bad but he secretly respects the good.

BUT, AH! Think what you do when you run in debt: *you give to another power over your liberty.*

SINCE THOU art not sure of a minute, throw not away an hour:

BE AT WAR with your vices, at peace with your neighbors, and let every New Year find you a better man.

WANT OF CARE does us more damage than want of knowledge.

WHEN THE WELL is dry, we know the wealth of water.

GET WHAT YOU CAN, and what you get, hold; 'Tis the stone that will turn all your lead into gold.

FOR AGE AND WANT, save while you may; No morning sun lasts a whole day.

WISH NOT so much to live long as to live well.

ONE TODAY is worth two tomorrows.

. . . . *BENJAMIN FRANKLIN*

THE USED KEY is always bright.

HAVE YOU SOMETHING to do tomorrow? Do it today!

IF YOU WOULD have your business done, go; if not, send.

ALWAYS taking out of the meal-tub, and never putting in,
soon comes to the bottom.

AT THE working man's house, hunger looks in, but dares not enter.

LEARNING IS to the studious, and Riches to the careful; Power to the bold, **and**
Heaven to the virtuous.

A PLOUGHMAN on his legs is higher than a gentleman on his knees.

SELL NOT virtue to purchase wealth, nor liberty to purchase power.

THEN PLOUGH DEEP while sluggards sleep,
And you shall have corn to sell and to keep.

INDUSTRY pays debts, while despair increaseth them.

NEVER leave that till tomorrow which you can do today.

KEEP conscience clear,
Then never fear.

THE NOBLEST QUESTION in the world is,
"What good may I do in it?"

OBSERVE all men; thyself, most.

237

PAUL REVERE'S RIDE
HENRY WADSWORTH LONGFELLOW

Listen, my children, and you shall hear
Of the midnight ride of Paul Revere,
On the eighteenth of April, in Seventy-five;
Hardly a man is now alive
Who remembers that famous day and year.

He said to his friend, "If the British march
By land or sea from the town tonight,
Hang a lantern aloft in the belfry arch
Of the North Church tower as a signal light—
One, if by land, and two, if by sea;
And I on the opposite shore will be,
Ready to ride and spread the alarm
Through every Middlesex village and farm,
For the country folk to be up and to arm."
Then he said, "Good-night!" and with muffled oar
Silently rowed to the Charlestown shore,
Just as the moon rose over the bay,
Where swinging wide at her moorings lay
The *Somerset*, British man-of-war;
A phantom ship, with each mast and spar
Across the moon like a prison bar,
And a huge black hulk, that was magnified
By its own reflection in the tide.

Meanwhile, his friend, through alley and street,
Wanders and watches with eager ears,
Till in the silence around him he hears
The muster of men at the barrack door,
The sound of arms, and the tramp of feet,
And the measured tread of the grenadiers,
Marching down to their boats on the shore.
Then he climbed the tower of the Old North Church,
By the wooden stairs, with stealthy tread,
To the belfry-chamber overhead,
And startled the pigeons from their perch
On the sombre rafters, that round him made
Masses and moving shapes of shade,
By the trembling ladder, steep and tall,
To the highest window in the wall,
Where he paused to listen and look down

A moment on the roofs of the town
And the moonlight flowing over all.

Beneath, in the churchyard, lay the dead,
In their night-encampment on the hill,
Wrapped in silence so deep and still
That he could hear, like a sentinel's tread,
The watchful night-wind, as it went
Creeping along from tent to tent,
And seeming to whisper, "All is well!"
A moment only he feels the spell
Of the place and the hour, and the secret dread
Of the lonely belfry and the dead;
For suddenly all his thoughts are bent
On a shadowy something far away,
Where the river widens to meet the bay,
A line of black that bends and floats
On the rising tide, like a bridge of boats.

Meanwhile, impatient to mount and ride,
Booted and spurred, with a heavy stride
On the opposite shore walked Paul Revere.
Now he patted his horse's side,
Now gazed at the landscape far and near,
Then, impetuous, stamped the earth,
And turned and tightened his saddle girth;
But mostly he watched with eager search
The belfry-tower of the Old North Church,
As it rose above the graves on the hill,
Lonely and spectral and sombre and still.
And lo! as he looks, on the belfry's height
A glimmer, and then a gleam of light!
He springs to the saddle, the bridle he turns,
But lingers and gazes, till full on his sight
A second lamp in the belfry burns!

A hurry of hoofs in a village street,
A shape in the moonlight, a bulk in the dark,
And beneath, from the pebbles, in passing, a spark
Struck out by a steed flying fearless and fleet:
That was all! And yet, through the gloom and the light,
The fate of a nation was riding that night;
And the spark struck out by that steed, in his flight,
Kindled the land into flame with its heat.

He has left the village and mounted the steep,
And beneath him, tranquil and broad and deep,
Is the Mystic, meeting the ocean tides;
And under the alders that skirt its edge,
Now soft on the sand, now loud on the ledge,
Is heard the tramp of his steed as he rides.

It was twelve by the village clock,
When he crossed the bridge into Medford town.
He heard the crowing of the cock,
And the barking of the farmer's dog,
And he felt the damp of the river fog,
That rises after the sun goes down.

It was one by the village clock,
When he galloped into Lexington.
He saw the gilded weathercock
Swim in the moonlight as he passed,
And the meeting-house windows, blank and bare,
Gaze at him with a spectral glare,
As if they already stood aghast
At the bloody work they would look upon.

It was two by the village clock,
When he came to the bridge in Concord town.
He heard the bleating of the flock,
And the twitter of birds among the trees,
And felt the breath of the morning breeze
Blowing over the meadows brown.
And one was safe and asleep in his bed
Who at the bridge would be first to fall,
Who that day would be lying dead,
Pierced by a British musket-ball.

You know the rest. In books you have read,
How the British Regulars fired and fled,
How the farmers gave them ball for ball,
From behind each fence and farmyard wall,
Chasing the red-coats down the lane,
Then crossing the fields to emerge again
Under the trees at the turn of the road,
And only pausing to fire and load.

So through the night rode Paul Revere;

And so through the night went his cry of alarm
To every Middlesex village and farm,
A cry of defiance, and not of fear,
A voice in the darkness, a knock at the door,
And a word that shall echo for evermore!
For, borne on the night-wind of the Past,
Through all our history, to the last,
In the hour of darkness and peril and need,
The people will waken and listen to hear
The hurrying hoof-beats of that steed,
And the midnight message of Paul Revere.

JACK JOUETT'S RIDE
NANCY BYRD TURNER

Eleven o'clock on a quiet night of a hot Virginia June.
The Cuckoo Tavern had candle-light and the glow of a lifting moon,
When young Jack Jouett, a country lad who should have been abed,
Lounged in the door with an idle ear for what a gossip said:
The Legislature in Charlottesville—so word had traveled down—
(Patrick Henry, Harrison, Lee, all the pick of the land);
Governor Jefferson lodging high on his mountain above the town,
And enemy raiders heading west with Tarleton in command.

Tarleton's troopers, three hundred strong!
Jouett straightened, his young eyes hard.
Charlottesville sleeping the hills among,
And Monticello without a guard . . . .
Not for naught would the British ride:
Jefferson, Nelson—name by name—
Hope of the Cause and the country's pride,
Lost to freedom if Tarleton came!

Out in the yard a saddled mare was cropping the clover's edge,
Bronze and lean. Jack could see her there as the moon swung over a ledge.
Muscled with steel and wild of heel, supple and satin-skinned;
The touch of his hand on neck or side would send her down the wind.
"Molly, my girl," he whistled low, "the Redcoats ride, they say."
She whinnied lightly. Then all at once she flung up a startled head,
Keen ears pricking the silver dark. Out on the long highway,
Beat—beat—beat down the distance. "Hark! they are coming now!" he said.

Enemy troopers riding fleet,

241

Tarleton coming with mounted men!
He flung himself to the saddle seat
(Stiffened stirrup and quickened rein.)
His leather sang and his buckles flashed
Brightness sharper than any moon's
As into the highway Jouett dashed,
Ten yards after the dark dragoons.

The Britishers rode with the moon at their back and a wild dust in their
    wake,
"As ride ye'd better," said panting Jack, "with thirty miles to make!"
The regular road for the King's red troops, and let them go with a will,
He would take the trail that was three miles short to Monticello hill.
(Jefferson sleeping without a guard, prison, it meant, or death.)
The road 'cross country was half ravine, hazardous, rough, and dark.
But he reined to the right with bridle tight and a sharp word under his
    breath,
And his good steed gathered her strength and sprang like an arrow off for
    the mark.

Jouett riding by swamp and wood,
Through brush and thicket and crowding trees,
His heart like thunder along his blood
And a bolt of lightning between his knees!
Jefferson, Harrison, Henry, Lee . . . .
Enemies on the midnight road . . . .
Twenty-six miles . . . . "We must," said he,
"Ay, and we will, by the help of God!"

Two miles farther the trail would cross; he had sighted an old fence line.
"Steady, my lass!" as she caught her foot in a tangle of twisted vine.
"Steady!" again, as she slid to her hocks in the muck of a sudden bog,
Then crouched like a leopard to span a ditch and a length of fallen log.
There was blood on the bridle warm and thick where a splintered limb had
    lashed.
Beat—beat—beat down the open road, a clamor of hoofs again;
The moon looked out of a drifting cloud as a lonely horseman dashed
Into the highway, fifty feet ahead of Tarleton's men—

Jouett galloping. "Halt!" he heard,
"Who is this rides by the devil's rule?"
Into the moonlight Tarleton spurred:
"Trooper or traitor? Halt, you fool!"
Horsemen closing from every side . . . .

Jouett stood in his stirrups. "Right!
I halt at the crack of dawn!" he cried,
And cleared a fence and was off through the night.

On and on, down a stony slope with the hardest still to go;
Flint sparks struck from a flying heel. Then, "So, my beauty, so!"
Hot hoofs plunged with a plash and a splash in cool Rivanna's tide.
Crystal flinging from bit and spur, and the current swinging wide.
A little halt on the farther shore;—little enough, for still
Twenty-one miles unrolled beyond, with perils and snares and bars,
And starkly distant, a world away, looked Monticello hill,
Grim and tall as a castle wall, its turret in the stars.

> Challenging Monticello hill
> The brown mare, rocking and winded, now,
> But pushing on with her utmost will,
> On at last to the mountain's brow;
> A gully, a bank, a stubbled field,
> A looming hedge at the side of a lawn,
> And her rein came taut, and her rider reeled
> Out of the saddle at crack of dawn!

Three strides into the dusky porch; old hinges shook to his knock;
There were hasty steps in the dreaming hall; a loud key turned in a lock.
Then a candle's flare on the winding stair, and Jouett bared his head
To the tall, gaunt grace of his Governor. "The British are coming!" he
   said.
"Tarleton is hard behind me now. I ride to Charlottesville.
Sire, make haste!" Where the chestnut stood they could hear her heart in
   her breast,
And the pull of her broken breathing. Then, louder and louder still
They heard the thunder of hard hoof-beats coming over the crest.

> The enemy riding! Let them ride!
> Stumbling back to the weary mare,
> He stood for a moment against her side,
> And she nickered gently to feel him there.
> Carved like a statue against the light,
> So they rested a little while,
> Who had ridden for freedom half a night,
> And won by half a mile!

WORDS OF GREAT AMERICANS:

EVERY artist was first an amateur.

CURIOSITY is lying in wait for every secret.

A WEED is a plant whose virtues have not been discovered.

CAN ANYTHING be so elegant as to have few wants, and to serve them one's self?

SPEAK as you think; be what you are; pay your debts of all kinds.

NATURE NEVER SENDS a great man into the planet, without confiding the secret to another soul.

HIS HEART was as great as the world, but there was no room in it to hold the memory of a wrong.

GREAT MEN are they who see that spiritual is stronger than any material force; that thoughts rule the world.

A FRIEND is a person with whom I may be sincere. Before him, I may think aloud.

EVERY VIOLATION of truth is not only a sort of suicide in the liar, but a stab at the health of human society.

HE IS GREAT who is what he is from Nature, and who never reminds us of others.

TOO BUSY with the crowded hour to fear to live or die.

FOR WHAT AVAIL the plough or sail,
Or land or life, if freedom fail?

244

RALPH WALDO EMERSON

EVERY hero becomes a bore at last.

WHOSO would be a man must be a nonconformist.

A FOOLISH CONSISTENCY is the hobgoblin of little minds.

EVERY MAN alone is sincere; at the entrance of a second
person, hypocrisy begins.

WORKS of the intellect are great only by comparison with each other.

CONGRATULATE YOURSELVES if you have done something strange and
extravagant and have broken the monotony of a decorous age.

LITERARY HISTORY and all history is a record of the power of minorities, and
of minorities of one.

GREAT MEN have not been boasters and buffoons, but perceivers of the terror
of life who have manned themselves to face it.

GIVE NO BOUNTIES: make equal laws: secure life and prosperity,
and you need not give alms.

FOR EVERYTHING you have missed, you have gained something else; and for
everything you gain, you lose something.

WHAT YOU ARE, stands over you the while, and thunders so
that I cannot hear what you say.

TRUTH IS beautiful! Without doubt; and so are lies.

BUT WHAT TORMENTS of pain you endured
From evils that never arrived!

WORDS OF GREAT AMERICANS:

AMERICA is a country of young men.

THE SKY is the daily bread of the eyes.

CAN ANYBODY remember when the times were not hard, and money not scarce?

THERE CAN BE NO EXCESS to love, none to knowledge, none to beauty, when these attributes are considered in the purest sense.

IT REQUIRES a great deal of boldness and a great deal of caution to make a great fortune, and when you have got it, it requires ten times as much wit to keep it.

HE (LINCOLN) IS THE TRUE HISTORY of the American people in his time . . . . Step by step he walked before them; slow with their slowness, quickening his march to theirs, the true representative of this continent; an entirely public man, father of his country, the pulse of twenty millions throbbing in his heart, the thought of their minds articulated by his tongue.

I SHOULD AS SOON THINK of swimming across the Charles River when I wish to go to Boston, as of reading all my books in originals, when I have them rendered for me in my mother tongue.

SPEAK WHAT YOU THINK today in words as hard as cannon balls, and tomorrow speak what tomorrow thinks in hard words again, though it contradict everything you said today.

THERE is properly no history, only biography.

THE GREATEST MAN in history was the poorest.

ALL mankind loves a lover.

MEN lose their tempers in defending their taste.

246

RALPH WALDO EMERSON

IT IS as easy to be great as to be small.

AMERICA means opportunity, freedom, power.

BUT THE REAL and lasting victories are those of peace, and not of war.

THE TRUEST TEST of civilization is not the census, nor the size of cities, nor the crops; no, but the kind of man the country turns out.

RAPHAEL PAINTS WISDOM, Handel sings it, Phidias carves it, Shakespeare writes it, Wren builds it, Columbus sails it, Luther preaches it, Washington arms it, Watt mechanizes it.

AN INSTITUTION IS THE LENGTHENED SHADOW of one man; as, monachism of the hermit, Anthony, the Reformation of Luther, Quakerism of Fox, Methodism of Wesley, abolition of Clarkson. Scipio, Milton called "the height of Rome"; and all history resolves itself easily into the biography of a few stout and earnest persons. Let a man, then, know his worth, and keep things under his feet.

THE THINGS TAUGHT in schools and colleges are not an education, but the means of education.

WITHIN MAN IS THE SOUL of the whole; the wise silence;
the universal beauty, to which every part and particle
is equally related; the eternal One.

THE TEST of the poet is the knowledge of love.

THE YEARS teach much which the days never know.

FOR FAITH, AND PEACE, and mighty love,
That from the Godhead flow,
Show them the life of heaven above
Springs from the life below.

OLD IRONSIDES
OLIVER WENDELL HOLMES

Ay, tear her tattered ensign down!
Long has it waved on high,
And many an eye has danced to see
That banner in the sky;
Beneath it rung the battle shout,
And burst the cannon's roar—
The meteor of the ocean air
Shall sweep the clouds no more!

Her deck, once red with heroes' blood,
Where knelt the vanquished foe,
When winds were hurrying o'er the flood,
And waves were white below,
No more shall feel the victor's tread,
Or know the conquered knee—
The harpies of the shore shall pluck
The eagle of the sea!

O, better that her shattered hulk
Should sink beneath the wave;
Her thunders shook the mighty deep,
And there should be her grave;
Nail to the mast her holy flag,
Set every threadbare sail,
And give her to the god of storms,
The lightning and the gale!

From *DEMOCRACY*
JOHN GREENLEAF WHITTIER

Bearer of Freedom's holy light,
  Breaker of Slavery's chain and rod,
The foe of all which pains the sight,
  Or wounds the generous ear of God!

... The generous feeling, pure and warm,
  Which owns the rights of *all* divine—
The pitying heart, the helping arm,
  The prompt self-sacrifice—are thine.

248

... Thy name and watchword o'er this land
I hear in every breeze that stirs,
And round a thousand altars stand
Thy banded party worshippers.

BETSY ROSS

NANCY BYRD TURNER

She was five and twenty; the chisel of life
Had graved old lines on her girlish brow.
She had watched and waited, a soldier's wife,
A soldier's widow she sorrowed now.
Day by day, as her slim hands flew
Backward and forward weaving lace,
She counted the dark things fate can do;
Then—a light began in the dusky place.

This is the way the light began:
A sudden shadow was on the floor;
She turned and fronted a martial man
Gaunt and courteous in the door,
General Washington, come to say
He knew her skill and her needle's grace.
Would she make a flag for America?
A beauty broke in her wistful face,

A shining caught her . . . . They shaped and planned,
The tall man towering to the beams,
The young lace maker; for one dear land
They wove and worked in a mist of dreams.
Six white bands and seven bright bars—
Eager they watched the pattern come—
A fair blue field and a welter of stars,
Glory gathering in the gloom.

Hour by hour, left alone,
Singing she wrought for far-off years,
Fadeless color to stitch upon,
Starry stuff for her valiant shears;
Fretting no longer of fate and doom,
She labored loving, till free and high,
The light that had kindled in one small room
Flamed to the world in a nation's sky!

BARBARA FRIETCHIE
John Greenleaf Whittier

Up from the meadows rich with corn,
Clear in the cool September morn,

The clustered spires of Frederick stand
Green-walled by the hills of Maryland.

Round about them orchards sweep,
Apple and peach-tree fruited deep,

Fair as a garden of the Lord
To the eyes of the famished rebel horde,

On that pleasant morn of the early fall
When Lee marched over the mountain wall;

Over the mountains winding down,
Horse and foot, into Frederick town.

Forty flags with their silver stars,
Forty flags with their crimson bars,

Flapped in the morning wind: the sun
Of noon looked down, and saw not one.

Up rose old Barbara Frietchie then,
Bowed with her fourscore years and ten;

Bravest of all in Frederick town,
She took up the flag the men hauled down;

In her attic window the staff she set,
To show that one heart was loyal yet.

Up the street came the rebel tread,
Stonewall Jackson riding ahead.

Under his slouched hat left and right
He glanced; the old flag met his sight.

"Halt!"—the dust-brown ranks stood fast.
"Fire!"—out blazed the rifle blast.

It shivered the window, pane and sash;
It rent the banner with seam and gash.

Quick, as it fell, from the broken staff
Dame Barbara snatched the silken scarf.

She leaned far out on the window-sill,
And shook it forth with a royal will.

"Shoot, if you must, this old grey head,
But spare your country's flag," she said.

A shade of sadness, a blush of shame,
Over the face of the leader came;

The nobler nature within him stirred
To life at that woman's deed and word;

"Who touches a hair of yon grey head
Dies like a dog! March on!" he said.

All day long through Frederick street
Sounded the tread of marching feet:

All day long that free flag tost
Over the heads of the rebel host.

Ever its torn folds rose and fell
On the loyal winds that loved it well;

And through the hill-gaps sunset light
Shone over it with a warm good-night.

Barbara Frietchie's work is o'er,
And the rebel rides on his raids no more.

Honor to her! and let a tear
Fall, for her sake, on Stonewall's bier.
Over Barbara Frietchie's grave,
Flag of freedom and union, wave!
Peace, and order, and beauty draw
Round thy symbol of light and law;
And ever the stars above look down
On thy stars below in Frederick town!

WISDOM OF UNKNOWN AMERICANS

HE THAT lends money to a friend has a double loss.

LOVE, when founded in respect, is proof against all changes.

BE NOT simply good; be good for something.

THERMOPYLAE had its messenger of defeat but the Alamo had none.
(Epitaph on the Alamo)

HUMILITY, like darkness, reveals the heavenly lights.

PUT NOT your trust in money; put your money in trust.

WHERE THERE is a surfeit of words there is a famine of ideas.

SOME have been esteemed brave because afraid to run.

WHATEVER is worth doing at all is worth doing well.

REBELLION to tyrants is obedience to God.

THE SPUR of the moment is the key to opportunity.

FAITH will never die as long as colored seed
catalogues are printed.

DON'T DIG a mountain to rescue a mouse.

TO ENJOY a thing alone is to miss half the enjoyment.

ASK your purse what you should buy.

WISDOM OF NOTED AMERICANS

IMMORTALITY is the glorious discovery
of Christianity.—*Channing*

INTIMATE BOOKS, like intimate friends, are a selection of a lifetime.
I would not be happy without many friends and many books, but
the intimate ones of each boil down to but a precious little handful.
—*George Matthew Adams*

GENIUS WILL live and thrive without training, but it does not the less reward
the watering pot and pruning knife.—*Margaret Fuller*

HALF THE MISERY in the world comes of want of courage to speak and to hear
the truth plainly, and in a spirit of love.—*Harriet Beecher Stowe*

THERE IS VIRTUE in country houses, in gardens and orchards, in fields, streams,
and groves, in rustic recreations and plain manners, that neither cities nor uni-
versities enjoy.—*Bronson Alcott*

A LOVE OF BEAUTY is born with us. It is inherent. And God, the Creator, knew
of its power, so he planted it everywhere—and in His great realm of this earth
it is free to all, no matter what the circumstance of birth or fortune.—*George
Matthew Adams*

WERE MY MAKER TO GRANT me but a single glance through these sightless eyes of
mine . . . I would without question or recall choose to see first a child, then a dog.
—*Helen Keller*

EDUCATION in its widest sense includes everything that exerts a formative influence, and causes a young person to be, at a given point, what he is.—*Mark
Hopkins*

THOUGH I AM WEAK, yet God, when prayed,
Cannot withhold his conquering aid.
                              —*Emerson*

NOTHING is old but the mind.—*Emerson*

CREED
HAL BORLAND

I am an American:
That's the way we put it,
Simply, without any swagger, without any brag,
In those four plain words.
We speak them softly, just to ourselves.
We roll them on the tongue, touching every syllable, getting the feel of them,
  the enduring flavor.
We speak them humbly, thankfully, reverently:
I am an American.

They are more than words, really.
They are the sum of the lives of a vast multitude of men and women and
  wide-eyed children.
They are a manifesto to mankind; speak those four words anywhere in the
  world—yes, anywhere—and those who hear will recognize their
  meaning.
They are a pledge. A pledge that stems from a document which says: "When
  in the course of human events," and goes on from there.
A pledge to those who dreamed that dream before it was set to paper, to
  those who have lived it since, and died for it.
Those words are a covenant with a great host of plain Americans, Americans
  who put their share of meaning into them.
Listen, and you can hear the voices echoing through them, words that sprang
  white-hot from bloody lips, scornful lips, lips a-tremble with human
  pity:
"Don't give up the ship! Fight her till she dies . . . .
  Damn the torpedoes! Go ahead! . . . Do you want to live forever! . . .
  Send us more Japs! . . . Don't cheer, boys; the poor devils are dying."
Laughing words, June-warm words, words cold as January ice:
"Root, hog, or die . . . *I've come from Alabama with my banjo* . . . Pike's Peak or
  bust! . . . Busted, by God! . . . When you say that, smile. . . . Wait till
  you see the whites of their eyes. . . . With malice toward none, with
  charity for all, with firmness in the right . . . I am not a Virginian, but
  an American."

You can hear men in assembly summoned, there in Philadelphia, hear the
  scratch of their quills as they wrote words for the hour and produced a
  document for the ages.
You can hear them demanding guarantees for which they suffered through
  the hell of war, hear a Yankee voice intoning the text of ten brief
  amendments.

You can hear the slow cadences of a gaunt and weary man at Gettysburg, dedicating not a cemetery, but a nation.

You can hear those echoes as you walk along the streets, hear them in the rumble of traffic; you can hear them as you stand at the lathe, in the roaring factory; hear them in the clack of train wheels, in the drumming throb of the air liner; hear them in the corn fields and in the big woods and in the mine pits and the oil fields.
But they aren't words any longer; they're a way of life, a pattern of living.
They're the dawn that brings another day in which to get on with the job.
They're the noon whistle, with a chance to get the kinks out of your back, to get a bowl of soup, a plate of beans, a cup of coffee into your belly.
They're evening, with another day's work done; supper with the wife and kids; a movie, or the radio, or the newspaper or a magazine—and no Gestapo snooping at the door and threatening to kick your teeth in.

They are a pattern of life as lived by a free people, freedom that has its roots in rights and obligations:
The right to go to a church with a cross or a star or a dome or a steeple, or not to go to any church at all; and the obligation to respect others in that same right.
The right to harangue on a street corner, to hire a hall and shout your opinions till your tonsils are worn to a frazzle; and the obligation to curb your tongue now and then.
The right to go to school, to learn a trade, to enter a profession, to earn an honest living; and the obligation to do an honest day's work.
The right to put your side of the argument in the hands of a jury; and the obligation to abide by the laws that you and your delegates have written in the statute books.
The right to choose who shall run our government for us, the right to a secret vote that counts just as much as the next fellow's in the final tally; and the obligation to use that right, and guard it and keep it clean.
The right to hope, to dream, to pray; the obligation to serve.

These are some of the meanings of those four words, meanings we don't often stop to tally up or even list.
Only in the stillness of a moonless night, or in the quiet of a Sunday afternoon, or in the thin dawn of a new day, when our world is close about us, do they rise up in our memories and stir in our sentient hearts.
Only then? That is not wholly so—not today!
For today we are drilling holes and driving rivets, shaping barrels and loading shells, fitting wings and welding hulls,
And we are remembering Wake Island, and Bataan, and Corregidor, and Hong Kong and Singapore and Batavia;

255

We are remembering Warsaw and Rotterdam and Rouen and Coventry.
Remembering, and muttering with each rivet driven home: "There's another
one for remembrance!"

They're plain words, those four. Simple words.
You could write them on your thumbnail, if you chose,
Or you could sweep them all across the sky, horizon to horizon.
You could grave them on stone, you could carve them on the mountain
ranges.
You could sing them, to the tune of *Yankee Doodle*.
But you needn't. You needn't do any of those things,
For those words are graven in the hearts of 130,000,000 people,
They are familiar to 130,000,000 tongues, every sound and every syllable.
But when we speak them we speak them softly, proudly, gratefully:
I am an American.

THE TUFT OF FLOWERS
ROBERT FROST

I went to turn the grass once after one
Who mowed it in the dew before the sun.

The dew was gone that made his blade so keen
Before I came to view the levelled scene.

I looked for him behind an isle of trees;
I listened for his whetstone on the breeze.

But he had gone his way, the grass all mown,
And I must be, as he had been,—alone,

'As all must be,' I said within my heart,
'Whether they work together or apart.'

But as I said it, swift there passed me by
On noiseless wing a bewildered butterfly,

Seeking with memories grown dim o'er night
Some resting flower of yesterday's delight.

And once I marked his flight go round and round,
As where some flower lay withering on the ground.

And then he flew as far as eye could see,
And then on tremulous wing came back to me.

I thought of questions that have no reply,
And would have turned to toss the grass to dry;

But he turned first, and led my eye to look
At a tall tuft of flowers beside a brook,

A leaping tongue of bloom the scythe had spared
Beside a reedy brook the scythe had bared.

I left my place to know them by their name,
Finding them butterfly weed when I came.

The mower in the dew had loved them thus,
By leaving them to flourish, not for us,

Nor yet to draw one thought of ours to him,
But from sheer morning gladness at the brim.

The butterfly and I had lit upon,
Nevertheless, a message from the dawn,

That made me hear the wakening birds around,
And hear his long scythe whispering to the ground,

And feel a spirit kindred to my own;
So that henceforth I worked no more alone;

But glad with him, I worked as with his aid,
And weary, sought at noon with him the shade;

And dreaming, as it were, held brotherly speech
With one whose thought I had not hoped to reach.

'Men work together,' I told him from the heart,
'Whether they work together or apart.'

ALL MEN desire to be immortal.—*Theodore Parker*

"I CAN FORGIVE, but I cannot forget," is only another way of saying, "I cannot forgive."—*Henry Ward Beecher*

GOD PARDONS like a mother, who kisses the offense into everlasting forgetfulness.—*Henry Ward Beecher*

THE DUTY OF LABOR is written on a man's body: in the stout muscle of the arm, and the delicate machinery of the hand.—*Theodore Parker*

LIKE A MAN, ON TRIAL for the murder of his father and mother, is one who pleads for clemency on the grounds that he is an orphan.—*Phillips Brooks*

A DEMOCRACY,—that is a government of all the people, by all the people, for all the people; of course, a government of the principles of eternal justice, the unchanging law of God; for shortness' sake I will call it the idea of Freedom.—*Theodore Parker*

ALL MEN NEED SOMETHING to poetize and idealize their life a little— something which they value for more than its use, and which is a symbol of their emancipation from the mere materialism and drudgery of daily life.—*Theodore Parker*

THY TRUTH IS still the light which guides the nations groping on their way.—*Theodore Parker*

BUT GIVE ME, LORD, eyes to behold the truth;
A seeing sense that knows the eternal right;
A heart with pity filled, and gentlest truth;
A manly faith that makes all darkness light;
Give me the power to labor for mankind.
—*Theodore Parker*

A PRAYER, in its simplest definition, is merely a wish turned heavenward.—*Phillips Brooks*

258

RELIGIOUS LEADERS

HUMANITY is the Son of God.—*Theodore Parker*

THE SUN does not shine for a few trees and flowers,
but for the wide world's joy.—*Henry Ward Beecher*

No GREAT ADVANCE has ever been made in science, politics,
or religion, without controversy.—*Lyman Beecher*

IT (HOLINESS) MADE the soul like a field or garden of God,
with all manner of pleasant flowers.—*Jonathan Edwards*

TODAY, TOMORROW, EVERY DAY, to thousands the end of the world is
close at hand. And why should we fear it? We walk here, as it were, in
the crypts of life; at times, from the great cathedral above us, we can
hear the organ and the chanting choir; we see the light stream through
the open door, when some friend goes up before us; and shall we fear
to mount the narrow staircase of the grave that leads us out of the
uncertain twilight into life eternal.—*Samuel Longfellow*

MANY MEN BUILD as cathedrals were built: the part nearest the ground
finished; but that part which soars toward heaven, the turrets and the
spires, forever incomplete.—*Henry Ward Beecher*

LIVE FOR THE GOOD, taking the ill thou must;
Toil with thy might; with manly labor pray;
Living and loving, learn thy God to trust,
And he will shed upon thy soul the blessings of the just.
　　　　　　　　　　　—*Theodore Parker*

GOD BE THANKED for books. They are the voices of the distant and the
dead, and make us heirs of the spiritual life of past ages.—*Channing*

MAN NEVER FALLS so low that he can see nothing higher than
himself.—*Theodore Parker*

ONE on God's side is a majority.—*Wendell Phillips*

259

I AM AN AMERICAN
By R. L. DUFFUS

I AM AN AMERICAN. The things I shall say about myself may seem at first to contradict one another, but in the end they add up. I am almost always recognized at once wherever I go about the world. Some say it is my clothes that give me away. Some say it is my way of talking. I think it is more than that.

I have had an unusual history. My ancestors came over in the *Mayflower*. They also came over during the hungry Forties of the last century, in the hopeful Eighties, in the troubled Nineties. Or I came five years ago and have just become a citizen. Name any race—I belong to it.

I have been around. I have seen the earth. No plain, no river, no mountain, no ocean, no race is alien to me, but now *I am an American. I am an American* because my father, or his father, or some other one of my ancestors, grew tired of being ordered about by persons no better or wiser than himself; or had more ambition or more energy than there was room for in the place where he was born; or was eager for new experience, or was hungry for land.

I, or some one for me, bought my share of America at a price. I have known hardships, sickness and danger.

I could not be held within the limits set for me by kings and lordlings on the other side of the water. I pushed forward. I hunted far beyond the mountains. I returned and took my wife and our brood and our wagons over. I crossed the great river and the little rivers. I crossed the ocean of plains. I crossed the deserts and the further ranges.

The life I lived shaped me into a new kind of human being. I will not say a better kind, only a different kind.

I have not loved arrogant authority. I have not respected any man because of the accident of birth. I have judged my fellows by what they were and what they did. I have relied upon myself. I have hoped greatly.

Out of the hate for power not answerable to the people, out of the bravest words and the boldest acts of my ancestors in other lands, out of the necessities of a new and untamed world, out of the knowledge learned by pioneers, that no man lives to himself alone; out of the desire for freedom, for peace and moderation, I have tried to create my government. I have not been wholly successful. I hope to be. I shall be.

In my struggle with this continent, out of my dreams, out of my griefs, out of my sins, I have laid by a great store of memories. They are a part of what I am. No torrent of words can tell of them. Some of them are too deeply hidden for words. But no new world, no new order in the world, can wipe them out.

I remember great men and great deeds. I remember great sayings.

But I remember, also, sayings that were never written down and deeds known only to a few: the pioneer greeting his wife as he came in from his new cornfield, in the dappled shade of ringed and dying trees; the strong surge of discussion in remote crossroads stores; the young man in Georgia or Ohio kissing his mother good-bye as he goes to enlist; a Mississippi Negro, a Texas cowboy, a round-house wiper making a song; a small-town William Tell standing up to a petty tyrant; all manner of men and women planning, working, saving, seeing that the children had better schooling than the parents; reformers crying out against brutality and corruption; dreamers battling against the full tide of materialism.

I remember all these things. They help to steady me when I lie awake at night, or when I walk the streets or go about the countryside in the darker night of injustice and violence that has come over the earth.

I stand up straighter. These are my people that have said and done these things.

MY AMERICA
THOMAS CURTIS CLARK

More famed than Rome, as splendid as old Greece,
And saintlier than Hebrew prophet's dream;
A shrine of beauty, Italy-inspired;
A nobler France, by truth and freedom fired;
As hale as England, treasuring the gleam
Of knightly Arthur; though a land of peace,
As brave as Sparta—till all hellish wars shall cease.

In thoughts, as wise as is her prairie sea;
In deeds, as splendid as her mountain piles;
As noble as her mighty river tides.
Let her be true, a land where right abides;
Let her be clean, as sweet as summer isles;
And let her sound the note of liberty
For all the earth, till every man and child be free!

THIS LAND AND FLAG
ANONYMOUS

WHAT IS the love of country for which our flag stands? Maybe it begins with love of the land itself. It is the fog rolling in with the tide at Eastport, or through the Golden Gate and among the towers of San Francisco. It is the sun coming up behind the White Mountains, over the Green, throwing a shining glory on Lake Champlain and above the Adirondacks. It is the storied Mississippi rolling swift and muddy past St. Louis, rolling past Cairo, pouring down past the levees of New Orleans. It is lazy noontide in the pines of Carolina, it is a sea of wheat rippling in western Kansas, it is the San Francisco peaks far north across the glowing nakedness of Arizona, it is the Grand Canyon, and a little stream coming down out of a New England ridge, in which are trout.

It is men at work. It is the storm-tossed fishermen coming into Gloucester and Provincetown and Astoria. It is the farmer riding his great machine in the dust of harvest, the dairyman going to the barn before sunrise, the lineman mending the broken wire, the miner drilling for the blast. It is the servants of fire in the murky splendor of Pittsburgh, between the Allegheny and the Monongahela, the trucks rumbling through the night, the locomotive engineer bringing the train in on time, the pilot in the clouds, the riveter running along the beam a hundred feet in air. It is the clerk in the office, the housewife doing the dishes and sending the children off to school. It is the teacher, doctor, and parson tending and helping, body and soul, for small reward.

It is small things remembered, the little corners of the land, the houses, the people that each one loves. We love our country because there was a little tree on a hill, and grass thereon, and a sweet valley below; because the hurdy-gurdy man came along on a sunny morning in a city street; because a beach or a farm or a lane or a house that might not seem much to others was once, for each of us, made magic. It is voices that are remembered only, no longer heard. It is parents, friends, the lazy chat of street and store and office, and the ease of mind that makes life tranquil. It is summer and winter, rain and sun and storm. These are flesh of our flesh, bone of our bone, blood of our blood, a lasting part of what we are, each of us and all of us together.

It is stories told. It is the Pilgrims dying in their first dreadful winter.

It is the Minute Man standing his ground at Concord Bridge, and dying there. It is the army in rags, sick, freezing, starving at Valley Forge. It is the wagons and the men on foot going westward over Cumberland Gap, floating down the great rivers, rolling over the great plains. It is the settler hacking fiercely at the primeval forest on his new, his own lands. It is Thoreau at Walden Pond, Lincoln at Cooper Union, and Lee riding home from Appomattox. It is corruption and disgrace, answered always by men who would not let the flag lie in the dust, who have stood up in every generation to fight for the old ideals and the old rights, at risk of ruin or of life itself.

It is a great multitude of people on pilgrimage, common and ordinary people, charged with the usual human failings, yet filled with such a hope as never caught the imaginations and the hearts of any nation on earth before. The hope of liberty. The hope of justice. The hope of a land in which a man can stand straight, without fear, without rancor.

The land and the people and the flag—the land a continent, the people of every race, the flag a symbol of what humanity may aspire to when the wars are over and the barriers are down; to these each generation must be dedicated and consecrated anew, to defend with life itself, if need be, but, above all, in friendliness, in hope, in courage, to live for.

MEETING WITH FRIENDS
By Henry David Thoreau

I HAVE certain friends whom I visit occasionally, but I commonly part from them early with a certain bitter-sweet sentiment. That which we love is so mixed and entangled with that which we hate in one another that we are more grieved and disappointed, aye, and estranged from one another, by meeting than by absence. Some men may be my acquaintances merely, but one whom I have been accustomed to regard, to idealize, to have dreams about as a friend, and mix up intimately with myself, can never degenerate into an acquaintance. I must know him on that higher ground or not know him at all. We do not confess and explain, because we would fain be so intimately related as to understand each other without speech. Our friend must be broad. His must be an atmosphere coextensive with the universe, in which we can expand and breathe. For the most part we are smothered and stifled by one another. I go and see my friend and try his atmosphere. If our atmospheres do not mingle, if we repel each other strongly, it is of no use to stay.

FOR YOU, O DEMOCRACY!
WALT WHITMAN

Come, I will make the continent indissoluble,
I will make the most splendid race the sun ever shone upon,
I will make divine magnetic lands,
 With the love of comrades,
 With the life-long love of comrades.

I will plant companionship thick as trees along all the rivers of
 America, and along the shores of the great lakes, and all over
 the prairies,
I will make inseparable cities with their arms about each other's
 necks,
 By the love of comrades,
 By the manly love of comrades.

For you these from me, O Democracy, to serve you,
For you, for you I am trilling these songs.

THAT DIVINE IDEA
By RALPH WALDO EMERSON

WE BUT HALF express ourselves, and are ashamed of that divine idea which each of us represents. It may be safely trusted as proportionate and of good issues, so it be faithfully imparted, but God will not have His work made manifest by cowards ... A man is relieved and gay when he has put his heart into his work and has done his best; but what he has said or done otherwise shall give him no peace. It is a deliverance which does not deliver. In the attempt his genius deserts him; no muse befriends; no invention, no hope.

263

WORDS OF GREAT AMERICANS:

MAN is the artificer of his own happiness.

HE ENJOYS true leisure who has time to improve his soul.

TO READ WELL, that is, to read true books in a true spirit, is a noble exercise.

WHAT WISDOM, what warning can prevail against gladness? There is no law so strong which a little gladness may not transgress.

WHAT OTHER LIBERTY is there worth having, if we have not freedom and peace in our minds,—if our inmost and most private man is but a sour and turbid pool?

MOST OF THE LUXURIES and many of the so-called comforts of life are not only not indispensable, but positive hindrances to the elevation of mankind.

MAN'S CAPACITIES have never been measured; nor are we to judge of what he can do by any precedents, so little has been tried.

NOTHING can be more useful to a man than a determination not to be hurried.

CULTIVATE POVERTY like a garden herb, like sage. . . . It is life near the bone, where it is sweetest.

I WOULD RATHER SIT on a pumpkin, and have it all to myself, than to be crowded on a velvet cushion.

THERE is never an instant's truce between virtue and vice.

THERE IS no remedy for love but to love more.

HENRY DAVID THOREAU

THE BLUEBIRD carries the sky on his back.

I THINK we may safely trust a good deal more than we do.

I SHOULD NOT TALK so much about myself if
there were anybody else whom I knew so well.

OUR LIFE IS but the soul made known by its fruits, the body. The whole duty
of man: make to yourself a perfect body.

IT IS A REMARKABLE SIGHT, THIS SNOW-CLAD LANDSCAPE, the fences and bushes
half buried, and the warm sun on it . . . . The town and country is now so still,
no rattle of wagons nor even jingle of sleigh bells, every tread being as with
woolen feet . . . . In such a day as this, the crowing of a cock is heard very far
and distinctly . . . . There are a few sounds still which never fail to affect me,
the notes of a wood thrush and the sound of a vibrating chord . . . . The strain
of the aeolian harp and of the wood thrush are the truest and loftiest preachers
that I know now left on this earth . . . . As I hear, I realize and see clearly what
at other times I only dimly remember. I get the value of the earth's extent and
the sky's depth.

MY DWELLING was small, and I could hardly entertain an echo in it.

A MAN is rich in proportion to the number of things
which he can afford to let alone.

EVERY MAN IS THE BUILDER of a temple, called his body, to the god he worships,
after a style purely his own.

TO HIM WHOSE elastic and vigorous thought keeps pace with the sun,
the day is a perpetual morning.

THAT MAN is the richest whose pleasures are the cheapest.

I LEAVE this world without a regret.

RANDOM MUSINGS:

GOOD MANNERS are made up of petty sacrifices.

ADOPT the pace of nature: her secret is patience.

OUR FAITH comes in moments; our vice is habitual.

THE ONLY WAY to have a friend is to be one. You shall not come nearer to a man by getting into his house.

THE WORLD belongs to the energetic man. His will gives him new eyes. He sees expedients and means where we saw none.

THE HIGHEST MERIT we ascribe to Moses, Plato, and Milton is, that they set at naught books and traditions, and spake not what men said but what they thought. A man should learn to detect and watch that gleam of light which flashes across his mind from within, more than the luster of the firmament of bards and sages.

IT IS EASY in the world to live after the world's opinion; it is easy in solitude to live after our own: but the great man is he who in the midst of the crowd keeps with perfect sweetness the independence of solitude.

STEAM IS NO STRONGER now than it was a hundred years ago, but it is put to better use.

THOUGHT IS THE PROPERTY of him who can entertain it, and of him who can adequately place it.

THE LANDSCAPE belongs to the man who looks at it.

YOU cannot do wrong without suffering wrong.

EVERY noble activity makes room for itself.

RALPH WALDO EMERSON

ALL great men come out of the middle classes.

DO HAVE the courage not to adopt another's courage.

LIFE IS NOT so short but that there is always time enough for courtesy.

THE PARTY of virility rules the hour, the party of ideas and sentiments rules the age.

HERE IS THE WORLD, sound as a nut, perfect, not the smallest piece of chaos left, never a stitch nor an end, not a mark of haste, or botching, or second thought; but the theory of the world is a thing of shreds and patches.

THE MARTYR can not be dishonored. Every lash inflicted is a tongue of fame; every prison, a more illustrious abode; every burned book or house enlightens the world; every suppressed or expunged word reverberates through the earth from side to side.

WE SOMETIMES MEET an original gentleman who, if manners had not existed, would have invented them.

DON'T WASTE YOUR LIFE in doubts and fears: spend yourself on the work before you, well assured that the right performance of this hour's duties will be the best preparation for the hours or ages that follow it.

THE ONE PRUDENCE of life is concentration.

IT IS BETTER to suffer injustice than to do it.

SEEING ONLY what is fair,
Sipping only what is sweet,
Thou dost mock at fate and care.

FEAR always springs from ignorance.

The Land Is Sleeping

By ROSE C. FELD

*T*HERE ARE SEVERAL WAYS of becoming an American. You can be born here, you can be naturalized, or you can grow a cabbage. Marya Vozech grew a cabbage. To be sure, she did it for other reasons—to provide food for her four fatherless children—but it was the cabbage that brought her out of the shadowed world of the alien into the sunlit warmth of American equality. It happened ten years ago, but it all came back to me today when I received a card announcing the marriage of Miss Helen Vozech to Mr. Donald Metcalfe.

I shall never forget my first meeting with Marya. It was a bitter cold day, early in March, when the ground was still hard and the trees stood shivering and bare against a bleak wind-swept sky. I had driven over to Lem Gaylord's general store to do my week's shopping.

Lem's place is a unique institution in our small Connecticut town. Or perhaps I should say our town is unique in the possession of a store like Lem's. It has stood on Main Street, flanked by the Congregational church on one side and the Town Hall on the other, for over a century.

There has always been a Gaylord, lean and gaunt, and friendly in his own Yankee fashion, behind one of the counters. The shop has been enlarged with the years, but it still retains the atmosphere and the services of a bygone day. You can buy practically anything at Lem's. If you want a ham and the fixings for a Sunday dinner, Lem has them; if you want a bag of fertilizer or lawn seed; if you want a lamp, hinges, a doorknob; if you want a pair of overalls or a wheelbarrow or cough medicine—if you want anything, in short—Lem can produce it for you. The oldtimers in our town go to Lem's out of habit, the newcomers either because they think its amusing or simply because he has something they want.

The lighting in Lem's store is a little on the thrifty side. He has an electric bulb over each counter and he assumes that you'll have the intelligence to pull the string if you want to examine anything. On a Saturday afternoon or evening, when there's a sizable crowd in the place, all the bulbs are lighted, but on a mid-week day most of Lem's wares are usually shrouded in semidarkness.

This bleak March morning I spotted Lem at the far end of the store, where he keeps his farm tools. He stood under the glaring light talking to someone in the shadows about the virtues of a hoe he was holding in his hands. I heard his customer before I saw her. Two words traveled across the counters laden with merchandise: "Is wonderful!"

I have often heard these words since, and they still retain a quality compounded of awe and delight, but this first time they struck me with special force. As I look back now, they hold the complete picture of Marya: foreign, courageous, glowingly appreciative of the good things of life.

Unashamedly curious, I walked over to Lem. He greeted me with a wave of his hand, but my eyes were not on him. They were on the woman who stood beside him, fingering the hoe he had surrendered to her. She was short and, even though wrapped up in an enormous shawl which covered her from head to below the waist, was obviously slight. Her features were not unusual except for a pair of very bright brown eyes set above wide cheekbones. It was not until I was quite close to her that I saw she had a child with her, a little boy about six, who clung with a bare, red little hand to her skirts. Like her, he was wrapped in a shawl, but, in respect to his sex, no doubt, his head was covered by a cap. He looked up at me shyly for a moment, then buried his head in his mother's skirts.

"Nah, Anton," she chided him as she gently released herself and said something more to him in a foreign language. She smiled at me. "Is six years old," she explained. "But yet like a baby." She turned to Lem. "You fix for the lady. No? I got plenty time."

Her eyes traveled to the racks which held other farm tools—shovels, spades, pitchforks, rakes. I expostulated, saying I was in no hurry and would wait my turn. As Lem leaned against the counter, I saw that he was in one of his talkative moods.

"This here is Mrs. Vozech," he said to me. "She's taken over Dave Stebbins' place."

He waited for me to make a comment, but before I could express the surprise he anticipated, Marya broke in.

"Is wonderful! No? We have a house in the country and land to grow things. Twenty-seven acres,

Mr. Stebbins tell me."

I looked at Lem and Lem looked at me. We knew Dave Stebbins' place. For twenty years it had stood, deserted and forlorn, on a rutted, washed-out, blind-alley road. It was picturesque if your eyes could find beauty in sagging chimneys and doorways, in broken windows, rotting clapboards and tottering porch. It may have been a good house when it was built, but neglect for many decades had turned it into a grim hag of a ruin. Even New Yorkers going in for restoring old property shuddered when they looked at it.

"Did you buy the place?" I asked Marya.

"No," she answered. "Mr. Stebbins say we can live there for nothing. I buy it later."

"She's figurin' on growin' things there," Lem interrupted. "I've told her it's hopeless. You'd need a tractor and bulldozer to turn that soil. Mostly stones, anyhow."

Marya's hands reached out to the tool racks again. "An ax I need. Also a shovel. And this." Her hand touched a brush scythe. "And for after, those." She pointed to a spade, a pitchfork, a sickle. She looked up at me. "Already I buy the things to plant." She nodded toward a large bag on the counter. "Potatoes, onions, cabbages, carrots. We live good this year."

She smiled shyly at Lem, as though asking him for confirmation of her words. But Lem, in the honesty of his soul, could not give it to her.

"It's a losing fight," he said to her. "It's a shame to waste your money on the seed."

"I don't lose," Marya answered quietly. "You see." She fumbled in the folds of her shawl and extracted a worn change purse. "How much I owe you for everything?"

He figured the sum quickly, with a look of embarrassment on his face. Besides the seed for planting, she had bought a peck of potatoes, a bag of flour, a pound of coffee and two cans of evaporated milk. Lem said the whole thing came to $2.78. I suspect it was more. An inaudible sigh escaped her lips as she counted out the money. I could see there was very little left in the purse when she closed it. Her transaction was over, but she could not bring herself to leave the tools she coveted. She touched the ax and the scythe handle with a caressing movement of her fingers.

"Is beautiful," she said to me.

"Yes," I answered uncomfortably.

"You have something to keep them sharp?" she asked Lem.

"Well, sure," he answered. "Sure."

"How much it cost?"

"I'll throw that in with the stuff when you buy it," he replied.

"Is good to begin early," she said. "Is much to do. The land is all choked up."

"That land is dead, Mrs. Vozech."

"No," she said softly. "Is sleeping under. I wake it up. When we come last week, the house is dead too. But we clean it and now is alive. Is the same with land. Needs good strong hands."

She paused for a moment as though listening to her own words, and a frown of concentration gathered on her wide brow.

"Excuse me, please," she said to Lem, in sudden decision. "But you are married?"

"Shucks, yes," said Lem, his blue eyes showing his surprise at her question.

"Good," commented Marya.

"Your wife have a clean house?"

Lem looked at me in complete bewilderment and I answered for him. "Mrs. Gaylord's house is spotless," I declared.

Marya's face fell. "Is too bad," she said, and her voice went dead. "I think, maybe, I clean for your wife," she explained to Lem, "and you pay me with the things what I need. First, the ax."

"Look," I said, "I could use somebody for my spring cleaning. So could others in this town. When could you come?"

"I come right away. Now," she answered, her face alight. "Maybe I make enough to buy the ax. No?"

"We'll start tomorrow," I declared. "And you can take the ax now. I'll pay for it and take it off from what I'll owe you."

Marya's eyes were wide with triumph as she looked at Lem. "We take it now," she said. "And you give me the thing to keep it sharp, like you say. No?"

Lem's lean, lined face was stern as he lifted the ax off the rack. He put it on the counter and then, in turn, he picked up the scythe, the shovel, the spade, the pitchfork, the hoe, the sickle, and placed them beside the ax. He looked around and added a few other things—a rake, a watering pot and a hand trowel. Marya watched him with amazement as he piled them on the counter.

"No," she expostulated. "Only the ax. I buy the other things later."

"Three can play the game, as well as two," he answered. "You can pay for them when you have the money."

"Oh, no," whispered Marya, and I could see the effort it cost her to say it. "Is not right. I must pay for what I take."

"Sure," agreed Lem. "I'm not making you a present. You get your cleaning jobs and pay me when you have the cash." Seeing the unbelief and doubt in her eyes he added, "Shucks, everybody around here buys things on credit. It's a good American custom."

Her eyes wide, Marya turned to me. "Is true? Is American like that?"

"Certainly," I answered. "We all owe money to Mr. Gaylord."

"America," said Marya. She breathed the word as though it were a prayer.

"Tell you what," added Lem. "When you find out you're licked by the job, you can return these things to me for half the price. How's that?"

Marya's lips set in a grim line. She seemed to grow several inches as she faced him. "You never get those things back." There was iron in her voice. "I buy more after."

Lem shook his head as he went to work making out the bill for Marya. She took it from him and folded it carefully into her purse. Then she lifted the ax and the scythe and hefted them over her shoulder.

"These I take now. I come back later with the children for the other things."

"You're not going to lug those home yourself, together with your groceries?" I asked.

"Oh, is all right," Marya assured me. "I carry these, and the other things we put in the little wagon." She indicated a child's cart standing beside her and began piling it up with her purchases. "Anton help me pull. He is strong, like me. Eh, Anton?"

The boy nodded in happy agreement.

"But it's over two miles," I argued.

"Sure," agreed Marya. "Is nothing. Is good roads. Better than the old country."

"Don't go," I said. "I've got my station wagon outside. If you'll wait until I get my groceries, I'll give you a lift to your house. Besides," I added, seeing signs of protest in her eyes, "we've got to talk about your cleaning job."

The old Stebbins place looked even worse than I remembered it. Weeds were growing up to the doors and windows, the fences were down, the fields were stifled with brush. But there was smoke coming out of a crooked chimney and there was bedding airing on the sagging porch. Against the wall of the house was propped a large, framed portrait of a swarthy man with a luxuriant mustache.

Marya laughed as she introduced me to him. "This is my husband, Jan. I put him on the porch so he can see the wonderful land we have."

Three little girls came out of the house while she was speaking. The oldest was about twelve; the youngest, four.

"Elena, Marya and Lisa," Marya introduced them.

"Helen, Mary and Louise," the one she had called Elena corrected her, and Marya nodded gravely.

"Sure. And Anthony. Always I forget. Is good you remind me." She turned to me. "You come in, please, and have a cup of coffee. Is first time we have a visitor. Is good."

I went through the crooked doorway into the large farmhouse kitchen. There wasn't much in the way of furniture—a stove, a couple of old tables, a few chairs. But what there was, was immaculate. The windows

271

had been washed, the wide, cracked floor boards and the woodwork scrubbed clean. In honor of the occasion, Marya brought out a fringed red tablecloth and spread it lovingly over the table.

"Is from the old country," she explained to me. "Is nice for company. No?"

"What brought you to Connecticut?" I asked her when we had settled down to the strong black coffee which she had brewed.

"Jan always want to come. He say America is a wonderful country. But he has no money and is ashamed to ask for help. When Jan die, I write to my brother Josef and he bring us. Two years we are here already."

"Your brother lives in Connecticut?" I asked.

"Oh, no," she replied. "Josef, he live in New York. He is a waiter in a restaurant. He got a wife and two children. They have four rooms in a big house with a lotta people. But is not America."

"What do you mean?" I queried.

Marya wrinkled her brows, seeking some way to make me understand. "Is not America," she continued, after a long moment. "Is not what Jan talk about. Is no trees, is no sky, is no land. Is no place to grow things to eat. The children stay in the streets. Josef get me some cleaning jobs, but I am afraid all the time to leave the children. Anton and Lisa are so small. Then Josef get me a janitor job where I can stay home all the time. We have three rooms downstairs. Is dark and it smell bad. Is no good. I think we make a big mistake to come to America. Then I meet Mr. Stebbins. You know him?"

"Yes," I said. "I used to know

Dave Stebbins."

Dave had always been a misfit in the country and had simply locked the door of his house and walked out the day after his mother's funeral. What he did in New York I never knew until Marya told me.

"Mr. Stebbins work for a wet-wash laundry," she informed me. "He pick up dirty clothes in a truck and he bring them back clean. He live in the same house where I am a janitor. One day he tell me about this house and he say we can come here for nothing. He bring us out here in the wet-wash truck last Sunday. His boss say is all right." She looked around the room with a deep, possessive glance. "Is wonderful! Someday, we buy this house."

She talked in her limping English of raising chickens, of buying a pig, perhaps a cow, later on. She put her hand on the shoulder of the little boy who stood leaning against her knee.

"Is good for children to have milk and eggs," she explained. "You help me, Anton. No?" she said to him. He nuzzled against her like a puppy. "They good children," she went on. "They help me with the land."

"You're going to send them to school, aren't you?" I asked her, a little aghast at her plans for them.

"Sure," she said. "Tomorrow they begin. Is all fixed. The bus take them. But they work after they come home. We all work."

She nodded encouragingly at them and they responded with eager smiles.

"Lisa—excuse, Louise, I mean —is too young for school, but not too young to plant potatoes," she added, looking at her youngest. "I plant potatoes when I am small like her." The thought of Louise made her frown. "Is all right I bring her with me tomorrow to your house? She don't make noise."

I assured her that Louise would be no trouble and left.

Before many weeks had passed, Marya had become a fixture in the homes of several of my friends. Lem, also, had recommended her to some of his customers. She was a marvelous worker, with an enormous pride in accomplishment. She washed and ironed curtains, she polished silver, she dusted furniture and waxed floors with a passion for perfection. The four-year-old Louise became a problem only in the sense that I felt guilty about the work her mother made her do. Marya would place a stack of books on the floor and show the child how to dust them. Or she would give her a cloth and tell her to wipe the window sills and corners of the room. When I expostulated, Marya would argue with me:

"Is no more hard work than to play. Later, when it get warm, you give her something to do in the sun. That make her strong."

But it was not the eight hours that Marya put in five days a week at the various households that filled me with respect and admiration for her; it was what went on at the Stebbins place before and after her regular working hours. When I came to fetch Marya at eight in the morning, she had already put in several hours of work on the land; and in the afternoons, when I brought her back, her three children, returned from school, were busy with hoe or rake in the large garden patch that Marya had staked out. Where there had been brush and choking weeds, there was now a smooth expanse of brown earth sifted by little hands into life-bearing soil.

"I do the work with the ax and spade before I go to clean," Marya explained to me, "and the children make it soft after. The big stones they leave for me."

With the few implements she had, she cut, she dug, she harrowed, she manured. But it was not the cold steel that woke the land that Marya said had been sleeping; it was Marya's yearning tenderness for its fertility. Once, I remember, when I was taking her home, she made me stop the car suddenly. She had seen a heap of horse manure in the road and couldn't bear to have it go to waste. She wrapped it in an old newspaper she found in the back seat and held it in her lap all the way home. Her apology to me was not for the burden she carried, but for keeping me on the road for the few minutes it took her to collect her find.

Saturdays and Sundays were days she loved, for then there was nothing to interfere with her labors. She was in her garden soon after the first spears of sunlight turned night into day, and she did not leave it until the last glow had sunk behind the horizon. Like a general commanding an army, she assigned projects to her helpers. To Helen, the eldest, fell the task of housework and cooking; to the others, definite chores of hoeing and weeding the long, straight rows of potatoes, onions, cabbages and carrots. Though she had never read a book in her life, Marya knew the essentials of psychology. She knew the value of commendation and encouragement, of turning labor into an exciting game, of stopping work for a treat of cookies or lemonade when she saw the signs of fatigue. Nor did she scold when the children, attracted by a toad or a rabbit or the antics of a chattering squirrel, slipped for a while into their natural world of play.

Each week when I came to Marya's place, I stopped to marvel at the magic of hands that had turned an angry wilderness into a plot of fruitfulness. The varying tints of green rose fair and fresh above the cool, dark, breathing earth.

It was I who suggested to Marya that she show her vegetables at Lem Gaylord's harvest fair. To call it a fair is a little extravagant, perhaps, but that was Lem's word for it. He liked to think he was in competition with the Danbury Fair, and it gave him a sense of satisfaction that he held his two weeks earlier. Every September, Lem cleared the rear of his store for the display of products that had been grown from seed or plants bought from him. A committee of three farmers from the state Grange were the judges, and the prizes were anything on Lem's shelves or counters, up to the value of five dollars. Competition, though keen, was always friendly and neighborly. Rivals for prizes for potatoes or corn or cabbages would slap one another on the back and chaff one another about the size and quality of their entries.

Marya was at first reluctant to enter the competition, partly out of shyness and partly out of an un-willingness to let any of her cherished vegetables out of sight. To her, they meant food, and food belonged in the cellar for winter's keeping. It was Helen, her twelve-year-old, who persuaded Marya. All the boys and girls at school were talking about the fair, she said, and she wanted to share in something that was as near

a game as she knew. She didn't say it that way, but when I heard her pleading with her mother I realized to what an extent she had missed the comradeship and the interests of those of her own years.

Marya must have sensed it, too, for in agreeing she added, "Don't worry, Elena. Someday we don't work so hard."

I helped Marya choose and ar-range her vegetables when the day for bringing them to Lem's arrived. We scrubbed the potatoes and carrots, we washed the onions. All of them were of a size and shape to bring pride to any grower's heart. But it was the cabbage that was breath-taking—an enormous ball of crisp, flawless green leaves, tightly packed around a firm core of white. Marya washed it under the kitchen pump and then shook it.

"I don't dry it," she said, standing off to look at it. "Is wonderful with the drops of water on it. Is like in the morning, with the dew. You think Mr. Gaylord let me put water on it tomorrow?"

"I think he will," I said, touched by her feeling for beauty.

Marya again looked at her cab-bage and then went to a cupboard and brought out a red-checkered napkin. "Is for company," she ex-plained, "but it look nice under the cabbage. Like a party. I show it like that."

Just as we were ready to leave for Lem Gaylord's store, I remembered that Marya's exhibit had no card, telling who the owner was. I was just going to print "Marya Vozech" on the bit of cardboard she brought me when she said, " 'Family Vozech.' That what you write on the card."
I hesitated for a moment, knowing

it was unusual, but finally wrote it as she wanted it.

Lem's blue eyes opened wide with unbelief when we put the baskets on his counter. It was a little over six months since the day when he had tried to discourage Marya from trying to do anything on Dave Stebbins' land. He looked at Marya standing small and shy but deeply triumphant beside me, and he looked at the vegetables she had brought.

"Well, I'll be danged!" he declared at last, and then, feeling the need for greater expression, added, "I'll be double-danged!"

"Is wonderful. No?" asked Marya.

"It's a miracle!" said Lem. "Hank Metcalfe'll have a job matching that head of cabbage. Hank grows the best cabbage around here. Been getting the prize for heaven knows how many years."

A look of doubt crossed Marya's face. "Maybe is bad I bring my cabbage," she told Lem. "Maybe this Mr. Hank don't like it."

"Don't be foolish, woman," Lem declared. "Hank's a fair man and cabbages is cabbages." He chuckled. "I reckon his wife won't like it much if he don't get the prize. She's got her eyes on some aluminum pots."

"Can I see the cabbage what Mr. Hank bring?" asked Marya.

"He ain't brought it in yet," answered Lem. "There's other cabbages here, but they don't stand a chance against this one. Durn it, Mrs. Vozech, prize or no prize, you ought to be mighty proud of this specimen. So'm I. Didn't think my seeds had it in 'em."

"Thanks," said Marya. "I am very proud."

Lem fingered the potatoes, the carrots and the onions in a state of wonderment, shaking his head all the time, but his appreciation of the cabbage was boundless. Made courageous by his approval and admiration, Marya asked him to wet it down before the showing tomorrow.

"Sure," said Lem. "I always sprinkle the green vegetables with water. Makes 'em come alive."

"Thanks," said Marya again.

"Two o'clock tomorrow," Lem called after us as we made our way out.

Main Street was crowded with people and cars when I drove in with Marya and her family the next day. It was Saturday afternoon; it was the day of Lem's fair. The whole town was out. I left my passengers in front of Lem's store and went on to find a place to park.

"You see us inside," Marya called after me. "I go in to look at my cabbage."

I had a little difficulty in finding her when I returned. The aisles of Lem's store were packed with laughing, talking men, women and children. There was an air of festivity and neighborliness in the place that was heart-warming. At the rear of the store, on counters covered with green tissue paper, were ranged the exhibits, impressive tributes to the age-old partnership between man and nature. They shone in splendor under the bright lights that Lem had provided for this occasion. Their colors ranged through all the hues of the rainbow, from the delicate yellow of bleached celery to the deep tones of purple beets. Within the small space of Lem's store was packed a microcosm of the country's rich bounty.

This is America, I thought, looking at the rewards of patient toil, the

275

gnarled hands, the weather-beaten, smiling faces.

Marya's voice brought me out of my reverie. "Is beautiful," she whispered to me. "It make me ashamed I do so little. Next year we plant corn and beans and tomatoes. Lotta things."

"You've done plenty," I declared. "How's the Vozech cabbage?"

"Good," she replied. "But I don't get no prize. Mr. Hank Metcalfe bring three. They are wonderful."

"Better than yours?" I asked.

"No. Like mine. But three." She smiled tremulously. "Is all right," she added. "Is wonderful to be here."

Promptly at two, Lem took his place at a table set up on a platform and pounded a gavel. With jocular remarks about their virtues, he introduced the three judges. The first item to come up was corn. There were fourteen contestants. Each man brought his entry to the table and placed it with his card before the experts. There was a hush as the three men conferred over size, weight, color and whatever else was important in their decision. A shout went up as Lem announced the judges' choice, a batch of Golden Bantam corn grown by Matt Edwards. Matt came forward sheepishly but proudly to claim his award. It was part of the fun at Lem's fair that each winner had to call out what he wanted as his prize.

"What'll you have, Matt?" asked Lem. "Anything in this emporium up to five dollars."

"I'll let the missus decide," said Matt.

"Fair enough," said Lem as a wave of laughter filled the place. "What'll it be, Mrs. Edwards?"

"A pair of overalls for Matt. And a pair of rubber gloves for me. I'll take credit on the rest."

Again a wave of laughter filled the store, and then Lem went on to the pumpkin contest. After the pumpkins came potatoes, beans and carrots. The choice of prizes was as individual as the owners—farm implements, clothing, groceries, a ham. Marya watched the proceedings with the breathless enjoyment of a child at its first circus. When the potato and carrot judgings were announced, I urged her to bring her entries, but she shook her head.

"Is not good enough," she said. "The others is better than what I bring."

It was almost four when the cabbages were announced. Gravely, Marya carried her cabbage on its checkered red napkin to the judges' stand. A burst of applause greeted her. I didn't realize until that moment that she was the only woman contestant in the store.

Hank Metcalfe and his son, Don, a lanky lad of thirteen or fourteen, brought his three cabbages and placed them beside hers. There were four other entries, but it was clear from the start that the choice would be made between Marya's and Hank's.

There was the tenseness of drama as the judges examined the specimens, feeling the heads for texture and firmness, hefting them for weight. The moments grew tenser when they weighed each of Hank's three cabbages and put the heaviest aside. Then they weighed Marya's. To the naked eye there seemed no difference between them, but obviously there was. The judges whispered to Lem, who, with a wide grin on his face, raised his hand.

276

"The cabbage award goes to"—he paused and a quizzical look came into his eyes as he read Marya's card—"the cabbage award goes to 'Family Vozech.'"

I must admit the name sounded strange after the Edwardses, the Hopkinses and the other typical Yankee names that had preceded this one. Intermingled with the applause, I heard short bursts of laughter. The sound of it made me uncomfortable, for it held something that wasn't friendly.

"Who is Family Vozech?" a wit from the crowd called forth. "Never heard of him?"

This time the laughter grew heavier. A woman's voice answered the question:

"It's those foreign peasants on Dave Stebbins' place."

I turned around to see who had had the indecency and the cruelty to make that insulting remark. It was Martha Metcalfe, Hank's wife.

And then a beautiful and wonderful thing happened. Hank Metcalfe pushed forward to the platform and put his hand on Marya's cabbage. A deep silence fell over the crowd as his short, heavy fingers stroked it.

"I'd like to say something," he said. "I reckon my wife don't rightly understand about such things as growin' cabbages. I don't think she meant any harm. She was just kind of disappointed. But I want to say my hat's off to anyone who can grow a cabbage like this one, much less on land like Dave Stebbins left."

Somebody started clapping, and it was taken up by every pair of hands. Hank waited until the applause was over, then he went on.

"I want to say," he continued, "that there ain't nothin' funny about a family workin' together. My son here, Don, helps me. Always has. It's nothin' to be ashamed of. This country was built by families workin' together. We used to call them pioneers. I think the Family Vozech is a good American family. I'm proud to lose to people like that."

Again there was a burst of applause, this time mingled with clearing of throats and blowing of noses. When my eyes cleared, I saw Marya standing at the side of Hank Metcalfe, looking up at his face with an expression of complete and awesome happiness. I also noticed that young Don Metcalfe had joined the group of Marya's children.

Lem rapped on the table for order. "Couldn't have said it better myself, Hank," he declared. He turned to Marya. "And now, Mrs. Vozech, what'll you and your family take as a prize?"

Marya's voice was hoarse as she answered, "I like a sled for my children to play this winter."

SCHOOLHOUSES are the republican line of fortifications.—
Horace Mann

To PITY distress is but human; to relieve it is Godlike.—*Horace Mann*

WHERE THERE is a mother in the house, matters speed well.—*Bronson Alcott*

HABIT IS a cable. We weave a thread of it every day, and at last we cannot break it.—*Horace Mann*

TRUTH IS THE NURSING MOTHER of genius. No man can be absolutely true to himself, eschewing cant, compromise, servile imitation, and complaisance, without becoming original, for there is in every creature a fountain of life which, if not choked back by stones and other dead rubbish, will create a fresh atmosphere, and bring to life fresh beauty.—*Margaret Fuller*

YET THE DEEPEST truths are best read between the lines, and, for the most part, refuse to be written.—*Bronson Alcott*

GENIUS may conceive, but patient labor must consummate.—*Horace Mann*

WE MOUNT to heaven mostly on the ruins of our cherished schemes, finding our failures were successes.—*Bronson Alcott*

EVERY MAN is a volume, if you can read him.—*Channing*

MANY can argue; not many converse.—*Bronson Alcott*

GREATER IS HE who is above temptation than he, who being tempted, overcomes.
—*Bronson Alcott*

AMERICAN WOMEN SPEAK

LIFE is my college. May I
graduate well, and earn
some honors.—*Louisa Alcott*

HE WHO aids another strengthens
more than one.—*Lucy Larcom*

KEEP YOUR FACE to the sunshine and you cannot
see the shadow!—*Helen Keller*

NO MAN EVER PROSPERED in the world, without the consent and co-operation
of his wife.—*Abigail Adams*

I SHOULD LIKE TO THINK THAT AMERICA should stand as a land of opportunity
and enthusiasm and riches. By riches I mean not only raw materials, armies,
navies, railroads, ships and cities, but a whole people full of good will toward
the world, loyal to its own flag and beautiful continent, ready to work to educate
its whole people.—*Mrs. J. Borden Harriman*

THERE IS nothing in the universe that I fear, except that I
may not know my duty, or may fail to do it.—*Mary Lyon*

THE WAY to a man's heart is through his stomach.—*Mrs. Fanny Fern*

NEXT TO INVENTION is the power of interpreting invention; next
to beauty, the power of appreciating beauty.—*Margaret Fuller*

FOR PRECOCITY some great price is always demanded.—*Margaret Fuller*

I FEEL the flame of Eternity in my soul!—*Helen Keller*

YOU HAVE NOT ONE MAN to spare;
a woman will not be missed
in the defense of the fort.
—*Elizabeth Zane*

279

From *COMMEMORATION ODE*
James Russell Lowell

Many loved Truth, and lavished life's best oil
  Amid the dusk of books to find her,
Content at last, for guerdon of their toil,
   With the cast mantle she hath left behind her.
    Many in sad faith sought for her,
    Many with crossed hands sighed for her.
    But these, our brothers, fought for her,
    At life's dear peril wrought for her,
    So loved her that they died for her,
    Tasting the raptured fleetness
    Of her divine completeness:
      Their higher instinct knew
Those love her best who to themselves are true,
And what they dare to dream of, dare to do;
    They followed her and found her
    Where all may hope to find,
Not in the ashes of the burnt-out mind,
But beautiful, with danger's sweetness round her.
    Where faith made whole with deed,
    Breathes its awakening breath
    Into the lifeless creed,
    They saw her, plumed and mailed,
    With sweet stern face unveiled,
And all-repaying eyes, look proud on them in death.

...We sit here in the Promised Land
That flows with Freedom's honey and milk;
  But 'twas they won it, sword in hand,
Making the nettle danger soft for us as silk.
  We welcome back our bravest and our best—
  Ah me! not all! some come not with the rest,
Who went forth brave and bright as any here!
I strive to mix some gladness with my strain,
      But the sad strings complain,
      And will not please the ear:
I sweep them for a paean, but they wane
      Again and yet again
Into a dirge, and die away, in pain.
In these brave ranks I only see the gaps,
Thinking of dear ones whom the dumb turf wraps,
Dark to the triumph which they died to gain:

Fitlier may others greet the living,
For me the past is unforgiving;
   I with uncovered head
   Salute the sacred dead,
Who went, and who return not.—Say not so!
'Tis not the grapes of Canaan that repay,
But the high faith that failed not by the way;
Virtue treads paths that end not in the grave;
No bar of endless night exiles the brave;
   And to the saner mind
We rather seem the dead that stayed behind.
Blow, trumpets, all your exultations blow!
For never shall their aureoled presence lack:
I see them muster in a gleaming row,
With ever-youthful brows that nobler show;
We find in our dull road their shining track;
   In every nobler mood
We feel the orient of their spirit glow,
Part of our life's unalterable good,
Of all our saintlier aspiration;
   They come transfigured back,
Secure from change in their high-hearted ways,
Beautiful evermore, and with the rays
Of morn on their white Shields of Expectation!

...Bow down, dear Land, for thou hast found release!
   Thy God, in these distempered days,
   Hath taught thee the sure wisdom of His ways,
And through thine enemies hath wrought thy peace!
   Bow down in prayer and praise!
...O Beautiful! my Country! ours once more!
Smoothing thy gold of war-dishevelled hair
O'er such sweet brows as never other wore,
   And letting thy set lips,
   Freed from wrath's pale eclipse,
The rosy edges of their smile lay bare,
What words divine of lover or of poet
Could tell our love and make thee know it,
Among the Nations bright beyond compare?
   What were our lives without thee?
   What all our lives to save thee!
   We reck not what we gave thee;
   We will not dare to doubt thee,
But ask whatever else, and we will dare!

AMERICA
By Dorothy Thompson

IN THE PREFACE to the 1855 edition of *Leaves of Grass*, which is one of the greatest essays ever written in this country, on the poet and America, and the poet's relation to America, Walt Whitman wrote: "The largeness of Nature and of this nation were *monstrous* without a corresponding largeness and generosity of the spirit of the citizen." And without a breed of men full-sized, capable of universal sympathy, full of pride and affection and generosity, this country would indeed be monstrous. Here it lies in the center of the world, looking out on the two great oceans, looking out on the east to the old world, the cradle of white western civilization, looking out here on the west to a still older world, of still older races, out of which have come all the great religions and the deepest of human wisdoms. Here lives no race, but a race of races—a new kind of man bred out of many old kinds of men—in a climate more fierce, more radioactive, less temperate than that of Europe—in a climate that encompasses all climates. Here is no nation, but a nation of nations, a continent enclosing many different kinds of cultures and slowly making them into one culture.

When I think of America, I see it in a series of pictures—of moving pictures. I see the tight white and green farms of Vermont; the quick lush summers knee-deep in fern and field flowers; the narrow faces and the ironic grins of the Vermonters; the love of thrift and the strange inhibited hospitality of the people; the deep quiet lakes, the hills that are never too high for cattle to graze on them, the long, long bitter winters; small friendly communities where free, independent farmers still help build each other's barns and cut each other's wood; where the hired man calls the farmer by his first name; where the women from the farms and villages will come to cook for you, to help out, but where you never can find anyone with the spirit or attitude of a servant.

I think of the incredible city of Manhattan—sometimes I think it too incredible to last—where the languages of a dozen nations are heard on the streets; where there are more Italians than in any Italian city except Rome; more Jews than there are in Jerusalem or in any other town on earth; where there are more Irish than there are in Dublin.

I think of the temperate and civilized—and uncivilized—Carolinas; of Annapolis, the most beautiful eighteenth-century town in the whole English-speaking world; of the long quays of Savannah and the opulent laziness of the South, and the queer intellectual vigor that has always come up in the South whenever people thought that it was dead—from the South that has repeatedly given us our greatest statesmen.

I think of the great Southwest with a climate in which it is almost impossible to die. Texas, where you could settle a whole nation—yes, even now, when they say our frontiers are exhausted. And here, California, the earth's *Eldorado*, bigger than all of Italy, with a population only one-seventh that of Italy; great glittery beaches out of which rise the towers of oil wells. The finest fruits on earth. The most enchanting American city: San Francisco.

Yes, this country would be monstrous without a corresponding largeness and generosity of the spirit of its citizens.

This country is only five generations old. In the days of our great-great-great-grandfathers it was still a howling wilderness, still unexplored. Today it is the most powerful single nation on the face of the earth.

This country has seven million farms valued at thirty-three billion dollars. It produces three and a half times as much corn as any other nation in the world. It produces more wheat than any other nation on earth except Soviet Russia. In the great industrial towns of the East and the Middle West—in twenty-six counties of this vast nation—it produces almost as much steel and four times as many automobiles as all the rest of the world combined.

It is so enormous and so powerful that gigantic public works are lost in it; they are done casually without any ballyhoo. We have the greatest roads ever built since the Romans, and they were built without Fascism and without forced labor. In our lifetimes we have undertaken one of the greatest reclamation jobs ever done in the history of mankind. We have taken the Columbia and the Colorado Rivers and bent them, diverted them, stopped them, and pushed them around to create a whole new province in which men can settle and live, to create a lake so vast that it is an internal sea—and most people in the United States don't even know about it.

Here is the imagination which could conceive Wilson's dream of a world-state. Is it so fantastic? Is it more fantastic than what this country is? Here is the imagination which could conceive a frontier on another nation, three thousand miles long and at all places vulnerable, and without a single fort. You think that is not something to have accomplished in history? Maybe it is the greatest thing that we have accomplished in history: the idea that two continental nations could live in permanent friendship.

And because of our geography, our position between two oceans, the largeness of the nation, the necessary wideness of sympathy and imagination, this country is of all countries in the world the most susceptible to what happens outside its own boundaries. Throughout our history, we have counseled isolation. Never in our history have we been isolationists. Upon this country beat all the ideas and all the conflicts of the whole world—for in this country are the peoples of the whole world, and in this country is a certain type of mind, which is impatient of boundaries; which is able to contemplate things near and very far—nothing too far.

For five generations people have been coming here with a dream. Sometimes the dream was grandiose. The men who built New England came here with a dream of religious freedom. They came here as refugees, persecuted because they wouldn't bend their consciences. Acadians trekked to Louisiana also to find a world in which they could be themselves. And some came here hoping to find gold in the streets. And some came because they were herded up in Hungarian and Slavic villages and brought over here like cattle under false pretentions, full of false hopes. But in all of their minds there was something common. For all of them there was a magnet. And the magnet was that they thought that here, in their own way, they could stand up,

283

and look their neighbors in the face, and call themselves men, and not slaves.

And in five generations we have produced on this continent a race. You think there's not an American race? It's funny. Here we are made up of every stock in the world, and yet you can tell an American if you see him on the streets of Berlin, or Vienna, or Paris. What is an American? A typical American? An American is a fellow whose grandfather was a German forty-eighter who settled in Wisconsin and married a Swede, whose mother's father married an Englishwoman, whose son met a girl at college, whose mother was an Austrian and whose father was a Hungarian Jew and their son in the twentieth century right now is six feet tall—we are perhaps the tallest race on earth—goes to a state college, plays football, can't speak a word of any known language except American, and is doubtful whether he ever had a grandfather.

This American has several characteristics. He doesn't like to take orders. If you speak to him in a friendly way, he will do almost anything you ask him—inside reason. If you once get him into a war, he is a very good fighter, but he has a very low opinion of war. He doesn't like to commit himself to stay forever in one place. He is restless, and an inveterate traveler in his own country or elsewhere if he can afford it. He is incredibly ingenious. He can devise more ways to save himself work than any other known race of human beings; that's probably why he has invented so many gadgets. He is enormously inventive. This is one of the greatest races of inventors ever produced. He was born free and he shows it by the way he moves. He is

the best-nourished human being on the face of the earth. I know there are parts of this country where this is not true. It's got to be made better. But just the same the per capita consumption of food in the United States is higher than it is anywhere else, and the food that is consumed is more expensive and more various than it is anywhere else, taken for the country as a whole.

Now, what I am saying is this: we have got as far as we have, not only because we have a continent rich in resources—there are other continents rich in resources—we have got as far as we have because we produced a certain kind of human being and a certain type of mind. That human being is, first of all, a fellow with his eye on the future and not on the past. He is skeptical, and yet he has eternal faith. He constantly tries to think why something doesn't work as well as it should and how you can make it better. He is the kind of human being who likes to go off on his own and start something. If anyone wants to come with him, that's all right, too. He's a born democrat—and democrats are born, not made. He hates a stuffed shirt and he doesn't like to be high-hatted. He is suspicious of anybody who pretends to be better than he is. Nobody except the Scots and the Jews has such a passion for education as has the American.

I say all this because I hope that we are going to keep this kind of race alive. This race has emerged out of the concept of equality. Now don't misunderstand this word "equality." Equality does not mean that everybody is as good as everybody else. The American concept of equality is that every person has a right to a break. It is based on the belief in the immense value of every individual, and the right of every individual to make out of himself the very best human being that he can. The questions that Americans naturally ask concerning other human beings are: "What does he do?" and, "What sort of a guy is he?" and, "Does he know his stuff?"

The attitude of Americans toward themselves and toward all other human beings, the fact that we are a race of races, and a nation of nations, the fact of our outlook upon two oceans—and the miracle of the creation of this country out of stock that for such a large part represents the frustrations of European dreams and the rejection of human material—all these combine to make us a messianic people, with a feeling of mission not only for ourselves but for the world. This has been true from our very beginnings. Our whole political literature, which is one of the greatest possessed by any nation, reiterates the conception that the values that we cherish are of universal validity.

The Declaration of Independence contains these words:

"We hold these truths to be self-evident, that all *men* are created equal —[not all Americans]—and that they are endowed by their Creator with certain unalienable rights, among them life, liberty, and the pursuit of happiness."

And when we wrote the Constitution, we made one which is not confined to any geographic area, but is infinitely expandable.

In all the great speeches of Lincoln, there is the same sense of the American mission. In his farewell speech at Springfield, he spoke of the United States as "the last great hope of earth." And he closed the Gettysburg Address, that great apostrophe to popular government, with the words: "Shall not perish from the earth." He did not say "from this soil." He, like all great Americans, and above all the poets, conceived that there was some cosmic significance about this country and about this great experiment. And that feeling is still in the American heart. It is expressed in our reaction, our spontaneous reaction, to all assaults against human rights, to the degradation of personality, to all crimes against human freedom, to all persecutions and bigotries, and, above all, to all tyranny wherever it raises its head, in the most remote quarters of the globe. And since we are a free people, and are not inhibited in our expression, all such crimes have been protested by the American people as individuals long in advance of the protests of their government. Time and again in our history we have broken off diplomatic relations with countries because they have persecuted Jews or Armenians, or any other branch of the human race. We have been told that it is none of our business; but in some undefined way, we know it is some of our business; that the sense and meaning of our life is that we should be sensitive to such things.

285

WORDS OF GREAT AMERICANS:

WEALTH is not his that hath it,
but his that enjoys it.

WHERE liberty dwells, there is my country.

THE WORST WHEEL of the cart makes the most noise.

WHAT is a butterfly? At best he's but a caterpillar dressed.

IF YOU WOULD be wealthy, think of saving as well as of getting.

A LITTLE NEGLECT may breed mischief: for want of a nail
the shoe was lost; for want of a shoe the horse was lost; and
for want of a horse the rider was lost.

SLOTH MAKES ALL THINGS DIFFICULT, but industry all easy; and he that riseth late
must trot all day, and shall scarce overtake his business at night; while laziness
travels so slowly that poverty soon overtakes him.

GOD GRANT THAT not only the love of liberty but a thorough knowledge
of the rights of man may pervade all the nations of the earth, so that a
philosopher may set his foot anywhere on its surface and say: "This is
my country."

LET HIM that scatters thorns not go barefoot.

HE that would catch fish must venture his bait.

HE that cannot obey cannot command.

WRITE injuries in dust; benefits in marble.

IN HUMILITY imitate Jesus and Socrates.

286

BENJAMIN FRANKLIN

EARLY TO BED and early to rise,
Makes a man healthy, wealthy, and wise.

HE that lives on hope will die fasting.

KEEP thy shop, and thy shop will keep thee.

THE USE of money is all the advantage there is in having money.

IF A MAN could have half his wishes, he would double his troubles.

A MAN MUST HAVE a good deal of vanity who believes, and a good deal
of boldness who affirms, that all the doctrines he holds are true, and all
he rejects are false.

THE WAY TO WEALTH, if you desire it, is as plain as the way to market. It depends
chiefly on two words, industry and frugality; that is, waste neither time nor money,
but make the best use of both.

IF A MAN empties his purse into his head, no one can take it from him.

IF PRINCIPLE is good for anything, it is worth living up to.

WE MUST all hang together, else we shall all hang separately.

IN MY OPINION, there never was a good war or a bad peace.

IN THIS WORLD, nothing is certain but death and taxes.

HE that falls in love with himself will have no rivals.

THE DOORS of wisdom are never shut.

The Happy Journey to Trenton and Camden

By THORNTON WILDER

No scenery is required for this play. Perhaps a few dusty flats may be seen leaning against the brick wall at the back of the stage.

The five members of the Kirby *family and the* Stage Manager *compose the cast.*

The Stage Manager *not only moves forward and withdraws the few properties that are required, but he reads from a typescript the lines of all the minor characters. He reads them clearly, but with little attempt at characterization, scarcely troubling himself to alter his voice, even when he responds in the person of a child or a woman.*

As the curtain rises, the Stage Manager *is leaning lazily against the proscenium pillar at the audience's left. He is smoking.*

Arthur *is playing marbles in the center of the stage.*

Caroline *is at the remote back right talking to some girls who are invisible to us.*

Ma Kirby *is anxiously putting on her hat before an imaginary mirror.*

MA. Where's your pa? Why isn't he here? I declare we'll never get started.

ARTHUR. Ma, where's my hat? I guess I don't go if I can't find my hat.

MA. Go out into the hall and see if it isn't there. Where's Caroline gone to now, the plagued child?

ARTHUR. She's out waitin' in the street talkin' to the Jones girls.—I just looked in the hall a thousand times, Ma, and it isn't there. (*He spits for good luck before a difficult shot and mutters:*) Come on, baby.

MA. Go and look again, I say. Look carefully.

Arthur *rises, runs to the right, turns around swiftly, returns to his game, flinging himself on the floor with a terrible impact and starts shooting an aggie.*

ARTHUR. No, Ma, it's not there.

MA (*serenely*). Well, you don't leave Newark without that hat, make up your mind to that. I don't go no journeys with a hoodlum.

ARTHUR. Aw, Ma!

Ma *comes down to the footlights and talks toward the audience as through a window.*

MA. Oh, Mrs. Schwartz!

THE STAGE MANAGER (*consulting his script*). Here I am, Mrs. Kirby. Are you going yet?

MA. I guess we're going in just a minute. How's the baby?

THE STAGE MANAGER. She's all right now. We slapped her on the back and she spat it up.

MA. Isn't that fine!—Well now, if you'll be good enough to give the cat a saucer of milk in the morning and the evening, Mrs. Schwartz, I'll be ever so grateful to you.— Oh, good afternoon, Mrs. Hobmeyer!

THE STAGE MANAGER. Good afternoon, Mrs. Kirby, I hear you're going away.

MA (*modest*). Oh, just for three days, Mrs. Hobmeyer, to see my married daughter, Beulah, in Camden. Elmer's got his vacation week from the laundry early this year, and he's just the best driver in the world.

Caroline *comes "into the house" and stands by her mother.*

THE STAGE MANAGER. Is the whole family going?

MA. Yes, all four of us that's here. The change ought to be good for the children. My married daughter was downright sick a while ago—

THE STAGE MANAGER. Tchk—Tchk —Tchk! Yes. I remember you tellin' us.

MA. And I just want to go down and see the child. I ain't seen her since then. I just won't rest easy in my mind without I see her. (*To Caroline*) Can't you say good afternoon to Mrs. Hobmeyer?

CAROLINE (*blushes and lowers her eyes and says woodenly*). Good afternoon, Mrs. Hobmeyer.

THE STAGE MANAGER. Good afternoon, dear.—Well, I'll wait and beat these rugs until after you're gone, because I don't want to choke you. I hope you have a good time and find everything all right.

MA. Thank you, Mrs. Hobmeyer, I hope I will.—Well, I guess that milk for the cat is all, Mrs. Schwartz, if you're sure you don't mind. If anything should come up, the key to the back door is hanging by the ice box.

ARTHUR AND CAROLINE. Ma! Not so loud. Everybody can hear yuh.

MA. Stop pullin' my dress, children. (*In a loud whisper*) The key to the back door I'll leave hangin' by the ice box and I'll leave the screen door unhooked.

THE STAGE MANAGER. Now have a good trip, dear, and give my love to Loolie.

MA. I will, and thank you a thousand times.

She returns "into the room."

What can be keeping your pa?

ARTHUR. I can't find my hat, Ma.

Enter Elmer *holding a hat.*

ELMER. Here's Arthur's hat. He musta left it in the car Sunday.

MA. That's a mercy. Now we can start.—Caroline Kirby, what you done to your cheeks?

CAROLINE (*defiant-abashed*). Nothin'.

MA. If you've put anything on 'em, I'll slap you.

CAROLINE. No, Ma, of course I haven't. (*hanging her head*) I just rubbed 'm to make 'm red. All the girls do that at High School when they're goin' places.

MA. Such silliness I never saw. Elmer, what kep' you?

ELMER (*always even-voiced and always looking out a little anxiously through his spectacles*). I just went to the garage and had Charlie give a last look at it, Kate.

MA. I'm glad you did. I wouldn't like to have no breakdown miles from anywhere. Now we can start. Arthur, put those marbles away. Anybody'd think you didn't want to go on a journey to look at yuh.

They go out through the hall, take the short steps that denote going downstairs, and find themselves in the street.

ELMER. Here, you boys, you keep away from that car.

MA. Those Sullivan boys put their heads into everything.

The Stage Manager *has moved forward four chairs and a low platform. This is the automobile. It is in the center of the stage and faces the audience. The platform slightly raises the two chairs in the rear.*

Pa's *hands hold an imaginary steering wheel and continually shift gears.* Caroline *sits beside him.* Arthur *is behind him and* Ma *behind* Caroline.

CAROLINE (*self-consciously*). Goodbye, Mildred. Goodbye, Helen.

THE STAGE MANAGER. Goodbye, Caroline. Goodbye, Mrs. Kirby. I hope y'have a good time.

MA. Goodbye, girls.

THE STAGE MANAGER. Goodbye, Kate. The car looks fine.

MA (*looking upward toward a window*). Oh, goodbye, Emma! (*modestly*) We think it's the best little Chevrolet in the world.—Oh, goodbye, Mrs. Adler!

THE STAGE MANAGER. What, are you going away, Mrs. Kirby?

MA. Just for three days, Mrs. Adler, to see my married daughter in Camden.

THE STAGE MANAGER. Have a good time.

Now Ma, Caroline, *and the* Stage Manager *break out into a tremendous chorus of goodbyes. The whole street is saying goodbye.* Arthur *takes out his pea shooter and lets fly happily into the air. There is a lurch or two and they are off.*

ARTHUR (*in sudden fright*). Pa! Pa! Don't go by the school. Mr. Biedenbach might see us!

MA. I don't care if he does see us. I guess I can take my children out of school for one day without having to hide down back streets about it.

Elmer *nods to a passerby.*

Ma *asks without sharpness:*

Who was that you spoke to, Elmer?

ELMER. That was the fellow who arranges our banquets down to the Lodge, Kate.

MA. Is he the one who had to buy four hundred steaks? (Pa *nods.*) I declare, I'm glad I'm not him.

ELMER. The air's getting better already. Take deep breaths, children.

They inhale noisily.

ARTHUR. Gee, it's almost open fields already. "*Weber and Heilbronner Suits for Well-dressed Men.*" Ma, can I have one of them some day?

MA. If you graduate with good marks perhaps your father'll let you have one for graduation.

CAROLINE (*whining*). Oh, Pa! do we have to wait while that whole funeral goes by?

Pa *takes off his hat.*

Ma *cranes forward with absorbed curiosity.*

MA. Take off your hat, Arthur. Look at your father.—Why, Elmer, I do believe that's a lodge-brother of yours. See the banner? I suppose this is the Elizabeth branch.

Elmer *nods.* Ma *sighs: Tchk—tchk—tchk. They all lean forward and watch the funeral in silence, growing momentarily more solemnized. After a pause,* Ma *continues almost dreamily:*

Well, we haven't forgotten the one that went on, have we? We haven't forgotten our good Harold. He gave his life for his country, we mustn't forget that. (*She passes her finger from the corner of her eye across her cheek. There is another pause.*) Well, we'll all hold up the traffic for a few minutes some day.

THE CHILDREN (*very uncomfortable*). Ma!

MA (*without self-pity*). Well I'm "ready," children. I hope everybody in this car is "ready." (*She puts her hand on* Pa's *shoulder.*) And I pray to go first, Elmer. Yes. (Pa *touches her hand.*)

THE CHILDREN. Ma, everybody's

looking at you. Everybody's laughing at you.

MA. Oh, hold your tongues! I don't care what a lot of silly people in Elizabeth, New Jersey, think of me.—Now we can go on. That's the last.

There is another lurch and the car goes on.

CAROLINE. *"Fit-Rite Suspenders. The Working Man's Choice."* Pa, why do they spell Rite that way?

ELMER. So that it'll make you stop and ask about it, Missy.

CAROLINE. Papa, you're teasing me. —Ma, why do they say *"Three Hundred Rooms Three Hundred Baths?"*

ARTHUR. *"Miller's Spaghetti: The Family's Favorite Dish."* Ma, why don't you ever have spaghetti?

MA. Go along, you'd never eat it.

ARTHUR. Ma, I like it now.

CAROLINE (*with gesture*). Yum-yum. It looks wonderful up there. Ma, make some when we get home?

MA (*dryly*). "The management is always happy to receive suggestions. We aim to please."

The whole family finds this exquisitely funny. The children scream with laughter. Even Elmer *smiles.* Ma *remains modest.*

ELMER. Well, I guess no one's complaining, Kate. Everybody knows you're a good cook.

MA. I don't know whether I'm a good cook or not, but I know I've had practice. At least I've cooked three meals a day for twenty-five years.

ARTHUR. Aw, Ma, you went out to eat once in a while.

MA. Yes. That made it a leap year. *This joke is no less successful than its predecessor. When the laughter dies down,* Caroline *turns around in an ecstasy of well-being and kneeling on the cushions says:*

CAROLINE. Ma, I love going out in the country like this. Let's do it often, Ma.

MA. Goodness, smell that air will you! It's got the whole ocean in it.—Elmer, drive careful over that bridge. This must be New Brunswick we're coming to.

ARTHUR (*jealous of his mother's successes*). Ma, when is the next comfort station?

MA (*unruffled*). You don't want one. You just said that to be awful.

CAROLINE (*shrilly*). Yes, he did, Ma. He's terrible. He says that kind of thing right out in school and I want to sink through the floor, Ma. He's terrible.

MA. Oh, don't get so excited about nothing, Miss Proper! I guess we're all yewman-beings in this car, at least as far as I know. And, Arthur, you try and be a gentleman.— Elmer, don't run over that collie dog. (*She follows the dog with her eyes.*) Looked kinda peakéd to me. Needs a good honest bowl of leavings. Pretty dog, too. (*Her eyes fall on a billboard.*) That's a pretty advertisement for Chesterfield cigarettes, isn't it? Looks like Beulah, a little.

ARTHUR. Ma?

MA. Yes.

ARTHUR (*"route" rhymes with "out"*). Can't I take a paper route with the Newark *Daily Post*?

MA. No, you cannot. No, sir. I hear they make the paper boys get up at four-thirty in the morning. No son of mine is going to get up at four-thirty every morning, not if it's to make a million dollars. Your *Saturday Evening Post* route on Thursday mornings is enough.

ARTHUR. Aw, Ma.

MA. No, sir. No son of mine is going to get up at four-thirty and miss the sleep God meant him to have.

ARTHUR (*sullenly*). Hhm! Ma's always talking about God. I guess she got a letter from him this morning.

Ma *rises, outraged*.

MA. Elmer, stop that automobile this minute. I don't go another step with anybody that says things like that, Arthur, you get out of this car. Elmer, you give him another dollar bill. He can go back to Newark, by himself. I don't want him.

ARTHUR. What did I say? There wasn't anything terrible about that.

ELMER. I didn't hear what he said, Kate.

MA. God has done a lot of things for me and I won't have him made fun of by anybody. Go away. Go away from me.

CAROLINE. Aw, Ma,—don't spoil the ride.

MA. No.

ELMER. We might as well go on, Kate, since we've got started. I'll talk to the boy tonight.

MA (*slowly conceding*). All right, if you say so, Elmer. But I won't sit beside him. Caroline, you come, and sit by me.

ARTHUR (*frightened*). Aw, Ma, that wasn't so terrible.

MA. I don't want to talk about it. I hope your father washes your mouth out with soap and water.—Where'd we all be if I started talking about God like that, I'd like to know! We'd be in the speakeasies and night-clubs and places like that, that's where we'd be.—All right, Elmer, you can go on now.

CAROLINE. What did he say, Ma? I didn't hear what he said.

MA. I don't want to talk about it.

*They drive on in silence for a mo-*ment, *the shocked silence after a scandal.*

ELMER. I'm going to stop and give the car a little water, I guess.

MA. All right, Elmer. You know best.

ELMER (*to garage hand*). Could I have a little water in the radiator—to make sure?

THE STAGE MANAGER (*in this scene alone he lays aside his script and enters into a rôle seriously*). You sure can. (*He punches the tires.*) Air, all right? Do you need any oil or gas?

ELMER. No, I think not. I just got fixed up in Newark.

MA. We're on the right road for Camden, are we?

THE STAGE MANAGER. Yes, keep straight ahead. You can't miss it. You'll be in Trenton in a few minutes.

He carefully pours some water into the hood.

Camden's a great town, lady, believe me.

MA. My daughter likes it fine,—my married daughter.

THE STAGE MANAGER. Ye'? It's a a great burg all right. I guess I think so because I was born near there.

MA. Well, well. Your folks still live there?

THE STAGE MANAGER. No, my old man sold the farm and they built a factory on it. So the folks moved to Philadelphia.

MA. My married daughter Beulah lives there because her husband works in the telephone company. —Stop pokin' me, Caroline!— We're all going down to see her for a few days.

THE STAGE MANAGER. Ye'?

MA. She's been sick, you see, and I just felt I had to go and see her. My husband and my boy are going to stay at the Y.M.C.A. I

292

hear they've got a dormitory on the top floor that's real clean and comfortable. Had you ever been there?

THE STAGE MANAGER. No, I'm Knights of Columbus myself.

MA. Oh.

THE STAGE MANAGER. I used to play basketball at the Y though. It looked all right to me.

He has been standing with one foot on the rung of Ma's chair. They have taken a great fancy to one another. He reluctantly shakes himself out of it and pretends to examine the car again, whistling.

Well, I guess you're all set now, lady. I hope you have a good trip; you can't miss it.

EVERYBODY. Thanks. Thanks a lot. Good luck to you.

Jolts and lurches.

MA (*with a sigh*). The world's full of nice people.—That's what I call a nice young man.

CAROLINE (*earnestly*). Ma, you ought-n't to tell'm all everything about yourself.

MA. Well, Caroline, you do your way and I'll do mine.—He looked kinda thin to me. I'd like to feed him up for a few days. His mother lives in Philadelphia and I expect he eats at those dreadful Greek places.

CAROLINE. I'm hungry. Pa, there's a hot dog stand. K'n I have one?

ELMER. We'll all have one, eh, Kate? We had such an early lunch.

MA. Just as you think best, Elmer.

ELMER. Arthur, here's half a dollar. —Run over and see what they have. Not too much mustard either.

Arthur descends from the car and goes off stage right. Ma and Caroline get out and walk a bit.

MA. What's that flower over there?

—I'll take some of those to Beulah.

CAROLINE. It's just a weed, Ma.

MA. I like it.—My, look at the sky, wouldya! I'm glad I was born in New Jersey. I've always said it was the best state in the Union. Every state has something no other state has got.

They stroll about humming.

Presently Arthur *returns with his hands full of imaginary hot dogs which he distributes. He is still very much cast down by the recent scandal. He finally approaches his mother and says falteringly:*

ARTHUR. Ma, I'm sorry. I'm sorry for what I said.

He bursts into tears and puts his forehead against her elbow.

MA. There. There. We all say wicked things at times. I know you didn't mean it like it sounded.

He weeps still more violently than before.

Why, now, now! I forgive you, Arthur, and tonight before you go to bed you . . . (*she whispers.*) You're a good boy at heart, Arthur, and we all know it.

Caroline *starts to cry too.*

Ma *is suddenly joyously alive and happy.*

Sakes alive, it's too nice a day for us all to be cryin'. Come now, get in. You go up in front with your father, Caroline. Ma wants to sit with her beau. I never saw such children. Your hot dogs are all getting wet. Now chew them fine, everybody.—All right, Elmer, forward march.—Caroline, what-ever are you doing?

CAROLINE. I'm spitting out the leather, Ma.

MA. Then say: Excuse me.

CAROLINE. Excuse me, please.

MA. What's this place? Arthur, did you see the post office?

ARTHUR. It said Laurenceville.

MA. Hhm. School kinda. Nice. I wonder what that big yellow house set back was.—Now it's beginning to be Trenton.

CAROLINE. Papa, it was near here that George Washington crossed the Delaware. It was near Trenton, Mama. He was first in war and first in peace, and first in the hearts of his countrymen.

MA (*surveying the passing world, serene and didactic*). Well, the thing I like about him best was that he never told a lie.

The children are duly cast down. There is a pause.

There's a sunset for you. There's nothing like a good sunset.

ARTHUR. There's an Ohio license in front of us. Ma, have you ever been to Ohio?

MA. No.

A dreamy silence descends upon them. Caroline sits closer to her father. Ma puts her arm around Arthur.

ARTHUR. Ma, what a lotta people there are in the world, Ma. There must be thousands and thousands in the United States. Ma, how many are there?

MA. I don't know. Ask your father.

ARTHUR. Pa, how many are there?

ELMER. There are a hundred and twenty-six million, Kate.

MA (*giving a pressure about Arthur's shoulder*). And they all like to drive out in the evening with their children beside'm.

Another pause.

Why doesn't somebody sing something? Arthur, you're always singing something; what's the matter with you?

ARTHUR. All right. What'll we sing? (*He sketches:*)

"In the Blue Ridge Mountains of Virginia,

On the trail of the lonesome pine . . ."

No, I don't like that any more. Let's do:

"I been workin' on de railroad
All de liblong day.
I been workin' on de railroad
Just to pass de time away."

Caroline joins in at once. Finally even Ma is singing. Even Pa is singing. Ma suddenly jumps up with a wild cry:

MA. Elmer, that signpost said Camden, I saw it.

ELMER. All right, Kate, if you're sure.

Much shifting of gears, backing, and jolting.

MA. Yes, there it is. Camden—five miles. Dear old Beulah.—Now children, you be good and quiet during dinner. She's just got out of bed after a big sorta operation, and we must all move around kinda quiet. First you drop me and Caroline at the door and just say hello, and then you men-folk go over to the Y.M.C.A. and come back for dinner in about an hour.

CAROLINE (*shutting her eyes and pressing her fists passionately against her nose*). I see the first star. Everybody make a wish.

"Star light, star bright,
First star I seen tonight.
I wish I may, I wish I might
Have the wish I wish tonight."

(*then solemnly*) Pins. Mama, you say "needles."

She interlocks little fingers with her mother.

MA. Needles.

CAROLINE. Shakespeare. Ma, you say "Longfellow."

MA. Longfellow.

CAROLINE. Now it's a secret and I

294

can't tell it to anybody. Ma, you make a wish.

MA (*with almost grim humor*). No, I can make wishes without waiting for no star. And I can tell my wishes right out loud too. Do you want to hear them?

CAROLINE (*resignedly*). No, Ma, we know'm already. We've heard'm. (*She hangs her head affectedly on her left shoulder and says with unmalicious mimicry:*) You want me to be a good girl and you want Arthur to be honest-in-word-and-deed.

MA (*majestically*). Yes. So mind yourself.

ELMER. Caroline, take out that letter from Beulah in my coat pocket by you and read aloud the places I marked with red pencil.

CAROLINE (*working*). "A few blocks after you pass the two big oil tanks on your left . . ."

EVERYBODY (*pointing backward*). There they are!

CAROLINE. " . . . you come to a corner where there's an A and P store on the left and a firehouse kitty-corner to it . . ."

They all jubilantly identify these landmarks. " . . . turn right, go two blocks, and our house is Weyerhauser St. Number 471."

MA. It's an even nicer street than they used to live in. And right handy to an A and P.

CAROLINE (*whispering*). Ma, it's better than our street. It's richer than our street.—Ma, isn't Beulah richer than we are?

MA (*looking at her with a firm and glassy eye*). Mind yourself, missy. I don't want to hear anybody talking about rich or not rich when I'm around. If people aren't nice I don't care how rich they are. I live in the best street in the world because my husband and children live there.

She glares impressively at Caroline *a moment to let this lesson sink in, then looks up, sees* Beulah *and waves.*

There's Beulah standing on the steps lookin' for us.

Beulah *has appeared and is waving.*

They all call out: Hello, Beulah— Hello.

Presently they are all getting out of the car.

Beulah *kisses her father long and affectionately.*

BEULAH. Hello, Papa. Good old Papa. You look tired, Pa.—Hello, Mama.—Lookit how Arthur and Caroline are growing!

MA. They're bursting all their clothes!—Yes, your pa needs a rest. Thank Heaven, his vacation has come just now. We'll feed him up and let him sleep late. Pa has a present for you, Loolie. He would go and buy it.

BEULAH. Why, Pa, you're terrible to go and buy anything for me. Isn't he terrible?

MA. Well it's a secret. You can open it at dinner.

ELMER. Where's Horace, Loolie?

BEULAH. He was kep' over a little at the office. He'll be here any minute. He's crazy to see you all.

MA. All right. You men go over to the Y and come back in about an hour.

BEULAH (*as her father returns to the wheel, stands out in the street beside him*). Go straight along, Pa, you can't miss it. It just stares at yuh. (*She puts her arm around his neck and rubs her nose against his temple.*) Crazy old Pa, goin' buyin' things! It's me that ought to be buyin' things for you, Pa.

ELMER. Oh, no! There's only one Loolie in the world.

BEULAH (*whispering, as her eyes fill with tears*). Are you glad I'm still alive, Pa?

She kisses him abruptly and goes back to the house steps. The Stage Manager *removes the automobile with the help of* Elmer *and* Arthur *who go off waving their goodbyes.*

Well, come on upstairs, Ma, and take off your things.

Caroline, there's a surprise for you in the back yard.

CAROLINE. Rabbits?

BEULAH. No.

CAROLINE. Chickens?

BEULAH. No. Go and see.

Caroline runs off stage.

Beulah and Ma gradually go upstairs.

There are two new puppies. You be thinking over whether you can keep one in Newark.

MA. I guess we can. It's a nice house, Beulah. You just got a *lovely* home.

BEULAH. When I got back from the hospital, Horace had moved everything into it, and there wasn't anything for me to do.

MA. It's lovely.

The Stage Manager pushes out a bed from the left. Its foot is toward the right. Beulah *sits on it, testing the springs.*

BEULAH. I think you'll find the bed comfortable, Ma.

MA (*taking off her hat*). Oh, I could sleep on a heapa shoes, Loolie! I don't have no trouble sleepin'. (*She sits down beside her.*) Now let me look at my girl. Well, well, when I last saw you, you didn't know me. You kep' saying: *When's Mama comin'? When's Mama comin'?* But the doctor sent me away.

BEULAH (*puts her head on her mother's shoulder and weeps*). It was awful, Mama. It was awful. She didn't even live a few minutes, Mama. It was awful.

MA (*looking far away*). God thought best, dear. God thought best. We don't understand why. We go on, honey, doin' our business.

Then almost abruptly—passing the back of her hand across her cheek.

Well, now, what are we giving the men to eat tonight?

BEULAH. There's a chicken in the oven.

MA. What time didya put it in?

BEULAH (*restraining her*). Aw, Ma, don't go yet. I like to sit here with you this way. You always get the fidgets when we try and pet yuh, Mama.

MA (*ruefully laughing*). Yes, it's kinda foolish. I'm just an old Newark bag-a-bones. (*She glances at the backs of her hands.*)

BEULAH (*indignantly*). Why, Ma, you're good-lookin'! We always said you were good-lookin'.—And besides, you're the best Ma we could ever have.

MA (*uncomfortable*). Well, I hope you like me. There's nothin' like being liked by your family.—Now I'm going downstairs to look at the chicken. You stretch out here for a minute and shut your eyes.—Have you got everything laid in for breakfast before the shops close?

BEULAH. Oh, you know! Ham and eggs.

They both laugh.

MA. I declare I never could understand what men see in ham and eggs. I think they're horrible.—What time did you put the chicken in?

BEULAH. Five o'clock.

MA. Well, now, you shut your eyes for ten minutes.

> Beulah *stretches out and shuts her eyes.*
>
> Ma *descends the stairs absent-mindedly singing:*

"There were ninety and nine that safely lay
In the shelter of the fold,
But one was out on the hills away,
Far off from the gates of gold. . . ."
> *And the curtain falls.*

From *PASSAGE TO INDIA*
WALT WHITMAN

Have we not stood here like trees in the ground long enough?
Have we not groveled here long enough, eating and drinking, like mere brutes?
Have we not darkened and dazed ourselves with books long enough?
Sail forth—steer for the deep waters only.
Reckless, O soul, exploring, I with thee, and thou with me,
For we are bound where mariner has not yet dared to go,
And we will risk the ship, ourselves and all!

O my brave soul!
O farther, farther sail!
O daring joy, but safe! are they not all the seas of God?
O farther, farther, farther sail!

TO AMERICANS
GAIL BROOK BURKET

They chose a pioneer's harsh life: strange land,
Cold, loneliness, a rough-hewn cabin home,
And blood-marked trails worn deep across grim sand,
High hostile peaks, and rutted prairie loam.
A dream led them, a dream undreamed before;
A dream of people unafraid and free.
From many nations, ancient scars, and war,
They wrought a new triumphant unity.

We will not disavow their dream. We stand
With eager faces turned toward future days,
Ready to march ahead until our land
Has reached the heights by yet untraveled ways.
United, old in wisdom, young in might,
We bear the living flame of freedom's light.

CHARACTER is a reserve force, which acts directly,
by presence, and without means.

BOOKS ARE THE BEST things, well used; abused, among the worst.

IF YOU would learn to write, 'tis in the street you must learn it.

I DO with my friends as I do with my books. I would have them where I can find
them, but I seldom use them.

THE HONEST MAN must keep faith with himself; his sheet anchor is sincerity.

EVERY MAN TAKES CARE that his neighbor does not cheat him. But
a day comes when he begins to care that he does not cheat his
neighbor. Then all goes well.

THE MANLY PART is to do with might and main what you can do.

CITIES FORCE GROWTH, and make men talkative and entertaining, but they make
them artificial.

SHALLOW MEN believe in luck, believe in circumstances.
Strong men believe in cause and effect.

AT THE GATES of the forest, the surprised man of the world is forced to leave his
city estimate of great and small, wise and foolish.

TRUST MEN, and they will be true to you; treat them gently,
and they will show themselves great.

THE SHOEMAKER makes a good shoe because he makes nothing else.

No MAN ever prayed heartily without learning something.

RALPH WALDO EMERSON

THE DIFFERENCE between landscape and landscape is small,
but there is great difference in the beholders.

CONVERSATION is the laboratory and workshop of the student.

OUR HIGH RESPECT for a well-read man is praise enough of literature.

IDEAS MUST WORK through the brains and the arms of good and brave men,
or they are no better than dreams.

NATURE IS METHODICAL, and doeth her work well. Time is never to be hurried.

NO MAN EVER FORGOT the visitations of that power to his heart and brain,
which created all things new; which was the dawn in him of music, poetry,
and art.

I ALWAYS SEEM to suffer some loss of faith on entering cities.

CONCENTRATION is the secret of strength in politics, in war, in trade, in short
in all management of human affairs.

EVERYTHING IN NATURE contains all the powers of Nature.
Everything is made of one hidden stuff.

AND IT IS so plain to me that eloquence, like swimming, is an art which all men
might learn, though so few do.

WE GRANT NO DUKEDOMS to the few, we hold like rights and shall;
Equal on Sunday in the pew, on Monday in the mall.

DISCONTENT is the want of self-reliance: it is infirmity of will.

NO MAN ever stated his griefs as lightly as he might.

WORDS OF GREAT AMERICANS:

NECESSITY has no law.

A WORD to the wise is enough.

FLY pleasures, and they'll follow you.

WORK AS IF you were to live a hundred years;
pray as if you were to die tomorrow.

WORDS may show a man's wit, but actions his meaning.

EVERY MAN WILL OWN that an author, as such, ought to be tried by the merit
of his productions only.

AMERICA, where people do not inquire of a stranger, "What is he?" but "What
can he do?"

WITHOUT INDUSTRY and frugality nothing will do, and with them everything.

CAESAR DID not merit the triumphal car more than he that conquers himself.

CONTENT makes poor men rich; discontent makes rich men poor.

A LONG LIFE may not be good enough,
but a good life is long enough.

NONE preaches better than the ant,
and she says nothing.

GREAT MODESTY often hides great merit.

INDUSTRY need not wish.

BENJAMIN FRANKLIN

HASTE makes waste.

THE CAT in gloves catches no mice.

THE WISE and brave dares own that he was wrong.

IF YOU KNOW how to spend less than you get you
have the philosopher's stone.

MODESTY makes the most homely virgin amiable and charming.

HE THAT GETS all he can honestly, and saves all he gets (necessary expenses
excepted), will certainly become *rich*.

THEY THAT CAN GIVE up essential liberty to obtain a little temporary safety deserve
neither liberty nor safety.

NOTHING can contribute to true happiness that is inconsistent with duty.

DIFFERENT SECTS, like different clocks, may all be near the matter,
though they don't quite agree.

ONE CANNOT always be a hero, but one can always be a man.

VESSELS LARGE may venture more,
But little boats should keep near shore.

THREE may keep a secret, if two of them are dead.

THINK of saving as well as of getting.

WHAT you would seem to be, be really.

Going to the Fourth

By DORA AYDELOTTE

Here is a little girl's picture of an old-fashioned Fourth of July.

PA SAID more than once, "Now, you work good, and mebbe we'll all go to the Fourth."

So you got up early and weeded the veg'table patch. You gathered up the eggs, fed the chickens. You drove the cows home from pasture. You helped Ma in the kitchen—washing dishes, peeling potatoes, stirring batter in a huge bowl, churning until your thin arms ached. And Ma would encourage you with, "That's right. You help good and mebbe Pa'll take us to the Fourth."

"Going to the Fourth" was a dazzling dream, a glorious adventure. You watched the weather anxiously. Rain on that day of days would be sheer calamity. You couldn't quite forget that dismal Fourth when it had rained for hours. You wept in woe until Ma, pestered to death by your whining around, made you sit down by yourself in the front room a long time.

The night of the third was still and hot—so still that even the big maple by the house didn't stir and whisper to itself. Pa was sitting on the barrel-stave hammock, smoking his pipe. You went out and asked if he thought it would rain. He squinted up at the sky, all bright with stars, and said, "Oh, I guess we'll have nice weather."

Joyfully you went to the kitchen where Ma was still at work. The others—Bill, Jimmie, and your little sister, Minnie—had gone to bed right after supper. But you wanted to stay up and help. The big cookstove sent out waves of sultry heat. Ma had baked bread that day. She had made an amazing number of cakes and pies. A boiled ham was cooling on the table. A big roast of beef stood beside it. May was busy frying chicken in two huge iron skillets. Your little nose sniffed ecstatically. "Can I do anything?" you asked.

Ma turned around from the stove, pushing back a lock of wet hair from her perspiring forehead. Tall, angular figure in faded blue calico. Thin, sallow face. Thin lips not given to much smiling. Tired, kindly gray eyes. Dark hair strained back from her forehead, twisted into a tight, hard knot on top of her head. Your eagerness must have touched that weary woman. She found the grace to smile as she told you to run on to bed.

You climbed the stairs to that stifling little room under the eaves where you and Minnie slept. You got out your "best" clothes. Black buttoned shoes with spring heels. Black cotton stockings. White ruffled petticoats. Stiffly starched white dress, with tucks in the skirt so it could be let down. Straw sailor with a blue band. Everything spread out grandly on a chair by your bed. In bed, your hand stroked lovingly the crisp folds of that white dress. . . .

You leaped from bed as Pa called, "Git up, Barbry—all of ye!" Roosters were crowing valiantly. Dogs barked. A wagon went rattling by. You washed and dressed in a happy flurry.

You buttoned little Minnie's shoes, braided her hair, silky and soft as yellow corn "tossels," tied it with a blue ribbon.

Your shoes squeaked delightfully as you ran downstairs. Breakfast was waiting on the long table in the kitchen. A fat milk pitcher with two blue stripes encircling its portliness. A tin coffee pot, its snout steaming fragrantly. Thick, stubby goblets, thick white stoneware plates and cups. Knives and forks with bone handles, pewter spoons. Fried eggs, fried ham, fried potatoes, hot biscuits, apple butter, pear preserves.

Pa said, "Go on and eat. I already asked the blessing." You gazed at him with admiration verging upon awe. He did look grand in his Sunday-go-to-meeting black suit. Pa was a big man. He had big black eyes and black hair, and the longest black mustache. He was drinking coffee out of the mustache cup you gave him for Christmas. Ed, the hired man, gulped hot coffee from his saucer. He was all dressed up in his best suit.

Ma was flying around getting the dinner ready. Everything was packed in a big wooden washtub, covered with a clean red-and-white tablecloth. After Pa and Ed carried the tub out to the wagon, they came back and Bill helped them take out the chairs. You couldn't go to the Fourth in proper style unless you sat on chairs in the back of the wagon. Some folks put down straw and spread old quilts over, but that was tacky.

The two extra chairs were for Gramma and Aunt Min. You would stop by for them on the way to town.

Ma came out last, locking the back door, shooing the chickens away from the step. She had on her nice black lawn with white ruching in the collar. Her good black hat, too, with a red rose in front. Her white petticoats rustled as she climbed up to the high front seat by Pa and Jimmie. Pa jerked the lines, shouted, "Giddap there!" and the wagon rolled down the lane to the big road.

The air was fresh and cool. You smelled the sweet clover, the dewy grass. Wagons jogged in from every side road. Young men with their best girls dashed past in buggies. You wished you could go to the Fourth in some young man's shiny buggy, behind a team of prancing bay horses. Then you looked down at your hands, all sunburned and briar-scratched, and sighingly remembered your face, dotted over with fat brown freckles.

Gramma and Aunt Min came down the path as Pa drove up. Gramma had on her black calico with white dots, and her black sateen sunbonnet, and she wore black silk mitts. Aunt Min wore her white mull with lace on the ruffles. A pink bow at her neck—another pink bow on her hat. And—loveliest of all to your admiring eyes—she wore pink silk mitts. Aunt Min looked real nice. Ma said so.

As you drove into town, there was a delightful pop-pop of torpedoes on the wooden sidewalks. Firecrackers exploded sharply. Tom and Jerry snorted and rared up, but Pa held them in. Ma said, "Look at the way those fellows tried to pass us. Somebody's due to get killed, driving so fast." The dust rose in stifling, swirling clouds.

You went by a big white house, with a picket fence all around. Two little girls swung on the gate. They had lovely bangs. You wished Ma would let you wear bangs. You hated having your hair jerked back and braided in a tight pigtail. The little girls stared at you. One of them stuck out her tongue. You stuck your tongue out at her and made a snoot. Smarty—just because she lived in town!

When you got to Green's Grove it seemed like you must be the last ones there. But you looked back, and there were wagons and buggies and buckboards and men riding horseback, and some folks walking—and all coming to the Fourth! Gramma said, "Look at all them folks. I bet they's come from as far as Pickaway." Bill and Jimmie climbed out and went tearing off the minute Pa drove in. Aunt Min shook out her skirts and Ed helped her over the side of the wagon, and they went off together.

You wanted to hippity-hop as you started out with Minnie and Pa. It was such a grand place—flags and bunting on the stands, and boys shooting off fire-crackers right under your feet to make you jump and yell. Folks were fanning and saying, "My, ain't it turned off hot?" Pa took off his coat and carried it. You got thirsty, and Pa took you to a barrel of water with a piece of ice in it and a tin cup tied on a string, and said, "Drink all you want—it's free."

You went over to the speaker's stand. The Antioch band was playing, "My Country 'Tis of Thee." Then they played, "Marching Through Georgia." A fat man got up and made a speech—you didn't know what about—but everybody clapped hard and you did, too. Then Miss Sue Miggles, the red-headed old maid that gave music lessons, came switching out and played the organ. Some girls in white dresses, with red and blue sashes, sang, "On, On, Steadily On." More speaking,

more clapping. You wanted to go and have some fun. Pa told you, "Well, don't stay long. And hold onto Minnie's hand."

Proudly you swung your shell purse, with its treasured two nickels, hoarded specially for the Fourth. And Minnie had a nickel tied up in a corner of her handkerchief. Your very first purchase was to be a sody pop, but when you walked up to a stand and opened your purse, your cherished wealth was gone! You were stunned by your loss. Minnie said she'd buy the pop and you could drink it together, but you shook your head.

Minnie was starting in to cry because you wouldn't take her nickel, when Aunt Min and Ed came by. They asked what was the matter and you told them. Ed took some money out of his pocket and gave you and Minnie twenty cents apiece. You wanted to thank him, but a man who bestowed dimes so lavishly must not be hailed as Ed. You started to say, "Much obliged to you, Mr. Ah—h —" "Just call me Ed," he told you, and strolled on, Aunt Min's hand in its pink silk mitt resting lightly on his arm.

Proudly you ordered Lemon pop, while Minnie got straw-ry. Then you both got white chewing gum hearts with pictures on them, and some cocoanut candy flags, and some "lickerish."

Somebody was beating on a dishpan, so you and Minnie went running back to the wagon. Dinner was all spread out on the red-and-white tablecloth. Dishpan full of fried chicken in the middle. Platters of ham and beef. Dishes of pickled beets, of coleslaw, bowls of hard-boiled eggs. Cakes and pies and jelly— everything good. Gramma shooed flies away with a green branch.

Then Pa came up with some folks. Pa always went around inviting anybody that hadn't brought their dinners—town folks, mostly. Pa reached for the chicken and started passing it along. Ma said, "Just help yourselves to what there is. It ain't much, but mebbe it'll do." And the folks all told her how good it was. Of course you had to go and drop some beet juice on your dress, and get some grease from chicken on it, but you pinned your handkerchief over the worst spots and hoped Ma wouldn't notice it.

After dinner, you and Minnie went right over to the merry-go-round. It was a dazzling thing, all painted in light blue and red. An old mule went round and round the post to make it go. The man cracked his whip and shouted, "All 'board here—fi' cents a ride! Lady 'at sets with the fiddler gits to ride free!" You and Minnie sat entranced through your first ride. Minnie wanted to ride again. So did you—if you could ride with the fiddler. That had been your heart's fond wish for a long time. Now you were big enough to try it.

You shoved and pushed through the crowd around the swings, trying to scrouge in ahead. You lost a hair-ribbon, your hat was knocked over your eyes, and one big girl slapped you when you pushed her aside. But with a flying leap you made it as the merry-go-round started—right by the old fiddler. He scraped his fiddle and played, "Turkey in the Straw." Your heart swelled with a sense of victory. You smiled proudly across at Minnie. You wished Pa and Ma could see you now—you, Barbry Miller, a freckle-face country girl, sitting up there in the free seat by the fiddler!

When that glamorous ride was over, you and Minnie walked around some more. It was getting hotter, and your feet hurt. A hack drove up, and you saw Aunt Min and Ed get in. You ran over and asked, "Aunt Min, where you going?" Everybody looked around and laughed. Aunt Min leaned out and whispered, "We'll be back. But you mustn't tell, you and Minnie. Remember—not one word."

You made the sacred sign—crossed your heart, held your right hand high, mumbled the phrase, "Hope I may die." You nudged Minnie to go through the same ritual. Aunt Min waved at you as the hack lunged off and was swallowed up in a cloud of dust.

Slowly you made your way back to the wagon. There seemed nothing else to do. You started in to tell Ma how you got to ride with the fiddler, but right away she saw your hair-ribbon gone, your sailor broken in one place, and the incriminating spots on your dress—for somehow your handkerchief was gone. Gramma was washing Bill's face. He had got in a fight with some town boys, and cut his lip. Jimmie was hot and tired, and he was crying.

Pa had his coat and collar off, and was hitching up. He looked at you real stern and said, "You know better than to stay so long. We got to start, soon as Ed and Min come." After you'd waited a while, Pa went out to look around. He came back and said, "I don't know what to think—can't find a trace of 'em." You kicked your feet against the side of the wagon, tried to seem unconcerned. You gave Minnie a warning glance.

Gramma said, real quivery, "I told Min she ortn't to go with that wild Ed Pearson," and she took off her specs and wiped her eyes. Pa kept asking folks that passed, did they see Aunt Min and Ed anywhere. But they all said they didn't b'lieve they had, come to think of it. Somebody said mebbe they'd gone to town. So Pa whipped up Tom and Jerry, and you jounced and rattled through the dust haze to town.

Pa stopped in front of Gregory's store and let Bill hold the horses while he went to look for Ed and Aunt Min. Ma looked back at you and said, "Seems like you keepin' mighty still back there. Didn't you see your Aunt Min and Ed?" You shook your head —that wasn't really telling a lie. But Ma kept on. "What's wrong with you, anyway? It ain't like you to mope around." You muttered something about being tired. At the same time you kicked Minnie on the shin, as a hint to keep still. She whimpered softly, looking at you with reproachful blue eyes.

When Pa came back, Ma said to him, "I just feel like they've run off to get married. I never would uv thought it of Min, but you never can tell." Then Gramma told Pa to go right over to Redford. Min wasn't of age till October, and they might get there in time to stop them. Then you felt worse than ever. Of course you didn't know where they'd gone, or anything, but you'd crossed your heart and promised not to tell. Ma gave you a funny look and said, "Barbry Miller, if you're keeping anything back from me, it'll be worse for you when I find out." That made you utterly miserable. You just sat there and wished there never had been a Fourth of July—or anything!

Everybody with a team of fast horses tried to pass you as you bumped along to Redford. Bill said he was spitting mudballs, and you kept squinching your eyes to keep the dust out. The blackest clouds came up and it thundered hard. Ma kept telling Pa to hurry.

When you got to Redford, Pa tied the horses at the hitchrack by the courthouse, and said you'd better all pile out and come inside, because that storm wasn't far off. You were going up the steps when Ma said there was a whole dishpan of dinner in the wagon and no use letting the rain spoil it. You and Bill ran back to get it. The storm came before you could get back—rain and hail and a wind that almost blew you over. Your hat blew away, your dress was soaked. Somebody inside started to come out just as you got to the door. You fell and went rolling down the steps, the dishpan, with everything in it, falling on top of you. A man picked you up and asked if you were hurt. You told him no, you were just mad all over. The jar of coleslaw had broken and it was all in your hair. You had sticky lemon cake on your hands, and your dress was a sight.

Ma grabbed you when you got inside, and right before everybody she shook you real hard by both shoulders. And she said, "All that good dinner gone and the dishes broke! As if I didn't have enough, with Min gone and you acting like this!"

Just then Minnie called out, "There they are!" You rubbed tears and cake crumbs out of your eyes and looked—and there was Pa and Aunt Min and Ed coming down the hall, and they were all smiling. Aunt Min came running up and threw her arms around Gramma's neck and kissed her. And Ed came and kissed Gramma, too, and called her "Mother Warren." Everybody was kissing everybody else—even Ma wasn't mad at Aunt Min, and you thought she would be. Ed kissed you and Minnie and said, "Call me Uncle Ed now."

306

Folks stood around in the hall and grinned and whispered behind their hands. Pa said something to Ed and all of you went into a room off the hall—a big room with a table and chairs, and two hanging lamps.

You couldn't stand it another minute. You looked at Aunt Min and asked, "Now can I tell?" And Minnie piped up with, "Can I tell, too?" Ma looked sharp at you and said, "Tell what?"

Aunt Min's cheeks got red as fire but she laughed and said to go ahead. So you told how you saw them get in the hack and Aunt Min made you promise not to tell, so you crossed your heart and promised—"Hope to die." You didn't understand why Pa put his arm around you, and why Ma kissed you and gave you a big hug, but it was nice, anyway.

Pa said, "Well, we got to stay here till the rain lets up. Too bad all that good dinner's gone." Uncle Ed winked at Pa, and they went out and came back with the best things to eat—buns and pickles and cookies and sardines and cheese, and a whole cocoanut cake from the bakery.

Ma and Gramma spread out papers on the table, and you all sat down. Ma said this was a wedding feast, and the bride and groom must sit at the head of the table. She put the cake in front of them, and Aunt Min cut it with Pa's pocket knife. Everything tasted so good and everybody acted so happy—you forgot your messy dress and your hair and your lost sailor hat. You didn't see why Bill and Jimmie could get so sleepy and go sound asleep. Pa put them on the floor and laid his coat over them.

You kept looking at Aunt Min. She looked so pretty with her cheeks so rosy, her light yellow hair curling around her face. You wondered why she didn't wear a veil and a long white dress, like the picture in Ma's album. You wondered if *you'd* ever be a bride and wear a veil and—

The next thing you knew Ma was shaking your arm and saying, "Wake up, Barbry! The idea—a big girl like you going sound asleep right at the table. Come on, now. The rain's over and we must get home."

Outside there was a cool, sweet wind, and the stars were shining. It was good to roll along home—to hear the horses' feet sloshing in the mud. At Gramma's house the bride and groom got out. Gramma was coming on to stay all night at your house. You would always call them "bride and groom"—that sounded nicer than just "Aunt Min and Uncle Ed." They hollered good-bye, and Ma called back, "Come and stay to dinner Sunday."

MY CREED
By Theodore Roosevelt

I BELIEVE in honesty, sincerity, and the square deal; in making up one's mind what to do—and doing it.

I believe in fearing God and taking one's own part.

I believe in hitting the line hard when you are right.

I believe in speaking softly and carrying a big stick.

I believe in hard work and honest sport.

I believe in a sane mind in a sane body.

I believe we have room for but one soul loyalty, and that is loyalty to the American people.

You cannot hide the soul.—*Melville*

GLITTER—and in that one word how much of all that is detestable do we express!—*Poe*

A SHARP TONGUE is the only edged tool that grows keener with constant use.—*Washington Irving*

THERE RISE AUTHORS now and then, who seem proof against the mutability of language, because they have rooted themselves in the unchanging principles of human nature.—*Washington Irving*

APOLOGY is only egotism wrong side out.—*Oliver Wendell Holmes*

HOW CONVENIENT IT WOULD BE to many of our great men and great families of doubtful origin, could they have the privilege of the heroes of yore, who, whenever their origin was involved in obscurity, modestly announced themselves descended from a god.—*Washington Irving*

HONEST GOOD HUMOR is the oil and wine of a merry meeting, and there is no jovial companionship equal to that where the jokes are rather small, and the laughter abundant.—*Washington Irving*

IT IS TO THE CREDIT of human nature, that, except where its selfishness is brought into play, it loves more readily than it hates.—*Hawthorne*

EASY-CRYING WIDOWS take new husbands soonest. There's nothing like wet weather for transplanting.—*Oliver Wendell Holmes*

THERE IS CERTAINLY SOMETHING in angling . . . that tends to produce a gentleness of spirit, and a pure serenity of mind. —*Washington Irving*

HIS VERY FAULTS smack of the raciness of his good qualities.—*Washington Irving*

AMERICAN WRITERS

No one can disgrace us but ourselves.—*J. G. Holland*

A goose flies by a chart which the Royal Geographical Society could not improve.—*Oliver Wendell Holmes*

A soul,—a spark of the never-dying flame that separates man from all the other beings of earth.—*James Fenimore Cooper*

There is in every true woman's heart a spark of heavenly fire, which lies dormant in the broad daylight of prosperity; but which kindles up, and beams and blazes in the dark hour of adversity.—*Washington Irving*

Life is a great bundle of little things.—*Oliver Wendell Holmes*

The greatest obstacle to being heroic is the doubt whether one may not be going to prove one's self a fool; the truest heroism is to resist the doubt, and the profoundest wisdom to know when it ought to be resisted, and when to be obeyed.—*Hawthorne*

Human nature will not flourish, any more than a potato, if it be planted and replanted for too long a series of generations, in the same worn-out soil.—*Hawthorne*

There is a healthful hardiness about real dignity that never dreads contact and communion with others, however humble.—*Washington Irving*

Every individual has a place to fill in the world, and is important in some respect, whether he chooses to be so or not.—*Hawthorne*

A woman in love is a very poor judge of character.—*J. G. Holland*

The groves were God's first temples.—*William Cullen Bryant*

Eloquence is the poetry of prose.—*William Cullen Bryant*

HOME is the nursery of the infinite.—*Channing*

MEN ARE never very wise and select in the exercise of a new power.—*Channing*

LABOR IS DISCOVERED to be the grand conqueror, enriching and building up nations more surely than the proudest battles.—*Channing*

THE CONSTANT INTERCHANGE of those thousand little courtesies which imperceptibly sweeten life has a happy effect upon the features, and spreads a mellow evening charm over the wrinkles of old age.—*Washington Irving*

No MAN should part with his own individuality and become that of another.—*Channing*

THERE IS ONE kind of a laugh that I always did recommend; it looks out of the eye first with a merry twinkle, then it creeps down on its hands and knees and plays around the mouth like a pretty moth around the blaze of a candle, then it steals over into the dimples of the cheeks and rides around in those little whirlpools for a while, then it lights up the whole face like the mellow bloom on a damask rose, then it swims up on the air, with a peal as clear and as happy as a dinner bell, then it goes back again on gold tiptoes like an angel out for an airing, and lies down on its little bed of violets in the heart where it came from.—*Josh Billings*

GREAT MINDS HAVE PURPOSES, others have wishes. Little minds are tamed and subdued by misfortune; but great minds rise above them.—*Washington Irving*

A MAN in earnest finds means, or if he cannot find, creates them.—*Channing*

A SPECIALIST is a man who knows more and more about less and less.
—*Dr. William James Mayo*

NOTED AMERICANS

We have many modern inconveniences.—*Samuel Clemens*

One o' the finest accomplishments is makin'
a long story short.—*Kin Hubbard*

I have seen folks who had traveled all over the world,
and all they could tell you about it waz, how mutch
it had kost them.—*Josh Billings*

I am happiest when I am idle. I could live for months without performing any
kind of labor, and at the expiration of that time I should feel fresh and vigorous
enough to go right on in the same way for numerous more months.—*Artemus
Ward*

Plezzures make folks acquainted with each other, but it takes trials and grief
tew make them know each other.—*Josh Billings*

"How 'bout my Cabinit, Mister Ward?" sed Abe. "Fill it up with showmen,
sir! Showmen is devoid of pollertics. They hain't got any principles! They know
how to cater for the public. They know what the public wants, North and South.
Showmen, sir, is honest men. Ef you doubt their literary ability, look at their
posters. Ef you want a Cabinit as is a Cabinit, fill it up with showmen."—*Artemus
Ward*

The trouble with lots o' us is that we prepare fer the
best instead o' the worst.—*Kin Hubbard*

If a man should happen to reach perfection in this world, he would have to die
immediately to enjoy himself.—*Josh Billings*

It is easy to assume a habit; but when you try to cast it
off, it will take skin and all.—*Josh Billings*

It don't make no difference what it is, a
woman'll buy anything she thinks a store is
losin' money on.—*Kin Hubbard*

311

From *NEW YORK TO PARIS*

[*May 20, 1927*]

By CHARLES A. LINDBERGH

Here is a thrilling chapter of American history—the first flight across the Atlantic.

. . . WE WENT to Curtiss Field as quickly as possible and made arrangements for the barograph to be sealed and installed, and for the plane to be serviced and checked.

We decided partially to fill the fuel tanks in the hangar before towing the ship on a truck to Roosevelt Field, which adjoins Curtiss Field on the east, where the servicing would be completed.

I left the responsibility for conditioning the plane in the hands of the men on the field while I went into the hotel for about two and one-half hours of rest; but at the hotel there were several more details which had to be completed and I was unable to get any sleep that night.

I returned to the field before daybreak on the morning of the twentieth. A light rain was falling which continued until almost dawn; consequently we did not move the ship to Roosevelt Field until much later than we had planned, and the take-off was delayed from daybreak until nearly eight o'clock.

At dawn the shower had passed, although the sky was overcast, and occasionally there would be some slight precipitation. The tail of the plane was lashed to a truck and escorted by a number of motorcycle police. The slow trip from Curtiss to Roosevelt was begun. The ship was placed at the extreme west end of the field heading along the east and west runway, and the final fueling commenced.

About 7:40 A.M. the motor was started, and at 7:52 I took off on the flight for Paris.

The field was a little soft, due to the rain during the night, and the heavily loaded plane gathered speed very slowly. After passing the halfway mark, however, it was apparent that I would be able to clear the obstructions at the end. I passed over a tractor by about fifteen feet and a telephone line by about twenty, with a fair reserve of flying speed. I believe that the ship would have taken off from a hard field with at least five hundred pounds more weight.

I turned slightly to the right to avoid some high trees on a hill directly ahead, but by the time I had gone a few hundred yards I had sufficient altitude to clear all obstructions and throttled the engine down to 1750 R.P.M. I took up a compass course at once and soon reached Long Island Sound, where the Curtiss *Oriole* with its photographer, which had been escorting me, turned back.

The haze soon cleared, and from Cape Cod through the southern half of Nova Scotia the weather and visibility were excellent. I was flying very low, sometimes as close as ten feet from the trees and water. On the three hundred mile stretch of water between Cape Cod and Nova Scotia I passed within view of numerous fishing vessels.

The northern part of Nova Scotia contained a number of storm areas, and several times I flew through cloudbursts.

As I neared the northern coast, snow appeared in patches on the ground, and far to the eastward the coastline was covered with fog.

For many miles between Nova Scotia and Newfoundland the ocean was covered with caked ice, but as I approached the coast the ice disappeared entirely and I saw several ships in this area.

I had taken up a course for St. Johns, which is south of the great Circle from New York to Paris, so that there would be no question of the fact that I had passed Newfoundland in case I was forced down in the North Atlantic. I passed over numerous icebergs after leaving St. Johns, but saw no ships except near the coast.

Darkness set in about 8:15, New York time, and a thin, low fog formed, through which the white bergs showed up with surprising clearness. This fog became thicker and increased in height until within two hours I was just skimming the top of storm clouds at about ten thousand feet. Even at this altitude there was a thick haze through which only the stars directly overhead could be seen.

There was no moon, and it was very dark. The tops of some of the storm clouds were several thousand feet above me, and at one time, when I attempted to fly through one of the larger clouds, sleet started to collect on the plane, and I was forced to turn around and get back into clear air immediately and then fly around any clouds which I could not get over.

The moon appeared on the horizon after about two hours of darkness; then the flying was much less complicated. Dawn came at about 1 A.M., New York time, and the temperature had risen until there was practically no remaining danger of sleet.

Shortly after sunrise the clouds became more broken, although some of them were far above me and it was often necessary to fly through them, navigating by instruments only.

As the sun became higher, holes appeared in the fog. Through one the open water was visible, and I dropped down until less than a hundred feet above the waves. There was a strong wind blowing from the northwest, and the ocean was covered with whitecaps.

After a few miles of fairly clear weather the ceiling lowered to zero, and for nearly two hours I flew entirely blind through the fog at an altitude of about 1500 feet. Then the fog raised, and the water was visible again.

On several more occasions it was necessary to fly by instrument for short periods; then the fog broke up into patches. These patches took on forms of every description. Numerous shorelines appeared, with trees perfectly outlined against the horizon. In fact, the mirages were so natural that, had I not been in mid-Atlantic and known that no land existed along my route, I would have taken them to be actual islands.

As the fog cleared, I dropped down closer to the water, sometimes flying within ten feet of the waves and seldom higher than two hundred. There is a cushion of air close to the ground or water through which a plane flies with less effort than when at a higher altitude, and for hours at a time I took advantage of this factor.

Also, it was less difficult to determine the wind drift near the water. During the entire flight the wind was strong enough to produce whitecaps on the waves. When one of these formed, the foam would be blown off, showing the wind's direction and

313

approximate velocity. This foam remained on the water long enough for me to obtain a general idea of my drift.

During the day I saw a number of porpoises and a few birds but no ships, although I understand that two different boats reported me passing over.

The first indication of my approach to the European coast was a small fishing boat which I first noticed a few miles ahead and slightly to the south of my course. There were several of these fishing boats grouped within a few miles of each other.

I flew over the first boat without seeing any signs of life. As I circled over the second, however, a man's face appeared, looking out of the cabin window.

I have carried on short conversations with people on the ground by flying low with throttled engine, shouting a question, and receiving the answer by some signal. When I saw this fisherman, I decided to try to get him to point towards land. I had no sooner made the decision than the futility of the effort became apparent. In all likelihood he could not speak English, and even if he could, he would undoubtedly be far too astounded to answer. However, I circled again and closing the throttle as the plane passed within a few feet of the boat I shouted, "Which way is Ireland?" Of course the attempt was useless, and I continued on my course.

Less than an hour later a rugged and semi-mountainous coastline appeared to the northeast. I was flying less than two hundred feet from the water when I sighted it. The shore was fairly distinct and not over ten or fifteen miles away. A light haze coupled with numerous local storm areas had prevented my seeing it from a long distance.

The coastline came down from the north, curved over towards the east. I had very little doubt that it was the southwestern end of Ireland, but in order to make sure, I changed my course toward the nearest point of land. I located Cape Valentia and Dingle Bay, then resumed my compass course towards Paris.

After leaving Ireland I passed a number of steamers and was seldom out of sight of a ship.

In a little over two hours the coast of England appeared. My course passed over southern England and a little south of Plymouth; then across the English Channel, striking France over Cherbourg. The English farms were very impressive from the air in contrast to ours in America. They appeared extremely small and unusually neat and tidy with their stone and hedge fences.

I was flying at about a fifteen hundred foot altitude over England, and as I crossed the Channel and passed over Cherbourg, France, I had probably seen more of that part of Europe than many native Europeans. The visibility was good, and the country could be seen for miles around. People who have taken their first flight often remark that no one knows what the locality he lives in is like until he has seen it from above. Countries take on different characteristics from the air.

The sun went down shortly after I passed Cherbourg, and soon the beacons along the Paris-London airway became visible.

I first saw the lights of Paris a little before 10 P.M., or 5 P.M., New York time, and a few minutes later I was circling the Eiffel Tower at an altitude of about four thousand feet.

The lights of Le Bourget were plainly visible, but appeared to be very close to Paris. I had understood that the field was farther from the city; so I continued out to the northeast into the country for four or five miles to make sure that there was not another field farther out which might be Le Bourget. Then I returned and spiraled down closer to the lights. Presently I could make out long lines of hangars, and the roads appeared to be jammed with cars.

I flew low over the field once, then circled around into the wind and landed.

After the plane stopped rolling I turned it around and started to taxi back to the lights. The entire field ahead, however, was covered with thousands of people all running toward my ship. When the first few arrived, I attempted to get them to hold the rest of the crowd back, away from the plane, but apparently no one could understand or would have been able to conform to my request if he had.

I cut the switch to keep the propeller from killing someone, and attempted to organize an impromptu guard for the plane. The impossibility of any immediate organization became apparent, and when parts of the ship began to crack from the pressure of the multitude, I decided to climb out of the cockpit in order to draw the crowd away.

Speaking was impossible; no words could be heard in the uproar, and nobody apparently cared to hear any. I started to climb out of the cockpit, but as soon as one foot appeared through the door, I was dragged the rest of the way without assistance on my part.

For nearly half an hour I was un-able to touch the ground, during which time I was ardently carried around in what seemed to be a very small area, and in every position it is possible to be in. Everyone had the best of intentions, but no one seemed to know just what they were.

The French military flyers very resourcefully took the situation in hand. A number of them mingled with the crowd; then, at a given signal, they placed my helmet on an American correspondent and cried: "Here is Lindbergh." That helmet on an American was sufficient evidence. The correspondent immediately became the center of attraction, and while he was being taken protestingly to the Reception Committee via a rather devious route, I managed to get inside one of the hangars.

Meanwhile a second group of soldiers and police had surrounded the plane and soon placed it out of danger in another hangar. The French ability to handle an unusual situation with speed and capability was remarkably demonstrated that night at Le Bourget.

Ambassador Herrick extended me an invitation to remain at his Embassy while I was in Paris, which I gladly accepted. But grateful as I was at the time, it did not take me long to realize that a kind Providence had placed me in Ambassador Herrick's hands. The ensuing days found me in situations that I had certainly never expected to be in and in which I relied on Ambassador Herrick's sympathetic aid.

These situations were brought about by the whole-hearted welcome to me—an American—that touched me beyond any point that any words can express. . . .

315

The Defeat of the City

By O. HENRY

*A great American writer here shows us that many
American men are really country boys at heart.*

*R*OBERT WALMSLEY'S DESCENT upon
the city resulted in a Kilkenny struggle. He came out of the fight
victor by a fortune and a reputation. On the other hand, he was
swallowed up by the city. The city gave him what he demanded and
then branded him with its brand. It remodelled, cut, trimmed and stamped him to the pattern it approves. It opened its social gates to him and shut him in on a close-cropped, formal lawn with the select herd of ruminants. In dress, habits, manners, provincialism, routine and narrowness he acquired that charming insolence, that irritating completeness, that sophisticated crassness, that overbalanced poise that makes the Manhattan gentleman so delightfully small in his greatness.

One of the up-state rural counties pointed with pride to the successful young metropolitan lawyer as a product of its soil. Six years earlier this county had removed the wheat straw from between its huckleberry-stained teeth and emitted a derisive and bucolic laugh as old man Walmsley's frecklefaced "Bob" abandoned the certain three-per-diem meals of the one-horse farm for the discontinuous quick lunch counters of the three-ringed metropolis. At the end of the six years no murder trial, coaching party, automobile accident or cotillion was complete in which the name of Robert Walmsley did not figure. Tailors waylaid him in the street to get a new wrinkle from the cut of his unwrinkled trousers. Hyphenated fellows in the clubs and members of the oldest subpoenaed families were glad to clap him on the back and allow him three letters of his name.

But the Matterhorn of Robert Walmsley's success was not scaled until he married Alicia Van Der Pool. I cite the Matterhorn, for just so high and cool and white and inaccessible was this daughter of the old burghers. The social Alps that ranged about her—over whose bleak passes a thousand climbers struggled —reached only to her knees. She towered in her own atmosphere, serene, chaste, prideful, wading in no fountains, dining no monkeys, breeding no dogs for bench shows. She was a Van Der Pool. Fountains were made to play for her; monkeys were made for other people's ancestors; dogs, she understood, were created to be companions of blind persons and objectionable characters who smoked pipes.

This was the Matterhorn that Robert Walmsley accomplished. If he found, with the good poet with the game foot and artificially curled hair, that he who ascends to mountain tops will find the loftiest peaks most wrapped in clouds and snow, he concealed his chilblains beneath a brave and smiling exterior. He was a lucky man and knew it, even though he were imitating the Spartan boy with an ice-cream freezer beneath his doublet frappéeing the region of his heart.

After a brief wedding tour abroad, the couple returned to create a decided ripple in the calm cistern (so placid and cool and sunless it is) of the best society. They entertained at their red brick mausoleum of ancient greatness in an old square that is a cemetery of crumbled glory. And Robert Walmsley was proud of his wife; although while one of his hands shook his guests' the other held tightly to his alpenstock and thermometer.

One day Alicia found a letter written to Robert by his mother. It was an unerudite letter, full of crops and motherly love and farm notes. It chronicled the health of the pig and the recent red calf, and asked concerning Robert's in return. It was a letter direct from the soil, straight from home, full of biographies of bees, tales of turnips, paeans of new-laid eggs, neglected parents and the slump in dried apples.

"Why have I not been shown your mother's letters?" asked Alicia. There was always something in her voice that made you think of lorgnettes, of accounts at Tiffany's, of sledges smoothly gliding on the trail from Dawson to Forty Mile, of the tinkling of pendant prisms on your grandmothers' chandeliers, of snow lying on a convent roof; of a police sergeant refusing bail. "Your mother," continued Alicia, "invites us to make a visit to the farm. I have never seen a farm. We will go there for a week or two, Robert."

"We will," said Robert, with the grand air of an associate Supreme Justice concurring in an opinion. "I did not lay the invitation before you because I thought you would not care to go. I am much pleased at your decision."

"I will write to her myself," answered Alicia, with a faint foreshadowing of enthusiasm. "Félice shall pack my trunks at once. Seven, I think, will be enough. I do not suppose that your mother entertains a great deal. Does she give many house parties?"

Robert arose, and as attorney for rural places filed a demurrer against six of the seven trunks. He endeavored to define, picture, elucidate, set forth and describe a farm. His own words sounded strange in his ears. He had not realized how thoroughly urbsidized he had become.

A week passed and found them landed at the little country station five hours out from the city. A grinning, stentorian, sarcastic youth, driving a mule to a spring wagon, hailed Robert savagely.

"Hallo, Mr. Walmsley. Found your way back at last, have you? Sorry I couldn't bring in the automobile for you, but Dad's bull-tonguing the ten-acre clover patch with it today. Guess you'll excuse my not wearing a dress suit over to meet you—it ain't six o'clock yet, you know."

"I'm glad to see you, Tom," said Robert, grasping his brother's hand. "Yes, I've found my way at last. You've a right to say 'at last.' It's been over two years since the last time. But it will be oftener after this, my boy."

Alicia, cool in the summer heat as an Arctic wraith, white as a Norse snow maiden in her flimsy muslin and fluttering lace parasol, came around the corner of the station; and

Tom was stripped of his assurance. He became chiefly eyesight clothed in blue jeans, and on the homeward drive to the mule alone did he confide in language the inwardness of his thoughts.

They drove homeward. The low sun dropped a spendthrift flood of gold upon the fortunate fields of wheat. The cities were far away. The road lay curling around wood and dale and hill like a ribbon lost from the robe of careless summer. The wind followed like a whinnying colt in the track of Phoebus's steeds.

By and by the farmhouse peeped gray out of its faithful grove; they saw the long lane, with its convoy of walnut trees, running from the road to the house; they smelled the wild rose and the breath of cool, damp willows in the creek's bed. And then, in unison, all the voices of the soil began a chant addressed to the soul of Robert Walmsley. Out of the tilted aisles of the dim wood they came hollowly; they chirped and buzzed from the parched grass; they trilled from the ripples of the creek ford; they floated up in clear Pan's pipe notes from the dimming meadows; the whippoorwills joined in as they pursued midges in the upper air; slow-going cow-bells struck out a homely accompaniment—and this was what each one said: "You've found your way back at last, have you?"

The old voices of the soil spoke to him. Leaf and bud and blossom conversed with him in the old vocabulary of his careless youth—the inanimate things, the familiar stones and rails, the gates and furrows and roofs and turns of road had an eloquence, too, and a power in the transformation. The country had smiled and he had felt the breath of it, and his heart was drawn, as if in a moment, back to his old love. The city was far away.

This rural atavism, then, seized Robert Walmsley and possessed him. A queer thing he noticed in connection with it was that Alicia, sitting at his side, suddenly seemed to him a stranger. She did not belong to this recurrent phase. Never before had she seemed so remote, so colorless and high—so intangible and unreal. And yet he had never admired her more than when she sat there by him in the rickety spring wagon, chiming no more with his mood and with her environment than the Matterhorn chimes with a peasant's cabbage garden.

That night when the greetings and the supper were over, the entire family, including Buff, the yellow dog, bestrewed itself upon the front porch. Alicia, not haughty but silent, sat in the shadow dressed in an exquisite pale-gray tea gown. Robert's mother discoursed to her happily concerning marmalade and lumbago. Tom sat on the top step; Sisters Millie and Pam on the lowest step to catch the lightning bugs. Mother had the willow rocker. Father sat in the big armchair with one of its arms gone. Buff sprawled in the middle of the porch in everybody's way. The twilight pixies and pucks stole forth unseen, and plunged other poignant shafts of memory into the heart of Robert. A rural madness entered his soul. The city was far away.

Father sat without his pipe, writhing in his heavy boots, a sacrifice to rigid courtesy. Robert shouted: "No, you don't!" He fetched the pipe and lit it; he seized the old gentleman's boots and tore them off. The last one slipped suddenly, and Mr. Robert Walmsley, of Washington Square, tumbled off the porch backward with Buff on top of him, howling fearfully. Tom laughed sarcastically.

Robert tore off his coat and vest and hurled them into a lilac bush.

"Come out here, you landlubber," he cried to Tom, "and I'll put grass seed on your back. I think you called me a 'dude' a while ago. Come along and cut your capers."

Tom understood the invitation and accepted it with delight. Three times they wrestled on the grass, "side holds," even as the giants of the mat. And twice was Tom forced to bite grass at the hands of the distinguished lawyer. Dishevelled, panting, each still boasting of his own prowess, they stumbled back to the porch. Millie cast a pert reflection upon the qualities of a city brother. In an instant Robert had secured a horrid katydid in his fingers and bore down upon her. Screaming wildly, she fled up the lane, pursued by the avenging glass of form. A quarter of a mile and they returned, she full of apology to the victorious dude. The rustic mania possessed him unabatedly.

"I can do up a cowpenful of you slow hayseeds," he proclaimed, vaingloriously. "Bring on your bulldogs, your hired men and your log-rollers."

He turned handsprings on the grass that prodded Tom to envious sarcasm. And then, with a whoop, he clattered to the rear and brought back Uncle Ike, a battered colored retainer of the family, with his banjo, and strewed sand on the porch and danced *Chicken in the Bread Tray* and did buck-and-wing wonders for half an hour longer. Incredibly wild and boisterous things he did. He sang, he told stories that set all but one shrieking, he played the yokel, the humorous clodhopper; he was mad, mad with the revival of the old life in his blood.

He became so extravagant that once his mother sought gently to reprove him. Then Alicia moved as though she were about to speak, but she did not. Through it all she sat immovable, a slim, white spirit in the dusk that no man might question or read.

By and by she asked permission to ascend to her room, saying that she was tired. On her way she passed Robert. He was standing in the door, the figure of vulgar comedy, with ruffled hair, reddened face and unpardonable confusion of attire—no trace there of the immaculate Robert Walmsley, the courted clubman and ornament of select circles. He was doing a conjuring trick with some household utensils, and the family, now won over to him without exception, was beholding him with worshipful admiration.

As Alicia passed in, Robert started suddenly. He had forgotten for the moment that she was present. Without a glance at him, she went on upstairs.

After that the fun grew quiet. An hour passed in talk, and then Robert went up himself.

She was standing by the window when he entered their room. She was still clothed as when they were on the porch. Outside, and crowding against the window, was a giant apple tree, full blossomed.

Robert sighed and went near the window. He was ready to meet his fate. A confessed vulgarian, he foresaw the verdict of justice in the shape of that still, whiteclad form. He knew the rigid lines that a Van Der Pool would draw. He was a peasant, gambolling indecorously in the valley, and the pure, cold, white, unthawed summit of the Matterhorn could not but frown on him. He had been unmasked by his own actions. All the polish, the poise, the form that the city had given him had fallen from him like an ill-fitting mantle at the first breath of a country breeze. Dully he awaited the approaching condemnation.

"Robert," said the calm, cool voice of his judge, "I thought I married a gentleman."

Yes, it was coming. And yet, in the face of it, Robert Walmsley was eagerly regarding a certain branch of the apple tree, upon which he used to climb out of that very window. He believed he could do it now. He wondered how many blossoms there were on the tree—ten millions? But here was someone speaking again:

"I thought I married a gentleman," the voice went on, "but—"

Why had she come and was standing so close by his side?

"But I find that I have married"—was this Alicia talking?—"something better—a man— Bob, dear, kiss me, won't you?"

The city was far away.

The Statue

By COREY FORD

*H*IS HEAD WAS ERECT, and his eyes were straight ahead. They were fine eyes, set deep in his face. He stood with feet planted a little apart, the broad Army belt straining across his chest, the pants of his tight-fitting uniform pulling in sharp folds against the bigness of his calves. His long-visored G.A.R. cap was gripped in his left hand, and his right hand was raised shoulder-high in a gesture of response, as though he were about to answer to his name at roll call. He was only eighteen when he died, eighty-three years ago in the Northern drive on Richmond.

"Bean, his name was," a young man working near the monument said. "He was a Brownfield boy. There's always been a family of that name here in Brownfield." They had found his daguerreotype in the town records, the young man said, and a famous sculptor had made the statue in his likeness, and it stood on a granite boulder in the center of the square of what had been the town of Brownfield. There was no town now. The forest fire, sweeping down out of the Maine hills two nights ago on a thirty-five-mile wind, had leveled every building for almost a mile. From where the statue stood, looking up the main street, the town was a

320

gray wasteland of cellar holes and chimneys and twisted metal. The fire had burned across the grass of the village square to the very base of the monument, but a small American flag stuck in the turf was not even scorched. "To her sons," the bronze plaque on the boulder read, "who upheld the flag. 1861–1865." In front of the monument, where the Congregational church had been, was a rectangle of split stone littered with broken, colored glass, and beyond that, was another hole filled with ashes that had been the Grange hall. Behind the town the fire had run through the cemetery, blackening the grass and withering the ancient cedars and yews.

"It came too fast," the young man said. "There wasn't anything we could do. I was back of town fighting the fire, and the next thing I knew, the wind had shifted, and I jumped in my car—but it got here first. People had to leave everything and run."

Only the statue had seen the town burn. The flames rolling down the main street had lighted his bronze face, and thrown a monstrous shadow leaping against the reddening walls of the church. For a timeless moment, in the silence of the empty square, he had stood alone with feet planted solidly and head erect, watching the fire come. His right hand was raised as if to shield his face from the heat.

"Nobody saved anything. There wasn't time," the young man said. He was wearing old Army pants and a pair of soot-blackened combat boots; evidently they were the same clothes he had on during the fire. "I never even saw my house until I came back the next day and saw where it was."

He bent over and pulled a sheet of tin roofing from the cellar hole of his house, and tossed it on a pile; the crash echoed in the ghost town. Here and there, amid the ashes, people were moving aimlessly like drifting wisps of smoke, poking in the ruins. An old woman across the street was gathering the rust-colored nails that had dropped on the ground when the beams of the house burned away.

"Where are you going to live now?"

"Where?" the young man said, looking up in surprise. "Why, here."

Even the double row of elms that lined the main street were dead; their bark had peeled off in the fierce heat. Telephone lines looped crazily from the leaning poles, and at the top of the hill, where a roadside sign said SCHOOL, several burned bicycle frames stood in a rack beside a flight of granite steps. The swamp behind the town was still smoldering; a sickly sweet smell like death hung in the air.

"They're shipping in sixty prefab houses next week," he said, "and we're setting up a portable sawmill. There's a lot of burned timber we can use for two-by-fours. The selectmen are handling town business in a freight car down where the station was. Of course, some people are moving away," he said, "but a lot of people like to live in Brownfield." Evidently he felt that didn't quite express what he meant, for he groped a moment for words, and then he raised his right hand shoulder-high in a gesture toward the statue. "Only the houses are gone," he said. "Brownfield's still here."

His combat boots were planted solidly on the split-stone foundations of his house. His head was erect as he said it, and his eyes were straight ahead. They were the same eyes.

321

AMERICAN WORDS

WAR is hell!—*General William T. Sherman*

HE gains much who loses vain hope.—*Anonymous*

TAKE THINGS always by their smooth handles.—*Jefferson*

HOME IS the kingdom and love is the king!—*William Rankin Duryea*

DUTY is the sublimest word in the English language.—*General Robert E. Lee*

YOU MUST OBEY THIS, now, for a law—that "he that will not work shall not eat."
—*Captain John Smith*

MANKIND THROUGHOUT THE WORLD will improve and better his condition, in proportion, as he comes to see, know, and understand, that what a man sows, that must he also reap, somewhere, somehow, and at sometime. And that, by the operation of a reign of laws, so wise and good, they will never require to be altered, amended or revoked.—*Peter Cooper*

THE BIBLE IS A BOOK of faith, and a book of doctrine, and a book of morals, and a book of religion, of especial revelation from God.—*Webster*

GOD BRINGS men into deep waters, not to drown them, but to cleanse them.—
Aughey

I PREFER the honestly simple to the ingeniously wicked.—*Penn*

HELL is paved with good intentions.—*Anonymous*

DEATH SHALL NEVER harm thee,
Shrink not from his blow,
For thy God shall arm thee,
And victory bestow.
—*Francis Scott Key*

322

OF WISDOM

E pluribus unum. From many, one.—*Anonymous*

THE PEN is mightier than the sword.—*Anonymous*

NEVER spend your money before you have it.—*Jefferson*

ABANDON ALL THESE local animosities, and make your sons Americans!
—*General Robert E. Lee*

YOU HAVE BEEN good soldiers; you can be good citizens.—*General Forrest*

THE FORCE OF SELFISHNESS is as inevitable and as calculable as the force of gravitation.—*Hilliard*

I SEE THE MARKS of God in the heavens and the earth; but how much more in a liberal intellect, in magnanimity, in unconquerable rectitude, in a philanthropy which forgives every wrong, and which never despairs of the cause of Christ and human virtue; I do and I must reverence human nature. I bless it for its kind affections. I honor it for its achievements in science and art, and still more for its examples of heroic and saintly virtue. These are marks of a divine origin and the pledges of a celestial inheritance; and I thank God that my own lot is bound up with that of the human race.—*Channing*

THE WAY of the world is to praise dead saints and persecute living ones.—*Nathaniel Howe*

NEVER put off till tomorrow what you can do today.—*Jefferson*

CHARACTER is heaven's passport.—*Anonymous*

THE UNION OF LAKES, the union of lands,
The union of States none can sever;
The union of hearts, the union of hands,
And the Flag of our Union forever!
         —*George Pope Morris*

323

Beyond Price . . .

By HUGH B. CAVE

*T*HE FLAGPOLE was Jeff Graham's idea. He brought the matter up at town meeting.

We were pretty patriotic by this time. Wadrey Anderson's fertilizer plant was being turned into a gunpowder factory, and government men, acting mysterious, had set up a radio listening station on Henry Whipple's farm. The flagpole seemed like a fine idea, especially when Jeff warmed up to his oratory. You wouldn't think a six-footer weighing over two hundred pounds would have any flair for elocution, but Jeff always could talk!

"What we've got to do in Farmville," he said, "is set an example for other small towns and villages in this neck of the woods! They need waking up! Patriotism—that's what we've got to show 'em! We're Americans. Citizens of the finest country on earth. We're free people, and it's our solemn duty to show the free people of other lands that we mean business.

"What we need," Jeff shouted, "is a symbol of our Americanism. Yes, sir. Something big, that people will sit up and take notice of. What we need is the biggest flagpole you ever laid eyes on, set up right in the middle of the town-hall lawn! With Old Glory waving from the top!"

Jeff had always told us what to do, more or less, and this time he didn't need to bear down much. We agreed there ought to be a flagpole, and it had to be a whopper.

"What we'll do," Wadrey Anderson declared, "is go out right now and locate a tree that will suit." This was on a Saturday afternoon.

Jeff said he liked our spirit. Yes, sir, that was the way to do things, while they were piping hot. But we didn't need to hunt up a tree. "The tree we want is less than a mile from here. You men come along with me."

We did, and Jeff had sure picked out a beauty.

I said, "That's the finest Norway pine I ever saw, Jeff."

"That isn't a Norway, Will. It's a genuine red pine, and there aren't many left in these parts. The ancestors of that tree traveled the world over, as masts and spars on the old clipper ships."

He was proud of having picked out that tree. It was American. Had roots in the past.

The tree was straight as a ramrod, and high enough, and it grew on land owned by a fellow name of Joe Wilczek, who worked at the fertilizer plant. It was on the corner of his property, a hundred feet from the house. While we were looking it over, Wilczek came from his vegetable garden to see what we wanted.

He was a big, unsociable sort of fellow, born in one of those Baltic countries. He was about forty-five, wore old clothes most of the time, and worked around in different places whenever there was work to be had.

His father, who brought him to America when he was around thirteen, was buried in Birch Hill cemetery, along with most of Farmville's dead, and now Joe was married to a Polish girl he'd met while working in a mill in Montpelier, I think it was, and he had a little girl nine years old. The child went to school and was smart, but Joe hadn't any education to speak of.

He came over and nodded, by way of saying how do, and looked kind of puzzled at the way we were studying the pine. His little girl came over, too. She was a pretty thing, with dark hair and big black eyes. She just looked at us.

"Wilczek," said Jeff Graham, "we have just come from a town hall meeting." He told Wilczek what we'd decided. Then he waved a hand at the tree and said, "There'll be no finer flagpole in the State of Vermont!"

Wilczek was not what you'd call quick to understand. He scowled at the pine for some time, and then looked hard at Jeff. "You want to cut down my tree?" he said.

Jeff said that was the idea.

"No," Wilczek said, and shook his head.

This was something we hadn't looked for, and it struck us as being mighty narrow. After all, Wilczek was a citizen of Farmville like the rest of us, and ought to have some feeling for the town, even if he was a queer sort who never attended town meetings.

Jeff had more patience than the rest of us. When we began muttering and sending dark looks at Wilczek, Jeff gave us a stare that shut us up. Then he explained to Wilczek, so even a child could understand, why the town had to have that tree. "It's not as if we wanted your tree for some mercenary reason. This tree will fly Old Glory. Doesn't that mean anything to you?"

Wilczek was stubborn. "She is my tree, on my land. You have to find some other."

"But you've got any number of trees! You won't feel the loss of this one!"

"Some other tree," Wilczek said. "I am sorry."

His little girl stepped forward then, shy as a rabbit but anxious to say something. "You gentlemen don't understand. My father doesn't know how to say it, but—"

Wilczek turned her away from us. "Ella," he said, "you go in the house."

"But, Pa—"

"Go in the house!"

The little girl went away, looking back at us. Wilczek said again, "I am sorry. Some other tree." Then he went away.

"Well," I said, "that's that."

We were all pretty sore, because we hadn't foreseen anything like this and didn't have any idea what to do about it. Delbert Hubbard said there was a white pine back of his place we could have, but he thought it was pretty old and might break up when we felled it.

Matthew Selley, who runs the Main Street garage, thought he'd seen a good tree—he didn't know what kind—near the falls on Hemlock Brook.

Jeff Graham just glared at them. "The town wants this tree," he said, "and the town's going to get this tree!"

"It's his property," I pointed out.

"Then we'll buy the tree. We'll take up a collection."

It was my job to keep track of the money that came in. I also called on half the townspeople personally, including Miss Watlet, the school-teacher. "We're collecting money for a flagpole to stand in front of the town hall," I told her.

She gave me a dollar and seemed real interested. "It's high time," she declared, "that this town developed some patriotism! Heavens knows I've been working on it hard enough. I've even had the children writing essays on why they are glad to be Americans!"

Miss Watlet is a brisk kind of woman, who speaks her mind at great length. I didn't want to get into any argument with her.

She said, "Are you planning a ceremony at the dedication of the flagpole, Mr. Evans?"

"Well, we haven't talked about it."

"You certainly should!" she declared. "But I'll take care of that. You leave that part of it to me, and I assure you it will be in capable hands. Among other things"—and she was already planning away like a politician—"we must have a reading of our prize essay on Americanism. Indeed we must!"

I'd meant to tell her about Joe Wilczek and his tree, but I let it go because she was wound up for fair. "That will be mighty nice, Miss Watlet, I'm sure," I said, and got away quick as I could, with her dollar.

We got $47.20 in all. Jeff said that would change Joe Wilczek's mind all right. "That's a lot of money," he said. "Perhaps we should set aside some of it to pay for the flag."

We talked it over and decided no, we'd give every cent of that money to Wilczek for his tree, and pay for the flag some other way. The money was raised for the flagpole, and we decided Wilczek was entitled to it.

It was a lot of money, though. "More than he makes in two weeks," Wadrey Anderson said, "working in my fertilizer plant."

Jeff and Wadrey and myself went over there of a Thursday evening, and Joe Wilczek was working in his garden. "Joe," Jeff said, "the town has decided to buy your tree and pay you good money for it. We've got forty-seven dollars and twenty cents here. I guess that will change your mind, won't it?"

He held out the envelope of money, and Joe looked at it. It was a fat envelope.

You could tell Joe was thinking what a lot of money that was. He needed money, too. His house needed lots of fixing up, and his clothes were in mighty sad shape. Yes, sir, forty-seven dollars meant a lot to Joe Wilczek.

But you know what he did? He looked at us and shook his head and said, "No."

I said, "What? You won't even sell that tree?"

"No," he said. "I am sorry."

Jeff got mad. "Look here, Wilczek," he said, pushing his jaw out, "you're being pigheaded obstinate about this! A tree's only a tree, and we're offering you a deal more than it's worth. What you need is a grain of good American patriotism!"

"I am sorry. You do not understand."

"You're right, we don't understand!" Jeff shouted, and proceeded to tell this stubborn foreigner just what was wrong with him. He laid it on good and heavy.

Wadrey Anderson was sore, too. He planted himself in front of Wilczek when Jeff got through. "Is this final, Wilczek?"

Wilczek just stared at him.

"All right then," Wadrey shouted, "get yourself another job! I won't have any pigheaded foreigners working in my place!"

Joe Wilczek didn't say anything. He sort of shrugged his shoulders, helplessly, and went into the house.

But that didn't end it. Jeff wouldn't let the matter drop. We talked it over and he had an idea. We'd go over there at night, he said, and take the tree, whether Joe Wilczek liked it or not. If he tried to stop us, we could handle him all right.

Yes, sir, we'd take that tree. So long as Wilczek got paid for it, he'd have no complaint. And we were determined not to let any dumb foreigner's obstinacy stand in the way of Farmville's patriotism. By this time we were calling Joe Wilczek a foreigner.

The three of us met at my house the following night, and I had my shotgun in case Joe Wilczek decided to get ugly.

We took a big two-handled saw and some ropes and an ax.

Just the three of us, mind you. What we meant to do was get that tree and have it standing in front of the town hall by morning. "It will show Wilczek and others of his kind that real Americans are a determined, fighting lot of people," Jeff said, "especially when they're in the right and know it."

We left my house a little after ten o'clock, and were at the Wilczek place in twenty minutes. There was a light burning in Wilczek's kitchen, at the back.

The front was dark. We stood there at the corner of the property, close to the tree, and talked a while, and decided to get started. We wouldn't go up to the house and tell him. He'd hear us soon enough and come out to see what was going on, and then we'd deal with him in whatever way was necessary.

"I just hope he gets ugly," I said. "These foreigners ought to be taught some respect."

We looked the tree over and decided how to cut it down. And just then the headlights of a car swung around the bend of the road, forcing us to move back.

The car stopped in front of the house, not forty feet from us, and I can tell you we looked at it good and hard. It had yellow New York license plates, and was covered with mud and dirt, but it was worth a lot of money, that car.

A dark, little man got out, went up the steps and rang the bell. None of us spoke a word. Just watched. The car's lights were still on. Pretty soon a light went on in Joe's front room, and Joe opened the door.

We couldn't hear what was said. It looked mighty suspicious, though, I can tell you. The dark little man did most of the talking, and Joe just listened. Then he hurried back to his car, lifted a black suitcase out of the trunk, put out the car's lights, and lugged this big suitcase into the house. The door closed, but the light in the front room stayed on.

"You see that?" I whispered, trembling some with excitement. "A New York car, and him taking that big suitcase into Wilczek's house! At this time of night!"

It looked queer, all right. You couldn't ever be sure of these foreigners, Jeff pointed out. With Wadrey's fertilizer plant being turned into a powder factory, and the government operating that radio listening station over on Henry Whipple's farm, most anything was likely to happen.

"First he wouldn't let us have that

327

tree," Jeff muttered, "and now this happens! You ask me, he'd have given us the tree quick enough if it was some *other* kind of flag we'd wanted to fly on it!" We talked like that, getting more and more worked up. I finally suggested it was our duty to find out what was going on. "We can creep up close and look in a window."

Jeff carried the ax and I gripped my shotgun in both hands as we crept silently to the veranda. If the dark little man was dangerous, he would be armed with something a lot easier to use than an ax or a shotgun. We got to a window, and could see in.

It looked bad. Wilczek and his wife were sitting on an old sofa, and the dark man was in a chair facing them, his back to us. The suitcase was on the floor in front of him, and it wasn't a suitcase.

It was a machine of some sort. The sides of the box were flat on the floor now, and the top was raised up on a hinge.

We couldn't see much of the machine itself, but we could see metal gleaming, and something turning, and a row of dials along one edge of it.

The stranger was hunched over the machine, turning the dials and talking to the Wilczeks at the same time, with his head tipped up like a bird's. I didn't like his looks.

"He's a foreigner, too," I muttered. Jeff poked me to shut up.

"What are we going to do?" I whispered.

The dark man stopped talking, and Mrs. Wilczek got up off the sofa. She went upstairs. For a while the stranger and Joe Wilczek just sat there, talking in low tones. We couldn't hear what they were saying,

because they were clear over on the other side of the room.

"What are we to do?" I whispered again. "We ought to do something!"

Neither Jeff nor Wadrey answered, because right then Mrs. Wilczek came downstairs, and the little girl was with her. The dark man stood up and said something to Ella and shook hands with her, and smiled. He had a paper of some sort in his other hand.

You could see Ella had just got out of bed, because she was wearing pajamas. She was still sleepy and kept rubbing her eyes as she looked at the machine. The stranger spent a long time showing her the machine. Then he handed her the paper and she unfolded it and read what was on it. We could see her lips move and we knew she was reading it aloud, but we couldn't hear a word.

The stranger listened and kept nodding. When she got to the end of the paper, he took her arm and led her across the room. He stood her right close to the window. We could hear him now. "You just stand over here, young lady, where the machine won't make you nervous," he said, "and read it again. Read it just as you did the first time. And talk into this," he said, handing her something on the end of a wire. Ella waited for him to go back to the machine. Then she began reading, and the Wilczeks and the dark man sat very still, listening. We listened, too.

"Why I am glad to be an American," Ella read. "I am glad to be an American because this is a free and wonderful country. My grandfather came here thirty-two years ago, to escape oppression in the land where he was born. He worked hard, and saved enough money to buy some land. 'This,' he said then, 'is my home. I have worked for it and now it is mine. No one in this country will take it away from me.'

"The first thing he did on his land was to build a house. Then he planted a tree. It was not a large tree, but to him it was a symbol. My father, Joseph, was thirteen years old then, and helped plant the tree.

"'Joseph,' my grandfather said, 'this tree will grow, and you will grow with it. This land will be yours, and then your children's, and their children's. Long after I am gone, this tree will be here. Take good care of it. Never let anything happen to it. It is an everlasting symbol of your allegiance to America. It means that you belong here!'

"The tree is still on our land, but I am old enough now to know for myself what it means, and my father, Joseph, no longer has to tell me. It is a beautiful tree. Its roots are deep and strong. They are like the roots of America. Its trunk is straight and true, and has weathered every storm. No doubt there will be other storms, such as the one raging today, and some of them will be savage and terrible. But I know that my tree will be standing when they have passed."

That was the end of the paper. Ella Wilczek stopped reading, and the dark man smiled at her. He shut off the machine. "Fine, young lady! And I want to congratulate you on winning our contest. We're very proud of you. And we're grateful to your teacher for sending your essay in to us."

He closed the machine and shook hands with the Wilczeks, and with their little girl. "You listen to the radio next Monday evening," he said, "and you'll hear your essay exactly as I've recorded it."

Mrs. Wilczek said something that we couldn't hear, and the man shook his head.

"Thank you, no," he said. "It's very late. It was an imposition for me to come at all at this hour, but schedules have to be kept, broken axles or not."

We didn't wait to watch him leave! Oh, no! We picked up our tools and got out of there, and made for home. And I can tell you we were mighty glad we hadn't announced to anyone else that we were going to cut down Joe Wilczek's tree! It was bad enough for us to have to face each other.

We got our flagpole—a white pine from Delbert Hubbard's place. We had our ceremony, too, and Ella Wilczek read her essay. But Ella didn't read it in front of the town hall. No, sir. Right after the pole was up and Old Glory was run to the top of it, the people of Farmville went down to Joe Wilczek's place and sat on the grass, and Ella read her essay under the tree that Joe Wilczek's father had planted.

Then Jeff announced that since we'd got the flagpole for nothing, the money we'd raised was to be presented to Ella Wilczek, for winning the radio contest.

"And," said Jeff, "for teaching the town of Farmville what it means to be an American."

How sweet and gracious, even in common speech,
Is that fine sense which men call courtesy!
—*J. T. Fields*

Calumny is a vice of curious constitution; trying to kill it keeps it
alive; leave it to itself and it will die a natural death.—*Thomas Paine*

As years go by, and only the large outlines of lofty American characters and careers remain, the wide republic will confess the benediction of a life like this, and gladly own that, if with perfect faith, and
hope assured, America would still stand and "bid the distant generations hail:" the inspiration of her national life must be the sublime
moral courage, the all-embracing humanity, the spotless integrity, the
absolutely unselfish devotion of great powers to great public ends,
which were the glory of Wendell Phillips.—*George William Curtis*

And the final event to himself (Mr. Burke) has been, that, as he rose
like a rocket, he fell like the stick.—*Thomas Paine*

Wherever there is a human being, I see God-given rights inherent in that
being, whatever may be the sex or complexion.—*William Lloyd Garrison*

The sublime and the ridiculous are often so nearly related, that it is
difficult to class them separately. One step above the sublime makes the
ridiculous, and one step above the ridiculous makes the sublime again.
—*Thomas Paine*

Whatever has a tendency to promote the civil intercourse of nations
by an exchange of benefits is a subject as worthy of philosophy as of
politics.—*Thomas Paine*

The best use of a journal is to print the largest practical amounts
of important truth,—truth which tends to make mankind wiser, and
thus happier.—*Greeley*

Better to be driven out from among men than to be disliked
of children.—*Richard Henry Dana*

OF AMERICAN JOURNALISTS

TALENT without tact is only half talent.—*Greeley*

IT IS but a step from the sublime to the ridiculous.—*Thomas Paine*

HAPPINESS lies, first of all, in health.—*George William Curtis*

THOUGH I APPEAR a sort of wanderer, the married state has not a sincerer friend than I am. It is the harbor of human life, and is, with respect to the things of this world, what the next world is to this. It is home; and that one word conveys more than any other word can express.—*Thomas Paine*

YOU CANNOT POSSIBLY have a broader basis for any government than that which includes all the people, with all their rights in their hands, and with an equal power to maintain their rights.—*William Lloyd Garrison*

WITH REASONABLE MEN, I will reason; with humane men I will plead; but to tyrants I will give no quarter, nor waste arguments where they will certainly be lost.—*William Lloyd Garrison*

IT IS ERROR only, and not truth, that shrinks from inquiry.—*Thomas Paine*

THOSE WHO EXPECT to reap the blessings of freedom, must, like men, undergo the fatigue of supporting it.—*Thomas Paine*

PATIENT ENDURANCE OF SUFFERINGS, bold resistance of power, forgiveness of injuries, hard-tried and faithful friendship, and self-sacrificing love, are seen in beautiful relief over the flat uniformity of life, or stand out in steady and bright grandeur in the midst of the dark deeds of men.—*Richard Henry Dana*

COMMON SENSE is very uncommon.—*Greeley*

THE MAN who tells me an indelicate story does me an injury.—*J. T. Fields*

331

LOVELIEST of lovely things are they
On earth, that soonest pass away.
The rose that lives its little hour
Is prized beyond the sculptured flower.
—*William Cullen Bryant*

DIFFICULTIES are meant to rouse, not discourage.—*Channing*

EVERY MAN has a right to his opinion, but no man has a right to be wrong
in his facts.—*Bernard Baruch*

THE MAN WHO MAKES it the habit of his life to go to bed at nine o'clock,
usually gets rich and is always reliable. . . Rogues do their work at night.
Honest men work by day. It's all a matter of habit, and good habits in
America make any man rich. Wealth is largely a result of habit.—
John Jacob Astor

FAME IS THE SCENTLESS SUNFLOWER, with gaudy crown of gold;
But friendship is the breathing rose, with sweets in every fold.
—*Oliver Wendell Holmes*

GREAT MEN have to be lifted upon the shoulders of the whole world, in
order to conceive their great ideas, or perform their great deeds.—
Hawthorne

NATURE IS a revelation of God; art a revelation of man.—*Longfellow*

THE ALMIGHTY DOLLAR, that great object of universal devotion throughout our land, seems to have no genuine devotees in these peculiar
villages.—*Washington Irving*

FAITH is love, taking the form of aspiration.—*Channing*

ACTION, not talk, has shaped and
reshaped the world, and made
history.—*George Matthew Adams*

332

OF WISDOM

HERE THE FREE SPIRIT of mankind at length,
Throws its last fetters off; and who shall place
A limit to the giant's unchained strength,
Or curb his swiftness in the forward race?
        —William Cullen Bryant

TODAY is yesterday's plan put into action.*—George Matthew Adams*

LET A YOUNG MAN get a job and work so hard at it that he has no time to fall into temptation.*—Edison*

"THE LITERARY WORLD," said he, "is made up of little confederacies, each looking upon its own members as the lights of the universe; and considering all others as mere transient meteors, doomed soon to fall and be forgotten, while its own luminaries are to shine steadily on to immortality."*—Washington Irving*

ALL THINGS that are on earth shall wholly pass away,
Except the love of God, which shall live and last for aye.
        —William Cullen Bryant

AS A WORK OF ART, I know few things more pleasing to the eye, or more capable of affording scope and gratification to a taste for the beautiful, than a well-situated, well-cultivated farm.*—Edward Everett*

BOOKS ARE the true levelers. They give to all who faithfully use them the society, the spiritual presence, of the best and greatest of our race.*—Channing*

I MUST ARRANGE my pillows for another weary night. (Last words)*—Washington Irving*

BE TRUE to your own highest convictions.*—Channing*

THE REAL DANGER in our situation lies in the
fact that so many people see clearly what
they are revolting from and so few see at all
what they are revolting to.*—Fosdick*

The Citizen

By JAMES FRANCIS DWYER

Woodrow Wilson, talking to a large group of recently naturalized citizens, inspired this story. He welcomed these two thousand foreign-born men into American citizenship in 1915, during World War I.

THE PRESIDENT OF THE UNITED STATES was speaking. His audience comprised two thousand foreign-born men who had just been admitted to citizenship. They listened intently, their faces, aglow with the light of a newborn patriotism, upturned to the calm, intellectual face of the first citizen of the country they now claimed as their own.

Here and there among the newly-made citizens were wives and children. The women were proud of their men. They looked at them from time to time, their faces showing pride and awe.

One little woman, sitting immediately in front of the President, held the hand of a big, muscular man and stroked it softly. The big man was looking at the speaker with great blue eyes that were the eyes of a dreamer.

The President's words came clear and distinct:

You were drawn across the ocean by some beckoning finger of hope, by some belief, by some vision of a new kind of justice, by some expectation of a better kind of life. You dreamed dreams of this country, and I hope you brought the dreams with you. A man enriches the country to which he brings dreams, and you who have brought them have enriched America.

The big man made a curious choking noise and his wife breathed a soft "Hush!" The giant was strangely affected.

The President continued:

No doubt you have been disappointed in some of us, but remember this, if we have grown at all poor in the ideal, you brought some of it with you. A man does not go out to seek the thing that is not in him. A man does not hope for the thing that he does not believe in, and if some of us have forgotten what America believed in, you at any rate imported in your own hearts a renewal of the belief. Each of you, I am sure, brought a dream, a glorious, shining dream, a dream worth more than gold or silver, and that is the reason that I, for one, make you welcome.

The big man's eyes were fixed. His wife shook him gently, but he did not heed her. He was looking through the presidential rostrum, through the big buildings behind it, looking out over leagues of space to a snow-swept village that huddled on an island in the Beresina, the swift-flowing tributary of the mighty Dnieper, an island that looked like a black bone stuck tight in the maw of the stream.

It was in the little village on the Beresina that the Dream came to Ivan Berloff, Big Ivan of the Bridge.

The Dream came in the spring. All great dreams come in the spring, and the Spring Maiden who brought Big Ivan's Dream was more than ordinarily beautiful. She swept up

334

the Beresina, trailing wondrous draperies of vivid green. Her feet touched the snow-hardened ground, and armies of little white and blue flowers sprang up in her footsteps. Soft breezes escorted her, velvety breezes that carried the aromas of the far-off places from which they came, places far to the southward, and more distant towns beyond the Black Sea whose people were not under the sway of the Great Czar.

The father of Big Ivan, who had fought under Prince Menshikov at Alma fifty-five years before, hobbled out to see the sunbeams eat up the snow hummocks that hid in the shady places, and he told his son it was the most wonderful spring he had ever seen.

"The little breezes are hot and sweet," he said, sniffing hungrily with his face turned toward the south. "I know them, Ivan! I know them! They have the spice odor that I sniffed on the winds that came to us when we lay in the trenches at Balaklava. Praise God for the warmth!"

And that day the Dream came to Big Ivan as he plowed. It was a wonder dream. It sprang into his brain as he walked behind the plow, and for a few minutes he quivered as the big bridge quivers when the Beresina sends her ice squadrons to hammer the arches. It made his heart pound mightily, and his lips and throat became very dry.

Big Ivan stopped at the end of the furrow and tried to discover what had brought the Dream. Where had it come from? Why had it clutched him so suddenly? Was he the only man in the village to whom it had come?

Like his father, he sniffed the sweet-smelling breezes. He thrust his great hands into the sunbeams. He reached down and plucked one of a bunch of white flowers that had sprung up overnight. The Dream was born of the breezes and the sunshine and the spring flowers. It came from them and it had sprung into his mind because he was young and strong. He knew! It couldn't come to his father or Donkov, the tailor, or Poborino, the smith. They were old and weak, and Ivan's dream was one that called for youth and strength.

"Ay, for youth and strength," he muttered as he gripped the plow. "And I have it!"

That evening Big Ivan of the Bridge spoke to his wife, Anna, a little woman, who had a sweet face and a wealth of fair hair.

"Wife, we are going away from here," he said.

"Where are we going, Ivan?" she asked.

"Where do you think, Anna?" he said, looking down at her as she stood by his side.

"To Bobruisk," she murmured. "No."

"Farther?"

"Ay, a long way farther."

Fear sprang into her soft eyes. Bobruisk was eighty-nine versts away, yet Ivan said they were going farther.

"We—we are not going to Minsk?" she cried.

"Ay, and beyond Minsk!"

"Ivan, tell me!" she gasped. "Tell me where we are going!"

"We are going to America."

"*To America?*"

"Yes, to America!"

Big Ivan of the Bridge lifted up his voice when he cried out the words "To America," and then a sudden fear sprang upon him as those words dashed through the little window out into the darkness of the village street. Was he mad? America was 8,000 versts away! It was far across the ocean, a place that was only a name to him, a place where he knew no one. He wondered in the strange little silence that followed his words if the crippled son of Poborino, the smith, had heard him. The cripple would jeer at him if the night wind had carried the words to his ear.

Anna remained staring at her big husband for a few minutes, then she sat down quietly at his side. There was a strange look in his big blue eyes, the look of a man to whom has come a vision, the look which came into the eyes of those shepherds of Judea long, long ago.

"What is it, Ivan?" she murmured softly, patting his big hand. "Tell me."

And Big Ivan of the Bridge, slow of tongue, told of the Dream. To no one else would he have told it. Anna understood. She had a way of patting his hands and saying soft things when his tongue could not find words to express his thoughts.

Ivan told how the Dream had come to him as he plowed. He told her how it had sprung upon him, a wonderful dream born of the soft breezes, of the sunshine, of the sweet smell of the upturned sod and of his own strength. "It wouldn't come to weak men," he said, baring an arm that showed great snaky muscles rippling beneath the clear skin. "It is a dream that comes only to those who are strong and those who want —who want something that they haven't got." Then in a lower voice he said: "What is it that we want, Anna?"

The little wife looked out into the darkness with fear-filled eyes. There were spies even there in that little village on the Beresina, and it was dangerous to say words that might be construed into a reflection on the Government. But she answered Ivan. She stooped and whispered one word into his ear, and he slapped his thigh with his big hand.

"Ay," he cried. "That is what we want! You and I and millions like us want it, and over there, Anna, over there we will get it. It is the country where a muzhik is as good as a prince of the blood!"

Anna stood up, took a small earthenware jar from a side shelf, dusted it carefully and placed it upon the mantel. From a knotted cloth about her neck she took a ruble and dropped the coin into the jar. Big Ivan looked at her curiously.

"It is to make legs for your Dream," she explained. "It is many versts to America, and one rides on rubles."

"You are a good wife," he said. "I was afraid that you might laugh at me."

"It is a great dream," she murmured. "Come, we will go to sleep."

The Dream maddened Ivan during the days that followed. It pounded within his brain as he followed the plow. It bred a discontent that made him hate the little village, the swift-flowing Beresina and the gray stretches that ran toward Mogilev. He wanted to be moving, but Anna had said that one rode on rubles, and rubles were hard to find.

And in some mysterious way the village became aware of the secret. Donkov, the tailor, discovered it. Donkov lived in one-half of the cottage occupied by Ivan and Anna, and Donkov had long ears. The tailor spread the news, and Poborino, the smith, and Yanansk, the baker, would jeer at Ivan as he passed.

"When are you going to America?" they would ask.

"Soon," Ivan would answer.

"Take us with you!" they would cry in chorus.

"It is no place for cowards," Ivan would answer. "It is a long way, and only brave men can make the journey."

"Are you brave?" the baker screamed one day as he went by.

"I am brave enough to want liberty!" cried Ivan angrily. "I am brave enough to want——"

"Be careful! Be careful!" interrupted the smith. "A long tongue has given many a man a train journey that he never expected."

That night Ivan and Anna counted the rubles in the earthenware pot. The giant looked down at his wife with a gloomy face, but she smiled and patted his hand.

"It is slow work," he said.

"We must be patient," she answered. "You have the Dream."

"Ay," he said. "I have the Dream."

Through the hot, languorous summertime the Dream grew within the brain of Big Ivan. He saw visions in the smoky haze that hung above the Beresina. At times he would stand, hoe in hand, and look toward the west, the wonderful west into which the sun slipped down each evening like a coin dropped from the fingers of the dying day.

Autumn came, and the fretful whining winds that came down from the north chilled the Dream. The winds whispered of the coming of the Snow King, and the river grumbled as it listened. Big Ivan kept out of the way of Poborino, the smith, and Yanansk, the baker. The Dream was still with him, but autumn is a bad time for dreams.

Winter came, and the Dream weakened. It was only the earthenware pot that kept it alive, the pot into which the industrious Anna put every coin that could be spared. Often Big Ivan would stare at the pot as he sat beside the stove. The pot was the cord which kept the Dream alive.

"You are a good woman, Anna," Ivan would say again and again. "It was you who thought of saving the rubles."

"But it was you who dreamed," she would answer. "Wait for the spring, husband mine. Wait."

It was strange how the spring came to the Beresina that year. It sprang upon the flanks of winter before the Ice King had given the order to retreat into the fastnesses of the north. It swept up the river escorted by a million little breezes, and housewives opened their windows and peered out with surprise upon their faces. A wonderful guest had come to them and found them unprepared.

Big Ivan of the Bridge was fixing a fence in the meadow on the morning the Spring Maiden reached the village. For a little while he was not aware of her arrival. His mind was upon his work, but suddenly he discovered that he was hot, and he took off his overcoat. He turned to hang the coat upon a bush, then he sniffed the air, and a puzzled look came upon his face. He sniffed again, hurriedly, hungrily. He drew in great breaths of it, and his eyes shone with a strange light. It was wonderful air. It brought life to the Dream. It rose up within him, ten times more lusty than on the day it was born, and his limbs trembled as he drew in the hot, scented breezes that breed the *Wan-*

derlust and shorten the long trails of the world.

Big Ivan clutched his coat and ran to the little cottage. He burst through the door, startling Anna, who was busy with her housework.

"The Spring!" he cried. "*The Spring!*"

He took her arm and dragged her to the door. Standing together they sniffed the sweet breezes. In silence they listened to the song of the river. The Beresina had changed from a whining, fretful tune into a lilting, sweet song that would set the legs of lovers dancing. Anna pointed to a green bud on a bush beside the door.

"It came this minute," she murmured.

"Yes," said Ivan. "The little fairies brought it there to show us that spring has come to stay."

Together they turned and walked to the mantel. Big Ivan took up the earthenware pot, carried it to the table, and spilled its contents upon the well-scrubbed boards. He counted while Anna stood beside him, her fingers clutching his coarse blouse. It was a slow business, because Ivan's big blunt fingers were not used to such work, but it was over at last. He stacked the coins into neat piles, then he straightened himself and turned to the woman at his side.

"It is enough," he said quietly. "We will go at once. If it was not enough, we would have to go because the Dream is upon me and I hate this place."

"As you say," murmured Anna. "The wife of Littin, the butcher, will buy our chairs and our bed. I spoke to her yesterday."

Poborino, the smith; his crippled son; Yanansk, the baker; Dankov, the tailor, and a score of others were out upon the village street on the morning that Big Ivan and Anna set out. They were inclined to jeer at Ivan, but something upon the face of the giant made them afraid. Hand in hand the big man and his wife walked down the street, their faces turned toward Bobruisk, Ivan balancing upon his head a heavy trunk that no other man in the village could have lifted.

At the end of the street a stripling with bright eyes and yellow curls clutched the hand of Ivan and looked into his face.

"I know what is sending you," he cried.

"Ay, *you* know," said Ivan, looking into the eyes of the other.

"It came to me yesterday," murmured the stripling. "I got it from the breezes. They are free, so are the birds and the little clouds and the river. I wish I could go."

"Keep your dream," said Ivan softly. "Nurse it, for it is the dream of a man."

Anna, who was crying softly, touched the blouse of the boy. "At the back of our cottage, near the bush that bears the red berries, a pot is buried," she said. "Dig it up and take it home with you and when you have a kopeck drop it in. It is a good pot."

The stripling understood. He stooped and kissed the hand of Anna, and Big Ivan patted him upon the back. They were brother dreamers and they understood each other.

Boris Lugan has sung the song of the versts that eat up one's courage as well as the leather of one's shoes.

"Versts! Versts! Scores and scores of them!

Versts! Versts! A million or more of them!

338

Dust! Dust! And the devils who play in it,
Blinding us fools who forever must stay in it."

Big Ivan and Anna faced the long versts to Bobruisk, but they were not afraid of the dust devils. They had the Dream. It made their hearts light and took the weary feeling from their feet. They were on their way. America was a long, long journey, but they had started, and every verst they covered lessened the number that lay between them and the Promised Land.

"I am glad the boy spoke to us," said Anna.

"And I am glad," said Ivan. "Some day he will come and eat with us in America."

They came to Bobruisk. Holding hands, they walked into it late one afternoon. They were eighty-nine versts from the little village on the Beresina, but they were not afraid. The Dream spoke to Ivan, and his big hand held the hand of Anna. The railway ran through Bobruisk, and that evening they stood and looked at the shining rails that went out in the moonlight like silver tongs reaching out for a low-hanging star.

And they came face to face with the Terror that evening, the Terror that had helped the spring breezes and the sunshine to plant the Dream in the brain of Big Ivan.

They were walking down a dark side street when they saw a score of men and women creep from the door of a squat, unpainted building. The little group remained on the sidewalk for a minute as if uncertain about the way they should go, then from the corner of the street came a cry of "Police!" and the twenty pedestrians ran in different directions.

It was no false alarm. Mounted police charged down the dark thoroughfare swinging their swords as they rode at the scurrying men and women who raced for shelter. Big Ivan dragged Anna into a doorway, and toward their hiding place ran a young boy who, like themselves, had no connection with the group and who merely desired to get out of harm's way till the storm was over.

The boy was not quick enough to escape the charge. A trooper pursued him, overtook him before he reached the sidewalk, and knocked him down with a quick stroke given with the flat of his blade. His horse struck the boy with one of his hoofs as the lad stumbled on his face.

Big Ivan growled like an angry bear, and sprang from his hiding place. The trooper's horse had carried him on to the sidewalk, and Ivan seized the bridle and flung the animal on its haunches. The policeman leaned forward to strike at the giant, but Ivan of the Bridge gripped the left leg of the horseman and tore him from the saddle.

The horse galloped off, leaving its rider lying beside the moaning boy who was unlucky enough to be in a street where a score of students were holding a meeting.

Anna dragged Ivan back into the passageway. More police were charging down the street, and their position was a dangerous one.

"Ivan!" she cried, "Ivan! Remember the Dream! America, Ivan! America! Come this way! Quick!"

With strong hands she dragged him down the passage. It opened into a narrow lane, and, holding each other's hands, they hurried toward the place where they had taken lodgings. From far off came screams and hoarse orders, curses and the

339

sound of galloping hoofs. The Terror was abroad.

Big Ivan spoke softly as they entered the little room they had taken. "He had a face like the boy to whom you gave the lucky pot," he said. "Did you notice it in the moonlight when the trooper struck him down?"

"Yes," she answered. "I saw."

They left Bobruisk next morning. They rode away on a great, puffing, snorting train that terrified Anna. The engineer turned a stopcock as they were passing the engine, and Anna screamed while Ivan nearly dropped the big trunk. The engineer grinned, but the giant looked up at him and the grin faded. Ivan of the Bridge was startled by the rush of hot steam, but he was afraid of no man.

The train went roaring by little villages and great pasture stretches. The real journey had begun. They began to love the powerful engine. It was eating up the versts at a tremendous rate. They looked at each other from time to time and smiled like two children.

They came to Minsk, the biggest town they had ever seen. They looked out from the car windows at the miles of wooden buildings, at the big church of St. Catharine, and the woolen mills. Minsk would have frightened them if they hadn't had the Dream. The farther they went from the little village on the Beresina the more courage the Dream gave to them.

On and on went the train, the wheels singing the song of the road. Fellow travelers asked them where they were going. "To America," Ivan would answer.

"To America?" they would cry. "May the little saints guide you. It is a long way, and you will be lonely."

"No, we shall not be lonely," Ivan would say.

"Ha! you are going with friends?"

"No, we have no friends, but we have something that keeps us from being lonely." And when Ivan would make that reply Anna would pat his hand and the questioner would wonder if it was a charm or a holy relic that the bright-eyed couple possessed.

They ran through Vilna, on through flat stretches of Courland to Libau, where they saw the sea. They sat and stared at it for a whole day, talking little but watching it with wide, wondering eyes. And they stared at the great ships that came rocking in from distant ports, their sides gray with the salt from the big combers which they had battled with.

No wonder this America of ours is big. We draw the brave ones from the old lands, the brave ones whose dreams are like the guiding sign that was given to the Israelites of old—a pillar of cloud by day, a pillar of fire by night.

The harbor master spoke to Ivan and Anna as they watched the restless waters.

"Where are you going, children?"

"To America," answered Ivan.

"A long way. Three ships bound for America went down last month."

"Our ship will not sink," said Ivan.

"Why?"

"Because I know it will not."

The harbor master looked at the strange blue eyes of the giant, and spoke softly. "You have the eyes of a man who sees things," he said. "There was a Norwegian sailor in the *White Queen*, who had eyes like yours, and he could see death."

"I see life!" said Ivan boldly. "A free life——"

340

"Hush!" said the harbor master. "Do not speak so loud." He walked swiftly away, but he dropped a ruble into Anna's hand as he passed her by. "For luck," he murmured. "May the little saints look after you on the big waters."

They boarded the ship, and the Dream gave them a courage that surprised them. There were others going aboard, and Ivan and Anna felt that those others were also persons who possessed dreams. She saw the dreams in their eyes. There were Slavs, Poles, Letts, Jews, and Livonians, all bound for the land where dreams come true. They were a little afraid—not two per cent of them had ever seen a ship before—yet their dreams gave them courage.

The emigrant ship was dragged from her pier by a grunting tug and went floundering down the Baltic Sea. Night came down, and the devils who, according to the Esthonian fishermen, live in the bottom of the Baltic, got their shoulders under the stern of the ship and tried to stand her on her head. They whipped up white combers that sprang on her flanks and tried to crush her, and the wind played a devil's lament in her rigging. Anna lay sick in the stuffy women's quarters, and Ivan could not get near her. But he sent her messages. He told her not to mind the sea devils, to think of the Dream, the Great Dream that would become real in the land to which they were bound. Ivan of the Bridge grew to full stature on that first night out from Libau. The battered old craft that carried him slouched before the waves that swept over her decks, but he was not afraid. Down among the million and one smells of the steerage he induced a thin-faced Livonian to play upon a

mouth organ, and Big Ivan sang Paleer's "Song of Freedom" in a voice that drowned the creaking of the old vessel's timbers, and made the seasick ones forget their sickness. They sat up in their berths and joined in the chorus, their eyes shining brightly in the half gloom:

"Freedom for serf and for slave,
Freedom for all men who crave
Their right to be free
And who hate to bend knee
But to Him who this right to them gave."

It was well that these emigrants had dreams. They wanted them. The sea devils chased the lumbering steamer. They hung to her bows and pulled her for'ard deck under emerald-green rollers. They clung to her stern and hoisted her nose till Big Ivan thought that he could touch the door of heaven by standing on her blunt snout. Miserable, cold, ill, and sleepless, the emigrants crouched in their quarters, and to them Ivan and the thin-faced Livonian sang the "Song of Freedom."

The emigrant ship pounded through the Cattegat, swung southward through the Skagerrack and the bleak North Sea. But the storm pursued her. The big waves snarled and bit at her, and the captain and the chief officer consulted with each other. They decided to run into the Thames, and the harried steamer nosed her way in and anchored off Gravesend.

An examination was made, and the agents decided to transship the emigrants. They were taken to London and thence by train to Liverpool, and Ivan and Anna sat again side by side, holding hands and smiling at each other as the third-class emigrant train from Euston raced down through the green Midland counties to grimy Liverpool.

"You are not afraid?" Ivan would say to her each time she looked at him.

"It is a long way, but the Dream has given me much courage," she said.

"Today I spoke to a Lett whose brother works in New York City," said the giant. "Do you know how much money he earns each day?"

"How much?" she questioned.

"Three rubles, and he calls the policemen by their first names."

"You will earn five rubles, my Ivan," she murmured. "There is no one as strong as you."

Once again they were herded into the bowels of a big ship that steamed away through the fog banks of the Mersey out into the Irish Sea. There were more dreamers now, nine hundred of them, and Anna and Ivan were more comfortable. And these new emigrants, English, Irish, Scotch, French, and German, knew much concerning America. Ivan was certain that he would earn at least three rubles a day. He was very strong.

On the deck he defeated all comers in a tug of war, and the captain of the ship came up to him and felt his muscles.

"The country that lets men like you get away from it is run badly," he said. "Why did you leave it?"

The interpreter translated what the captain said and through the interpreter Ivan answered.

"I had a Dream," he said, "a Dream of freedom."

"Good," cried the captain. "Why should a man with muscles like yours have his face ground into the dust?"

The soul of Big Ivan grew during those days. He felt himself a man, a man who was born upright to speak his thoughts without fear.

The ship rolled into Queenstown one bright morning, and Ivan and his nine hundred steerage companions crowded the for'ard deck. A boy in a rowboat threw a line to the deck, and after it had been fastened to a stanchion he came up hand over hand. The emigrants watched him curiously. An old woman sitting in the boat pulled off her shoes, sat in a loop of the rope, and lifted her hand as a signal to her son on deck.

"Hey, fellers," said the boy, "help me pull me muvver up. She wants to sell a few dozen apples, an' they won't let her up the gangway!"

Big Ivan didn't understand the words, but he guessed what the boy wanted. He made one of a half dozen who gripped the rope and started to pull the ancient apple-woman to the deck.

They had her halfway up the side when an undersized third officer discovered what they were doing. He called to a steward and the steward sprang to obey.

"Turn a hose on her!" cried the officer. "Turn a hose on the old woman!"

The steward rushed for the hose. He ran with it to the side of the ship with the intention of squirting on the old woman, who was swinging in midair and exhorting the six men who were dragging her to the deck.

"Pull!" she cried. "Sure, I'll give every one of ye a rosy red apple an' me blessing with it."

The steward aimed the muzzle of the hose, and Big Ivan of the Bridge let go of the rope and sprang at him. The fist of the great Russian went out like a battering ram; it struck the steward between the eyes, and he dropped upon the deck. He lay like

342

one dead, the muzzle of the hose wriggling from his limp hands.

The third officer and the interpreter rushed at Big Ivan, who stood erect, his hands clenched.

"Ask the big swine why he did it," roared the officer.

"Because he is a coward!" cried Ivan. "They wouldn't do that in America!"

"What does the big brute know about America?" cried the officer.

"Tell him I have dreamed of it," shouted Ivan. "Tell him it is in my Dream. Tell him I will kill him if he turns the water on this old woman."

The apple-seller was on deck then, and with the wisdom of the Celt she understood. She put her lean hand upon the great head of the Russian and blessed him in Gaelic. Ivan bowed before her, then as she offered him a rosy apple he led her toward Anna, a great Viking leading a withered old woman who walked with the grace of a duchess.

"Please don't touch him," she cried, turning to the officer. "We have been waiting for your ship for six hours, and we have only five dozen apples to sell. It's a great man he is. Sure he's as big as Finn Mac-Cool."

Some one pulled the steward behind a ventilator and revived him by squirting him with water from the hose which he had tried to turn upon the old woman. The third officer slipped quietly away.

The Atlantic was kind to the ship that carried Ivan and Anna. Through sunny days they sat up on deck and watched the horizon. They wanted to be among those who would get the first glimpse of the wonderland.

They saw it on a morning with sunshine and soft wind. Standing together in the bow, they looked at the smear upon the horizon, and their eyes filled with tears. They forgot the long road to Bobruisk, the rocking journey to Libau, the mad buck-jumping boat in whose timbers the sea devils of the Baltic had bored holes. Everything unpleasant was forgotten, because the Dream filled them with a great happiness.

The inspectors at Ellis Island were interested in Ivan. They walked around him and prodded his muscles, and he smiled down upon them good-naturedly.

"A fine animal," said one. "Gee, he's a new white hope! Ask him can he fight?"

An interpreter put the question, and Ivan nodded. "I have fought," he said.

"Gee!" cried the inspector. "Ask him was it for purses or what?"

"For freedom," answered Ivan. "For freedom to stretch my legs and straighten my neck!"

Ivan and Anna left the Government ferryboat at the Battery. They started to walk uptown, making for the East Side, Ivan carrying the big trunk that no other man could lift.

It was a wonderful morning. The city was bathed in warm sunshine, and the well-dressed men and women who crowded the sidewalks made the two immigrants think that it was a festival day. Ivan and Anna stared at each other in amazement. They had never seen such dresses as those worn by the smiling women who passed them by; they had never seen such well-groomed men.

"It is a feast day for certain," said Anna.

"They are dressed like princes and princesses," murmured Ivan. "There are no poor here, Anna. None."

Like two simple children, they walked along the streets of the City of Wonder. What a contrast it was to the gray, stupid towns where the Terror waited to spring upon the cowed people! In Bobruisk, Minsk, Vilna, and Libau the people were sullen and afraid. They walked in dread, but in the City of Wonder beside the glorious Hudson every person seemed happy and contented.

They lost their way, but they walked on, looking at the wonderful shop windows, the roaring elevated trains, and the huge skyscrapers. Hours afterward they found themselves in Fifth Avenue near Thirty-third Street, and there the miracle happened to the two Russian immigrants. It was a big miracle inasmuch as it proved the Dream a truth, a great truth.

Ivan and Anna attempted to cross the avenue, but they became confused in the snarl of traffic. They dodged backward and forward as the stream of automobiles swept by them. Anna screamed, and, in response to her scream, a traffic policeman, resplendent in a new uniform, rushed to her side. He took the arm of Anna and flung up a commanding hand. The charging autos halted. For five blocks north and south they jammed on the brakes when the unexpected interruption occurred, and Big Ivan gasped.

"Don't be flurried, little woman," said the cop. "Sure I can tame 'em by liftin' me hand."

Anna didn't understand what he said, but she knew it was something nice by the manner in which his Irish eyes smiled down upon her. And in front of the waiting automobiles he led her with the same care that he would give to a duchess, while Ivan, carrying the big trunk, followed them, wondering much. Ivan's mind went back to Bobruisk on the night the

Terror was abroad.

The policeman led Anna to the sidewalk, patted Ivan good-naturedly upon the shoulder, and then with a sharp whistle unloosed the waiting stream of cars that had been held up so that two Russian immigrants could cross the avenue.

Big Ivan of the Bridge took the trunk from his head and put it on the ground. He reached out his arms and folded Anna in a great embrace. His eyes were wet.

"The Dream is true!" he cried. "Did you see, Anna? We are as good as they! This is the land where a muzhik is as good as a prince of the blood!"

The President was nearing the close of his address. Anna shook Ivan, and Ivan came out of the trance which the President's words had brought upon him. He sat up and listened intently:

We grow great by dreams. All big men are dreamers. They see things in the soft haze of a spring day or in the red fire of a long winter's evening. Some of us let those great dreams die, but others nourish and protect them, nurse them through bad days till they bring them to the sunshine and light which come always to those who sincerely hope that their dreams will come true.

The President finished. For a moment he stood looking down at the faces turned up to him, and Big Ivan of the Bridge thought that the President smiled at him. Ivan seized Anna's hand and held it tight.

"He knew of my Dream!" he cried. "He knew of it. Did you hear what he said about the dreams of a spring day?"

"Of course he knew," said Anna. "He is the wisest man in America, where there are many wise men.

344

Ivan, you are a citizen now."
"And you are a citizen, Anna."
The band started to play "My Country, 'tis of Thee," and Ivan and Anna got to their feet. Standing side by side, holding hands, they joined in with the others who had found after long days of journeying the blessed land where dreams come true.

DUSK OVER WISCONSIN
AUGUST DERLETH

Wisconsin is still a young man with names remembered.

He can think of Black Hawk and Red Bird and Yellow
    Thunder,
and he can think how slowly years turn past things under.

Hearing the long cry of locomotives in the night and
    motors humming in the air,
he can remember how canoes came down his waters,
    and how the rafts, and how the river boats went up and
    down.
And he can think of ox-carts trailing into valleys from the
    hills.

Every spring and every summer he can hear the whippoor-
    wills
singing in the early evening, and in this nostalgic sound
    he can tell himself again a round
    of memories:

        legend-tired Frontenac, wanting knowledge
        of the stream called Father of Waters:
John Jacob Astor and the outposts of his fur empire:
imprisoned Black Hawk sick with longing for his
    hills and prairies, for his dying sons and daughters:
Senator La Follette fighting lumber kings and railroad kings,
    all despoilers of his land with his death-bound fire . . .
Wisconsin is still a young man with centuries remembered.

Carver and Marquette and Joliet
drowsing down his yesterday:
Dewey and La Follette scarcely gone,
Schurz and Garland fingering his dawn.

345

Still a young man sprawled in the deep grass of a summer
    afternoon,
remembering how Sacs and Foxes, and how Chippewas fell
    back, and how soon
the forests came to end, dreaming memoried footfalls
    soft against unquiet earth:
Quebec and New Orleans, and Pere Marquette seeing in a
    dawn, how the Ouisconsin gave birth
to that elder stream, proud Black Hawk fronting General
    Street on the Prairie of the Dog: "I am Black Hawk of the
    Sacs, surrendering."

      Wisconsin is a young man knowing kinship
    with the whickering hawk above, as on a stair—
but restless, restless, nostrils distended to the change,
    knowing some time night comes where hangs at thicken-
    ing twilight, sharpened air.

SING, AMERICA, SING!
GAIL BROOK BURKET

Take up your harp, America,
This is the hour for song.
Let myriad-throated harmony
Rise jubilant and strong.

Forward, invincible with song,
Loved homeland of the free.
With mighty steps and mighty songs,
Achieve your destiny.

A singing nation can prevail
Against the strongest foe.
A singing people marches on,
Undaunted as they go.

Then sweep the strings with valiant song,
Let hill and valley ring.
Lift up your hearts and voices, all
America, and sing!

A CREED FOR AMERICANS
By STEPHEN VINCENT BENÉT

WE BELIEVE in the dignity of man and the worth and value of every living soul, no matter in what body housed, no matter whether born in comfort or born in poverty, no matter to what stock he belongs, what creed he professes, what job he holds.

We believe that every man should have a free and equal chance to develop his own best abilities under a free system of government, where the people themselves choose those who are to rule them and where no one man can set himself up as a tyrant or oppress the many for the benefit of the few.

We believe that free speech, free assembly, free elections, free practice of religion are the cornerstones of such a government. We believe that the Declaration of Independence, the Constitution and the Bill of Rights of the United States of America offer the best and most workable framework yet devised for such a government.

We believe in justice and law. We do not believe in curing an evil by substituting for it another and opposite evil. We are unalterably opposed to class hatred, race hatred, religious hatred, however manifested, by whomsoever instilled.

We believe that political freedom implies and acknowledges economic responsibility. We do not believe that any state is an admirable state that lets its people go hungry when they might be fed, ragged when they might be clothed, sick when they might be well, workless when they might have work. We believe that it is the duty of all of us, the whole people, working through our demo-cratic system, to see that such conditions are remedied, whenever and wherever they exist in our country.

We believe that political freedom implies and acknowledges personal responsibility. We believe that we have a great and priceless heritage as a nation—not only a heritage of material resources but of liberties, dreams, ideals, ways of going forward. We believe it is our business, our right and our inescapable duty to maintain and expand that heritage. We believe that such a heritage cannot be maintained by the lacklustre, the selfish, the bitterly partisan or the amiably doubtful. We believe it is something bigger than party, bigger than our own small ambitions. We believe it is worth the sacrifice of ease, the long toil of years, the expense of our heart's blood.

We know that our democratic system is not perfect. We know that it permits injustices and wrongs. But with our whole hearts we believe in its continuous power of self-remedy. That power is not a theory—it has been proven. Through the years, democracy has given more people freedom, less persecution and a higher standard of living than any other system we know. Under it, evils have been abolished, injustices remedied, old wounds healed, not by terror and revolution but by the slow revolution of consent in the minds of all the people. While we maintain democracy, we maintain the greatest power a people can possess—the power of gradual, efficient, and lawful change.

Most of all, we believe in democracy itself—in its past, its present and its future—in democracy as a political system to live by—in democracy as the great hope in the minds of the free. We believe it so deeply rooted in the earth of this country that neither assault from without nor dissension from within can ever wipe it entirely from that earth. But, because it was established for us by the free-minded and the daring, it is our duty now, in danger as in security, to uphold and sustain it with all that we have and are. We believe that its future shall and must be even greater than its past. And to the future—as to the past of our forebears and the present of our hard-won freedom—we pledge all we have to give.

OUR AMERICA
By Marjorie Barrows

America! America!
We'll sing our love for you
From prairie farms and mountain homes
And towered cities too.

O land of Washington and Lincoln,
Land of pioneers,
Our gratitude to you we'll show
Throughout the coming years!

Your stars and stripes wave in the breeze
And thrill us all today,
In God we trust, America,
He'll lead us on our way.

America, we'll work with you
For what we know is good,
We'll work for Truth and Liberty
And Peace and Brotherhood!

From THE PREFACE TO THE 1857 EDITION OF LEAVES OF GRASS
By Walt Whitman

DRAW NEAR and learn the faithful American lesson. Liberty is poorly served by those who are quelled by one failure or any number of failures, or from the casual indifference of the people, or from the sharp show of the tushes of power . . . . Liberty relies on itself, invites no one, promises nothing, sits in calmness and light and knows no discouragement.

The battle rages, with many a loud alarm and frequent advance and retreat; the enemy triumphs; the prison, the handcuffs, the iron necklace and anklet, the scaffold, the garrote do their work; the cause is asleep; the strong throats are choked in their own blood; the young men drop their eyelids toward the ground when they pass one another.

And is Liberty gone out of that place? No, never. When Liberty goes it is not the first to go, nor the second or third to go; it waits for all the rest to go. It is the last.

When the memories of the old martyrs are faded utterly away; when the boys are no more christened after them, but christened after tyrants and traitors instead; when the laws of the free are grudgingly permitted and laws for informers and blood money are sweet to the taste of the people; when you and I walk abroad on the earth, stung with compassion at the sight of numberless brothers answering our equal friendship and calling no man master— and are elated with noble joy, at the sight of slaves; when the swarms of cringers, doughfaces, lice of politics, planners of sly involutions . . . obtain a response of love and deference from the people; when it is better to be a bound booby and rogue in office than the poorest free mechanic or farmer, with his hat unmoved from his head and firm eyes and a candid and generous heart; and when servility can be tried on by any government without its own punishment following duly and in exact proportion, against the smallest chance of escape . . . .

Or rather when all the souls of men and women are discharged from any part of the earth,

Then only shall the instinct of Liberty be discharged from that part of the earth.

HOME, SWEET HOME

JOHN HOWARD PAYNE

'Mid pleasures and palaces though we may roam,
Be it ever so humble, there's no place like home;
A charm from the sky seems to hallow us there,
Which, seek through the world, is ne'er met with elsewhere.
　　Home, home, sweet, sweet home!
There's no place like home, oh, there's no place like home!

An exile from home, splendor dazzles in vain;
Oh! give me my lowly thatched cottage again!
The birds singing gayly, that came at my call—
Give me them—and the peace of mind, dearer than all!
　　Home, home, sweet, sweet home!
There's no place like home, oh, there's no place like home!

WISDOM OF WHITTIER

God is, and all is well.

Who never wins can rarely lose,
Who never climbs as rarely falls.

One brave deed makes no hero;

Tradition wears a snowy beard, romance is always young.

To worship rightly is to love each other,
Each smile a hymn, each kindly deed a prayer.

Then shall all shackles fall; the stormy clangor of wild
war music o'er the earth shall cease;
Love shall tread out the baleful fire of anger, and in
its ashes plant the tree of peace!

And, step by step, since time began, I see the steady gain of man.

I know not where His islands lift
Their fronded palms in air;
I only know I cannot drift
Beyond His love and care.

Beauty seen is never lost.

Follow with reverent steps, the great example
Of Him whose holy work was "doing good;"
So shall the wide earth seem our Father's temple,
Each loving life a psalm of gratitude.

God blesses still the generous thought,
And still the fitting word He speeds,
And Truth, at His requiring taught,
He quickens into deeds.

WISDOM OF EMERSON

SKILL to do comes of doing.

NOR KNOWEST THOU what argument
Thy life to thy neighbor's creed has lent.
All are needed by each one;
Nothing is fair or good alone.

EVERY sweet has its sour; every evil its good.

ONLY so much do I know, as I have lived.

A SUFFICIENT MEASURE of civilization is the influence of good women.

ONLY AN INVENTOR knows how to borrow, and every man is or
should be an inventor.

LET US TREAT MEN and women well: treat them as if they were real:
perhaps they are.

AH, if the rich were rich, as the poor fancy riches!

NOTHING can be preserved that is not good.

MAN IS a piece of the universe made alive.

WITHOUT a rich heart, wealth is an ugly beggar.

MEN are what their mothers made them.

THERE is always safety in valor.

A MAN in debt is so far a slave.

WORDS OF HOSEA BALLOU

THE greatest truths are the simplest.

MODERATION is the keynote of lasting enjoyment.

BETWEEN THE HUMBLE and contrite heart and the majesty of heaven
there are no barriers; the only password is prayer.

THEORIES are very thin and unsubstantial; experience only is tangible.

THE OPPRESSION of any people for opinion's sake has rarely had any other
effect than to fix those opinions deeper, and render them more important.

REAL HAPPINESS is cheap enough, yet how dearly we pay for its counterfeit.

EDUCATION commences at the mother's knee, and every word
spoken within the hearsay of little children tends towards
the formation of character.

PRETENSION almost always overdoes the original, and hence exposes itself.

NOT THE LEAST misfortune in a prominent falsehood is the fact
that tradition is apt to repeat it for truth.

IDLENESS IS emptiness; the tree in which the sap is stagnant,
remains fruitless.

IT IS WHAT we give up, not what we lay up,
that adds to our lasting store.

ENERGY, even like the Biblical grain of mustard-seed,
will remove mountains.

TRUE repentance also involves reform.

WORDS OF WENDELL PHILLIPS

HEARTS are stronger than swords.

WHAT THE PURITANS gave the world was not thought, but action.

TO BE AS GOOD as our fathers, we must be better.

RIGHT IS the eternal sun; the world cannot delay its coming.

HEALTH LIES in labor, and there is no royal road to it but through toil.

COURAGE, purpose, endurance,—these are the tests. He did plant a state so deep that all the world has not been able to root it up.

GOVERNMENTS EXIST to protect the rights of minorities. The loved and the rich need no protection; they have many friends and few enemies.

TAKE THE WHOLE RANGE of imaginative literature, and we are all wholesale borrowers. In every matter that relates to invention, to use, or beauty or form, we are borrowers.

EXIGENCIES CREATE the necessary ability to meet and to conquer them.

GIVE IT ONLY the fulcrum of Plymouth Rock; an idea will upheave the continent.

ETERNAL VIGILANCE is the price of liberty.

WE LIVE under a government of men and morning newspapers.

POWER is ever stealing from the many to the few.

REVOLUTIONS are not made; they come.

When You Have Love

By GLADYS TABER

*J*ENNY PRITCHARD woke up and saw it was a sunny day. Out of all the days in the year, it had to be sunny. She hadn't slept much, but she hurried to the window and looked out and saw a cloud no bigger than a powder puff at the edge of sky beyond the water tower.

Bob was stirring, making little unhappy masculine morning sounds. "Ugh," he said, "woof." He opened a gray eye, whacked at his dark hair sleepily. "Rain?" he asked.

"No, Bob, it's sunny. Just one little cloud beyond the river."

"Time get up, s'pose," he muttered.

Jenny ran up the blinds and let the sun cascade in like a golden river. "I could never have gotten through this day if it had rained," she said solemnly.

"You look awful," said Bob.

Jenny went to the bathroom and started a tub. After all these years, Bob still left his towels in a swatch on the tub edge, and the cap off the toothpaste tube, and splashes of shaving cream on the mirror.

He'd done so when he came in last night. *People don't change much,* she thought. She wiped the mirror and splashed cold water on her face. She felt about ninety-eight. Dark circles underlined her wide dark eyes, her lips were pale, and she had lashed around so much in the bed that the careful wave in her fair hair was decidedly at ebb tide. She looked for wrinkles, but none had come overnight. She hurried with her bath, and started one for Bob.

"You've just got to get up," she said. "Time is flying."

"Ugh," said Bob lucidly. "If the groom feels as bad as I do, he'll call the whole thing off."

"Pull yourself together," said Jenny. "I told you not to racket around half the night with the boys."

"We had to drown our sorrow," he said. "Drowned me, too." But he rolled out and staggered sleepily to the bathroom, stepped into the tub without testing it and howled. "You always try to scald me to death," he yelled.

"You can't get clean with cold water," retorted Jenny. "And please don't wallow. I can't ask Minnie to clean that bathroom this morning again, with all she's got to do."

Just like any other morning, Jenny got into a clean blue wash dress, brushed back her hair, made up her face. Picked up after Bob.

The wedding was at four-thirty. The florist was already downstairs embroiled with delphinium, roses, lilies and chicken wire. From the kitchen came the smell of chicken, light rolls rising and the faint cool scent of cucumber being grated. Minnie and two of her friends were clattering about like nervous jitneys. The doorbell was ringing like a five-alarm fire and the telephone sounded a continual alert.

Banging from the cellar indicated that Michael, the groom, was trying madly to crate a few wedding presents that Mary Lou said had to go with them to the Army post.

More wedding presents were streaming in, and the front door slammed incessantly.

"You'd think buffaloes lived here," grumbled Bob. "Think we ought to sing *Headin' for the Last Roundup* instead of *Lohengrin*."

"Bob," said Jenny, "Bob—how do we know this isn't a terrible mistake? How can we tell? How can we—" She let her hands fall and turned away to hide quick tears.

"Call for Mr. Pritchard!" Minnie bellowed up the stairs.

"I got to have my breakfast," he yelled back. "Tell 'em—never mind, I'll tell 'em myself." He pulled on his soft brown shirt and hurried out.

Jenny made the bed, her hands shaking. *You've made your bed; you have to lie in it,* she thought to herself. She went down the hall, and Mary Lou's door was ajar, and she put her cold hand on the still colder knob and looked in.

Mary Lou was asleep. The way you sleep at nineteen, even in a time of stress—with relaxed hands and quiet breathing! The young, clean, bright hair tumbled on the pillow, her mouth was sweet as a song. Clothes lay strewn everywhere; the dressing case was open on the floor with the handmade ivory wedding nightgown on top, folded over pale blue tissue paper. Beside it was the silver frame holding Mike's picture —Mike in uniform standing by his plane, eyes screwed against sharp desert light, mouth smiling.

Jenny trembled, leaning in the doorway. *Oh, it's a mistake—it should be stopped! It's wrong! Why did I let her? I could have taken her away that first time. Going off to this life, too young, too sheltered—what does she know? I haven't raised her the way I should—she's too innocent, too soft; going away in a dream. Oh, it just can't be!*

Fear tightened her breathing until she opened her mouth to pull the air in stifled lungs. Fear was a sickness, a black icy sickness. She went blindly downstairs, clutching the freshly waxed rail. Mary Lou was to come down those stairs in her misty bridal dress in a few hours, facing a doubtful future with her starry eyes.

But it isn't too late yet! Weddings have been called off before. It can be done. I can have an accident: that will put it off.

Jenny had black coffee. Bob was eating chicken liver and scrambled eggs and a couple of the light rolls that were done, with buckwheat honey. "No use wasting all them livers," Minnie had said.

Three neighbors had come in; they were counting silver and folding linen napkins and tying fruitcake with silver ribbon. The whole house was rioting with people, all busy, all competent, all helping push Mary Lou away to that dreadful desert hole, that two-room shack, that future.

"You're not wanted at all for at least two hours," they said in a Greek chorus. "You just go away and relax, Jenny, so you'll be fresh for the ceremony and the reception."

Michael stuck his head up the cellar stairs. "Hey, Mother Pritchard," he yelled, "do I have to ship all this junk?"

Bob said, "I'll run it down right away."

"Do I smell livers?" Mike mounted the stairs from below. He got a

355

plate and ate ravenously. "I don't suppose I could—just say good morning to her?" Mike looked over a dripping roll.

"You may not," said Jenny.

The two men went away. Jenny looked out, but she didn't want to speak to a single neighbor or child or dog. She had to be alone; she had to work this out. She started upstairs, and the bridesmaids were upstairs in the guest room and the maid of honor was in the sewing room and Mary Lou was still asleep. In Jenny's room the dressmaker was pinning up somebody's slip that was too long.

At one, Minnie was going to serve a buffet luncheon to everybody who was around, on the lawn on the big picnic table. And when Jenny looked out she saw that even that was being fixed—two women were laying a cloth on the table.

Where could she go to hide away? Well, there was only the attic. Silently Jenny slipped up the stairs and managed to lift the trap door that sealed it away when the house was insulated.

The attic was dim and warm and cobwebby, but the sun came in just clearly enough for her to pick her way to the little chair by the desk with the broken front leg. Mary Lou used to play up here on rainy days, cracking butternuts and munching Baldwin apples while she rummaged in old trunks and cut paper dolls from old magazines.

Jenny sat down in the chair and wiped away the filtered dust from the desk top and rested her head on her arms. She could still hear the wedding sounds, but they were faint and remote, like sounds over quiet water. The house fell away from her, fatigue and the still attic and her fear all made her a little lightheaded all at once.

She drowsed a few minutes, and woke, and looked at her watch. Time left. Absently she pulled open the desk drawer; it stuck a little and she wrenched at it. The drawer had old road maps and folders from Sun Valley and Lucerne and a diploma and her D.A.R. certificate. Jenny reached farther, and closed her hand on an old snapshot album. She took it out. There were milky spots of mold on it; she brushed them off carefully.

"My goodness," she said, "I haven't seen this in years."

The album fell open in her lax hands.

"Why, there's Mamma," she said aloud. "I didn't know we had that picture left anywhere."

Mamma wore a duster of linen, and a big flat hat tied down with thick veiling. Voluminous folds of linen hung to her ankles, and her shoes were very pointed and high-heeled. She had on large goggles and gloves. About all you could see of her except for the swaddling was a firm, sensitive mouth and a good chin above the crisp jabot.

That was the day they went to the Dells.

Jenny had a new Peter Thompson middy suit—a scarlet silk tie around the blouse neck, the pleated skirt very trim. Her hair was in braids. Mamma had packed a fried-chicken picnic lunch in the big hamper. Mamma always went everywhere with plenty of food, just in case of emergency. Jenny's first beau, though not really a beau at that age, was allowed to go, too; he and Jenny sat in the back seat, slipping on the seat a little. Father, in duster, goggles and a brimmed straw hat, drove furiously at twenty miles an hour. Dust rose in clouds, the car roared, the horn sounded at every crossroad. Every half hour they waited while Father got a watering can out and filled the big radiator from a farm well.

It was an all-day trip. They had supper on the way back, on a grassy bluff overlooking the river. Two tires were flat and Father had to stop anyway to get out the vulcanizing kit and fix them and pump them up by hand. Mother spread the supper on a clean old tablecloth: the rest of the chicken, sandwiches, spice cookies, crisp dill pickles, green-apple tarts, apples and pears and bananas, coffee and milk, just a snack.

There was a snapshot of them eating, taken by Father. Jenny and the boy were partly hidden by the wicker hamper. You could see one of his gray eyes and his dark hair, and the ribbon on Jenny's fair braids.

Jenny and the boy wandered down to the edge of the water, where sunset made a soft haze of gold. They sat under a willow tree; gray-green leaves trailed in the water, drawn away forever by the tide, and forever held by the tree. They had played so much tennis together, ridden their bicycles, yelled "Gray wolf, gray wolf," dealt out the Flinch cards the winter evenings, these two children sitting there. And now it was different all at once. The all-day trip, the bouncing, beating of the car, the dark clear water of the Dells, the excitement, the fatigue—all these and the sense of being so far from home gave Jenny a strange feeling as she looked at him. The dark head bent above her;

the gray eyes were dark, too, in the pale light. "Jenny," he said, "I love you."

"I love you, too."

The first kiss, drawing them away into the tide like the trailing willow leaves, forever holding them back in a childish dream. The first kiss, his boy's mouth on her cheek, awkward and full of wonder, and her whole body in the Peter Thompson middy suit suddenly not just bones and flesh, but a glory and a fire and a beat of wings.

When they went back, Mamma had gathered up the supper and Father was wiping his hands on a towel, and the car was packed up.

"Come on, children, we're ready to go now. We'll have to hurry to get home before dark. You know we can't drive at night," said Mamma. "I called you. Where have you been?"

"At the edge of the river," said Jenny dreamily.

"Did you get your feet wet?" Young girls in that day never got their feet wet. You could sicken and die of it mysteriously.

They held hands all the way home, under the plaid auto robe. Jenny's hand was small and light in his, and burning hot. She could feel the clasp of his fingers all through her.

Jenny turned the page: snapshots of slumber parties, snapshots of canoeing, snaps of the high-school play, a little out of focus. A fairly clear picture of the class president, who had his head blown off at Verdun—a pleasant smiling boy with blue eyes and a shock of red hair.

"My favorite evening dress," she said aloud.

It was a full-length snap, slightly

brown from glue leaking through. Jenny wore her new chemise frock, slipped over her head; it was rose chiffon, with a low sash of pale blue. She had rose satin slippers, very pointed and narrow, with high heels and real silk stockings. Her hair was piled up in a soft mass of curls. That year she wore a girdle and silk knickers and her slip had real lace around the neck.

The boys were going away to war, singly and in groups. But a lot of them came home all the time from the nearest camps; they were gorgeous in their uniforms, their legs incased to the knees, almost, in putties or wound-up fabric. The pants flared out above, making them all look slim-waisted and flat-hipped. They wore their stiff-brimmed hats at an angle, had their pictures taken with the chin straps down.

Jenny was engaged to Paul Harrison. She had been around with a lot of boys since the picnic at the Dells. The first beau had moved away that fall, gone East to school; his mother and father had died, their house was closed and shuttered. Since then, Mark, of the arrogant mouth and sullen jaw, had come and gone; and Ricky, who died of pneumonia; and Jim, who taught her the tango; and Willis, who promised to build her a yacht someday; and Tony, who gave her the Airedale. She really just had an understanding with Paul, on account of the war and all. But she was embroidering teacups and saucers in red on Irish-linen dish towels, and Mamma was hemstitching pillowslips. Her hope chest was cedar and very big.

The dance was at the Riverview Country Club; Japanese lanterns strung all along the shadowy verandas, clusters of red and gold balloons tied to the pillars to be loosed at the end when they played *Home, Sweet Home.* Paul was tall and handsome in his cavalry officer's uniform. They were dancing while the band played *It's a Long Way to Tipperary.* The moon was like a gardenia.

They were standing near the door, waiting for the next dance, and Paul was laughing down at her and saying, "Maybe we ought to get married right away—what do you think?"

Jenny looked up and saw someone coming down the veranda, the peach glow of the paper lanterns and the white glow of moonlight on his straight easy figure and his dark hair and gray eyes. *Now where,* she thought, *and who*—He came in and stood at the door, and his eyes swept the whole room. They rested on her, and he walked directly over, just as Paul put his arm around her for the dance.

"Hello, Jenny," he said. "That was a wonderful picnic that day we went to the Dells."

The next night they walked in the rain. Jenny had told Paul she was in bed with a headache.

"I'm engaged to Paul," she said soberly.

"Why, Jenny, I thought you were going to wait for me."

"You never even wrote me."

"I did so. I sent you a post card of Bunker Hill."

Jenny laughed. The rain was cool on her face, but her face was hot. The rain was splashing up a little on her white spats and on her snow-white coat, and the brim of her white tricorn hat was soaked. He didn't even notice it. He just walked along in his uniform with the hat tilted over his eyes, and his hand on her arm very firm. It was her best coat, with kimono sleeves and big pearl buttons.

"Well," she said, "now you're going right away again to France. You came back too late."

"Did I?" he asked.

They went up the steps to the porch and he took his handkerchief and wiped the rain from her face, and his fingers brushed her mouth and it was trembling and hot.

"Kiss me, Jenny," he said.

The train left at four in the morning, the long inevitable troop train Fortunately, Mamma and Papa were away for the week end at the papermakers' convention. Mrs. Bascom, the chaperon, went to bed with lumbago. So they sat together on the mohair davenport, sometimes just holding hands, sometimes swept together in a passion of grief that made Jenny cling to him. Her heart was a burning heavy thing in a leaden breast. Her knees were shaky.

"Hey," he said, "you can't cry on me. I've only been back in your life three days." He got up and put a record on the phonograph. "Let's dance."

The fiber needle blurred the music. "There's a long, long trail a-winding, into the land of my dreams—" But when they tried to dance, he only held her close and kissed her hair and kissed her lips.

"Jenny," he said, "I'll come back. And there'll never be any more war to break people's hearts. We have to do this one. But if you weren't so young, so young, Jenny, I'd want to leave you differently."

"How?"

"I'd want to leave you my wife. It wouldn't be fair—but I wish it were." He said, "I want you to be really my own. My own."

"Yes," whispered Jenny.

The train jerked in, long dusty cars. The marching men were tired and pale in the pale light. Lines of women were crying softly or noisily. Flags were flying.

"Good-bye, Jenny," he said. He was grinning down at her now, the love and grief of the night only etched in lines around his tired gray eyes and set mouth. "I'll send you a post card from Paris."

"I still have the one from Bunker Hill," she said.

"I'll phone you if I can get another leave," he promised.

The train pulled away with its terribly precious burden. The townspeople drifted home; Jenny went back to face Paul.

"But you can't possibly be sure like this," he said.

"I know it. But I am."

"You'll change your mind. It's perfectly impossible."

"No, I won't change."

"We'll see. When the war is over, you'll see."

Jenny folded away the beautiful linens and silks and laces and locked the hope chest.

Two pages of the album stuck together. Jenny pulled and the soft paper tore. There she was in her black wool jersey, three yards for the whole dress. She had bobbed her hair that day; it was soft and low over her ears, and had a celluloid barrette holding it in place in back. Her rouge made two bright round spots on her cheeks. Mamma had taken the picture and slanted the camera so that it looked as if Jenny were on a ship, the ship sinking under her.

It was early autumn; the maples were scarlet and gold, Jenny remembered. Mamma was wearing

359

her wool suit with the otter collar and a hat with purple velvet ribbon on it.

"Mamma, I've got to go," Jenny had said, after the phone call. "He's got a four-day leave. We'll have four whole days."

"But, Jenny—"

"Afterward I'll get something to do. Or go back to school. They're having to change the rules now to let the girls who are married go back, just this fall."

Mamma clasped her little firm hands. "Jenny, getting married is—is—"

"Yes, I know."

Then Mamma had come over and kissed her and said, "I think the big Gladstone bag will do."

The tweed suit was packed, with the blue scarf to tuck in at the neck, the black satin sleeveless afternoon dress, the wool jersey, the crepe de Chine, beaded so beautifully, the heavy silk knickers, silk stockings, the white satin nightgown, square-necked, handmade lace framing the neck, the pink nightgown embroidered in blue forget-me-nots, the crepe de Chine robe. "And your galoshes," Mamma said. "It always rains in Boston." No time for a new coat; the old one with the kimono sleeves had to do. "But that satin lining never will show wear," said Mamma, packing a washcloth in a rubber bag, soap and towels and toothbrush and tooth paste in a fancy plaid traveling apron embroidered with flowing words, "Use Me!" High-heeled satin mules. Evening slippers came next with rubber-soled sports shoes, square-toed. On the top, folded in tissue, were the taffeta blouse and the pique shirtwaist and the white crepe de Chine waist, trailing lavender chiffon scarf, the Kewpie doll that Jenny had never left behind her. But the Good Fairy, with outstretched arms, that was luminous at night and she loved so dearly, she had to leave behind.

A last look at her room: the Maxfield Parrish pictures, blue and gold and purple and scarlet; the hand-painted china dresser set with her initials on the hair receiver and the ring tray; the walnut bed with the pink down puff and embroidered bolster cover.

At the station Jenny took a picture of the friends saying good-bye to her. They sat on the baggage truck, and it was because her hands shook so that all their heads were cut off. The picture was in the album, anyway. The serge skirt and arch-support shoes were Nina, the checked dress and patent pumps were Dodo. The fur-lined coat was Bethine. It was too early for it, but it was the new fashion.

There was Father looking grim, wearing his best suit. And Mamma, smiling, brown-eyed, her mouth trembling a little. Her brown broadcloth suit with the beaver collar, the long jacket, the flowered toque.

"Mamma!" said Jenny.

Mamma said, "Keep your money bag pinned in your corset all the time. You never know."

"All aboard—all aboard!" the man shouted down the platform.

Jenny and Mamma clung together and Mamma whispered, "You love him so much, it will be all right. It's fine. Don't worry. Everything will be fine."

The train pulled away. Everything was out of focus except Mamma's face, distinct, smiling, steady.

Jenny turned the last page, skipping the State House and the Sons

360

of Liberty and Paul Revere and Faneuil Hall and the pigeons on Boston Common and the library and the Copley-Plaza and the bronze Indian in front of the Museum of Fine Arts.

The flashlight powder had gone off too soon. It filled the hotel room with its hot brackish smell. Smoke billowed up. The snapshot caught Jenny sitting on the edge of the bed in her pink robe with her silver-backed hairbrush in her hand and her hair not combed at all, tumbled softly about her face. Her eyes had that look of surprise characteristic of all flash pictures, her mouth was partly open.

"Wait a minute!" she had been saying. "I look terrible."

"You're the loveliest thing in the world," he said. "I want this picture to carry right over my heart."

There was a big moon, and the air smelled of the sea, and somebody was playing *Poor Butterfly* somewhere near.

He put the camera down and came over and held her. "Jenny," he said, "no matter what happens, we have had this."

"Yes," she whispered.

"You'd never be sorry?"

"No. I'd never be sorry."

In the first light of dawn, Jenny propped herself up on her elbow and looked at him. He was sleeping soundly and his face looked strong and serene and awfully young. The lines of his body under the cover were strong, too, and young, alive and whole. The anguish that was to come for months and months had already made a darkness in Jenny's heart, but it had no power yet over him. He was in love, he was fulfilled, he had his desire and he was happy.

Jenny touched the dark hair, very gently, and he woke at once, muttering a little and making sleepy masculine movements.

"Ugh," he said, "woof." He looked at his watch and said, "Time get up, s'pose."

Jenny nodded. She raised the green window shade and let the sun pour in, a golden cascade. *I never could have gotten through this day if it had rained,* she said to herself.

She heard him splashing in the bathroom. When he came out and got into his uniform, she went to the tub and picked up the mass of scattered towels, put the cap on the toothpaste tube, wiped shaving cream from the mirror. People's hearts could break and go right on beating.

He came over, smelling of shaving lotion and his first cigarette, and took her in his arms. "I've had everything anyone could want in a lifetime," he said. "I just want you to know that. In case."

"So have I," said Jenny.

When they went out, the light in the street was dazzling. Some soldiers were marching down Summer Street, clean and spotless and young. They were singing, "There's a long, long trail a-winding, into the land of my dreams—"

Jenny looked at his grave, pale face. He gave her a smile. "There's a long, long night of waiting, until my dreams all come true," he sang under his breath. *This is it,* thought Jenny. *This is love. This racking pain, this loss, this fear, this ache in the breast —this is love. This tearing apart. This darkness. This crying in the long empty night. And this glory.*

Jenny closed the snapshot album and wiped the dust from her fingers. A mouse was gnawing inside the attic wall somewhere, a brittle sound. The insulation was supposed to keep mice out. But what insulation could keep the gnawing mice outside of one? Fear stole in the veins on small feet, gnawed at the heart.

She got up, and walked past the old trunks to the dusty window. A German helmet hung on a rusty nail—a canteen and a leather cartridge belt. She pushed them aside; the helmet was deep with dust. She had been so far away, she had to press her hands over her eyes to renew her actual vision. So far away, so long gone.

Under her soft hair, her forehead was damp. Her knees were stiff from sitting so still. She looked out and down and saw the spread of the lawn, and the gold and ivory and dark red of the roses in the border. It wasn't autumn at all, it was June, it was soft and tender June. The late iris was still pale amethyst by the garage. The table was spread; women were moving around it, laughing and talking, carrying big silver bowls and filled platters. They wore short white frocks and pastel uncrushable linens and the young ones had no stockings, little flat sandals on bare feet.

The sound of feet came to her, someone climbing the stairs. Someone had guessed where she was. It was late; her watch had stopped and she shook it, and still the hands did not move. The climbing feet hesitated, came on. Jenny pressed her handkerchief to her forehead, wiped her face, smoothed down her dress.

"Hello," said Bob. "They sent out a search warrant for the lady of the house."

"I just came up here," she said.

He threaded his way between old trunks, broken chairs and past the file of the *National Geographic Magazine*. "I thought this was the only place not too full of people," he said. "You'd think we were entertaining a convention. Michael's down at the hotel, and the women say it's time for lunch; we better appear and have something."

"Is it that late?"

"Yes," he said, "but everything's under control." He stood beside her and put his arm around her. "Jenny," he said, "don't take it so hard."

She rested her head against his shoulder. "I'm all right now," she told him.

"You'll have to clean up"—he ruffled her hair with his hand— "you're a sight! What have you been doing?"

Jenny looked at him with a little smile. "I've been on a long journey," she said.

"Back as far as Boston?" His voice was tender; his gray eyes smiled at her.

"Farther than that. Do you remember the day we went to the Dells?"

"The river," said Bob, "and the willow tree. The first time I kissed you." His hand closed on hers. "You wore a middy suit and a red silk tie and white rubber tennis shoes."

The river had caught them up, swept them along after all. The boy and the girl, innocent and eager, they were gone, gone.

"Well," said Bob, "hard days or easy, we've gotten along, haven't we?" He grinned. "It was a near thing, you almost taking Paul."

"And almost letting you go to France," said Jenny, "without marrying me first."

They went down the steep attic stairs together and Bob locked the door. Mary Lou's door was open, and she was having a tray by the window. The soft summer light came in on her; she had a dreamy look. But her eyes were wide with excitement.

"Hello, you two," she said. "Where have you been?"

"I had to dig your mother out of the attic," said Bob. "The crowd got to be too much for her."

The wedding dress was spread out carefully on the bed; the veil foamed over the edge. The bouquet was in a box and the smell of lilies of the valley came from the cover. Mary Lou had her old dressing gown on, the one that was being left behind for rags. It was the color of her eyes, a soft clear blue.

"Come in," she invited, waving toward the bed. "You could find a spot that isn't covered with junk."

Bob said, "I'll run on down and tell the gang that I've found the missing woman. And fix a plate for her." His hand closed hard once on Jenny's fingers, warm and sure and steady.

Mary Lou stood up and put the tray on the cluttered bed table.

"Mother," she said. "I feel funny inside. My stomach sort of floats."

"I know," said Jenny. What were the last words a mother said to her daughter in the hour before marriage? What distilled from time and living into a secret elixir? Jenny moved slowly across the room.

"Mother!" said Mary Lou, and they were clinging together.

"It's fine," said Jenny, "it will be all right. You love him. Even if you only had him four days," she said, "you would have happiness enough for a lifetime. That's the way it is," she said softly, "when you have love."

When she closed her eyes, she could see the river, flowing dark and swift, and the trailing green branches of the willow, forever pulled out to the flowing water.

LONE WOODSMAN
Ruth Crary

Unhesitatingly he tramps the trail;
Unerringly he turns to left or right,
Where other feet have found and pressed the Braille
Of forest paths long hidden from the sight:
There is no evidence that silently
As gathering mist, in other moons, once walked
Lone brother woodsmen silent here; yet he
Can feel the path that chief and brave have stalked.

So, even so, shall we, unfaltering,
Take up one day the hushed and hidden trail,
Companioned by the ghosts of one far spring.
Intrepid woodsmen, we shall seek the Grail,
Knowing no need of a divining rod,
And *feel* the paths the silent dead have trod.

MAN IS the only animal that is able to profit by past experience.—*William Allen White*

RIGHTEOUS INDIGNATION is your own wrath as opposed to the shocking bad temper of others.—*Elbert Hubbard*

GENIUS IS one per cent inspiration and ninety-nine per cent perspiration.—*Edison*

MY INTEREST IS in the future because I'm going to spend the rest of my life there.—*Charles F. Kettering*

I NEVER DID anything worth doing by accident, nor did any of my inventions come by accident; they came by work.—*Edison*

ART IS SOMETHING to make the heart beat a little warmer. It won't make life longer, but it will make it richer.—*Homer Saint-Gaudens*

IF A MAN'S MIND is filled with memories and reminiscences instead of anticipation, then he is growing old.—*William Lyon Phelps*

HUMAN SLAVERY will not have been fully abolished until every task now accomplished by human hands is turned out by some machine.—*Edison*

SUCCESS IN MARRIAGE is much more than finding the right person: it is a matter of being the right person.—*Rabbi Brickner*

IT IS THE FINAL TEST of a gentleman—his respect for those who can be of no possible service to him.
—*William Lyon Phelps*

DEMOCRACY IS BASED upon the conviction that there are extraordinary possibilities in ordinary people.—*Fosdick*

MODERN AMERICANS

CULTURE IS THE HABIT of being
pleased with the best, and knowing why.—*Henry van Dyke*

THERE IS NO EXPEDIENT to which a man will not go
to avoid the real labor of thinking.—*Edison*

WHEN WHAT YOU HAVE DONE in the past looks large to you,
you have not done much today.—*Elbert Hubbard*

IT IS THE SUPREME ART of the teacher to awaken joy in creative expression and
knowledge.—*Albert Einstein*

DOWN IN THEIR HEARTS, wise men know this truth: the only way to help yourself
is to help others.—*Elbert Hubbard*

AMERICANISM IS NOT alone a matter of birth or ancestry. The real American is
an ideal—a vision yet to be fulfilled.—*Edward W. Bok*

No AMOUNT of experimentation can ever prove me right; a single
experiment may at any time prove me wrong.—*Albert Einstein*

THERE EXIST limitless opportunities in every industry. Where there is an open
mind, there will always be a frontier.—*Charles F. Kettering*

THE CAPACITY OF the human brain is tremendous, but people put
it to no use. They live sedentary mental lives.—*Edison*

IF YOU DO NOT CULTIVATE a taste for music, you will have a miserable time for about a thousand years after you get to heaven.
—*Bishop Hughes*

IF I WERE RUNNING the world I would have it rain
only between two and five A.M. Anyone who was out
then ought to get wet.—*William Lyon Phelps*

365

HAIL COLUMBIA
JOSEPH HOPKINSON

Hail, Columbia! Happy land!
Hail, ye heroes! Heaven-born band!
  Who fought and bled in Freedom's cause,
  Who fought and bled in Freedom's cause,
And when the storm of war was gone,
Enjoyed the peace your valor won.
  Let independence be your boast,
  Ever mindful what it cost;
  Ever grateful for the prize,
  Let its altar reach the skies.

    Firm, united, let us be,
    Rallying round our Liberty;
    As a band of brothers joined,
    Peace and safety we shall find.

Immortal patriots! Rise once more:
Defend your rights, defend your shore:
  Let no rude foe with impious hand,
  Let no rude foe with impious hand,
Invade the shrine where sacred lies
Of toil and blood the well-earned prize.
  While offering peace sincere and just,
  In Heaven we place a manly trust,
  That truth and justice will prevail,
  And every scheme of bondage fail.

Sound, sound, the trump of Fame!
Let Washington's great name
  Ring through the world with loud applause;
  Ring through the world with loud applause;
Let every clime to Freedom dear,
Listen with a joyful ear.
  With equal skill, and godlike power,
  He governs in the fearful hour
  Of horrid war, or guides, with ease,
  The happier times of honest peace.

Behold the chief who now commands,
Once more to serve his country, stands—
  The rock on which the storm will beat;

The rock on which the storm will beat.
But, armed in virtue firm and true,
His hopes are fixed on Heaven and you.
When hope was sinking in dismay,
And glooms obscured Columbia's day,
His steady mind, from changes free,
Resolved on death or liberty.

Firm, united, let us be,
Rallying round our Liberty;
As a band of brothers joined,
Peace and safety we shall find.

FREEDOM FROM WANT

By CARLOS BULOSAN

IF YOU want to know what we are, look upon the farms or upon the hard pavements of the city. You usually see us working or waiting for work, and you think you know us, but our outward guise is more deceptive than our history.

Our history has many strands of fear and hope, that snarl and converge at several points in time and space. We clear the forest and the mountains of the land. We cross the river and the wind. We harness wild beast and living steel. We celebrate labor, wisdom, peace of the soul.

When our crops are burned or plowed under, we are angry and confused. Sometimes we ask if this is the real America. Sometimes we watch our long shadows and doubt the future. But we have learned to emulate our ideals from these trials. We know there were men who came and stayed to build America. We know they came because there is something in America that they needed, and which needed them.

We march on, though sometimes strange moods fill our children. Our march toward security and peace is the march of freedom—the freedom that we should like to become a living part of. It is the dignity of the individual to live in a society of free men, where the spirit of understanding and belief exist; of understanding that all men are equal; that all men, whatever their color, race, religion or estate, should be given equal opportunity to serve themselves and each other according to their needs and abilities.

But we are not really free unless we use what we produce. So long as the fruit of our labor is denied us, so long will want manifest itself in a world of slaves. It is only when we have plenty to eat—plenty of everything—that we begin to understand what freedom means. To us, freedom is not an intangible thing. When we have enough to eat, then we are healthy enough to enjoy what we eat. Then we have the time and ability to read and think and discuss things. Then we are not merely living but also becoming a creative part of life. It is only then that we become a

367

growing part of democracy.

We do not take democracy for granted. We feel it grow in our working together—many millions of us working toward a common purpose. If it took us several decades of sacrifices to arrive at this faith, it is because it took us that long to know what part of America is ours.

Our faith has been shaken many times, and now it is put to question. Our faith is a living thing, and it can be crippled or chained. It can be killed by denying us enough food or clothing, by blasting away our personalities and keeping us in constant fear. Unless we are properly prepared, the powers of darkness will have good reason to catch us unaware and trample our lives.

The totalitarian nations hate democracy. They hate us, because we ask for a definite guaranty of freedom of religion, freedom of expression and freedom from fear and want. Our challenge to tyranny is the depth of our faith in a democracy worth defending. Although they spread lies about us, the way of life we cherish is not dead. The American dream is only hidden away, and it will push its way up and grow again.

We have moved down the years steadily toward the practice of democracy. We become animate in the growth of Kansas wheat or in the ring of Mississippi rain. We tremble in the strong winds of the Great Lakes. We cut timbers in Oregon just as the wild flowers blossom in Maine. We are multitudes in Pennsylvania mines, in Alaskan canneries. We are millions from Puget Sound to Florida, in violent factories, crowded tenements, teeming cities. Our numbers increase as the war revolves into years and increases hunger, disease, death and fear.

But sometimes we wonder if we are really a part of America. We recognize the mainsprings of American democracy in our right to form unions and bargain through them collectively, our opportunity to sell our products at reasonable prices, and the privilege of our children to attend schools where they learn the truth about the world in which they live. We also recognize the forces which have been trying to falsify American history—the forces which drive many Americans to a corner of compromise with those who would distort the ideals of men that died for freedom.

Sometimes we walk across the land looking for something to hold on to. We cannot believe that the resources of this country are exhausted. Even when we see our children suffer humiliations, we cannot believe that America has no more place for us. We realize that what is wrong is not in our system of government, but in the ideals which were blasted away by a materialistic age. We know that we can truly find and identify ourselves with a living tradition if we walk proudly in familiar streets. It is a great honor to walk on the American earth.

If you want to know what we are, look at the men reading books, searching the dark pages of history for the lost word, the key to the mystery of living peace. We are factory hands, field hands, mill hands, searching, building and molding structures. We are doctors, scientists, chemists, discovering and eliminating disease, hunger and antagonism. We are soldiers, Navy men, citizens, guarding the imperishable dream of our fathers to live in freedom. We are the living dream of dead men. We are the living spirit of free men.

Everywhere we are on the march, passing through darkness into a sphere of economic peace. When we have the freedom to think and discuss things without fear, when peace and security are assured, when the futures of our children are ensured—then we have resurrected and cultivated the early beginnings of democracy. And America lives and becomes a growing part of our aspirations again.

We have been marching for the last one hundred and fifty years. We sacrifice our individual liberties, and sometimes we fail and suffer. Sometimes we divide into separate groups and our methods conflict, though we all aim at one common goal. The significant thing is that we march on without turning back. What we want is peace, not violence. We know that we thrive and prosper only in peace. We are the sufferers who suffer for natural love of man for another man, who commemorate the humanities of every man. We are the creators of abundance.

We are the desires of anonymous men. We are the subways of suffering, the well of dignities. We are the living testament of a flowering race.

But our march to freedom is not complete unless want is annihilated. The America we hope to see is not merely a physical but also a spiritual and an intellectual world. We are the mirror of what America *is*. If America wants us to be living and free, then we must be living and free. If we fail, then America fails.

What do we want? We want complete security and peace. We want to share the promises and fruits of American life. We want to be free from fear and hunger.

If you want to know what we are—We are Marching!

AMERICA
(1942)
Adelaide Love

I watch her as she climbs the steep,
A harsh wind tearing at her breast;
With what unfaltering strength and grace
She moves to stand upon the crest.

I mark her as she lifts the lamp
Of freedom over other lands;
For all the wounds upon their palms,
How firm, how beautiful her hands!

I look upon her face, now stained
With tears, and see upon her brow
The selfsame light that always shone—
But brighter now.

HAPPINESS is a habit—cultivate it.—*Elbert Hubbard*

PROFIT IS a by-product of work; happiness is its chief product.—*Henry Ford*

THE UNITED STATES never lost a war or won a conference.—*Will Rogers*

MY PHILOSOPHY OF LIFE: work. Bringing out the secrets of nature, and applying them for the happiness of man. Looking on the bright side of everything.—*Edison*

IT IS ALWAYS the minorities that hold the key of progress; it is always through those who are unafraid to be different that advance comes to human society.—*Raymond Blaine Fosdick*

IN EDUCATION WE ARE STRIVING not to teach youth to make a living, but to teach youth to make a life, in the sense that a life is useful happiness and well-spent leisure.—*William Allen White*

LIFE SEEMS TO ME not a state of being, but a process of becoming. It is an adventure, a training, a testing to try the soul's strength on, to educate the man.—*Henry van Dyke*

THERE IS no substitute for hard work.—*Edison*

EVERY GREAT ADVANCE in science has issued from a new audacity of imagination.—*John Dewey*

A CRITIC is a legless man who teaches running.—*Channing Pollock*

To AVOID criticism, do nothing, say nothing, be nothing.—*Elbert Hubbard*

THE MOST useful virtue is patience.—*John Dewey*

MODERN AMERICANS

RECIPE for having friends: be one.—*Elbert Hubbard*

ONCE PEOPLE were driven . . . . *Someday* they will be inspired.
—*Dr. Walter Dill Scott*

AN IDEAL WIFE is any woman who has an ideal husband.—*Booth Tarkington*

DON'T LOSE FAITH in humanity. Think of the hundred ten million
people in the United States who have never played you a single
nasty trick.—*Elbert Hubbard*

IT IS NOT TOLERANCE that one is entitled to in America. It is the
right of every citizen in America to be treated by other citizens as
an equal.—*Wendell L. Willkie*

ALL TRUE CIVILIZATION is ninety per cent heirlooms and memories—an
accumulation of small but precious deposits left by the countless generations that have gone before us.—*Robert I. Gannon, S. J.*

I CAN'T STAND JINGLE—where the thought is twisted out of shape
just to make it rime. But I like *Evangeline*, *Enoch Arden*, and things
like that. These I call poetry. But ah, Shakespeare! That's where
you get ideas. He would have been an inventor, a wonderful
inventor, if he had turned his mind to it. He seemed to see the
inside of everything.—*Edison*

I LIKE TO SEE a man get mad sometimes and have some bad habits too. I don't
like them when they're too good.—*Edison*

IMAGINATION is more important than knowledge.—*Albert Einstein*

EVERYTHING comes to him who hustles while he waits.—*Edison*

I WANT to do a lot more thinking
before I die.—*Edison*

MY AMERICA

By John Buchan (Lord Tweedsmuir)

A great Governor General of Canada, shortly before his death in 1940, talks about America.

THE TITLE of this chapter exactly defines its contents. It presents the American scene as it appears to one observer—a point of view which does not claim to be that mysterious thing, objective truth. There will be no attempt to portray the "typical" American, for I have never known one. I have met a multitude of individuals, but I should not dare to take any one of them as representing his country—as being that other mysterious thing, the average man. You can point to certain qualities which are more widely distributed in America than elsewhere, but you will scarcely find human beings who possess all these qualities. One good American will have most of them; another, equally good and not less representative, may have few or none. So I shall eschew generalities. If you cannot indict a nation, no more can you label it like a museum piece.

Half the misunderstandings between Britain and America are due to the fact that neither will regard the other as what it is—in an important sense of the word—a foreign country. Each thinks of the other as a part of itself which has somehow gone off the lines. An Englishman is always inclined to resent the unfamiliar when it is found under conditions for which he thinks he has some responsibility. He can appreciate complete and utter strangeness, and indeed show himself highly sympathetic towards it; but for variations upon his own ways—divergencies in speech, food, clothes, social habits—he has little tolerance. He is not very happy even in his own colonies and dominions, and in America he can be uncommonly ill at ease.

On a higher level, when it comes to assessing spiritual values, he often shows the same mixture of surprise and disappointment. America has lapsed from the family tradition; what would have been pardonable and even commendable in a foreigner is blameworthy in a cousin. Matthew Arnold, for example, was critical of certain American traits, not on their merits, but because they were out of tune with that essential European tradition of which he considered himself the guardian. The American critic can be not less intolerant, and for much the same reason. His expositions of England are often like sermons preached in a Home for Fallen Women, the point being that she has fallen, that her defects are a discredit to her relations, that she has let down her kin, and suffered the old home to fall into disrepute. This fretfulness can only be cured, I think, by a frank recognition of the real foreignness of the two peoples. No doubt they had a common ancestor, but he is of little avail against the passage of time and the estranging seas.

I first discovered America through books. Not the tales of Indians and the Wild West which entranced my boyhood; those seemed to belong to no particular quarter of the globe, but to an indefinable land of romance, and I was not cognisant of any nation behind them. But when I became interested in literature I came strongly under the spell of New England. Its culture seemed to me to include what was best in Europe's, winnowed and clarified. Perhaps it was especially fitted to attract youth, for it was not too difficult or too recondite, but followed the "main march of the human affections," and it had the morning freshness of a young people. Its cheerfulness atoned for its occasional bleakness and anaemia. Lowell was the kind of critic I wanted; learned, rational, never freakish, always intelligible. Emerson's gnomic wisdom was a sound manual for adolescence, and of Thoreau I became—and for long remained—an ardent disciple. To a Scot of my upbringing there was something congenial in the simplicity, the mild austerity, and the girded discipline of the New England tradition. I felt that it had been derived from the same sources as our own.

Then, while I was at Oxford, I read Colonel Henderson's *Stonewall Jackson* and became a student of the American Civil War. I cannot say what especially attracted me to that campaign: partly, no doubt, the romance of it, the chivalry and the supreme heroism; partly its extraordinary technical interest, both military and political; but chiefly, I think, because I fell in love with the protagonists. I had found the kind of man that I could wholeheartedly admire. Since those days my study of the Civil War has continued, I have visited most of its battlefields, I have followed the trail of its great marches, I have read widely in its literature; indeed, my memory has become so stored with its details that I have often found myself able to tell the

descendants of its leaders facts about their forbears of which they had never heard.

My interest soon extended from the soldiers to the civilians, and I acquired a new admiration for Abraham Lincoln. Then it was enlarged to include the rest of America's history —the first settlements, the crossing of the Appalachians, the Revolution, the building of the West. Soon America, instead of being the unstoried land which it appears to most English travellers, became for me the home of a long tradition and studded with sacred places. I dare to say that no American was ever more thrilled by the prospect of seeing Westminster Abbey and the Tower, Winchester and Oxford, than I was by the thought of Valley Forge and the Shenandoah and the Wilderness.

I came first into the United States by way of Canada—a good way to enter, for English eyes are already habituated to the shagginess of the landscape and can begin to realize its beauties. My first reflection was that no one had told me how lovely the country was. I mean *lovely*, not vast and magnificent. I am not thinking of the Grand Canyon and the Yosemite and the Pacific coast, but of the ordinary rural landscape. There is much of the land which I have not seen, but in the East and the South and the Northwest I have collected a gallery of delectable pictures. I think of the farms which are clearings in the Vermont and New Hampshire hills, the flowery summer meadows, the lush cowpastures with an occasional stump to remind one that it is old forest land, the quiet lakes and the singing streams, the friendly accessible mountains; the little country towns of

Massachusetts and Connecticut with their village greens and elms and two-century-old churches and court-houses; the secret glens of the Adirondacks and the mountain mea-dows of the Blue Ridge; the long-settled champaign of Maryland and Pennsylvania; Virginian manors more Old-England perhaps than anything we have at home; the exquisite links with the past like much of Boston and Charleston and all of Annapolis; the sunburnt aro-matic ranges of Montana and Wyo-ming; the Pacific shores where from snow mountains fishable streams descend through some of the noblest timber on earth to an enchanted sea.

It is a country most of which I feel to be in a special sense "habitable," designed for homes, adapted to hu-man uses, a friendly land. I like, too, the way in which the nomenclature reflects its history, its racial varieties, its odd cultural mixtures, the gran-diose and the homespun rubbing shoulders. That is how places should be named. I have no objection to Mechanicsville and Higginsville and Utica and Syracuse. They are a legitimate part of the record. And behind are the hoar-ancient memor-ials of the first dwellers, names like symphonies—Susquehanna, Ticon-deroga, Shenandoah, Wyoming.

"Ah, my cabbages!" Henry Adams wrote, "when will you ever fathom the American? Never in your sweet lives." He proceeds in his genial way to make epigrams about his own New Englanders: "Improvised Europeans we were and—Lord God!—how thin!"—"Thank God I never was cheerful. I come from the happy stock of the Mathers, who, as you remember, passed sweet mornings reflecting on the goodness of God and the damnation of infants." Where an Adams scrupled to tread it is not for a stranger to rush in. But I would humbly suggest a correction to one reading which, I think, has the authority of Robert Louis Stevenson. America is, no doubt, a vast country, though it can be comfortably put inside Canada. But it is not in every part a country of wide horizons. Dwellers on the Blue Ridge, on the prairies, and on the western ranges may indeed live habitually with huge spaces of land and sky, but most of America, and some of its most famous parts, is pockety, snug and cosy, a sanctuary rather than a watch-tower. To people so domiciled its vastness must be like the mathematician's space-time, a concept apprehended by the mind and not a percept of the eye. "The largeness of Nature and of this nation were monstrous without a corresponding largeness and gener-osity of the spirit of the citizen." That is one of Walt Whitman's best-known sayings, but let us remember that the bigness of their country is for most Americans something to be learned and imaginatively understood, and not a natural deduction from co-habiting with physical immensities.

Racially they are the most varie-gated people on earth. The prepon-derance of the Anglo-Saxon stock disappeared in the Civil War. Look today at any list of names in a society or a profession and you will find that, except in the Navy, the bulk are from the continent of Europe. In his day Matthew Arnold thought that the chief source of the strength of the American people lay in their homo-geneity and the absence of sharply defined classes, which made revolu-tion unthinkable. Other observers, like Henry James, have deplored the lack of such homogeneity and wished

374

for their country the "close and complete consciousness of the Scots." (I pause to note that I cannot imagine a more nightmare conception. What would happen to the world if a hundred and thirty million Scotsmen, with their tight, compact nationalism, were living in the same country?) I am inclined to query the alleged absence of classes, for I have never been in any part of the United States where class distinctions did not hold. There is an easy friendliness of manner which conceals a strong class pride, and the basis of that pride is not always, or oftenest, plutocratic. Apart from the social snobbery of the big cities, there seems to be everywhere an innocent love of grades and distinctions which is enough to make a Communist weep. I have known places in the South where there was a magnificent aristocratic egalitarianism. Inside a charmed circle all were equal. The village postmistress, having had the right kind of great-great-grandmother, was an honoured member of society, while the immigrant millionaire, who had built himself a palace, might as well have been dead. And this is true not only of the New England F.F.M.'s and the Virginian F.F.V.'s, the districts with long traditions, but of the raw little townships in the Middle West. They, too, have their "best" people who had ancestors, though the family tree may only have sprouted for two generations.

No country can show such a wide range of type and character, and I am so constituted that in nearly all I find something to interest and attract me. This is more than a temperamental bias, for I am very ready to give reasons for my liking. I am as much alive as anyone to the weak and ugly things in American life: areas, both urban and rural, where the human economy has gone rotten; the melting-pot which does not always melt; the eternal coloured problem; a constitutional machine which I cannot think adequately represents the efficient good sense of the American people; a brand of journalism which fatigues with its ruthless snappiness and uses a speech so disintegrated that it is incapable of expressing any serious thought or emotion; the imbecile patter of high-pressure salesmanship; an academic jargon, used chiefly by psychologists and sociologists, which is hideous and almost meaningless. Honest Americans do not deny these blemishes; indeed they are apt to exaggerate them, for they are by far the sternest critics of their own country. For myself, I would make a double plea in extenuation. These are defects from which today no nation is exempt, for they are the fruits of a mechanical civilisation, which perhaps are more patent in America, since everything there is on a large scale. Again, you can set an achievement very much the same in kind against nearly every failure. If her historic apparatus of government is cranky, she is capable of meeting the "instant need of things" with brilliant improvisations. Against economic plague-spots she can set great experiments in charity; against journalistic baby-talk a standard of popular writing in her best papers which is a model of idiom and perspicuity; against catch-penny trade methods many solidly founded, perfectly organised commercial enterprises; against the jargon of the half-educated professor much noble English prose in the great tradition. That is why it is so foolish to generalise about America.

You no sooner construct a rule than it is shattered by the exceptions.

As I have said, I have a liking for almost every kind of American (except the kind who decry their country). I have even a sneaking fondness for George Babbitt, which I fancy is shared by his creator. But there are two types which I value especially, and which I have never met elsewhere in quite the same form. One is the pioneer. No doubt the physical frontier of the United States is now closed, but the pioneer still lives, though the day of the covered wagon is over. I have met him in the New England hills, where he is grave, sardonic, deliberate in speech; in the South, where he has a ready smile and a soft, caressing way of talking; in the ranges of the West, the cow-puncher with his gentle voice and his clear, friendly eyes which have not been dulled by reading print—the real thing, far removed from the vulgarities of film and fiction. At his best, I think, I have found him as a newcomer in Canada, where he is pushing north into districts like the Peace River, pioneering in the old sense. By what signs is he to be known? Principally by the fact that he is wholly secure, that he possesses his soul, that he is the true philosopher. He is one of the few aristocrats left in the world. He has a right sense of the values of life, because his cosmos embraces both nature and man. I think he is the most steadfast human being now alive.

The other type is at the opposite end of the social scale, the creature of a complex society who at the same time is not dominated by it, but, while reaping its benefits, stands a little aloof. In the older countries culture, as a rule, leaves some irregularity like an excrescence in a shapely tree-trunk, some irrational bias, some petulance or prejudice. You have to go to America, I think, for the wholly civilised man who has not lost his natural vigour or agreeable idiosyncrasies, but who sees life in its true proportions and has a fine balance of mind and spirit. It is a character hard to define, but anyone with a wide American acquaintance will know what I mean. They are people in whom education has not stunted any natural growth or fostered any abnormality. They are Greek in their justness of outlook, but Northern in their gusto. Their eyes are shrewd and candid, but always friendly. As examples I would cite, among friends who are dead, the names of Robert Bacon, Walter Page, Newton Baker, and Dwight Morrow.

But I am less concerned with special types than with the American people as a whole. Let me try to set down certain qualities which seem to me to flourish more lustily in the United States than elsewhere. Again, let me repeat, I speak of America only as I know it; an observer with a different experience might not agree with my conclusions.

First I would select what, for want of a better word, I should call home-liness. It is significant that the ordinary dwelling, though it be only a shack in the woods, is called not a house, but a home. This means that the family, the ultimate social unit, is given its proper status as the foundation of society. Even among the richer classes I seem to find a certain pleasing domesticity. English people of the same rank are separated by layers of servants from the basic work of the household, and know very little about it. In America the kitchen is not too far away from the drawing-room, and it is recognised, as Heraclitus said, that the gods may dwell there. But I am thinking chiefly of the ordinary folk, especially those of narrow means. It is often said that Americans are a nomad race, and it is true that they are very ready to shift their camp; but the camp, however bare, is always a home. The cohesion of the family is close, even when its members are scattered. This is due partly to the tradition of the first settlers, a handful in an unknown land; partly to the history of the frontier, where the hearth-fire burnt brighter when all around was cold and darkness. The later immigrants from Europe, feeling at last secure, were able for the first time to establish a family base, and they cherished it zealously. This ardent domesticity has had its bad effects on American literature, inducing a sentimentality which makes a too crude frontal attack on the emotions, and which has produced as a reaction a not less sentimental "toughness." But as a social cement it is beyond price. There have been many to laugh at the dullness and pettiness of the "small town." From what I know of small-town life elsewhere, I suspect obtuseness in the satirists.

Second, I would choose the sincere and widespread friendliness of the people. Americans are interested in the human race, and in each other. Deriving doubtless from the old frontier days, there is a general helpfulness which I have not found in the same degree elsewhere. A homesteader in Dakota will accompany a traveller for miles to set him on the right road. The neighbours will rally round one of their number in distress with the loyalty of a Highland clan. This friendliness is not a self-conscious duty so much as an instinct. A squatter in a cabin will share his scanty provender and never dream that he is doing anything unusual.

American hospitality, long as I have enjoyed it, still leaves me breathless. The lavishness with which a busy man will give up precious time to entertain a stranger to whom he is in no way bound remains for me one of the wonders of the world. No doubt this friendliness, since it is an established custom, has its fake side. The endless brotherhoods and sodalities into which people brigade themselves encourage a geniality which is more a mannerism than an index of character, a tiresome, noisy, back-slapping heartiness. But that is the exception, not the rule. Americans like company, but though they are gregarious they do not lose themselves in the crowd. Waves of mass emotion may sweep the country, but they are transient things and do not submerge for long the stubborn rock of individualism. That is to say, people can be led, but they will not be driven. Their love of human companionship is based not on self-distrust, but on a genuine liking for their kind. With them the sense of a common humanity is a warm and constant instinct and not a doctrine of the schools or a slogan of the hustings.

Lastly—and this may seem a paradox—I maintain that they are fundamentally modest. Their interest in others is a proof of it; the Aristotelian Magnificent Man was interested in nobody but himself. As a nation they are said to be sensitive to criticism; that surely is modesty, for the truly arrogant care nothing for the opinion of other people. Above all they can laugh at themselves, which is not possible for the immodest. They are their own shrewdest and most ribald critics. It is charged against them that they are inclined to boast unduly about those achievements and about the greatness of their country, but a smug glorying in them is found only in the American of the caricaturist. They rejoice in showing their marvels to a visitor with the gusto of children exhibiting their toys to a stranger, an innocent desire, without any unfriendly gloating, to make others partakers in their satisfaction. If now and then they are guilty of bombast, it is surely a venial fault. The excited American talks of his land very much, I suspect, as the Elizabethans in in their cups talked of England. The foreigner who strayed into the Mermaid Tavern must often have listened to heroics which upset his temper.

The native genius, in humour, and in many of the public and private relations of life, is for overstatement, a high-coloured, imaginative, paradoxical extravagance. The British gift is for understatement. Both are legitimate figures of speech. They serve the same purpose, for they call attention to a fact by startling the hearer, since manifestly they are not the plain truth. Personally I delight in both mannerisms and would not for the world have their possessors reject them. They serve the same purpose in another and a subtler sense, for they can be used to bring novel and terrible things within the pale of homely experience. I remember on the Western Front in 1918 that two divisions, British and American, aligned side by side, suffered a heavy shelling. An American sergeant described it in racy and imaginative speech which would have been appropriate to the Day of Judgment. A British sergeant merely observed that "Kaiser 'ad been a bit 'asty." Each had a twinkle in his eye; each in his national idiom was making frightfulness endurable by domesticating it.

The United States is the richest, and, both actually and potentially, the most powerful state on the globe. She has much, I believe, to give to the world; indeed, to her hands is chiefly entrusted the shaping of the future. If democracy in the broadest and truest sense is to survive, it will be mainly because of her guardianship. For, with all her imperfections, she has a clearer view than any other people of the democratic fundamentals.

She starts from the right basis, for she combines a firm grip on the past with a quick sense of present needs and a bold outlook on the future. This she owes to her history; the combination of the British tradition with the necessities of a new land; the New England township and the Virginian manor *plus* the frontier. Much of that tradition was relinquished as irrelevant to her needs, but much remains: a talent for law which is not incompatible with a lawless practice; respect for a certain type of excellence in character which has made her great men uncommonly like our own; a disposition to compromise, but only after a good deal of arguing; an intense dislike of dictation. To these instincts the long frontier struggles added courage in the face of novelties, adaptability, enterprise, a doggedness which was never lumpish, but alert and expectant.

That is the historic basis of America's democracy, and today she is the chief exponent of a creed which I believe on the whole to be the best in this imperfect world. She is the chief exponent for two reasons. The first is her size; she exhibits its technique in large type, so that he who runs may read. More important, she exhibits it in its most intelligible form, so that its constituents are obvious. Democracy has become with many an unpleasing parrot-cry, and, as I have urged elsewhere in this book, it is well to be clear what it means. It is primarily a spiritual testament, from which certain political and economic orders naturally follow. But the essence is the testament; the orders may change while the testament stands. This testament, this ideal of citizenship, she owes to no one teacher. There was a time when I fervently admired Alexander Hamilton and could not away with Jefferson; the latter only began to interest me, I think, after I had seen the University of Virginia, which he created. But I deprecate partisanship in those ultimate matters. The democratic testament derives from Hamilton as well as from Jefferson.

It has two main characteristics. The first is that the ordinary man believes in himself and in his ability, along with his fellows, to govern his country. It is when a people loses its self-confidence that it surrenders its soul to a dictator or an oligarchy. In Mr. Walter Lippmann's tremendous metaphor, it welcomes manacles to prevent its hands shaking. The second is the belief, which is fundamental also in Christianity, of the worth of every human soul—the worth, not the equality. This is partly an honest emotion, and partly a reasoned principle—that something may be made out of anybody, and that there is something likeable about everybody if you look for it—or, in canonical words, that ultimately there is nothing common or unclean.

The democratic testament is one lesson that America has to teach the world. A second is a new reading of nationalism. Some day and somehow the peoples must discover a way to brigade themselves for peace. Now, there are on the globe only two proven large-scale organisations of social units, the United States and the British Empire. The latter is not for export, and could not be duplicated; its strength depends upon a thousand-year-old monarchy and a store of unformulated traditions. But the United States was the conscious work of men's hands, and a task which has once been performed can be performed again. She is the supreme example of a federation in being, a federation which recognises the rights and individuality of the parts, but accepts the overriding interests of the whole. To achieve this compromise she fought a desperate war. If the world is ever to have prosperity and peace, there must be some kind of federation—I will not say of democracies, but of states which accept the reign of Law. In such a task she seems to me to be the predestined leader. Vigorous as her patriotism is, she has escaped the jealous, barricadoed nationalism of the Old World. Disraeli, so often a prophet in spite of himself, in 1863, at a critical moment of the Civil War, spoke memorable words:

"There is a grave misapprehension, both in the ranks of Her Majesty's Government and of Her Majesty's Opposition, as to what constitutes the true meaning of the American democracy. The American democracy is not made up of the scum of the great industrial cities of the United States, nor of an exhausted middle class that speculates in stocks and calls that progress. The American democracy is made up of something far more stable, that may ultimately decide the fate of the two Americas and of 'Europe.' "

For forty years I have regarded America not only with a student's interest in a fascinating problem, but with the affection of one to whom she has become almost a second motherland. Among her citizens I count many of my closest friends; I have known all her presidents, save one, since Theodore Roosevelt, and all her ambassadors to the Court of Saint James's since John Hay; for five years I have been her neighbour in Canada. But I am not blind to the grave problems which confront her. Democracy, after all, is a negative thing. It provides a fair field for the Good Life, but it is not in itself the Good Life. In these days when lovers of freedom may have to fight for their cause, the hope is that the ideal of the Good Life, in which alone freedom has any meaning, will acquire a stronger potency. It is the task of civilisation to raise every citizen above want, but in so doing to permit a free development and avoid the slavery of the beehive and the antheap. A humane economic policy must not be allowed to diminish the stature of man's spirit. It is because I believe that in the American people the two impulses are of equal strength that I see her in the vanguard of that slow upward trend, undulant or spiral, which today is our modest definition of progress. Her major prophet is still Whitman. "Everything comes out of the dirt—everything; everything comes out of the people, everyday people, the people as you find them and leave them; people, people, just people!"

It is only out of the dirt that things grow.

THE FAITH WHICH DWELLS WITHIN
Maxwell Anderson

A city is but the outer hull, or garment,
of the faith which dwells within. Its palaces
and walls that stand up nobly in the air
and seem so tough and durable, are blown
into these shapes by the spirit which inhabits—
blown like a bubble, and will subside again
when the spirit is withdrawn. And what is true
of cities is true of kingdoms. For a cycle of years
they keep their faith, and this faith holds them steady
against the winds. But when they cease to believe
only a little while, the high roofs take rain,
and the walls sink to the moat. There was once a city
whose walls were destroyed by music blown against them,
but the walls of every city are raised up
by music and are held foursquare in the sun
by a people's secret singing.

BEACONS

MILDRED PLEW MEIGS

Sometimes at evening like a wing
   Across my windowpane,
I watch the Lindbergh beacon swing
   My city on the plain;

And as it swings it seems to sweep
   The roofs and spires away,
Until the city sinks to sleep
   And prairie grasses sway.

Along the dark the beacon breaks
   To roll the record back;
Again the covered wagon takes
   The rutted prairie track;

Again the trapper traps for skins,
   The savage prowls the mire;
Again the prairie mother spins
   Beside the cabin fire;

Again small beacons shine by night
   Throughout the prairie gloam,
As little girls set candlelight
   To guide their fathers home.

And so the shadows shuffle past
   Until my picture wanes,
And overhead I hear at last
   The drone of aeroplanes;

And as the grasses cease to sway,
   The prairie disappears,
I think how signals shine today
   For other pioneers,

How light will never fail to break,
   On land and air and sea,
For men who give their lives to make
   The trails of history.

FLAG AT THE PEAK

A Holmes Letter recalled by Catherine Drinker Bowen

In February, 1931, Justice Oliver Wendell Holmes of the United States Supreme Court had a letter from President E. O. Holland of the State College of Washington. The boys out there wanted, it seemed, to celebrate the Justice's approaching ninetieth birthday. Would the Justice be kind enough to write a word of greeting for the occasion?

The Justice would. Sitting at the desk in his upstairs study on I street, in Washington, D.C., facing the mantel over which hung his sword with the colors of the Twentieth Regiment, Massachusetts Volunteer Infantry, Holmes wrote a few lines in that strong, too swift handwriting that is the despair of his biographers.

I do not know of a more magnificent message. Nor does it detract from the message to recall that when the Justice wrote it he was alone in the world; his wife had died the year before, his friends were gone. There was no one, he said, to call him by his first name. Even the work he loved, the daily routine of the Court, must soon, he knew, be relinquished because of his failing powers. Here is what the Justice wrote:

SUPREME COURT OF THE
UNITED STATES
WASHINGTON, D. C.

February 24, 1931
For March 8

MY DEAR SIR:

On the eighth of March, 1862, sixty-nine years ago, the sloop *Cumberland* was sunk by the *Merrimac*, off Newport News. The vessel went down with her flag flying—and when a little later my regiment arrived to begin the campaign on the Peninsula I saw the flag still flying above the waters beneath which the *Cumberland* lay. It was a lifelong text for a young man. Fight to the end and go down with your flag at the peak. I hope that I shall be able to do it—and that your students may live and die by the same text.

Very sincerely yours,
(*signed*) O. W. HOLMES

E. O. Holland
President, State College
of Washington

THE FOUR FREEDOMS
By FRANKLIN DELANO ROOSEVELT

"IN THE future days, which we seek to make secure, we look forward for a world founded upon four essential human freedoms.

"The first is freedom of speech and expression—everywhere in the world.

"The second is freedom of every person to worship God in his own way—everywhere in the world.

"The third is freedom from want—which, translated into world terms, means economic understandings which will secure to every nation a healthy peaceful life for its inhabitants—everywhere in the world.

"The fourth is freedom from fear—which, translated into world terms, means a worldwide reduction of armaments to such a point and in such a thorough fashion that no nation will be in a position to commit an act of aggression against any neighbor—anywhere in the world."

382

THE PROMISE OF AMERICA
By Thomas Wolfe

Go, SEEKER, if you will, throughout the land and you will find us burning in the night.

There where the hackles of the Rocky Mountains blaze in the blank and naked radiance of the moon, go make your resting stool upon the highest peak. Can you not see us now? The continental wall juts sheer and flat, its huge black shadow on the plain, and the plain sweeps out against the East, two thousand miles away. The great snake that you see there is the Mississippi River.

Behold the gem-strung towns and cities of the good, green East, flung like star-dust through the field of night. That spreading constellation to the north is called Chicago, and that giant wink that blazes in the moon is the pendant lake that it is built upon. Beyond, close-set and dense as a clenched fist, are all the jeweled cities of the eastern seaboard. There's Boston, ringed with the bracelet of its shining little towns, and all the lights that sparkle on the rocky indentations of New England. Here, southward and a little to the west, and yet still coasted to the sea, is our intensest ray, the splintered firmament of the towered island of Manhattan. Round about her, sown thick as grain, is the glitter of a hundred towns and cities. The long chain of lights there is the necklace of Long Island and the Jersey shore. Southward and inland, by a foot or two, behold the duller glare of Philadelphia. Southward further still, the twin constellations—Baltimore and Washington. Westward, but still within the borders of the good, green East, that night-time glow and

smolder of hell-fire is Pittsburgh. Here, St. Louis, hot and humid in the cornfield belly of the land, and bedded on the mid-length coil and fringes of the snake. There at the snake's mouth, southward six hundred miles or so, you see the jeweled crescent of old New Orleans. Here, west and south again, you see the gemmy glitter of the cities on the Texas border.

Turn now, seeker, on your resting stool atop the Rocky Mountains, and look another thousand miles or so across moon-blazing fiend-worlds of the Painted Desert and beyond Sierras' ridge. That magic congeries of lights there to the west, ringed like a studded belt around the magic setting of its lovely harbor, is the fabled town of San Francisco. Below it, Los Angeles and all the cities of the California shore. A thousand miles to north and west, the sparkling towns of Oregon and Washington.

Observe the whole of it, survey it as you might survey a field. Make it your garden, seeker, or your backyard patch. Be at ease in it. It's your oyster—yours to open if you will. Don't be frightened, it's not so big now, when your footstool is the Rocky Mountains. Reach out and dip a hatful of cold water from Lake Michigan. Drink it—we've tried it—you'll not find it bad. Take your shoes off and work your toes down in the river oozes of the Mississippi bottom—it's very refreshing on a hot night in the summertime. Help yourself to a bunch of Concord grapes up there in northern New York state—they're getting good now. Or raid that watermelon patch down there in Georgia. Or, if you like, you can try the Rocky Fords here at your elbow, in Colorado. Just make yourself at home, refresh yourself, get the feel of things, adjust your sights, and get the scale. It's your pasture now, and it's not so big—only three thousand miles from east to west, only two thousand miles from north to south— but all between, where ten thousand points of light prick out the cities, towns, and villages, there, seeker, you will find us burning in the night.

Here, as you pass through the brutal sprawl, the twenty miles of rails and rickets, of the South Chicago slums—here, in an unpainted shack, is a Negro boy, and, seeker, he is burning in the night. Behind him is a memory of the cotton fields, the flat and mournful pineland barrens of the lost and buried South, and at the fringes of the pine another shack, with mammy and eleven children. Farther still behind, the slave-driver's whip, the slave ship, and, far off, the jungle dirge of Africa. And before him, what? A roped-in ring, a blaze of lights, across from him a white champion; the bell, the opening, and all around the vast sea-roaring of the crowd. Then the lightning feint and stroke, the black panther's paw—the hot, rotating presses, and the rivers of sheeted print! O seeker, where is the slave ship now?

Or there, in the clay-baked piedmont of the South, that lean and tan-faced boy who sprawls there in the creaking chair among admiring cronies before the open doorways of the fire department, and tells them how he pitched the team to shut-out victory today. What visions burn, what dreams possess him, seeker of the night? The packed stands of the stadium, the bleachers sweltering with their unshaded hordes, the faultless velvet of the diamond, unlike the clay-baked outfields down in Georgia. The mounting roar of eighty thousand voices and Gehrig coming up to bat, the boy himself upon the pitching mound, the lean face steady as a hound's; then the nod, the signal, and the wind-up, the rawhide arm that snaps and crackles like a whip, the small white bullet of the blazing ball, its loud report in the oiled pocket of the catcher's mitt, the umpire's thumb jerked upward, the clean strike.

Or there again, in the east-side of Manhattan, two blocks away from the East River, a block away from the gas-house district and its thuggery, there in the swarming tenement, shut in his sweltering cell, breathing the sun-baked air through opened window at the fire escape, celled there away into a little semblance of privacy and solitude from all the brawling and vociferous life and argument of his family and the seething hive around him, the boy sits and pores upon his book. In shirt-sleeves, bent above his table to meet the hard glare of a naked bulb, he sits with gaunt, starved face converging to his huge nose, the weak eyes squinting painfully through his thick-lens glasses, his greasy hair roached back in oily scrolls above the slanting cage of his painful and constricted brow. And for what? For what this agony of concentration? For what this hell of effort? For what this intense withdrawal from the poverty and squalor of dirty brick and rusty fire escapes, from the raucous cries and violence and never-ending noise? For what? Because, brother, he is burning in the night. He sees the class, the lecture room, the shining apparatus of gigantic laboratories, the open field of scholarship and pure research, certain knowledge, and the world distinction of an Einstein name.

So, then, to every man his chance —to every man, regardless of his birth, his shining, golden opportunity—to every man the right to live, to work, to be himself, and to become whatever thing his manhood and his vision can combine to make him— this, seeker, is the promise of America.

CREED

By WENDELL L. WILLKIE

I BELIEVE in America because in it we are free—free to choose our government, to speak our minds, to observe our different religions.

Because we are generous with our freedom, we share our rights with those who disagree with us.

Because we hate no people and covet no people's lands.

Because we are blessed with a natural and varied abundance.

Because we have great dreams and because we have the opportunity to make those dreams come true.

WHO LOVES HIS COUNTRY

NANCY BYRD TURNER

Who loves his country will not rest
   Content with vow and pledge alone.
But flies her banner in his breast
   And counts her destiny his own—
Not only when the bugle plays
   Stands forth to give his life for her,
But on the field of common days
   Is strong to live his life for her;
He is not satisfied to claim
   As heritage, her power and fame,
But striving, gains the right to wear
   The shining honor of her name.

Author Index

387

388

Subject Index

395

POETS OF THE PAST